Speculations III

speculationsjournal@gmail.com
www.speculations-journal.org

EDITORS
Michael Austin
Paul J. Ennis
Fabio Gironi
Thomas Gokey
Robert Jackson

ISBN 978-0988234017

Front Cover: *unanswered: witness* Grace Lutheran Church Parking Lot, Linwell Road, St. Catharines, June 2003 by P. Elaine Sharpe
Back Cover: *unanswered: witness* Flight Simulation Training Center, Opa Locka Airport, FLA, December 2002 by P. Elaine Sharpe
Courtesy of P. Elaine Sharpe, used with permission. pesharpe.com

The focal distance in these photograph is at the normal range of human conversational distance, 3 meters. Although the image may appear to be out of focus, it is focused on the absence of human presence.

Designed by Thomas Gokey

V 1.0

 punctum books ✳ brooklyn, ny

 2012

Editorial Introduction 5

ARTICLES

Re-asking the Question of the Gendered Subject after 7
Non-Philosophy
Benjamin Norris

Thing Called Love 43
That Old, Substantive, Relation
Beatrice Marovich

The Other Face of God 69
Lacan, Theological Structure, and the Accursed Remainder
Levi R. Bryant

Improper Names for God 99
Religious Language and the "Spinoza-Effect"
Daniel Whistler

Namelessness and the Speculative Turn 135
A Response to Whistler
Daniel Colucciello Barber

Diagonals 150
Truth-Procedures in Derrida and Badiou
Christopher Norris

Synchronicity and Correlationism 189
Carl Jung as Speculative Realist
Michael Haworth

TRANSLATIONS

Über stellvertretende Verursachung 210
Graham Harman

Speculative Realism 241
After finitude, and beyond?
Louis Morelle

POSITION PAPERS AND INTERVIEW

273 Outward Bound
On Quentin Meillassoux's After Finitude
Christian Thorne

290 The Noumenon's New Clothes (Part 1)
Peter Wolfendale

367 Of Realist Turns
A conversation with Stathis Psillos
Fabio Gironi

REVIEWS

426 In Defense of Unfashionable Causes
The Democracy of Objects by Levi Bryant
Daniel Sacilotto

473 Assessing the French Atheistic Turn
Difficult Atheism: Post-theological thought in Badiou, Nancy and Meillassoux by Christpher Watkin
Fabio Gironi

491 Fight and Flight
Merrifield's Magical Convulsions
Magical Marxism: Subversive Politics and the Imagination by Andy Merrifield
Dave Mesing

499 *Circus Philosophicus* by Graham Harman
Maxwell Kennel

507 Joseph Nechvatal's nOise anusmOs Installation
Yuting Zou

Editorial Introduction

WE ARE PROUD TO SAY THAT this third volume of *Speculations* needs very little support from our editorial introduction. We have done our best to collect, in the pages that follow, outstanding contributions covering a wide range of topics (from the philosophy of religion to psychoanalysis, from the philosophy of science to gender studies), formats (articles, interviews, position pieces, translations and review essays) and authors (from well-published authors to the best among a new generation of philosophers).

We would like to thank all the contributors and the peer reviewers for their patient collaboration during the editorial phase. We are also very grateful to the Atelier de métaphysique et d'ontologie contemporaines at the École Normale Supérieure, and their group of English translators (Mark Ohm, Leah Orth, Jon Cogburn and Emily Beck) for allowing us to publish the translation of one of their publications.

Finally, we like to think that, with each new issue, Speculations grows and develops its own peculiar identity as more than just another academic journal: a space for the appraisal of, and critical reflection upon, the contemporary and ever-

Speculations III

developing philosophical scene. It is an ambitious aim, but there can be no speculations without a modicum of audacity. We hope you'll enjoy reading this new materialization of the Speculations project with as much excitement as we experienced while we were assembling it.

Re-asking the Question of the Gendered Subject after Non-Philosophy[1]

Benjamin Norris

The New School for Social Research, New York

IS A SCIENCE OF (NON-)GENDER Identity constitution possible? What would be the object and proper method of this science? And, most importantly, what new spaces of (non-)philosophical investigation can be opened in light of such an analysis?

At some point in time during its perpetual production and proliferation of problems, philosophy stumbled across a problem it called "the subject." As time passed and philosophy

---

[1] Three people in particular made this paper possible in its present form. I would first like to thank Professor Alan Bass, as much of the reading of Freud contained herein is largely influenced by his work and lectures. Although he is only directly cited once, his work on Freud and Derrida is responsible for my focus on the primacy of time and disavowal in Freud's thought. I would secondly like to thank Anthony Paul Smith for his criticisms and comments on the first two drafts of this paper. It is hard to come by informed and insightful feedback on Laruelle, especially in America (even in "continental" circles), and my understanding of Laruelle and hopefully the engagement with his work contained herein has been exponentially increased and aided by way of Anthony's help. Finally, I would like to thanks Professor Richard J. Bernstein for encouraging me to pursue my diverse interests in philosophy, including my work with Laruelle. He's says he'll "make a pragmatist out of me one day" and I in turn hope to convince him that non-philosophy is in spirit not that far from the work of thinkers like Peirce and Dewey.

roared on, the question of the subject has taken many different forms, been approached with many different methods and has yielded incredibly diverse and distinct answers. We have now come to a point where we no longer need to ask *philosophically* "what is the subject?" and "how is the subject's individuality constituted?" but instead ask *non-philosophically* "how has philosophy produced its hypotheses, conditioned its methods and pre-determined its conclusions regarding the subject?"

In the following, I will show that a non-philosophical analysis, as a form of rigorous and scientific analysis of philosophical problems, can point toward a science that investigates the fractal nature of the temporal (non-)interaction between the transcendental and the empirical selves. By bypassing the "empirico-transcendental" philosophical deadlock one can produce new and expansive (explosive even) methods of theorizing gender identity as always at once a playful, generative experiment and a unique unity that can provided an immediate site of resistance toward external (and internal) negative determinations. Non-philosophy affords us the seemingly contradictory ability to fall to neither a transcendent universalizing of gender by way of static categories that are then applied to individuals and distinct subjects, nor to a destruction of a unitary self that never persists in the wake of the flux and contingency of experience and thus marks the opportunity for the much needed expansion of the discourses driving theoretical feminisms, queer theories and, more generally, theories of subjective individuation and constitution.

I proceed in four parts. Part I is a non-genealogy, influenced by the non-philosophical method, of the philosophical permutations of the question of the subject. Part II explicitly introduces François Laruelle into the discussion and attempts to begin articulating the new spaces of study non-philosophy opens in the discourse of the subject. Part III builds on the opening developed in Part II in order to argue that a science of (non-)gender Identity constitution must psychoanalytically interpret the productive nature of an unconscious structured by a fractalized temporal inner sense. Part IV will then compare and contrast the account provided in Part III to a more "traditional" non-philosophical understanding of the unilateral relationship between a temporally driven unconscious, Identity and the Real.

Part I The (non-)Genealogy

In his extensive study of philosophies of difference, Laruelle warns the reader that "we do not pursue here the absurd project [...], of showing that Derrida 'amounts to the same thing' as Nietzsche or even Heidegger."[2] Here I will follow a similar method circling around the question of the subject instead of the question of difference. Although I will point out structural similarities between the seven thinkers discussed, it will be shown that these similarities are a result of the philosophical decision itself and not the result of a direct influence between the thinkers. "In general" Laruelle writes, "a philosophical decision is a cut—repeated or relaunched—with regard to an empirical singular, or more generally, some given and, at the same time, an identification with an idealizing law of this given, itself supposed as real, a transcendence towards a veritable real."[3] The philosophical decision, in an attempt to achieve the "philosophizable-all" (the "*telos*" of the principle of sufficient philosophy) is driven time and time again to universalize contingent givens and attribute to them a privileged access to the real and the true. The singular example is subsumed under the universal law, creating a *dueling* relationship of co-determination and auto-legitimation. What sets non-philosophy apart from this vicious philosophical circle that auto-affirms itself is its ability to isolate and then separate the empirical and the ideal, or the given and the idealizing law of the given, by way of an acceptance of the radically foreclosed nature of the Real. The non-philosopher is relieved of her passion for the real

---

[2] François Laruelle, *Philosophies of Difference: A Critical Introduction to Non-Philosophy* (London and New York: Continuum, 2010), 17.

[3] Ibid., 198.

by thinking alongside the Real, (of) the Real and not *of* the Real. Laruelle writes that "The hiatus between the empirical and the ideal, which we have posited the possibility of lifting (in the form of an a priori relation, before then lifting it really through the passage to transcendental essence), is now definitively re-opened and lets a *new kind of gap be glimpsed* that is no longer that of the empirical and the ideal, or of empiricism and rationalism."[4]

The non-decisional genealogy of the question of the subject in its various philosophical permutations can allow us to both identify and subsequently break philosophy's self-created empirico-transcendental deadlock regarding the question of the subject, and more particularly the gendered subject. This will be a non-genealogy in the sense that it will posit the equivalence of all the individual philosophical decisions discussed. The history of the question of the subject to be traced can be tentatively characterized as a continuing battle between the transcendent and the immanent in which the two categories oscillate, re-define and subordinate one another. By immanent I mean any theory that defines identity in terms of a flux of empirical and/or virtual elements that are self-organized by way of repetition and cannot be reduced to a universal, unexperienced category. By transcendent I mean any theory of identity that appeals to a universal, external and never experienced, "true" self. I will introduce the extremes of the immanent/transcendent stories of the subject to be traced later on by beginning with a contrasting of Descartes' individually discovered and purely transcendent *cogito* with Hume's decentralized and purely immanent self. I will then move to Kant and his attempt to preserve both Descartes' *cogito* as well as acknowledge Hume's theory regarding the flux of the immanent self. Here Kant presents himself with a problem: how can one reconcile the chaotic empirical self with the universal and transcendental self? We will see that introduction of time as a productive inner sense and "mediator" between the seemingly irreconcilable Cartesian and

---

[4] Laruelle, *Philosophies of Difference*, 198 [emphasis added, B.N.].

Benjamin Norris – *Re-asking the Question*

Humean selves was an invention of Kant's that opens a strange, and incredibly relevant, "third space." Next, in Husserl and Sartre, we will witness how the transcendental ego is lost in light of Sartre's analysis of Husserl in *The Transcendence of the Ego*. This loss of the transcendental ego in Sartre's early existentialism provides the space for all following theories of the de-centered, fragmented and/or "deconstructed" subject. Here the immanent seems to re-establishes primacy over the transcendent. The primacy of immanence, postulated by Hume and re-vitalized by Sartre retains its influence in the contemporary continental discourse on gender and identity. To exemplify this, I will briefly discuss the way Jacques Lacan and Judith Butler inherit and re-iterate this discourse and the limitations they inherit with it. This history will exemplify the role the "empirico-transcendental" philosophical deadlock has continuously played in discussions of subjective constitution and gender identity by extension.

In each analysis, we will not seek to argue for the validity or lack thereof in each account. We will instead seek to identify the "idealized law" or philosophically hallucinated transcendental concept and the contingent "empirical singular" in each theory as well as point toward the new kind of gap opened by a non-philosophical analysis of the philosophical decision as it pertains to the question of the subject.

I Descartes

Some credit Descartes with the honor of being the father of the question of the subject. This original account is often seen, rightly in my view, as a radically one sided answer to this question. Quite simply, for Descartes "I am, then, in the strict sense only a thing that thinks, that is, I am a mind, or intelligence, or intellect, or reason [...] But for all that I am a thing which is real and truly exists. But what kind of a thing? As I have just said—a thinking thing."[5] By privileging

---

[5] Rene Descartes, "Meditations on First Philosophy" in *Descartes selected Philosophical Writings* (New York: Cambridge University Press, 1998), 27.

the thinking self as the core of the subject, Descartes is infamously lead to completely dismiss the body ("I am not that structure of limbs which is called a human body"[6]) and the empirical because it cannot live up to the same universality and indubitability as the transcendent and unchanging *cogito*. The body and its senses are fallible, for Descartes, and can thus not ground any certain theory of the subject. The question of the subject is here, at its origins, answered firmly in favor of the transcendent over the immanent. The thinking self is posited as the idealized and universal law and the body and senses are merely contingent manifestations subordinated to the self as a universal thinking thing.

II Hume

Hume's theory of subjective constitution flattens all identity into a flux of empirical perceptions and passions and thus exemplifies the absolute opposite of a Cartesian thinking and unified self. Hume's strict empiricism leads him to conclude that any idea of an identity or self that pre-exists and persists throughout all experience is simply a constructed fiction, based only in habit (repetition), custom and belief. There is no transcendent ground for the subject's identity. The mind infers or ascribes an identity to an object when it observes only a gradual change in it. No impression of "Identity" is found in the object itself. It is instead only a product of the imagination relating different impressions to each other. The same thing holds true for personal identity. Beyond the immanent, there is no transcendent self: "the mind, in following the successive changes of the body, feels an easy passage from the surveying its condition in one moment to the viewing of another, and so at no time perceives any interruption in its actions. From which continu'd perception, it ascribes a continu'd existence and identity to the object."[7] We can only

---

[6] Descartes, "Meditations on First Philosophy," 27.

[7] David Hume, *A Treatise of Human Nature* (Oxford University Press: New York, 1967), 256.

infer and ascribe identity through artificial ideas that are not based on any simple impression found in experience.

Because there is no impression that corresponds to the idea of the self as universal and unchanging, Hume argues that the self is ultimately nothing more than a tumultuous collection of shifting passions and sensations; "I may venture to affirm of the rest of mankind, that they are nothing but a bundle or collection of different perceptions, which succeed each other with an inconceivable rapidity, and are in perpetual flux and movement."[8] We should recall that for Hume the very notion of an identity must be something fixed and unchanging throughout time. If the self is indeed nothing more than a changing flux of perceptions, then no such transcendent stability can be found. The point Hume is making is that when we ascribe to ourselves an Identity that depends on a concept of stability and universality, we lapse into a fictitious account. But if we are to instead consider the self as something that is the product, and not the producer, of changes in ideas, passions and perceptions over time, then we can speak of a self without contradiction.

What is important to draw out of Hume's work on the self is that he attempts to completely dismiss any sort of transcendent ground for a permanent self. For Hume, this self, as a fixed, stable and eternally self-identifying unity, cannot be found in the world and must therefore not exist at all. Any account of "self" as unified Identity is simply a fiction constructed by culture and produced by habituation. There are no secret or transcendent criteria that identity is measured against. Instead, experience internally produces customs and habits that constitute, in a largely contingent fashion, our conception of "self." This means that gender could never be universally and permanently constitutive. Individuation, on this account, is an empirical contingency, following a flow of passions that is only categorized by contingent socio-cultural categories established and re-established through the habitual repetitions of belief and customs. Here the immanent flux

---

[8] Hume, *A Treatise of Human Nature*, 252.

of perceptions is the idealized law of the self and the plastic formation of habits and beliefs by way of repetition is the empirical contingent.[9]

III Kant

In an attempt to both grant to Hume that causality, space and time do not appear directly in experience but also hold that space and time are necessary conditions for experience Kant invents a transcendental idealism to deduce that space, time, cause and effect are still necessary in order for there to be any experience even if they are never present/presented in experience, as Hume's copy-principle (ideas derived from impressions) would necessitate. Kant effectively bridges the two extremes of Descartes and Hume through the claim that the *cogito* is a necessary product of the transcendental imagination's temporal structure. Kant claims that:

> For the empirical consciousness, which accompanies different representations, is in itself diverse and without relation to the identity of the subject. [...] Only in so far, therefore, as I can unite a manifold of given representations in one consciousness, is it possible for me to represent myself to the identity of the consciousness in [i.e. throughout] these representations[10]

Here Kant identifies two aspects of consciousness. There is

---

[9] Hume gives us, in my opinion, the first true account of what will later come to be known as a philosophy of difference. His account of the influence of repetition on the contingency of beliefs and habits can in a way, unlike Descartes, account for both the iteration of the "illusion" (belief, habit) of the self as permanent identity based on alteration (the self as common wealth: "In this respect I cannot but compare the soul more properly to anything than to a republic or a common wealth, [...] as the same republic may not only change its members, but also its laws and constitutions; in a like manner the same person may vary his character and disposition, as well as his impressions and ideas, without losing his identity" [Hume, Ibid., 261]) accounting for the flux of the manifestation the "self" of individuals.

[10] Immanuel Kant, *Critique of Pure Reason* (Palgrave Macmillan: New York, 2003), B 133.

the diverse flux of empirical consciousness and the unifying identity that is exposed not in experience but in the very fact that we can have unified representations of experience. The former can evade the later but is incomprehensible without it. In this characterization we are presented with a strict binary between empirical (lived experience) and transcendental (reflective and determinative abstraction). Kant retains from Hume the idea that our experience of ourselves is always diverse and variable. But Kant does add another "level" of consciousness that is necessary for there to be any account of experience at all. By creating the binary between transcendental and empirical consciousness Kant is left with the trouble of explaining how the transcendental consciousness can have any relation at all to the empirical consciousness. In order to bridge this gap, Kant turns to time, the inner sense. Kant claims that:

> I exist as an intelligence which is conscious solely of its power of combination; but in respect to the manifold which it has to combine I am subjected to a limiting condition (entitled inner sense), namely, that this combination can be made intuitable only according to the relations of time, which lie entirely outside the concepts of the understanding, strictly regulated.[11]

Any relation of my empirical self to my transcendental self is both guided by and limited by the inner sense of time. For Kant, the I that accompanies all experience yet is never presented in any particular experience is only generated and reveled through the combination of manifolds into representations in the unity of apperception. This process of combination is necessarily regulated by a time that is an *a priori* form of intuition that can never be captured as a concept of the understanding. Hence, time, as the productive connecter between the empirical and the transcendental consciousness, is both necessary for and inaccessible to the understanding. Time is a bridge between the un-bridgeable

---

[11] Kant, *Critique of Pure Reason*, B 159.

that can never be reduced to that which it bridges. As a pure form of intuition it never subordinates the transcendental to the empirical or vice versa. Time is here what will be called below a fractalized free-play of the "between-two."

Several key aspects of the interplay between temporality and consciousness in Kant must be emphasized as they will become relevant in Part III of this paper. First, Kant preserves an element of Hume's thought by emphasizing the diverse and variable nature of the empirical consciousness that is "without relation to the identity of the subject." Secondly, identity is an accomplishment of the unification of a manifold through time as the inner sense, so Kant also retains a form of the necessary, universal yet never experienced self-created through a unique temporal synthesis. Third, although time as inner sense is the only source of our awareness of our transcendental consciousness and the only form of interaction between the empirical and transcendental consciousness, this inner sense is an *a priori* form of intuition which is itself both beyond conceptualization *by* the understanding and never encountered *in* experience. And finally, this temporal synthesis must be understood as a very particular form of synthesis that, when reinterpreted in light of Laruelle's work, can barely be called a synthesis. In a strange way, Kant allows for both a flux of the empirical self as well as a universal and unified "I" that accompanies all experiences yet is never in these experiences without subordinating one to the other automatically. The invention of time as an inner sense is, in my reading, the first glimpse of the gap non-philosophical analysis later opens.

IV Husserl-Sartre

At this point I want to continue the non-genealogy and move on to the distinct shift that takes place in the discourse of the subject manifested in the existentialist innovation. The transition from Husserl to Sartre chronicles a return to a more Humean understanding of the self. Instead of arguing for a unified I that structures all experience while remaining outside of experience, Sartre argues that it is *experience itself* that produces the ego. We once again return to a privileging of immanent or empirical criteria of personal constitution. The empirical no longer needs to be compared to or referred back to some category that is not experienced, in this case Husserl's transcendental ego. The discourse of the subject is at this point thrown in to the depth of the empirico-transcendental philosophical deadlock where it remains.

The ego, in Husserl's *Cartesian Meditations*, is transcendental and always outside of the world. Even though it is outside of the world, it shows itself through its various intentional acts toward objects. The ego then, through its decisions, shows itself in a style that presents or expresses a unified identity or personal character. The transcendental ego itself is personalized, in the sense that there is always an I that acts as a condition of possibility for experience, but there is also a personal character expressed in the world through the decisions of the transcendental I that lives through the multiplicity of decisions. This ego is always my ego. It is me before I am myself in the world. Personality is what is shown through my decisions, valuations, etc. during my interactions with the world but it is never in the world.

Sartre reverses Husserl's account of the ego and posits that experience precedes and produces the idea of a transcendental ego. Because experience creates the ego, the transcendental ego is rendered superfluous. Hence consciousness is first and foremost a pure spontaneity and freedom, and it must remain spontaneous and free at each moment. States, actions, and qualities are reflectively shown/created after the fact but are never determining factors at the start that emanate out of a transcendental ego pole.[12]

With existentialism, we find a return to a purely immanent I that reflectively and retrospectively produces a transcendent ego that it is not in turn dependent on or reducible to. The self is once again fragmented and has no dependence upon any

---

[12] Jean-Paul Sartre, *The Transcendence of the Ego: An Existentialist Theory of Consciousness* (Hill and Wang: New York, 1991), 71.

external criteria. It has gained a new freedom of expression, but it has, as a consequence, lost any form of pre-empirical unity. The history of thinkers surveyed, for the most part (Kant being our exception), exemplify not the *irreconcilability* of the question of the subject itself but instead the *un-decidability* of the oscillating battle between the privileging of either the permanent and un-experienced Cartesian self, or the chaotic flux of the Humean, immanent "self." The question of the subject has been answered in the form of either privileging the immanent flux and turning becoming into the ideal law and reducing universal categories to mere contingent illusions (Hume, Sartre) or by turning the transcendent unified self into the ideal law and subordinating the fluxes immanent self into an irrelevant or largely insignificant factor (Descartes, Husserl). This is and has been a problem for quite a while, but it becomes further complicated with the advent of the question of the gendered subject, especially the question of the gendered subject after queer theories. Thinkers now search for a way to completely decentralize and dismiss any binary category defining gender identity from the outside. If difference is privileged in theories of subjective gender constitution, fragmentation becomes the law, but, just as problematically, if the universal self is made the law, individual differences cannot be theoretically accounted for and practically respected.

V Butler-Lacan

Feminist theory, in a certain sense, was born through a critique of the applicability of universal determinations of "man" and "woman" to distinct individuals. Lived gender was found to be inaccurately described by and irreducible to the universal givens handed down, both pre-determined and unjustly determining. Thinkers began looking more closely at the *existential* conditions under which one *became* either a man or a woman (the Sartrean resonance should be stressed here). In some ways we return to a Humean theorizing of the self as an empirically contingent bundle of perceptions. As

Hume claims "I may venture to affirm of the rest of mankind, that they are nothing but a bundle or collection of different perceptions, which succeed each other with an inconceivable rapidity, and are in perpetual flux and movement."[13] The self is a flux; it is an ever changing and shifting bundle of perceptions. In a like fashion, Sartre emphasizes that, "the ego maintains its qualities through a genuine, continuous creation. Nevertheless, we do not finally apprehend the ego as a pure creative source apart from its qualities."[14] The ego, for Sartre, is also a creative product of ever-changing interactions with the world. The self by no means stays stable. It is instead, just as Hume suggested, a collection of changing experiences and perceptions placing the self in a state of "perpetual flux and movement." In both cases, the self shifts according to its experiences within the world. It is always a product and not a producer of these different experiences.

The existential account of gender constitution was then challenged by the advent of queer theories and their crucial critique of the heteronormative essence of even these more existential accounts. In order to expand our understanding of gender constitution in a way that can positively account for a multiplicity of gender identities, most of which cannot be simply reduced to "heterosexual man" or "heterosexual woman," fragmentation and flux seem to become the law. In this situation, the emphasis of the importance of lived difference is pushed to its most extreme limit but also encounters a very serious problem. The gendered identity is always an identity founded upon an experience of complete fragmentation and aggressive alienation from any form of unified identity in the wake of the chaos of their empirical and individual gendered experience. For Hume, the original thinker of the self as perpetual flux, there was no transcendent and universal criteria whatsoever to determine the self and there was thus no conflict between empirical reality and transcendent illusion. What comes to characterize a large

---

[13] Hume, *A Treatise of Human Nature*, 252.
[14] Sartre, *Transcendence of the Ego*, 78.

number of prevalent contemporary theories of subjective constitution is that they are actually *driven* by an inherent tension between the empirical flux and the transcendent illusion. Thus the current discussions of gender identity are characterized by what Laruelle would call a *duel* relationship between the transcendent illusion of the unified I and the empirical flexuous self. Furthermore, what we will see is that this duel is not simply a consequence of individual shortcomings in the theories presented that can be remedied philosophically. Laruelle argues that this is simply a consequence of the philosophical decision regarding the primacy of difference "Difference affirms the superiority if their [the law and the given] combat."[15] To exemplify this duel, let us turn to Lacan and Butler.

For Lacan, the I (as "*Je*") is the product of a necessary and fundamental mis-recognition/identification of oneself (as "*moi*") and one's specular image (as "ideal-I") during his infamous "mirror stage." This mis-recognition and the desire to remedy this fundamental fragmentation between the experienced body and the ideal *imago* of the body serves as the condition of possibility for both the subject's aggression and desire as well as the subject's entry into the symbolic register. This conflict is ultimately a battle between the irreconcilability of space and time. Space, in Lacan's account, includes the "imaginary space" of the universal, ideal and static *imagos* acquired in early infant experience and most dramatically in the mirror stage. The universal and timeless *imagos* stand in direct conflict with the temporal experience of the imperfect, fragile and dependent body. As a consequence, "man's ego is never reducible to his lived experience."[16] The temporal, dependent and vulnerable individual desires an ideal-I that can never be attained but only asymptotically approached.[17] The subject, now fragmented through a desire

---

[15] Laruelle, *Philosophies of Difference*, 8.

[16] Jacques Lacan, "Aggressiveness in Psychoanalysis," *Écrits* (New York: W.W. Norton, 2006), 114.

[17] See Lacan, "The Mirror Stage as Formative of the I Function as Revealed

for the transcendent universal, enters into the symbolic realm and attempts to complete herself through the desire of the other. The constitution of gender identity is now actually driven by an active and irreconcilable conflict between transcendent lack and immanent fragmentation. Fragmentation and conflict are now at the core of the development of the individual's gender identity. Differentiation and, more importantly, conflict become the law.

The most dominate theoretical continuation of this Lacanian perspective and its potential for providing an account of gender identity in its true state of diversity (non-heteronormative) is articulated by Judith Butler.[18] Here I want to briefly draw out the way Butler's 1988 essay "Preformative acts and Gender Constitution: An Essay in Phenomenology and Feminist Theory" exemplifies Butler's inheritance of the empirico-transcendental philosophical deadlock showing us that ultimately even philosophies of gender constitution founded in difference are equally susceptible to the non-philosophical critique. Butler begins her account with a reference to the founding figure of feminist existentialism:

> When Simone de Beauvoir claims, "one is not born, but, rather, becomes a woman," she is appropriating and reinterpreting this doctrine of constituting acts from the phenomenological tradition. In this sense, gender is in no way a stable identity or locus of agency from which various acts proceed; rather, it is an identity tenuously constituted in time—an identity instituted through a stylized repetition of acts.[19]

Hume and Sartre speak powerfully in this claim. The self, as immanent flux, is privileged above all else. Constitution of

---

in Psychoanalytic Experience," in *Écrits*, 94.

[18] I want to acknowledge here that this account of Butler's work is by no means extensive and is not meant to be a critique. Butler's work makes important advancements after her 1988 essay discussed here, distancing herself from Lacan, but due to space, these advancements cannot be discussed here.

[19] Judith Butler, "Performative Acts and Gender Constitution: An Essay in Phenomenology and Feminist Theory," in *Theatre Journal*, Vol. 40, No. 4, (Dec., 1988), 519.

gender is a repetition of stylized acts of expression. Gender is not pre-determined by some transcendent essence but is instead created continuously by the spontaneity of the immanent self.

> If the ground of gender identity is the stylized repetition of acts through time, and not a seemingly seamless identity, then the possibilities of gender transformation are to be found in the arbitrary relation between such acts, in the possibility of a different sort of repeating, in the breaking or subversive repetition of that style.[20]

The gender constituting act is an empirical expression and the very fragmentation of the self is what provides a site for "subversive repetition of that style."

In an attempt to account for the largest possible plurality of gendered expression, Butler decides in favor of difference and flux, standing in opposition to transcendence and binary universal categories. Yet the loss of the transcendent or transcendental ego does not completely rid discussions of subjective gender constitution of the *duel*-isms that have plagued it at least since Descartes nor of the oppositional structure inherent in the philosophical decision. Butler and Lacan both follow Hume and Sartre by turning the flux of the individual into the law but they, in addition to this, posit an inherent tension between the universal "ideal" and the fragmented self (taken in this decision to be the law of the Real) and seem to actually elevate *conflict itself* to the status of the ideal law governing subjective constitution. The purely transcendent I of Descartes is fundamentally unable to account for the diversity of the empirical expression of individual selves. On the other hand, the purely chaotic or fragmented self of Sartre, Lacan or Butler cannot account for or maintain any form of unity and ultimately becomes characterized only by opposition, lack or aporia. Through its decision, philosophy can only think *either* unity *or* difference and through its desire for sufficiency, the philosophical resolution of the

---

[20] Butler, "Performative Acts and Gender Constitution," 520.

either/or always determines and thus hallucinates the Real.

In the next Part, I will show how Laruelle's non-relational mode of thinking is able to remove us from the duel-istic deadlock between transcendental subject and the empirical subject, without privileging either one. This method provides a clue to why antimony, conflict, tautology, aporia and deadlock might not be the necessary consequence of any investigation into subjective gender constitution, even if they are a necessary consequence of any *philosophical* investigation into the matter. What comes to the fore in light of this is that the battle against dichotomous and oppositional gender logic can only come in the form of a redefinition of time and temporal experience itself and not either the collapsing of the transcendent into the immanent or in privileging the immanent over the transcendent. We must stop giving law to the Real in order to truly subvert the philosophical decision's deadlock.

Part II Non-Philosophy, Non-Photography and (non-)Gender Identity

Laruelle's *The Concept of Non-Photography* is nothing short than an accessible and insightful masterpiece of disguise and subtlety. In this text, Laruelle isolates and analyzes the way the philosophical decision has constrained philosophical discourse and interpretation of photography into an antinomical battle over the privileging, re-positing and re-privileging of binary relationships. The philosophical decision has an invariant effect upon any subject matter philosophy approaches. Therefore, the non-photography developed in this text can be easily and legitimately translated into a science of (non-)gender Identity constitution. In this section I will demonstrate and develop this claim in order to show how the non-philosophical de-coupling of the "empirico-transcendental doublet", which is actually the "empirico-transcendental deadlock," can make the space for a consideration of the purely temporal element of gender constitution that can bypass the deadlock philosophy still harbors in its core. What is unique about the opening Laruelle provides for our analysis is that it points to a "third" term in gender constitution yet does not require us to replace the law or given of the earlier theories of subjective constitution. Laruelle's position on the (non-)relationship of the transcendental and empirical self can be summarized by the following claim made in *The Concept of Non-Photography*:

> The cause [...] no longer corresponds to the "transcendental subject," nor do the conditions of existence correspond to an "empirical" conditioning in the sense in which the philosopher understands it. Photography [non-philosophy] along with symbolic modes of thought, radical phenomenologies, non-Euclidian generalizations and, in general in the spirit of "Abstraction," has contributed to identifying the transcendental and the empirical as functions of a specific process, and to the distinguishing of this usages from their philosophical putting-into-correlation, the "empirico-transcendental doublet."[21]

The non-philosophical gendered subject would be one that is immediately experienced apart from any empirical or transcendental philosophical determination. It would resemble what Laruelle terms the "identity photo" or "photographic identity." The proper photographic identity can only be "discovered" by way of a non-philosophical science because "science eliminates from itself the philosophical correlation between fact and principle, between the rational faktum and its possibility; it describes and manifests simultaneously the being-photo (of) the photo, *photographic identity as such*, such as it is deployed from its real cause to its effective conditions of existence and fills in this 'between-two.'"[22] The science of non-photography does not reduce the identity of the photo to either its transcendental conditions (the camera and other technological apparatuses of photographic production) or to the empirical content of the photo (the scene it "represents"

---

[21] François Laruelle, *The Concept of Non-Photography*, (Urbanomic/Sequence Press: New York. 2010), 42.

[22] Ibid., 42.

expresses etc.). The identity of the photo, and correlatively of the (non-)gendered Identity, is something that is not reducible to either the immanent (philosophically understood) or the transcendent. The photographic identity is more properly the "space between" the proposed doublet/deadlock.

Using *The Concept of Non-Photography* let us further develop a concept of (non-)gender Identity. For Laruelle, the photo (properly understood) is "an absolute reflection, without mirror, unique each time but capable of an infinite power ceaselessly to secrete multiple identities."[23] The photo is always immediate and unique, yet it retains the power of multiple and ceaseless iteration. It is never reducible to either the technology it is produced with (the "ideal law" of the photo) or the scene which it "represents" (the contingent empirical given). The surface of the photo, in its immediate experience, is always an infinite fractal surface, and its fractal nature provides the infinite surface without depth upon which the photographic experience is placed. Yet, "The fractalized wall carries no signification."[24] The fractal nature of the surface resists all signification not because it is "un-signifiable" but because it is "omni-significant," and the fractal nature of this omni-significance is what allows for the photo's ability to "secrete multiple identities" at any point in time while retaining a unique, unitary and inexhaustible identity.

In his analysis of the photo and theories of photography Laruelle attempts to show how the introduction of a fractal surface of the photo can provide us with a "synthesis of the modern and the postmodern"[25] How can this be possible and how is this claim in anyway different from previous attempt to reconcile empirical with transcendent consciousness? Laruelle writes that:

> If the ontological destination of Abstraction were the void as either Being, fractality realizes the synthesis of the most undifferentiated

---

[23] Laruelle, *The Concept of Non-Photography*, 82.

[24] Ibid., 126.

[25] Ibid., 137.

> void and of the most differentiated concreteness [...] Neither the empirical and transcendent content, nor the purified void, the purism of the abstract but a synthesis that reconciles the opposites without summarily hybridizing them.[26]

The fractal surface is the "plane" of synthesis that renders synthesis itself incomprehensible. It in no way reproduces hybridizations of the empirico-transcendental philosophical deadlock. It instead discards the never-ending co-production of subordination in order to discover an immediate unity, capable of infinite and never determinative or exhaustive differentiation.

Gender can now be understood as an immediately experienced unity that is never reducible to either its immanent expression or the transcendent category it is measured against. It is never stable yet never fragmented. It is a constant experiment, limited only by itself. Gender is no longer an oppositionally defined splitting into male or female, queer or straight, etc. Yet at the same time, the gendered subject is not simply a fragmented body of meaningless contingencies piled upon contingencies. We no longer need to define the gendered body in terms reducible to either the immanent or the transcendent, a method that has inevitable resulted in antinomical and auto-justifying philosophical deadlocks. We can instead turn to the fractal nature of temporality as the "between-two" to ground an experience of gender that is infinitely free, unitary and productive, always affirmative and self-realizing. Gender becomes a pure reflection without the funhouse mirror of custom, habit, transcendent gender categories, capitalist fabrication or other distorting effects. Gender is an expression of a fractal temporality that is always-already beyond, and more importantly indifferent to and before, any form of binary dicotomization.

But here I am presented with a problem. I claim that the object of a rigorous science of (non-)gender Identity constitution would be a fractal temporality. How can time and gender

---

[26] Laruelle, *The Concept of Non-Photography*, 139.

be connected at all, and can this be done in a way that does not fall prey to the philosophical deadlock I have attempted to exit from above? It is at this point when I must take a heretical turn. Although I do believe that non-philosophy can help us diagnose philosophy's constant stumbling block in the discourse of the subject as well as point toward a space for new considerations that might surpass and bypass the philosophical deadlock, Freudian psychoanalysis is needed to provide us with a working conceptual framework by with which to show how gender and time come together. It is here where we must turn to psychoanalysis in order to concretely lay out what a non-decisional investigation of the time (of) gender would look like. Ray Brassier argues that non-philosophy's "conceptual import can and should be philosophically interpreted."[27] I, on the other hand, will suggest that the import of non-philosophy, if it is going to open up a new discussion of the gendered subject, must be *psychoanalytically* interpreted.

Part III Temporality, Psychoanalysis and (non-)Gender Identity Constitution

How can an account that relies on the assumption of a productive unconscious that is temporally structured provide us with a theory of subjective gender constitution that can bypass the empirico-transcendental deadlock we used Laruelle's work to identify in the above non-genealogy?

In order to begin bringing time and gender together, let us here draw the work of Julia Kriseva into our discussion. Kriseva's 1981 article "Women's Time" is an investigation into a confrontation between two distinct temporal dimensions as they relate to gender identity. Kristeva writes that, "with sociocultural ensembles of the European type, we are constantly faced with a double problematic: that of their *identity* constituted by historical sedimentation, and that of

---

[27] Ray Brassier, *Nihil Unbound: Enlightenment and Extinction.* (New York: Palgrave Macmillan, 2007), 119.

their *loss of identity* which is produced by this connection of memories which escape from history only to encounter anthropology."[28] European ensembles, understood as historical products, present us with two distinct and oppositional trends: the constitution of identity and the dissolution of identity. How is this double process possible? To understand how the movement of identity formation and loss of identity are simultaneously possible in historical development, we must distinguish between two different temporal registers or dimensions: "we confront two temporal dimensions: the time of linear history or *cursive time* (as Nietzsche called it) and the time of another history, thus another time, *monumental time* (again according to Nietzsche), which englobes these supranational, sociocultural ensembles within even larger entities."[29] One time, the time that constitutes universal identity, is logical and linear. The other time, which dissolves identity into fragmented multiplicity, is a monumental movement, irreducible to a linear interpretation that seeks to bind and create larger entities through the dissolution of individual identities.

In addition to the cursive and linear generations of temporal experience, which both entail a conflict between transcendent universals and immanent flux, Kristeva posits the possibility of a third generation. This third generation is also defined by a distinct experience of temporality, but this is a time that is neither foreign to women, as linear time is, nor a rejection of the historical time exemplified by the second generation's post '68 rejection of universal categories. Instead, "it can be argued that as of now a third attitude is possible, thus a third generation, which does not exclude [...] the *parallel* existence of all three in the same historical time, or even that they be interwoven one with the other."[30] This third generation offers the promise of both the previous generations without the exclusion or subordination of either temporal dimension.

---

[28] Julia Kristeva, "Women's Time" *Signs*, Vol. 7. No. 1. (Autumn, 1981), pp. 13-35. 14.

[29] Ibid., 14.

[30] Ibid., 33.

For Kristeva, the temporality of the third generation, can signal to an outside of the traditional metaphysics of gender:

> In this third attitude, which I strongly advocate [...] the very dichotomy man/woman as an opposition between two rival entities may be understood as belonging to *metaphysics*. What can "identity," even "sexual identity," mean in a new theoretical and scientific space where the very notion of identity is challenged?[31]

A synthesis (a complete synthesis beyond opposition, negation, reconciliation, hybridization, etc.) can yield an experience of temporality that dissolves the very notion of identity itself into something that can be both linear and cyclical. We achieve Nietzsche's dream of an affirmation of values based on the monumental repetitions that occur within the time of history. One could theoretically experience a time beyond binary constitution that does not just sublate the history of these binaries, but renders the entire binary theoretical construction obsolete.

At this point, I want to draw together three threads in the above paper. The first thread is the discussion of time in Kristeva and Kant and the role it can play in the interrelation between a historically experienced empirical, contingent self and an ahistorical and necessary self. The second thread is the deadlock produced by a long history of constitutional theories (exemplified by the series Descartes-Hume-Husserl-Sartre-Lacan-Butler) that rely solely on the privileging of either the ahistorical, transcendent self or the historical empirical self. The final thread, and the most speculative one, is the non-philosophical method's ability to return to a focus on temporal synthesis that is not reducible to either a historical, contingent account or a transcendent ahistorical account (in short, an account that gives no hallucinatory law to the Real). We will ultimately see how gender constitution is not simply structured by temporal experience, but our very desire for gender differentiation itself is a result of a dynamic and im-

---

[31] Kristeva, "Women's Time," 33-34.

mediate experience of a temporal synthesis that renders all synthesis incomprehensible. I have suggested that Laruelle can assist us in separating completely the empirical and transcendental aspects of theories of subjective constitution in order to avoid having to subordinate and determine one by the other. We saw that Laruelle accomplishes this separation by referring us to the fractal "between-two" of the photographic identity, now converted in to the fractal "between-two" of (non-)gender Identity. I now will argue that a particular reading of Freudian psychoanalysis can provide a legitimately non-philosophical method for studying the constitution of the individual's (non-)gender Identity without giving a philosophically understood law to the Real.

Let us here turn to one of the most puzzling yet important remarks Freud makes on temporality in *Beyond the Pleasure Principle*. Freud pauses for a moment in section IV, one of the most (in)famous speculations in the psychoanalytic tradition, and writes:

> At this point I shall venture to touch for a moment upon a subject which would merit the most exhaustive treatment. As a result of certain psycho-analytic discoveries, we are to-day in a position to embark on a discussion of the Kantian theorem that time and space are "necessary forms of thought." We have learnt that unconscious mental processes are in themselves *"timeless."* This means in the first place that they are not themselves ordered temporally, that time does not change them in any way and that the idea of time cannot be applied to them. These are the negative characteristics which can only be clearly understood if a comparison is made with *conscious* mental processes. On the other hand, our abstract idea of time seems to be wholly derived from the method of working of the system *Pcpt-Cs.* and corresponds to a perception on its own part of that method of working. This mode of functioning may perhaps constitute another way of providing a shield against stimuli. I know the remarks must sound very obscure, but I must limit myself to these hints.[32]

---

[32] Sigmund Freud, "Beyond the Pleasure Principle," *The Standard Edition of the Complete works of Sigmund Freud* (Hogarth Press: London, 1974) Volume. XVIII, 27.

Freud is here suggesting that the conscious experience of time as linear (what Kriesteva called cursive or historical time) is in fact a defense against another form of unknown yet always experienced unconscious time. The Kantian inner sense of time as a pure form of immediate *a priori* intuition is something that must necessarily be guarded against because of its dynamic implications. The battle between the insistent and dynamic inner sense of unconscious time and the Pcpt-Cs.'s protective linear time represents the original (non-) dialectic in the sense that it is interminable and never fully constitutive. This dialectic can never decide for it is lost in its own fractalization in peaceful fascination.[33]

Linear time, in the Freudian account, is not the starting point for psychic experience as a whole. It is instead a form of protection and defense against a primary dynamic experience of time as other than linear. This original experience of time is at the same time never surpassed, it is only repressed. This would mean that Kristeva's third generation is no longer some future category to be obtained or achieved. It is instead fundamental and generative of the desire to create linear, logical definitions of gendered identity and gendered experience. The fractal nature of temporality as the "between-two" is both the always present yet never presented source of salvation, re-iteration and radical recreation. The third generation

---

[33] Linear conscious temporality can be read in this light as similar to Sartre's reading of Husserl's *epoché*. For Sartre, the phenomenological reduction that Husserl uses to find the transcendental ego is no longer a method of bracketing the world in order to gain apodictic certainty; it is instead a therapeutic technique for buffering the inherent spontaneity of consciousness itself from itself. The *epoché* is, "no longer a miracle, an intellectual method, an erudite procedure: it is an anxiety which is imposed on us and which we cannot avoid"(Sartre, *Trancendence of the Ego*, 103). The immediate experience of consciousness is literally too much to bear. Personality, created through reflective reduction, is a guardian against the radical spontaneity of consciousness and not a necessary, pre-personalized transcendental ego. The ego, for Sartre, is not a uniting operation but instead a buffer against the nothingness that allows for the pure spontaneity of consciousness. In my account, the linear construction of narrative gender identity is not a universal necessity but instead a continent response to an original experience of individual constitution as a matter of fractal, unconscious temporality.

precedes the first two necessarily. The third generation does not need to be achieved; it instead needs to be remembered. Recall that, for Kristeva, in the third generation's temporal experience "the very dichotomy man/woman as an opposition between two rival entities may be understood as belonging to *metaphysics* What can 'identity,' even 'sexual identity,' mean in a new theoretical and scientific space where the very notion of identity is challenged?"[34] The unique experience of temporality as fractal is itself enough to dissolve the very notion of identity as it is conceived metaphysically and more importantly, *philosophically* as well. Now in order to fully grasp how a new experience of collapsed and dynamic unconscious, fractal temporality can explode the idea of gender constitution we must link the third generation's temporality to a fractal experience of temporality that lies in the "between-two" of the empirical-transcendental deadlock. Time itself must be fractalized in order to understand how any innovation in a theory of gender constitution could exit the dogmas it repeatedly inherits in the form of (seemingly) irreducible binaries. Freud's 1915 paper "The Unconscious" states that:

> *The processes of the system* Ucs. [Unconscious] *are timeless;* I.e they are not ordered temporally, are not altered by the passage of time; they have no reference to time at all. Reference to time is bound up, once again, with the work of the system Cs. [Consciousness]. [...] To sum up: *exemption from mutual contradiction, primary processes* (mobility of cathexis), *timelessness and replacement of external by psychic reality*—these are the characteristics which we may expect to find in processes belonging to the system Ucs.[35]

Timelessness is a central characteristic of the unconscious and the expression of unconscious processes. Yet, as Derrida notes in "Freud and the Scene of Writing,"

---

[34] Kristeva, "Women's Time," 33-34.

[35] Sigmund Freud, "The Unconscious," *The Standard Edition of the Complete works of Sigmund Freud* (Hogarth Press: London, 1974) Volume. XIV, 15.

> The Timelessness of the unconscious is no doubt determined only in opposition to a common concept of time, a traditional concept, the metaphysical concept: the time of mechanics or the time of consciousness. [...] the unconscious is no doubt timeless only from the stand point of a certain vulgar conception of time.[36]

This "vulgar time" has been recognized and discussed in the subsequent literature on the time of the unconscious, but it has, for the most part, remained vulgar, but only in the sense that it has remained *philosophical*. An example of this comes from Adrian Johnston's *Time Driven: Metapsychology and the Splitting of the Drive* in which he argues in a *philosophical* manner for the primacy of temporality in the productive unconscious and the drives themselves. Johnston claims that "Temporality—as the irreducible tension between timelessness (the atemporal subjectivity of unconscious enunciation) and time (the phenomenal subjectivity of diachronic utterances)—is the gap constitutive of the Kantian-Lacanian subject."[37] Temporality, in Johnson's account, remains constituted by an oppositional battle between two irreconcilable contraries: iteration and alteration or the monumental and the linear. "The temporality of the Kanitan-Lacanian subject is prefigured by the metapsychological condition of the (possible) emergence of all subjects, namely, drive."[38] Johnston's analysis here contributes important aspects to the discussion of the temporal nature of the drive, yet he still posits alterable, linear and cursive time in opposition to the monumental, repetitions, iterable "timelessness" of the noumenal unconscious. Johnston thus once again raises the conflict between two irreconcilables to the status of the "ideal law" of the psyche's temporal productivity. Fragmentation and conflict remain the law and the limit, and the philosophical decision lives on.

---

[36] Jacques Derrida, "Freud and the Scene of Writing," *Writing and Difference* (Chicago: University of Chicago Press, 1978), 215.

[37] Adrian Johnston, *Time Driven: Metapsychology and the Splitting of the Drive.* (Chicago :Northwestern University Press, 2005), 112.

[38] Ibid., 119

Can the idea of a fractal and not a fractured experience of temporality as the dynamic source of libidinal investment bypass the still clear philosophical threat? If we accept that drive, and by extension the constitution of (non-)gender Identity, and temporality are deeply connected but characterize the time of the unconscious not as timeless but instead as fractal then we can account for both the infinite alteration of the expression of gender as well as incorporate the monumental iteration of the flux of the drive itself. The fractal, like the unconscious, like the Real, is radically inexhaustible. It collapses any difference and repetition, iteration and alteration, cursive and monumental into a single, unified yet inexhaustible surface of creative play and possibility. The productive unconscious is, in this account, not characterized by lack, opposition or fragmentation. It is instead productive and "unique each time but capable of an infinite power ceaselessly to secrete multiple identities." In Kristeva's parlance, yet modified in light of our investigation, the time of the third generation must be akin to an inexhaustible fractal time such as described above.

To concisely summarize the dynamic, temporally structured unconscious that I am here proposing as the proper object of the psychoanalytic and scientific study of (non-)gender Identity constitution:

> 1: Like Kant, the temporality of our unconscious is the synthetic faculty "which lies entirely outside of the concepts of the understanding, strictly regulated": time is not the *content* of thought and the unconscious more generally, it is instead the subtle and dynamic *form*.

> 2: Like Kristeva's third generation, fractal temporality shows that "the very dichotomy man/woman as an opposition between two rival entities belonging to metaphysics;" extended in our analysis to the entirety of philosophy and universally amongst the plurality of philosophical decisions on the matter thus dissolving any determinative/determining relationship between dichotomy and gender identity e.g. male/female, gay/straight, Sadist/masochist etc.

3: Like Johsnton's drive theory, the drives themselves are temporally driven and this temporality supplies the drives with both their unity and their infinite diversity of vicissitudes. But unlike Johnston, our temporal unconscious is driven not due to an irreconcilable division between the experience of time and the transcendent timelessness of the noumenal unconscious, elevating conflict and difference to the status of an ideal law. The drive is instead driven, yet only in-the-last-instance, by the fractal nature (of) unconscious time itself.

4: Like the fractal surface of the identity photo, the fractal temporality of the unconscious is "an absolute reflection, without mirror, unique each time but capable of an infinite power ceaselessly to secrete multiple identities;" it is like the fractalized wall that "carries no signification;" it "realizes the synthesis of the most undifferentiated void and of the most differentiated concreteness [...] Neither the empirical and transcendent content, nor the purified void, the purism of the abstract but a synthesis that reconciles opposites without summarily hybridizing them."

Yes, a science of (non-)gender Identity constitution is possible. The object of this science would be the fractal "between-two" experience of temporality understood and analyzed in a rigorous psychoanalytic sense. Finally what new spaces of (non-)philosophical investigation can be opened in light of such an analysis? I have attempted to show that the shift in focus from either immanent or transcendent theories of gender constitution to the fractal experience of irreducible and inexhaustible unconscious temporality can lead us outside of the traditional binary philosophical deadlock and point toward a "third way" of temporal experience that is always-already upon us and not deferred *à venir* into an aporetic future. By collapsing the temporality of gender onto a flat, yet infinitely complex fractal surface we can explode the possibilities of gender expression as well as solidify a unitary core from which gendered resistance can proceed. We allow for ceaseless differentiation without turning either fragmentation or opposition into the law by way of a philosophical cut or decision and, in fact, attempt to apply no determinative final law to the dynamism of the temporal unconscious at all. We continue to study gender as only determined-in-the-last-instance by the vicissitudes (of) the fractal unconscious while at the same time respecting its inexhaustibility.

Part IV Possible Non-Philosophical Objections
The Analysis of a Heresy

I have argued that psychoanalysis provides a way to pragmatically apply the findings and principles of non-philosophy concretely to theories of gender constitution. How faithful is this positive account of gender constitution based on a fractal temporality to Laruelle's own accounts of the unconscious, temporality and Identity? Why can a psychoanalytic reinterpretation of the Kantian/Freudian notion of time as a constitutive inner sense in light of the findings of Laruelle's non-philosophy provide a better solution for the exiting of the empirico-transcendental philosophical deadlock the question of the subject finds itself in than a more strictly non-philosophical understanding of temporality and psychoanalysis more generally? Where is my heresy and what advantages, if any, does it give my account? In order to address this question I will have to briefly pit psychoanalysis against non-philosophy and ask if Freud is in fact making a philosophical decision, enforcing a "principle of sufficient psychoanalysis," and consequently hallucinating the unconscious as the Real, or more problematically for Laruelle, positing time and temporality itself as the ideal law of the Real. If the unconscious, and more specifically the temporal unconscious, is simply another philosophical hallucination then it could never constitute-in-the-last-instance a (non-) gender Identity, rendering a psychoanalytic science of (non-) gender Identity impossible. I simply mean here to show that Freudian psychoanalysis and Laruellean non-philosophy are not *contrary* but *complimentary*.

Benjamin Norris – *Re-asking the Question*

The first point of tension between a psychoanalytic account and a more traditionally non-philosophical interpretation of gender Identity revolves around a different understanding of the relationship between Identity, the unconscious, repression and time. The Freudian unconscious, strictly understood, does not truly capture the radical (non-philosophical) immanence of Laruelle's One. I have argued that an account of (non-)gender Identity constitution must be founded in the study of the way the fractal temporality of the unconscious both constitutes the desire for gender identification as an immediate unity of Identity as well as creates the possibility of productive and creative individual contingencies resulting in the expression of desire and the constitution of the gendered subject. It would seem at first as if an analysis of this type would depend on the operation of a Freudian notion of repression, memory and time that Laruelle attempts to radically distance himself from.[39] For Freud, and the psychoanalytic account I have argued for more generally, there must be some form of interaction between the past, memory and the constitution of sexual identity. The unconscious must in some fashion express itself through the individual's object choices and psychic hallucinations/duplications of the chosen objects in order for sexuality to be constituted.[40] This stands in strict

---

[39] Laruelle has more generally attempted to distance non-philosophy from psychoanalysis. He is for the most part effective in this attempt but concentrates on distancing himself from a Lacanian iteration of psychoanalysis. See Laruelle *Théorie des Etrangers* (Paris: Kimé, 1995). For a more extended secondary discussion of Laruelle and Lacan in english see Katerina Kolozova (in *The Real and 'I': On the Limit and the Self* (Skopje: Euro-Balkan Press, 2006) chapter 3) and John Mullarky (*Post-Continental Philosophy: An Outline* (New York: Continuum International Publishing Group, 2006) chapter 4). This focus on Lacan leads Laruelle to overlook certain affinities between non-philosophy and a more Freudian iteration of psychoanalysis. I will briefly expand on this at the end of the paper.

[40] See Freud's "Three Essays on Sexuality" in *The Standard Edition of the Complete works of Sigmund Freud* (Hogarth Press: London, 1974) Volume VII (1901-1905): A Case of Hysteria, Three Essays on Sexuality and Other Works, 123-246. Object choice, and the experience of libidinal satisfaction by extension, is determined (in-the-last-instance) by the contingent interaction of

contrast to Laruelle's "Past foreclosed to memory" and thus seems to stand at odds with non-philosophy, sinking back into a philosophical desire for the Real, unjustly exhausting the un-exhaustible immanence of the One. Laruelle claims that, from a philosophical perspective "memory has just been considered as an anthropological faculty or instance, the past and memory in general as functions of a worldly time or even reduced and immanent to consciousness, *always philosophizable or sufficient.*"[41] A non-philosophical consideration of memory, and symptomatology in general, would have to acknowledge the necessity yet radical insufficiency and foreclosure of the past and memory. The Identity could only be determined-in-the-last-instance by the past foreclosed to memory. This critique could be leveled against a form of psychoanalytic understanding centering on the primacy of repression as a mechanism of psychic defense. The One cannot be repressed and thus Identity, in a non-philosophical sense, cannot be captured by the traditional form of the Freudian "return of the repressed."

Laruelle wants to envision memory as a radically foreclosed, necessary yet also radically insufficient past or memory. If non-philosophical past or memory are to be consistent with the non-philosophical project they must respect the radically immanent and foreclosed nature (of) the One. In non-philosophy "The One cannot be forgotten or repressed by occidental memory but hallucinated, giving rise to a special form of symptom."[42] The non-philosophical unconscious is similarly foreclosed.

---

the individual infant unconscious and the contingent material/historical events of its early childhood. (It is at this point where Freud and Marx meet). Psychic reality requires necessarily an external (and ultimately internal [see. Freud's "The Project for a Scientific Psychology" *The Standard Edition of the Complete works of Sigmund Freud* (Hogarth Press: London, 1974) Volume I, 281-391]) material reality independent of the individual psyche.

[41] Laruelle, François, *Future Christ* (New York: Continuum, 2011), 75.

[42] Ibid., 89.

> Non-psychoanalysis extricates a radical transcendental unconscious from the result of the Real (the One). The unconscious is the syntactic side of jouissance, which is itself, in non-psychoanalysis, a concept on the same level as the Stranger. But, in opposition to the restrained unconscious or the unconscious determined by the signifier, logic, or the combinatory, the non-psychoanalytic unconscious has nothing to do with the transcendence of "the autonomy of the symbolic": it is the identity of jouissance and a unilateral duality[43]

This is clearly an attack on Lacan's unconscious. The non-philosophical unconscious, in contrast to the Lacanian unconscious, is characterized by a unilateral casual relation between jouissance, desire, and its expression in the Stranger-subject. Here I will speculate that the fractal temporality of the unconscious provides a picture of the necessary yet radically insufficient, foreclosed core of gender constitution due to its unity and it radical differentiation-without-fragmentation or exhaustion.

The account I have given runs into even deeper contradiction with Laruelle's direct consideration of temporality in *The Dictionary of Non-Philosophy*: "non-philosophy renounces to make of time (or history or even becoming) the essence of the Real, to desubstantialize the latter by the former."[44] In order to not turn time or temporality into the idealized and hallucinated law or essence of the Real Laruelle develops a concept of time in line with his concept of memory; radically immanent, foreclosed, necessary yet insufficient. For non-philosophy "Time as Given or Past-without-temporalization, as seen-in-One or 'in time,' etc" are all:

> first names of time [that] symbolize not a past time but a past which simultaneously possesses a primacy over synchrony and diachrony and determines these transcendent dimensions themselves at least as

---

[43] François Laruelle, *The Dictionary of Non-Philosophy* (http://speculativeheresy.wordpress.com/2009/03/25/dictionary-of-non-philosophy/), 80.

[44] Ibid., 75.

comprising the object of philosophical interpretations. The radical past is uni-versal immanent time, of which one could say that it is-without-existing or even that it is a non-temporal time. It is less a question of a memory capable of forgetting and anamnesis than of a *past which cannot be forgotten and which, precisely for this reason, is foreclosed to memory* which itself, in its sufficiency, believes to be able to forget and repeat by anamnesis. This One-time, even effectuated as future, remains in its necessary sterility and in no way participates in the present-world such as non-philosophy conceives it and no longer—this is what distinguishes it from the Levinasian Other, and from the "trace"—in the ontological present or the "Same."[45]

For time to be consistent with the One, it must possess a radical primacy to both synchrony and diachrony. I have argued that if the fractal nature of the temporality of the unconscious plays the constitutive role in the constitution of (non-)gender Identity in a way that turns neither empirical contingency, difference or fracture nor the timeless, universal and static into an ideal law of Identity constitution, hence respecting the an-archic nature of the One. Just as the fractal can never be exhausted, the time of the unconscious determines yet can never in turn be determined or exhausted.

Laruelle's characterizes the non-psychoanalytic Unconscious in a way that falls in line with the above discussions of "Past-without-temporalization" and "Past foreclosed to memory." As a consequence, the common or "vulgar" philosophical language of "repression," "temporality" and most importantly "unconscious" cannot adequately maintain non-philosophical rigor. But, I think we can find what seems at first to be a crucial oversight in Laruelle's understanding of the Freudian Unconscious. Laruelle claims that:

> Psychoanalysis treats under the name of the unconscious not only one of the local proprieties of the psychic apparatus—the product of repression constituted from the representation of things (Freud, Klein)—but also the dimension of the imaginary (Jung) or symbolic (Lacan) Other,

---

[45] Laruelle, *The Dictionary of Non-Philosophy*, 76.

nevertheless generally endowed with a "subject" that Lacan estimates as being "nothing but the Cartesian subject."[46]

What Laruelle seems to be missing here are some very important comments in Freud's later work on the inexhaustible and un-decidable nature of the unconscious[47] and ultimately Freud's final suggestions that repression may not be the primary form of psychic defense and begins to emphasize the mechanisms of disavowal, first articulated in his work with fetishism.[48]

Certain concepts borrowed from psychoanalysis can and should be rigorously re-worked by way of a non-philosophical analysis in order to truly show the expanded potential of both psychoanalysis and non-philosophy in their relation to queer theories and other theories of the constitution of individuality. Here I have argued that the key step in preforming this task

---

[46] Laruelle, *The Dictionary of Non-Philosophy* 79-80.

[47] "Everything that is repressed must remain unconscious; but let us state at the very outset that the repressed does not cover everything that is unconscious. The unconscious has the wider compass; the repressed is a part of the unconscious" Freud, "The Unconscious," 166. The unconscious, contra Laruelle's suggestion, is not simply a topographical psychic stores house for repressed contents. There is some "thing" else there "in" or (of) the unconscious, but it seems as if the philosophical question of "what is x" has nearly exhausted itself attempting to exhausted this "thing."

[48] More importantly, by the end of Freud's thinking, disavowal, as the simultaneous, undecidable registration and repudiation of trauma takes on a more central role in the construction of all psychic defenses (repression included). As Alan Bass puts it "let me emphasize Freud's words: 'whatever the ego does in its efforts of defense...' In other words, the disavowal and ego splitting first elaborated in order to understand fetishism have now become the basis of a changed understanding of psychopathology in general" Alan Bass, *Difference and Disavowal: The Trauma of Eros*, (California: Stanford University Press, 2000). We must be cautious here, due to the Derridian resonances, in a reading of the importance of disavowal as a mechanism of defense. We must analyze this phenomenon in a "non-deconstructive" manner. This would involve, from my point of view a re-reading of Derrida's reading of Hegel and Antigone in *Glas* (Lincoln: University of Nebraska Press, 1990) alongside Laruelle's engagement with Derrida in chapter 5 of *Philosophies of Difference*. With caution, and more space than I have here, one could expand the implications of disavowal and non-philosophy.

involves re-thinking the time(lessness) of the Unconscious as something radically other (but not in the Judeic [still philosophical] sense) than a lack that generates and sustains oppositional, fragmented and ultimately "false" identities, or as simply a determined stasis, defining individuals "once and for all" at the outset regardless of empirical and material factors. The non-vulgar time of the unconscious turns out to be a strange form of non-philosophical and fractal time. Productive in-the-last-instance yet never in turn produced, unified yet inexhaustible, "unique each time but capable of an infinite power ceaselessly to secrete multiple identities" yet a "wall carries no signification," etc...

Thing Called Love
That Old, Substantive, Relation

Beatrice Marovich

Drew University

The Love Object

INTO WHAT, PRECISELY, DO WE PLUMmet when we fall *into* love? What, exactly, is produced when we *make* it? When we are hungry for love, what stomach is nourished by that strange food? Colloquialisms are littered with a language that *objectifies* love, that turns it into a *thing*—not just something we can feel, but something we can touch, something that hits us, changes us, throws us, consumes us, drives us. Popular parlance makes the love relation into something almost tangible, concrete, autonomous: love is some thing we *fall into*, love is a master key, love is a war, love is a bite of heaven, love is a virus. Such language begins to suggest that the "love object" is not, exactly, the person for whom you pine. Instead, it begins to look as though the "love object" is the relation, itself. Love takes on thing-like contours, becomes its own sort of creature. It does its own little cosmic dance.

Such formulations are, you might say, fundamentally idealist in nature. This is not to say that they are unrealistic, or anti-realistic. Rather, as Iain Hamilton Grant, Jeremy Dunham, and Sean Watson suggest—in their history of idealism—this language might be idealist in the sense that it attempts to be realistic about the idea, itself.[1] Love, the idea of love, is taken seriously as an entity. This raises the possibility that a love is something *real* in the world—more than merely the emotive outcome of a human psychological engagement. A love with such a degree of autonomy, presents itself as mind-independent. This kind of a love—a love that is somehow *real* in the world—allows us to speculate in strange new directions. Could it have been, for instance, *love* that was made as the leaf was reaching for the sun?

Never mind the obvious absurdities of such a statement. That we tend not to think of love in this particular manner, I realize, should be obvious. I offer it as a thought exercise because—much as I recognize that the prospect of such a "love object" invites skepticism—this idealistic method of investigating love also commends certain practices and approaches. That is to say, an idealistic understanding of love (one that attempts to approach the *idea itself* realistically, to understand the idea of love as something real in the world) can also understand that this entity—like other creatures who move, act, or grow—is something fragile and vulnerable. It is something that demands recognition and requires nurture. This is as true for the loves that appear between human individuals as it is for the loves that act as bonds between tiny earthlings and the creaky old planet that birthed them, that sustains them. Love that is *real* in the world may not be something we can prolong through the cultivation of psychological states. Rather, this sticky bonding relation that connects bodies has certain tissues and fibers of its own (tissues that come into *contact* with, yet are not reduced to, the folds and fibers of our human brains and bodies) This love

---

[1] Jeremy Dunham, Iain Hamilton Grant & Sean Watson, *Idealism: The History of a Philosophy* (Montreal, Kingston & Ithaca: McGill University Press, 2011), 7. They clarify, further, that with regard to ideas, an idealism means "having a theory of what they are." In this sense, perhaps, my parallel falls apart. If colloquial language *sounds* idealist in nature (because it reflects the extent to which we take ideas seriously as things in themselves) it probably lacks a *theory* of what exactly these ideas are. Nonetheless, I do think that such language reflects a kind of stubborn underlying realism with respect to the idea of love.

needs room to breathe, nourishment, attention, recognition.

Such a pronouncement might seem religious, in the Jamesian sense: a drive to make real (and live in accord with) the *unseen*. "Were one asked to categorize the life of religion in the broadest and most general terms possible," William James writes, "one might say that it consists of the belief that there is an unseen order, and that our supreme good lies in harmoniously adjusting ourselves thereto."[2] James intimates that the building blocks of religion[3] are abstractions with their own lives. "The more concrete objects of most men's [sic] religion, the deities whom they worship, are known only to them in idea."[4] And yet, "strangely enough" in the sincerity of our fervor, these abstractions come to "have a definite meaning *for our practice*. We can act *as if* there were a God; feel *as if* we were free; consider Nature *as if* she were full of special designs; lay plans *as if* we were immortal; and we find then that these words do make a genuine difference in our moral life."[5] He suggests that religion is the sphere of life, in other words, where the reality of the unseen—the actuality of abstractions—is sanctioned, preserved, and protected.

In the Christian tradition, of course, love has long been one of those great abstractions. Love, in fact, has been effectively collapsed into the figure of the divine itself: love has been divinized. The biblical assertion that "God is love" (1 John 4:8) has driven attempts *not only* to divinize the love relation but more, to assert its independence from human emotions and psychology. If love is, itself, divine (following a rather standard and orthodox line of Christian theologic) it must indeed be mind-independent. It cannot be a human

---

[2] William James, "Lecture 3: The Reality of the Unseen" in *The Varieties of Religious Experience* (London & New York: Collier MacMillan Publishers, 1961, 1973), 59.

[3] "The building blocks of religion": a phrase that I am playfully cribbing from Ann Taves. See: Ann Taves, *Religious Experience Reconsidered: A Building-Block Approach to the Study of Religion and Other Special Things* (Princeton, New Jersey & Woodstock, Oxfordshire: Princeton University Press, 2009).

[4] James, *Varieties*, 59.

[5] Ibid., 60.

construct, or a psychological, emotive aftershock. It must be *real* in the cosmic sense. It must be something with the agential power to bear responsibility, to shape worlds. This may be, perhaps, the very reason that the theologian Augustine of Hippo gave thing-like contours to love—turning it into a "substance."[6] Such a theoretical move suggestively points to a need for the most abstract of entities to become the most real, the most concrete.

Consider this essay a contemplative exercise in relational ontology—a speculative excursion. In what follows I endeavor to take the idea of love seriously—to make the relation *real*. Given his claim that "Anything real can be regarded as an object"[7] (even, crucially, a relation) I will have cause to explore the extent to which the substantive nature of love that emerges with Augustine can be illuminated or elaborated within Graham Harman's Object Oriented Ontology. I will explore, in other words, whether there isn't something about the love relation that emerges more clearly when we risk a light objectification of its contours.

The Love Relation as Divine Substance

Christian theologians have traditionally been, of course, extremely cautious to uphold orthodox distinctions between things worldly (creaturely, material) and things divine. This is no less true for Augustine, who declares that God is not only "invisible and unchangeable" but fully immortal and beyond all human comprehension (available only in fits and starts to our quasi-divine intellectual faculties).[8] God is said to be locked fully into the transcendent.

---

[6] I will acknowledge, further along in the essay, the complications inherent in using the phrase "thing-like" to describe divine substance. Suffice it to say, for the time being, that Augustine himself verges in this direction in *De Trinitatae*.

[7] Graham Harman, *Guerilla Metaphysics: Phenomenology and the Carpentry of Things* (Peru, Illinois: Open Court Publishing, 2005), 76.

[8] Saint Augustine, *The Trinity*, trans. Stephen McKenna (Washington D.C.: The Catholic University of America Press, 1963), Book 2.15.

Augustine's interpretive skills are stretched and challenged, however, when he attempts to account for how the triune God (immortal, immutable, invisible) could *also* be the Son—that fleshy humanoid figure who walked on earth—without sacrificing his transcendently divine qualities. How, in other words, could the divinity of the fleshy incarnation be accounted for? It was important, of course, that Augustine figure out a way to do so, for to claim that Christ incarnate (the Son) was basically just a special sort of creature, or an actual earthling, would have been tantamount to heresy. It would have been improper to let Christ's divinity lapse. The negation of Christ's full unity with the divine was the Modalist mistake (Sabellianism), which claimed that the triune God was three *distinct modes*, rather than one unity. The mono-God has to be one, and all the unique *facets* of this divinity must play the same game of identity. Augustine's task in *De Trinitatae* is to convince his reader that God can indeed be three unique persons, while still remaining (somehow) unitary. The special challenge presented by Christ's (clearly not divine) creature carnality is chalked up to habit.

First, Augustine argues that creatures are *made* or produced by the creating divine. Christ, on the other hand, was "begotten not made."[9] His special creation means that, "he is not a creature." He may have walked like a creature and talked like a creature, but in his nature, he is no creature. If he is not a creature, what else could he be but God himself (given that everything which is *not* God can rightly be considered creaturely)? That is to say, "if He is not a creature, then He is of the same substance with the Father, since every substance which is not God is a creature, and that which is not a creature is God."[10] This is the important qualification that Augustine will hammer away at, chapter by chapter, in *De Trinitatae*: the triune God is one unified *substance*. Within this substance, there are three persons (Father, Son, Holy Spirit). But they

---

[9] Here Augustine makes reference to the Nicene Creed, and the interpretation of 1 John 1.14.

[10] Augustine, *The Trinity*, Book 1.6.

all remain relationally connected in the unitary, univocal, divine substance.

How does he then explain the Son's apparent creatureliness (when he takes on the form of an earthling—a humanoid)? Augustine determines that the Son has the *habit*[11] of taking on creaturely form (or, as Augustine more frequently phrases it, the form of a "slave.") The Latin term *habitus* is, of course, derived from the verb *habere*: to have, to hold, to own, to possess. The *habitus* might also be translated as a "condition," an "appearance," or a "state." The Son, in other words, might have the *appearance* of a creature, or might reside temporarily within the *state* of a creature. To speak of a creaturely *condition*, or a creaturely *state*, might make a more ready parallel to Pierre Bordieu's use of the term *habitus*: a "system of dispositions"[12] that governs and structures practices, perpetuating the past into the present. But the advantage of the term *habit* is the easy parallel to the language of a garment: a new nature is put on, like a garment, and taken off. The language of habit, I think, puts the ease and superficiality of this transition into sharper relief.

We might say that the Son, then, has a penchant for putting on the veil of creaturely materiality. This should be understood merely as a *personality* trait of the divine person—something he has the capacity to do, but that does not transform his nature. The Son is "equal to God the Father by nature, but less than he by habit."[13] The Son, we might say, has his own habits. And it is by virtue of such habits that the mechanism of incarnation is set in motion. Habit is the "mediator" between God and human.[14] It is, then, this habit that brings divine substance into the world in a form that humans can sense

---

[11] The Latin term is *habitus*, and the translation of this term in to the English "habit" can certainly be contested as inappropriate. I am exploiting, here, the language used in the 1963 translation by Stephen McKenna.

[12] Pierre Bordieu, *The Logic of Practice*, trans. Richard Nice (Stanford, Calif.: Stanford University Press, 1990) 54.

[13] Augustine, *The Trinity*, Book 1.7.

[14] Ibid., Book 1.8.

and comprehend. Divine substance can—in exceptional circumstances—become habituated to a creaturely form. The invisible, eternal, and immutable divine substance becomes comprehensible and sensible as a habit. Christ takes on the habit—he wears the veil of the creaturely world.

Christ, however, remains substantially divine. His habit may be creaturely, but his substance is divine. Augustine recognizes that the language of substance is tricky, risky. God must be a *substance* because God is certainly not an *accident*. Moreover, "we can in no way rightly say that anything is known while its substance is unknown."[15] We cannot claim to *know* God, in other words, if we do not know something about the divine substance. So it would seem that the language of substance can be appropriately applied to the divine. Or can it? "God is without a doubt a substance," Augustine pronounces, then muses more tentatively, "or perhaps essence would be a better term, which the Greeks call *ousia*."[16] Better for what reason? Because an essence is more clearly ethereal? More presciently spiritual? Augustine then begins to confuse himself further over other possible cognates for this slippery term. "They indeed also call it *hypostasis*," he ponders, "but I do not know what different meaning they wish to give to *ousia* and *hypostasis*."[17]

His confusion over the proper description of this divine substance signals that Augustine may be anxious about the possible consequences of substantializing the deity.

What interests me most, however, is that in the end Augustine does not fear—at least in brief flashes—*objectifying* the divine, giving it thing-like contours. What remains important, for Augustine, is that this divine object be wholly uncreaturely. It cannot be a *thing* in the same manner that a creature is a thing. It is (or should be) another sort of *thing*, entirely. The divine object, the divine thing, must be invisible, eternal, and immutable. "For the nature itself, or the substance, or

---

[15] Augustine, *The Trinity*, Book 10.10.

[16] Ibid., Book 5.2.

[17] Ibid., Book 5.8.

the essence" he writes almost on the verge of confusion, "or whatever name the *thing itself* that God is, whatever it should be called, cannot be seen corporeally."[18] I am interested in the fact that, in the end, the divine substance (or whatever it's most rightly named) is indeed a kind of *thing*. There is something thing-like about God. Is this part of what (for Augustine) "proves" the deity's reality, or actuality?

The incarnation, then, is not ultimately a roadblock in Augustine's path to discern divine substance. The language of substance becomes, however, even more risky when we begin to speak of high-ranking *spiritual creatures* such as angels, or the soul. These creatures, hovering around us or filling us up from the inside, might seem (in their very substance) as immutable, eternal, and invisible as the divine itself. They are, similarly, beyond the senses—they nag at the senses from some other realm. But Augustine works to cleverly distinguish these substances from God.

The human soul was, for Augustine, an extremely special cosmic substance—one that occupied a top rung in the hierarchical ladder of creation. The soul, for Augustine, was made *in the image* of God. The deity created the human "out of the dust of the earth" (not so special), but gave it "a soul of such a kind that because of it he surpassed all living creatures, on earth, in the sea, and in the sky in virtue of reason and intelligence; for no other creature had a mind like that."[19] The soul, then, was responsible for bringing the human closer to the angels, closer to God. But Augustine was also careful to distinguish that—when it comes to evaluating the human person—the *soul* of the human should not be considered in *isolation* from the body. Even *if* the soul was an awesome spiritual substance, it should not be divorced from the body. This is precisely why he disliked the Platonic doctrine of the soul—because it made the flesh abject, responsible for the evils of the world.[20] The emotions (which were acts of the

---

[18] Augustine, *The Trinity*, Book 2.18. *Emphasis mine.*

[19] Saint Augustine, *City of God*, trans. Henry Bettenson (New York: Penguin Classics, 2003), Book 12.24.

[20] Ibid., Book 14.5.

abstract will) were responsible for the perversions that drove the human to do evil.[21] This is also why Augustine contested Origen's claim that the soul was housed in the body, as if it were a prison.[22] Thus, the body could not be blamed for all perversion. The soul and the body could never be entirely separate. Certainly, in death the soul abandoned the body. So a moment of severance was inevitable. But, in Augustine's cosmology, the body and soul were reunited in the afterlife. We would get our actual bodies back (merged with our soul). Interestingly, however, they would be super-bodies, living in a state of superlative health, as "words cannot express the immense difference between what we call health in our present condition and the immortality which is to be ours in the future."[23] As human creatures, Augustine considered us a kind of soul/body package.

The fact that the soul is eternally related to the body gives some nuance to the claim that, for Augustine, the soul was a *creature* (and not a shard, or slice, of the creator). But it is important to note that the creatureliness of the soul held, even when the spiritual substance of the soul was contemplated *in abstraction* from the body. This is, Philip Cary argues, the crucial distinction between Plotinus' Neo-Platonism and Augustine. While Augustine agreed with the Plotinian claim that we must look *inward* to find the divine, what we find in the deep recesses of the human interior is not God, properly speaking. God starts to become *intelligible* when we look inward—the "eye of the soul" starts to get a glimpse of the divine. But there is not a collapse of distinction between the soul and God. One can indeed "look inside the self to find what is not self."[24] But to confess the soul's creatureliness is to repudiate its divinity. The soul, for instance, is a spiritual creature that can suffer a mortal death. The soul, Augustine

---

[21] Augustine, *City of God*, Book 14.6.

[22] Ibid., Book 11.23.

[23] Ibid., Book 13.18.

[24] Phillip Cary, *Augustine's Invention of the Inner Self: The Legacy of a Christian Platonist* (Oxford: Oxford University Press, 2000), 114.

clarifies, "is said to die, not because it is changed, or turned into a body or into any other substance, but because...[it] is found to be mortal inasmuch as that which it was has ceased to be."[25] The nature of the soul in its entirety, its basic substance, does not change. But something is altered in the mode of the soul—the soul's modality. Augustine suggests, in *City of God* that "the death of the soul results when God abandons it."[26] That which it was (blessed) has ceased to be. The soul dies when its blessedness dies.

Discerning divine substance is a messy business. And, realistically, to speak of divine substance is to make reference to an extremely long-lived and complicated series of debates in Christian theology. To contemplate the possible contours of divine substance would extend this essay far beyond the bounds of any reasonable limit. I have not even treated the subject exhaustively, in Augustine's own corpus. What I hope to have shown is merely that the thing-like contours of God, for Augustine, were thing-like in a way that does not seem concrete. Even the soul—a spiritual substance whose creaturely form is *so* abstract that it's commonly thought not to exist at all—is alleged to be thing-like in a more concrete sense than the deity. When it comes to the matter of divine substance, we have seen Augustine wrangling with Christ's creature carnality, searching for a way to determinately distinguish it from divine substance. We have seen him struggling with the strange substance of spiritual creatures—attempting to ensure that their insensible invisibility is not mistaken for some variant of divine substance. But it is love, I think, that presents Augustine with the most difficult challenge of all. For Augustine must give credence to the biblical injunction that "God is love" (he points, especially, to 1 John 4:8), while also recognizing the fact that there is nothing quite so creaturely, quite so carnal, quite so worldly and earth-bound as love itself. To charge that love is *thing-like*, but only thing-like in a *divine* way, was to set for himself a difficult metaphysical challenge.

---

[25] Augustine, *The Trinity*, Book 2.9.
[26] Augustine, *City of God*, Book 13.2.

What does Augustine talk about, when he talks about love? This, even for Augustine, is a perplexing question. For, when he loves *love*, he must love *God*. Yet what can it mean to love *love*, to love a relation? Passages in Augustine's work seem to reflect his own bewilderment over what it would mean to turn a relation into something metaphysically actual. "But what is it that I love in loving you?" he asks his god.[27] He loves a certain *manner of thing*. But he cannot, quite, discern what that thing might be. It is "not manna and honey, not the limbs embraced in physical love" that he loves, when he loves love. And yet neither is this *thing* that he loves, when he loves love, entirely without some sensual *thingness* itself. "I love a certain kind of light and sound and fragrance and food and embrace in loving my god."[28] Augustine stresses that love is certainly not nothing, it is not made of nothingness. It must, in some sense, be a *thing* that exists. "If love is nothing, how can it be said 'God is love?' If it is not a substance, how is God a substance?"[29] Augustine is careful to note that whatever this God stuff *is*, it must be more *spirit* than *body*.[30] Yet Augustine recognizes how odd it seems to call love a *thing*—namely, because it seems impossible to love love. That is to say, one cannot fall *in love* with love. "For I do not love love, except I love a lover, for there is no love where nothing is loved."[31] To repeat: Augustine discovers, I think, the strangeness of making a relation into something metaphysically *actual*.

Love must be *something* (because it cannot be *nothing*). Love must be a substance (according to the metaphysical rules he's set out for himself). Love must have some sort of thingness about it. And, yet, given that love is a relation, neither can he deny that this thingness is ever truly isolated, solitary, or wholly independent. Whatever thingness the love relation

---

[27] Saint Augustine, *Confessions*, trans. Albert C. Outler & Mark Vessey (New York: Barnes and Noble Classics), Book 10.5.7.

[28] Ibid., Book 10.6.8.

[29] Ibid., 6.5.

[30] Ibid., 9.2.

[31] Ibid.

has is tenuous and fragile—dependent, for its existence, on what it relates. Divine substance is not creaturely. And yet, it *does* take on a strange creaturely cast, glare, or contour: it begins to look (and perhaps smell) sensual, it begins to look *dependent*. Much as Augustine seeks to uphold the orthodox, rigid, distinction between the creaturely and the creatorly, the fleshy, dependent nature of the love relation seems to rope him into confounding these boundaries. It is necessary, here, to navigate through a resulting bifurcation that occurs in Augustine's development of love.

Eric Gregory argues that, for Augustine, love "like cholesterol, can be healthy or deadly."[32] He is making reference, of course, to Augustine's description of love as either *cupiditas* (desire) or *caritas* (charity, true love, good love). By this logic, it would seem, love is either good or bad: immanent, fleshy (and *of this world*), or heavenly, disembodied, and transcendent. This would split love into two variants, or strains. Thomas Carlson, for example, points to the "extraworldly tendency of love in Augustine and his heirs."[33] To speak of a "love of the world" was, says Carlson, to speak of "our human way of being with others."[34] Augustine, by this analysis, validates a love that is *out of this world*. For this reason, Carlson calls for a way of thinking love that reconnects the polarities, to think love "within the world, by making it a condition of the world."[35]

Hannah Arendt explored this distinction between *caritas* and *cupiditas* at great length in her doctoral dissertation, *Love and Saint Augustine*. As Arendt reads Augustine, there is a gap between lover and loved that begs to be filled. When I use the term "gap," I will be making reference to her analysis. But I think it clarifies something useful. Lover and loved need a connector. *Cupiditas*, she says, fills the gap between creatures

---

[32] Eric Gregory, *Politics and the Order of Love: An Augustinian Ethic of Democratic Citizenship* (Chicago & London: University of Chicago Press, 2008), 35.

[33] Thomas A. Carlson, *Indiscrete Image: Infinitude and the Creation of the Human* (Chicago: University of Chicago Press, 2008), 214.

[34] Ibid., 215.

[35] Ibid., 215.

while *caritas* fills the gap between creature and creator.[36] What I would especially like to underscore in Arendt's analysis is that both *caritas* and *cupiditas* "are distinguished by their objects, but they are not different kinds of emotion."[37] In other words, they belong to the same phenomenon. They are, in the last instance, the same thing. Love as *caritas*, Arendt clarifies, is a kind of ceaseless craving passion that turns whatever it craves into something to either ravish or consume. "The object of craving can only be a thing I can possess and enjoy, and it is therefore quite characteristic that in this context Augustine can even speak of God as an 'object of enjoyment.'"[38] Arendt thus underscores the importance, for Augustine, that when we (as human creatures) love, we must be careful to cast our love in the *proper direction*. We must be wary of where we cast our love. *Cupiditas* is a love of things in *this world*, it's a love *of* carnality and *in* carnality. *Caritas* aims outside of the world. It is directed toward the eternal God. One who loves the world via *caritas* will filter their love for the world through this *caritas* and will be able to love the world properly.

What I think we can get from this analysis is simply the complexity of this thing called love. Arendt claims that love is one form of "emotion" that is complicated in its directionality. This is, of course, an atheistic reading—one that reads love as purely emotive, rather than (in some sense) divine. For Augustine, I suggest, love is a form of *divine substance* that can be complicated in its directionality—pulled and tugged in various directions. I would stress that it is important to recognize the ambivalence inherent in Augustine's understanding of love, without understanding Augustine's love as something that is bifurcated *all the way down*—something that is eternally split between spheres (the temporal and the eternal). There are not kinds, variants, or strains of love. There

---

[36] Hannah Arendt, *Love and Saint Augustine*, Edited by Joanna Vecchiarelli Scott and Judith Chelius Stark (Chicago & London: University of Chicago Press, 1996), 30.

[37] Ibid., 18.

[38] Ibid., 16.

are distinct deployments of love, ways of directing it. It seems more accurate to me to say that love, for Augustine, is love. It is *one* thing. Thus, by this reading, to say that the God (who is one) is love (which is one) is to make a one-to-one correlation. The variations that create the *illusion* of different *kinds* of love are simply incremental distinctions in intensity. I am arguing that Augustine sees love deployed along a spectrum, or a continuum. Perhaps it is helpful, then, to imagine *caritas* and *cupiditas* as distinct points on a parabolic line of love.

Edward Morgan argues that *caritas* and *cupiditas* are at "intersecting but opposing points in an Augustinian ethical spectrum."[39] Morgan argues that the two are involved in a "transformative dialogue"[40] that happens through language—via the *word*. His claim, in other words, is that Augustine's *caritas* is "re-formed by engagement with scripture's prescriptive norm of *caritas*."[41] The medium of the text serves as the point of intersection. The text is what consolidates and reveals the continuity between *cupiditas* and *caritas*—the continuity that binds them within the more singular force of love. In their recent collaborative commentary on Augustine's *Confessions* Virginia Burrus, Mark Jordan, and Karmen MacKendrick also allude to the transformations that occur, for Augustine, through the medium of text. The "beauty of the text," they suggest, allows Augustine to slip "between flesh and words, words not always even about the flesh, though always, in sublime disregard of his own anti-rhetorical stance, words with a potent sensory appeal." The text is a point of intersection between flesh and abstraction. They claim that although "the *Confessions* seems—though, in real ways, it is—a text startlingly without a body, especially without a divine body" there is still a sense in which, "it is also a text in which every word is drawn toward the body."[42] Bodies burst into the text, and the

---

[39] Edward Morgan, *Incarnation of the Word: The Theology of Language of Augustine of Hippo* (New York & London: T&T Clark International, 2010), 73.

[40] Ibid., 74.

[41] Ibid., 75.

[42] Virginia Burrus, Mark D. Jordan, and Karmen Mackendrick, *Seducing*

text injects itself into bodies. We might see such slippage in, for example, Augustine's description of God's busty incarnations. Speaking of the breast milk that nourished him as a child, Augustine writes, "neither my mother nor my nurses filled their own breasts but you, through them."[43] God does not have a body, yet is present in the most intimate recesses of bodies. God may not have a distinct body, but does not leave bodies behind. There is, in the *Confessions*, a "mutual seduction of bodies and words."[44]

Augustine may claim to turn away from the flesh (from the world), when he turns toward God. But his own texts reveal the mutual transformation, the dialogue, between *caritas* and *cupiditas*. If scriptures are able to serve (as Morgan suggests) as a corrective to transform *cupiditas*, bodies (and images of bodies) also attach themselves to words and bring *caritas* back into the world, into the flesh. The text is the medium that reveals that *caritas* and *cupiditas* are not bifurcated into different kinds of love, but remain bound. As Augustine reports (textually) in his *Confessions*, he is seduced by his God, he burns for his God—divine love offers the most superlative erotic prospects. As MacKendrick has elsewhere argued, "Only God holds—or, as I suspect *is*—the promise of burning that hot."[45] The text reveals the entanglements of *caritas* and *cupiditas*. In this sense, there is a complex crossing of signals between *caritas* and *cupiditas* as different signals light up, on the spectrum of love.

If love moves back and forth, intensely and anxiously, between *cupiditas* and *caritas* on the parabola of love, does this mean that *cupiditas* is merely the side of the love spectrum most detached from the divine pinnacle of love? Would

---

Augustine: Bodies, Desires, Confesions (New York: Fordham University Press, 2010), 125.

[43] Augustine, *Confessions*, Book 1.6.7.

[44] Burrus, Jordan, and Mackendrick, *Seducing Augustine*, 125.

[45] Karmen MacKendrick, "Carthage Didn't Burn Hot Enough: Saint Augustine's Divine Seduction," in *Towards a Theology of Eros: Transfiguring Passion at the Limits of Discipline*, ed. Virginia Burrs and Catherine Keller (New York: Fordham University Press, 2006), 217.

cupiditas be a point on the end of the line, while the deity is located on the equidistant opposing point? It is not toward *cupiditas*, I submit, that we need to look if we seek the antithesis of love but, instead, to the love *of nothing*. That is to say, there *is* an end of the line—when it comes to love. Love (as God) may live eternally. But there is still a point when love becomes something else—when it undergoes a change of identity, when it stops being love. This happens when love loves *nothing*—when love is nullified.

In Book Two of the *Confessions*, Augustine gives a rather dramatic account of his youthful folly: the theft of some pears from a neighbor's tree. This narrative is a paradigmatic reflection on his sense of sin. In the end, it is not the *act* of stealing that appears most abhorrent to Augustine. Rather, what is most vile is that it revealed the nature and direction of his love: the nihilism of his love.[46] Given that there was no good, none at all, in the simple act of theft, Augustine claims that, "the theft itself was nothing."[47] Given that the act lacked any ontological good, it was evil (for Augustine, an ontological nothingness that is the antithesis of the profundity of creation). When he loved the theft, he was in love with nothing. He confesses that he had no love, whatsoever, for the pears that he stole. He took no pleasure at all in their juicy, fleshy, pear bodies. This was, in the end, a shame as it revealed to him that, "I did not desire to enjoy what I stole, but only the theft and the sin itself."[48] What this intimates, it seems, is that the love might have been less vile had it been mediated by something else. The theft might have been slightly less vile, had the love of the theft been interrupted or complicated by the love for a juicy, fleshy pear body.

Here, in this situation where Augustine loves nothing—by loving the sin of theft itself—it is the lack of mediation that I

---

[46] I have been aided in my analysis of this passage by: Kim Paffenroth, "Bad Habits and Bad Company: Education and Evil in the *Confessions*," in *Augustine and Liberal Education*, ed. Kim Paffenroth and Kevin L. Hughes (Lanham, Maryland: Lexington Books, 2008), 5.

[47] Augustine, *Confessions*, Book 2.8.16.

[48] Ibid., Book 2.3.8.

would like to highlight as central. As Arendt has articulated: the conundrum of love is that it exists to fill a gap between lover and loved. This is what makes love a trinity, by Augustine's account. "There are, therefore, three: the lover, the beloved, and the love."[49] It is the Trinitarian nature of love that allows him to draw an easy, and suggestive, parallel between love and God. When we love, we participate in a trinity. The substance of love can be *like* the divine substance because both are Trinitarian. What this means is that love exists, as a third. The death of love is when this third—this mediating element—is left out of the equation, or collapses. If the love of a thing in itself (in the very worst case, perhaps, a sin) is not interrupted or complicated by a mediating element, love is nullified. As James Wetzel puts it, sin is a void, "it is the lack in love,"[50] what becomes the lack *of* love. What the love of nothing lacks, says Wetzel, is "measure." God is "the beloved beyond measure."[51] In a love *of nothing* there is nothing to fill the gap between lover and loved. Nothingness is what fills the gap between lover and loved—rather than a love relation. To steal a pear in order to love the juicy, fleshy pear body wouldn't have been a holy act. But it would have mediated, or complicated, the love of theft with the love OF something good. For Augustine, the holiest sort of creature-to-creature connection is to love creaturely things with a love of God as the measure between them—to love things *in* God, to love microcosmic creatures within the macrocosm of God-love. This serves as a mediator, or complicator, in connections. We might imagine this holiest form of love as the vertex in the parabola of love, where the point of *caritas* crosses with that of *cupiditas*.

Love is a relation that binds. But, as the sort of relation I have been illuminating here, love is *always and already* a love

---

[49] Augustine, *The Trinity*, Book 9.2.

[50] James Wetzel, "Snares of Truth: Augustine on Free Will and Predestination," in *Augustine and His Critics*, ed. Robert Dodaro and George Lawless (London & new York: Routledge, 2000, 2005), 132.

[51] Wetzel, *Augustine and His Critics*, 135.

OF. That is to say (for example), when two humans love one another, the love that binds them is a relation. But this relation is not a simple knot between them, or a blob, or a plug. Rather, it is its own life and dynamic. The love that connects is, itself, already related (in a cosmic sense). In other words, love is something like a macrocosmic relation—a framework. To be *in love* is to be microscopically connected within the macrocosm of a connection: to be points on the parabolic line of love. The love *of God* becomes a framework for microcosmic loves between creatures. To love within the umbrage of this macrocosmic framework is what, I'm suggesting, it means to love *in God*. At the other extreme, the love *of nothing* is also a macrocosmic framework. But the love *of nothing* cuts love off from itself. Love is nullified as it's isolated from its connectivity. This is the negation of love, a putting-to-death of love, or nullification of love. Therefore, to love in the umbrage of this love *of nothing* is actually to pop or squash the fragile life of the relational connection. Connection is pursued without the mediator. We might imagine this, for example, as the quest to traverse a ravine without constructing a bridge, or finding a footpath. This might require, simply, convincing oneself that the ravine does not exist, which would be nothing more than a delusion.

Love's Ontological Dilemma: Object or Relation?

In the end, I am less interested in Augustine's metaphysics of love for its potential holiness. The function that it serves for me, here, is as a relational ontology that doggedly seeks to give reality, *actuality*, to the abstract figure of a relation. A relational ontology, like that of Bruno Latour, would deny Augustine's claim that a divine thing—like love—is a substance. Latour insists that the divinities (who he deems concrete and actual enough to dub creatures[52]) are "not substances." Instead, "they

---

[52] This is, of course, resonant with Alfred North Whitehead's process ontology where he follows up on William James' decoupling of the divine and the absolute (that emerges in his tirade against the British Hegelians in *A Pluralistic Universe*). God, says Whitehead, is the "primordial creature"

are all action."[53] Divinities are not substances but events that he calls "modus operandi."[54] This is, in fact, why he insists on calling them "divinities" rather than gods—because the gods, it is said, save through their very presence, they claim a kind of presence that only an ontology of substance might give them.

In his own analysis, however, Latour fails to "give a seat in existence" to the divinity I've been discussing: this divine relation, this divine thing called love. I'm simply suggesting that its agency and actuality is not sufficiently accounted for. Latour underscores the fact that love, in some crucial way, explains the function of religion—the way it works. Love, and specifically what he calls "love talk" (language exchanged between lovers) illustrates the critical distinction that Latour draws between religion and science. Both religion and science, he argues (echoing the passage from William James, cited earlier), are "regimes of invisibility." Neither of them (contrary, perhaps, to established belief) are much interested in the visible world. But the assumption, Latour argues, that religion is primarily preoccupied with the transcendent, the distant—that which is most far away—is erroneous. Instead, he suggests, "the long mediated chains of science" are what lead toward "the distant and the absent" while religion is actually preoccupied with "the representation of the close and the present."[55] Science seeks to get into the furthest reaches of the universe, while religion is concerned with bringing it close. Love talk, as he sees it, is exemplary of this process, this religious bringing-close-and-present. The words that lovers use are, in themselves, rather banal. There is nothing much thrilling in the confession: "I love you." What is significant about it, says Latour, is "the *transformation* it generates in

---

who is "transcended by the creativity which it qualifies." See: Alfred North Whitehead, *Process and Reality: An Essay in Cosmology* (New York: The Free Press, 1978), 31, 88.

[53] Bruno Latour, *On the Modern Cult of the Factish Gods* (Durham, NC: Duke University Press, 2010), 50.

[54] Ibid., 50.

[55] Ibid., 113.

the listener, as well as the speaker." Love talk possesses an incredible agency—the power to bring bodies close, the power to intimate. The power of religion, of religious talk, is not dissimilar. Religion "aims at jumping, dancing toward the present and the close: to redirect attention away from indifference and habituation, to prepare oneself to be seized again by this presence that breaks the usual, habituated passage of time."[56] Religion is about transforming the spaces between us and around us. Religion works to bring something (the divinities?) close and present.

What is interesting to note, however, is the role that Latour suggests *love* plays in religion. Love, in this discussion, is not a relation with any particular pride of place. Love is not a *site* where anything religiously significant is happening. Love talk exemplifies a *form of transmission*, a mode of relation. But this transmission, itself, is not concrete. Love talk is like a sign, or an icon, of the transmission that occurs. But the love, itself, is not a thing. Nor is love religiously meaningful (as anything more than an analogue). Latour avoids what he calls "freeze-framing" the love relation. Freeze-framing, he writes, takes an image (let us say, in this instance, the image of a love) and "interrupts the movement of the image" by "isolating it out of its flows of renewed images, in order to believe it has a meaning by itself."[57] Both religion and science, he states, are constituted by a "flowing character." And so he interprets the cardinal sin as nothing else but freeze-framing. Idolatary is not about the *making* of images, but the freeze-framing of them. "God did not ask us not to make images (what else do we have to produce objectivity, to generate piety?) but he told us not to freeze-frame, that is, not to isolate an image out of the flows that only produce them with their real—their constantly re-realized, re-represented meaning."[58] It may be, perhaps, that even a light objectification of love—such as that we witnessed in Augustine—is at risk of freeze-framing.

---

[56] Latour, *On the Modern Cult*, 122.

[57] Ibid., 121.

[58] Ibid., 123.

Yet there is something about the quality, or character, of love that both popular sentiment, as well as Augustine's metaphysical confessions, capture. Love talk *points* to a kind of transformation that happens across a gap (between lovers). But when a love becomes real (when two actors have "fallen into" the real thing in this gap between them) something *happens* in the world, something is born, something is made. There exists, between the lovers, an actual bond, a tie. The world itself readjusts to accommodate its presence. I would argue that this calls for a light objectification of the love relation—a sort of gentle freeze-framing, a willingness to see it as some real thing, with a presence: a *real* creature, an enduring thing, who calls out for recognition.

The metaphysical conflict between objects and relations has been explored at great length by Object Oriented Ontologist Graham Harman. Making the interesting move to read Latour (the Actor-Network theorist) as a metaphysician, Harman believes that Latour is object oriented in *some* senses, but not in others. While Latour does, indeed, account for the agency of non-human actors (such as, for example, divinities) the point of greatest difference between Latour and Object Oriented Ontology appears to be that Latour risks "reducing" real objects to the sum total of their relations—real objects are subsumed in his relationalism. Rather than fall error to Whitehead's "fallacy of misplaced concreteness"[59] Harman seems to suggest that Latour commits another sort of fallacy—of misplaced indeterminateness, perhaps. For Latour, Harman emphasizes, a *thing* is "nothing more than its sum total of perturbations of other entities. There is no mysterious residue in the things hiding behind their relations with other things."[60] This is what Harman calls the "weakest" form of relationalism—neither a "lump universe" that sees the entire cosmos as one connected relation, or a correlationism.

---

[59] "This fallacy consists in neglecting the degree of abstraction involved when an actual entity is considered merely so far as it exemplifies certain categories of thought." See: Whitehead, *Process and Reality*, 7.

[60] Graham Harman, *Prince of Networks: Bruno Latour and Metaphysics* (Melbourne: re.press, 2009), 158.

Latour's relationalism is, more, a kind of "theory of internal relations."[61]

Harman, on the other hand, has sought to underscore what he believes is a kind of "non-relational actuality" somewhere at the heart of things, their ability to "be actual without being registered by other things, or at least without being registered fully by them."[62] His sense is that reducing all objects to nothing more than their relations "does an injustice to the object in question."[63] There is a sense in which the actuality of a thing is exhausted by its connections. You are your connections, and nothing more: any entity is nothing other than a point in a network. This has given rise to Harman's somewhat polemical position—that the object is *always* more than its relations. The object is "a real thing apart from all foreign relations with the world, and apart from all domestic relations with its own pieces."[64] This holds *not only* for objects that we can touch (a rock, a hammer) but for relations as well. Relations, in other words, are themselves objects that are independent of (and more than) their own relations. Once a relation emerges into existence, it takes on the properties of what Harman calls an object. This may risk sounding nonsensical, but the emphasis falls on the fact that relations illustrate characteristics of an object and maintain a kind of non-relational core.

What is important to note, however, is that Harman wants to soften the sharp distinction between objects and relations (rather than deny the reality of relations). He argues that, "no simple distinction can be made between relational and nonrelational entities, since every entity is both of these."[65] Relations as objects (which I will simply refer to as "relational objects") play the cosmic role of acting as "the very carpentry

---

[61] Harman, *Prince of Networks*, 187.

[62] Ibid.

[63] Ibid., 186.

[64] Ibid., 188.

[65] Graham Harman, *Tool-Being: Heidegger and the Metaphysics of Objects* (Peru, Illinois: Open Court Publishing, 2002), 284.

of things, the joints and glue that hold the world together."⁶⁶ Relations are the objects that are created when two other objects come into contact. "When two objects come into genuine relation, even if they do not permanently fuse together, they generate a reality that has all of the features we require of an object."⁶⁷ This gives rise to what sounds like a rather hallucinogenic (and, perhaps, harmonious) interchange of objects and relations—what Harman calls the "wheel of substance and relation." "Substances are filled with relations; relations become substances. The wheel of substance and relation throws everything in the cosmos sometimes into one of these roles, sometimes into the other." More, "an object always plays both roles simultaneously, and it is only our reflection on them that places it more emphatically in one light or another."⁶⁸ It is only our ontological framework, in other words, that stops the wheel of substance and relation from spinning.

Up to this point, the object-oriented frame seems to provide a hospitable environment for the reality of a substantive relation like love. More intriguing parallels develop, however, when we ponder the connections between Augustine's substantive love relation and Harman's theory of "vicarious causation." The claim that all objects (even relations) withdraw into an autonomous and non-related core presents us with an ontological situation in which, "relations never directly encounter the autonomous reality of their components."⁶⁹ Objects hide from one another "endlessly, and inflict their mutual blows only through some vicar or intermediary."⁷⁰ This leads to the necessity of a mediator. This happens through the process of vicarious causation where "entities influence one another only by meeting on the interior of a third, where they exist side-by-side until something happens that allows them to

---

⁶⁶ Harman, *Guerilla Metaphysics*, 20.

⁶⁷ Ibid., 85.

⁶⁸ Ibid.

⁶⁹ Graham Harman, "On Vicarious Causation," *Collapse*, Vol II: Speculative Realism, Edited by Robin Mackay (March 2007): 171-205, 189.

⁷⁰ Ibid., 190.

interact."[71] The relation, as a third object, is born out of a kind of causal necessity: two objects are driven to connect, and so a relation is born. The site where the connections occur is not between the two objects' deep non-relational core, but along their sensual plane. "Something must happen on the sensual plane to allow them to make contact."[72] The sensual plane of objects gives birth to the relational object.

The vicarious causation that gives rise to a new relational object unfolds into a rather Trinitarian dynamic: one object can only touch another object by the creation of a third. In this sense, it resembles Augustine's substantive love relation: the gap between lovers is filled by the mediating relational substance of divine love. Even Harman's choice of language is interestingly relevant for the example at hand: the love object is created through the *sensual* point of contact between objects (by sensual objects). We might think, then, of the love object as read out of Augustine's metaphysics (which is also, coincidentally, God) as a third object that is borne from the gap between the lover objects. This also allows for an interesting explanation of how it is that love (which is a relation) can happen *in God*, as Augustine declares it to. Love can occur *within* an entity, because the entity is (itself) a relation. The ability to consider love more objectively opens new possibilities for (perhaps heretically) unpacking this orthodox claim.

All of this (the ability to contemplate love as *both* object and relation, the theory of vicarious causation that explains the birth of the new, thing-like, relation) would suggest that OOO offers a theoretical environment where the reality of love can be discerned at its most robust. And yet I am skeptical that, in the last instance, an object-oriented framework can accurately discern the reality of love—that substantive relation. The reason, I submit, is that Harman halts the wheel of substance and relation—forcing relations into the ontological position of objects. What this means is that, because entities are always objects, they are each "sealed away in a vacuum devoid of all

---

[71] Harman, "On Vicarious Causation," 190.
[72] Ibid., 197.

relation." These vacuums are "noncommunicating vacuous zones, ontological bubbles, none of them able to transmit energy or influence to the others."[73] Harman has described this withdrawal as "the single basic tenet" of an object-oriented philosophy.[74] The issue of withdrawal has been a subject of hot debate, on the blogosphere, between process-relational and object-oriented thinkers. I make, here, no claim about the possibility of withdrawal as a localized phenomenon. I merely question its universalizability.

What I mean to suggest is, merely, that withdrawal would nullify the reality (the very existence) of the substantive relation that I have illuminated in the preceding pages. To force the substantive relation into a purely objective status would be to take an anti-realist ontological approach to its actuality. For Augustine, the substantive love relation hovers in a paradoxical and anxious tension between object and relation. Indeed, I think it's appropriate to understand it as caught up within the wheel of substance and relation. But if the substantive relation that is love were to be located (at its *most real*) within a state of withdrawal, this would make the love relation something noncommunicating, cut off, existent within its own private vacuum. In Harman's ontology, it would seem entirely possible for a relation like love to exist, in its full reality, as a Platonically unconnected form. Particular loves would then be sensual instantiations of this great form. But for the substantive relation of love that I have explored, to be shut into a private vacuum (where it is disconnected and nonrelational) would essentially put an end to the love relation. It would be, in essence, a love *of nothing*. This was for Augustine, as we have seen, the end of love, the nullification of love. Love is born into existence (and remains real) to the extent that it is a love *of something*—in the best case (by Augustine's account) of the deity. The substance and essence of love is that it is a relation: a love *of*. When it is cut off from its relational status and loves *nothing*, the love relation col-

---

[73] Harman, *Tool Being*, 295.
[74] Harman, *Guerilla Metaphysics*, 20.

lapses and leaves nothing between lovers. It is in its love *of something* that a love relation becomes substantive enough to fill the gap between lovers.

This is, perhaps, the result of considering the love relation within a metaphysical frame that is purely objective. Harman suggests that ontology should be defined as "a description of the basic structural features" whereas metaphysics treats "fundamental traits."[75] To say that a given entity (like love) bears the *structural features* of an object does not preclude us from looking at those structural features from another angle (that of a relation). But to claim that the *fundamental traits* of an entity reveal the metaphysics of an object does seem to push its relational features aside. What I find compelling about Augustine's account is that he tenuously flirts with the notion that love (i.e. God) is an object, thing-like, actual. But he does not over-commit to this solidity. He allows love (because it also a relation) to remain just a bit more indeterminate, a bit more mysterious. I do not read this as a sign of analytical weakness. Rather, I see the suggestive contours of a more supple metaphysic.

---

[75] Harman, "On Vicarious Causation," 204.

The Other Face of God
Lacan, Theological Structure, and the Accursed Remainder

Levi R. Bryant

Collin College

I. Religion as a Social Structure

READING THE WORK OF CHRISTOpher Hitchens, Richard Dawkins, and Daniel Dennett, one gets the impression that questions of religion and theology revolve around whether or not these beliefs are accurate representations of the world.[1] However, as Levi-Strauss shows in *The Savage Mind*, the difference between mythological thought and scientific thought is not to be understood in terms of whether it is an accurate representation of the world, but rather both are variations of a common structural order. As Levi-Strauss understands it, both myth and scientific thought are characterized by identical mental operations, but are merely applied to different materials.[2] While not wishing to

---

[1] Cf. Richard Dawkins, *The God Delusion*, (New York: Houghton Mifflin Company, 2006); Daniel Dennett, *Breaking the Spell: Religion as a Natural Phenomenon*, (New York: Penguin Books: 2006); Christopher Hitchens, *God is Not Great: How Religion Poisons Everything*, (New York: Twelve Books: Hachette Book Group, 2007).

[2] "If our interpretation is correct, we are led toward a completely different view—namely, that the kind of logic in mythical thought is as rigorous as that of modern science, and that the difference lies, not in the quality of the intellectual process, but in the nature of things to which it is applied. This is well in agreement with the situation known to prevail in the field

follow Levi-Strauss all the way in arguing that structures are ahistorical invariants of the human mind, in this paper I do wish to argue—drawing heavily on Lacanian psychoanalytic theory—that religion is a particular *structure* of thought and human social formations. From this I will draw some *structural* or *systemic* consequences that follow from this structural organization. In particular, I wish to identify some structural features characteristic of a particular type of religious thought and social organization pertaining to monotheism in terms of the subject's precarious relationship to language, masculine sexuation, and the role that *objet a* plays in our economy of desire. I will argue that these features are not accidental by-products of unique historical conditions, but rather properties of a particular structural organization. While these structures might themselves be products of particular socio-historical conditions, these features will be seen to be part and parcel of these particular forms of structural organization, such that where these structural organizations are present, these features will be present as well in much the same way that the hypotenuse of a right-triangle is a ratio of its relation to the other two sides.

At the outset, it is important to note that it is extremely difficult to make generalizations about religion. As any theologian or philosopher of religion will tell you, "religion" is a polythetic concept, having characteristics of what Wittgenstein referred to as a set of family resemblances without an overarching essence. While we may anachronistically refer to the beliefs of the Aztec and the beliefs of the Christian as religions, we would be hard-put to find a common essence characteristic of both. In the course of this essay, I will be referring to collective formations that posit the transcendence

---

of technology: What makes a steel ax superior to a stone ax is not that the first one is better made than the second. They are equally well made, but steel is quite different from stone. In the same way we may be able to show that the same logical processes operate in myth as in science, and that man has always been thinking equally well; but the improvement lies not in an alleged progress of man's mind, but in the discovery of new areas to which it may apply its unchanged and unchanging powers." Claude Lévi-Strauss, *Structural Anthropology*, (New York: Basic Books, 1963), 230.

of the One. Moreover, following Russell McCutcheon, I here propose to treat these religious structures not as private, first person experiences, but rather as social formations.[3] This thesis necessarily follows from any Lacanian approach to religion, for as Lacan argues in Seminar 10, *Anxiety*, "...the subject is constituted in the locus of the Other. He constitutes himself from his mark in relationship to the signifier."[4] If this is indeed the case—and I won't rehearse the arguments here—then there can be no question of a private subject, or a subject characterized by immediate interiority and independence from the social field. If my thesis that religion is a structure of particular collective formations rather than a body of ontological claims and private experiences is correct, then it follows that certain social formations can be characterized as religious, regardless of whether they are secular or what we more commonly refer to as the religious. That is, questions of whether there is explanation of phenomena through the supernatural will be secondary to the nature of these structures, such that a strictly secular system could nonetheless exemplify these characteristics. As Manfred Frank puts it,

> ...*Structure* [is] in the first place only insofar as it is a finite context of assignments and references among a finite number of oppositive values. What can be *changed* in a structure are, at the most, the contentual and significational attributions, not the order of values itself.[5]

---

[3] Russell T. McCutcheon, *Critics Not Caretakers: Redescribing the Public Study of Religion*, (New York: SUNY, 2001).

[4] Jacques Lacan, *Seminar 10: L'Angoisse*, 1962 - 1963 trans. Cormac Gallagher, unpublished seminar, Seminar of 28 November 1962. Lacan develops his account of subject formation in terms of alienation and separation between seminars 9 and 14. Unfortunately I will be unable to develop this account here, but for excellent discussions of the Lacanian subject cf. Mladen Dolar, "The Cogito as Subject of the Unconscious" in Slavoj Zizek ed., *Cogito and the Unconscious*, (Durham: Duke University Press, 1998), 11-40; Paul Verhaeghe, "Causation and Destitution of a Pre-Ontological Non-entity: On the Lacanian Subject," in Dany Nobus ed., *Key Concepts of Lacanian Psychoanalysis*, (New York: Other Press, 1998), 164-189; and Bruce Fink, *The Lacanian Subject: Between Language and Jouissance*, (Princeton: Princeton University Press, 1995).

[5] Manfred Frank, *What is Neostructuralism?*, (Minneapolis: University of Minnesota Press, 1989), 65.

The terms that might fill a particular position in a structure might change—being supernatural in one instance and secular in another—but the value of the relations remains the same. But prior to this we need to pass through the discussion of a number of issues, ranging from linguistics to set theory, that will initially seem far removed from questions of religion and theology. This will provide the resources for discerning how this theological structure is a response to the problem of the Real. What I wish to understand is why there is a predominance of violence among social formations organized around the primacy of the One. The joke of this paper will be that this is the result of a set-theoretical paradox.

II. The Problem of Language

During the final phase of his work extending from roughly 1964 to the end of his life, Lacan came to focus increasingly on the role of the Real in the triad composing the Symbolic, Imaginary, and Real. This entailed understanding the formations of the unconscious—roughly symptoms—as attempts to recreate a harmony with the Real. As Lacan puts it,

> Whenever we speak of cause…there is always something anti-conceptual, something indefinite. The phases of the moon are the cause of tides—we know this from experience, we know that the word cause is correctly used here. Or again, miasmas are the cause of fever—that doesn't mean anything either, there is a hole, and something that oscillates in the interval. In short, there is a cause only in something that doesn't work. Well! It is at this point that I am trying to make you see by approximation that the Freudian unconscious is situated at that point, where, between cause and that which it affects, there is always something wrong. The important thing is not that the unconscious determines neurosis—of that one Freud can quite happily, like Pontius Pilot, wash his hands…For what the unconscious does is show us the gap through which neurosis recreates a harmony with a real—a real that may well not be determined.[6]

---

[6] Jacques Lacan, *The Four Fundamental Concepts of Psycho-Analysis*, (New York: W.W. Norton and Company, 1998), 22.

Importantly, Levi-Strauss makes an analogous claim in *Structural Anthropology*: "...since the purpose of myth is to provide a logical model capable of overcoming a contradiction (an impossible achievement if, as it happens, the contradiction is real), a theoretically infinite number of slates will be generated, each one slightly different from the others."[7] In short, it is a gap or Real in the social system or symbolic order that will generate mythic productions, just as it is a gap or Real in the unconscious that will generate symptoms, slips of the tongue, jokes, bungled actions, acts of forgetting, dreams, etc. The product of this attempt to re-create a harmony between the symbolic and the real is, of course, the symptom. A symptom can be anything from the dramatic compulsion to repeatedly wash one's hands to a simple slip of the tongue or a dream. What is important is that the symptom is a response to a gap, lack, or absence which is characterized as Real.

Lacan gives two key formulations in characterizing the specific difference of the Real: on the one hand, Lacan claims that the Real is that which always returns to its place. In the middle Lacan, something qualifies as Real if it has this quality of always returning to its place. Here, then, we might think of the movement of the planets. We can see how this characterization of the Real evolves over the course of his thought insofar as the symptom comes to increasingly be conceived as that which always returns to its place in the psychic economy of the subject. The symptom might occur in a variety of manifestations—a phobia of a weasel might turn into a phobia of planes—but these various manifestations will share a structural identity. In fact, we might even think of that final moment of analysis, which involves identification with the symptom, as consisting in the eternal return of the symptom. While it is certainly true that the movement of the symptom produces an endless variety of symptomatic formations, the lack or absence around which these formations occur is always the same. A good deal of analysis thus consists in the mapping of this lack in its sheer nonsensical

---

[7] Lévi-Strauss, *Structural Anthropology*, 229.

being (the movement from symptoms imbued with meaning to the sinthome as pure process without meaning). Part of traversing the fantasy consists in coming to stand before this fundamental void borne of castration covered over by fantasy.

On the other hand, Lacan characterizes the Real as the impossible. It is with this formulation of the Real that we truly enter Lacan's mature thought. Here the claim that the Real is the impossible should not be equated with idiotic common sense platitudes to the effect that pigs will never fly or pigs and donkeys cannot mate. As Lacan argues, impossibility is not to be understood as related to possibility, but necessity. Moreover, we ought not understand impossibility as being defined in terms of what people or a given culture believes is possible or impossible. Rather, the sort of impossibility Lacan has in mind are formal impossibilities like the sort that arise in logic or mathematics. Most often these formal impossibilities have to do with sets that do not include themselves, like the set of all sets that do not include themselves. Such entities generate irresolvable paradoxes. Thus there is a special relationship between paradox and impossibility as it pertains to the Lacanian Real. The Real is not reality—the latter, Lacan claims, is only ever approached through the frame of fantasy[8]—but rather is an impasse of formalization.[9] This impasse of formalization or the Real, Lacan will argue, does not cease writing itself;[10] which is to say, it does not cease producing symptoms in an attempt to recreate a harmony between the symbolic and the real. The graphs of sexuation,

---

[8] "To the right is the scant reality on which the pleasure principle is based, which is such that everything we are allowed to approach by way of reality remains rooted in fantasy." Jacques Lacan, Seminar 20: *Encore*, (New York: W.W. Norton & Company, 1998), p. 94-95.

[9] "This is where the real distinguishes itself. The real can only be inscribed on the basis of an impasse of formalization" (Ibid., 93).

[10] "The necessary—what I propose to accentuate for you with this mode—is that which doesn't stop what?—being written…'What doesn't stop being written' is a modal category, and its not the one you might have expected to be opposed to the necessary, which would have been the contingent. Can you imagine? The necessary is linked to the impossible, and this 'doesn't stop not being written' is the articulation whereof" (Ibid., 59).

along with the stances of hysteria ("am I a man or a woman?") and obsession ("am I alive or am I dead?") can be seen as variations on these set theoretical paradoxes.[11]

Thus, for instance, the problem with the set of all sets that do not include themselves is that if the set of all sets that do not include themselves includes itself, then it simultaneously must belong to itself and exclude itself. If it belongs to itself then it has violated the property defining membership to itself: Namely, it is no longer the set of all sets *are not members of themselves*. Likewise, if it is not a member of itself, then there is at least one signifier that does *not* belong to the set of all sets that are not members of themselves, thereby undermining the totality of this set. The set of all sets that are not members of themselves is consequently a paradoxical notion. The symbolic thus generates impasses of formalizations, these impasses express formal impossibilities, and these formal impossibilities are what characterize the Real. Moreover these impossibilities are intriguing in that they always return to their place. They always occur in the same place and thus mark a certain invariance in the symbolic which otherwise does not exist. Although I cannot develop this claim in detail here, Lacan will define three formal impasses that fundamental fantasy strives to surmount: the non-existence of the sexual relation, questions of our origin as subjects, and the non-existence of Woman.[12]

Now, having briefly unfolded Lacan's conception of the Real, it is worth noting that his conception of the signifier perfectly exemplifies Russell's paradox or the paradox of the set of all sets that do not include themselves. Lacan gives his most striking formulation of this feature of the signifier in Seminar 14, *The Logic of Fantasy*, when he remarks that, "...it is of the nature of each and every signifier not to be able in any

---

[11] Cf. Jacques Lacan, Seminar III: *The Psychoses*, (New York: W.W. Norton & Company, 1993), 178 - 179.

[12] On the primary questions underlying fundamental fantasy, cf. Paul Verhaeghe, *Does the Woman Exist? From Freud's Hysteric to Lacan's Feminine*, (New York: Other Press, 1999), 159 - 177.

case to signify itself."[13] To say that a signifier cannot signify itself is to say that no signifier is a member of itself. Rather, as Lacan's discourse of the master illustrates, the signifier must always refer to another signifier. Lacan immediately follows this up with reference to how this generates Russell's paradox or the paradox of the set of all sets that are not members of themselves.

> It is too late for me to impose on you, in a hurry, the writing of this inaugural point for the whole of set theory, which implies that this theory can only function starting from an axiom described as specification. Namely, that the only interest in making a set function is when there exists another set which can be defined by the definition of certain x's in the first as freely satisfying a certain proposition. "Freely" means: independently of any quantification: small number or all. The result of this…is that by positing any set whatsoever, by defining in it the proposition that I indicated as specifying x's in it, as being simply that x is not a member of itself—that which, as regards what interests us, namely, for the following, which is necessarily once one wishes to introduce the myth of a reduced language: that there is a language which is not one, namely, which constitutes, for example the totality of signifiers. What is proper to the totality of signifiers, I will show it to you in detail, involves the following as necessary—if we simply admit that the signifier cannot signify itself—involves the following as necessary: that there is something that does not belong to this set. It is not possible to reduce language, simply because of the fact that language cannot constitute a closed set; in other words: that there is no Universe of discourse.[14]

The consequences of this simple observation are profound. It will be recalled that at the outset I pointed out that the subject is constituted in the field of the Other or the field of language. Lacan develops his account of subject formation in seminars 10-14 in his account of alienation and separation.

---

[13] Jacques Lacan, Seminar 14: *The Logic of Fantasy*, 1966 - 1967, trans. Cormac Gallagher, unpublished seminar, Seminar of 16 November 1966.
[14] Ibid.

On the one hand, this will entail that the subject can never find a signifier for itself within the symbolic order that would adequately name it or fix its identity. Why? Simply because another signifier will always be required to engender the sense of any signifier. As Manfred Frank puts it speaking in the context of the Derridean notion of play,

> We are already familiar with the other object Derrida puts forward against the idea of a principle or a closure of structure. It is of a systematic nature and maintains that even the signification of a structural principle—in the semantic sense of the word "signification"—cannot escape the law of determination by means of opposition and thus can constitute itself only *within* the referential play of *signifiers* of structure. As a result, one has to give up the idea that the blueprint of structure, its transcendental principle, commandeers structure and keeps it in order from outside. One has to concede, on the contrary, that we are, as Derrida says, *entangled* in structures and have no possibility of getting beyond our Being-inside-structures.[15]

Although Frank is here referring to Derrida's critique of Lévi-Strauss's thesis of unchanging synchronic structures functioning as an infrastructure for the various myths we find about us, these claims equally characterize Lacan's understanding of the signifier. When Frank here refers to "determination," he is referring to the necessity of distinction in terms of what something is not for something to become determinate. As Hegel quotes Spinoza as saying, *omnis determinatio est negatio*. Lacan had begun developing these claims in 1961, in Seminar IX: *Identification*, nearly ten years before Derrida published *Speech and Phenomena* or *Writing and Difference*. Indeed, in Seminar 9, given between 1961-1962, one will even find a sophisticated discussion of writing and the trace. Questions of precedence aside, the upshot of this thesis is that the subject, insofar as it is constituted in the field of the Other, will experience its identity as precarious as it will be unable to fix on one signifier to ground or support that

---

[15] Frank, *What is Neostructuralism?*, 61-62.

identity. One more will always be needed. In certain respects, *this* is the hysterical core of neurotic subjectivity. The hysteric is perpetually asking the Other "what am I?," "tell me who I am?," but never finds a satisfactory answer.

However, matters are far worse than identities rendered precarious by virtue of every signifier requiring determination by another signifier; for if it is the case that the signifier is an example of a set characterized by not belonging to itself, then it follows that there cannot be a set of all signifiers or a totality of signifiers. As Lacan so forcefully puts it, "there is no Universe of discourse." This point will be expressed throughout Lacan's teaching in a variety of ways: Lacan will express it in the aphorism that "the Other does not exist," i.e., that it does not form a closed and consistent totality. Likewise, Lacan will claim that "there is no Other of the Other." The upshot of this, as we will see, is that not only is the subject, like Joseph K. in Kafka's *Trial* and *Castle*, unable to discover a stable name or identity for itself, it also discovers that there is no support for its very being. It is precisely here, I will argue, that the site of religion emerges.

III. Masculine Sexuation and Onto-Theology

As we have seen, there are thus two inter-related poles between which language is problematic. On the one hand, at the pole of the subject, there is no stable signifier that would anchor or fix the subject's identity. On the other hand, at the pole of the symbolic or the Other, language is unable to form a fixed or closed totality without falling into an impasse of formalization. As Lacan puts it, "the Other does not exist," which is to say, it does not form a closed totality. In a closely related vein, Lacan will also claim that "there is no Other of the Other," or signifier standing outside this play of the signifier (S_1), securing a foundation and stability for the endless sliding of the signifiers (S_2). As Lacan puts it in "Subversion of the Subject,"

> Let us begin with the conception of the Other as the locus of the signifier. No authoritative statement has any other guarantee here than

its very enunciation, since it would be pointless for the statement to seek it in another signifier, which could in no way appear outside that locus. I formulate this by saying that there is no metalanguage that can be spoken, or, more aphoristically, that there is no Other of the Other. And when the Legislator (he who claims to lay down the Law) comes forward to make up for this, he does so as an imposter.[16]

To say that there is no Other of the Other is to say that there is no signifier that would complete the set of all signifiers, establishing a totality and system of all possible relations, thereby guaranteeing speech. It is precisely this that Lacan illustrates in the discourse of the master:

Discourse of the Master

Impossibility

$$\uparrow \frac{S_1}{\$} \rightarrow \frac{S_2}{a} \downarrow$$

Impotence

In the upper left-hand portion of the discourse we have the master-signifier (S_1), while to the left we have the battery of signifiers (S_2). The master-signifier here functions as an "Other of the Other," totalizing and completing that battery in a finite and consistent whole. In terms of the passage we just saw from "Subversion of the Subject," this would be the so-called Legislator laying down the law. However, we note that in the position of the product we find the *objet a*. Despite this attempted totalization, a remainder is produced that fails to be integrated in the symbolic totality. The master-signifier proposes itself as outside the play of the signifier and therefore capable of forming a totality, yet it inevitably fails in this vocation. Why? Because no signifier, including the master-signifier, can signify itself. As Derrida so nicely puts it,

---

[16] Jacques Lacan, *Ecrits: The First Complete Edition in English* trans. Bruce Fink, (New York: W. W. Norton & Company, 2006), 688.

> The concept of centered structure is in fact the concept of a play based on a fundamental ground, a play constituted on the basis of a fundamental immobility and a reassuring certitude, which itself is beyond the reach of play. And on the basis of this certitude, anxiety can be master, for anxiety is invariably the result of a certain mode of being implicated in the game, of being caught by the game, of being as it were at stake in the game from the outset...This is why one perhaps could say that the movement of any archaeology, like that of any eschatology, is an accomplice of this reduction of the structurality of structure and always attempts to conceive of structure on the basis of a full presence which is beyond play.[17]

Derrida is here extremely close to Lacan. The upshot of the differential nature of the signifier is that any attempt to totalize the system of signifiers necessarily fails, leaving behind a remainder, that cannot be integrated in the system. It is for this reason that the barred subject ($) appears in the position of truth in this discourse, or as that which is unconscious or which must be excluded while animating the discourse. On the one hand, this discourse perpetually strives to surmount its division or lack produced in and through language ($), presenting itself in the semblance of completeness and totality (S_1). On the other hand, this discourse perpetually finds this gap or division returning in the form of the loss or remainder (a) produced by this discourse when the master-signifier intervenes in the battery of signifiers (S_2). For this reason, the upper level of the discourse is characterized by impossibility insofar as the master-signifier is never sufficient to produce the totality it aims at; while the lower level of the discourse is characterized by impotence insofar as the divided subject ($) is forever separated from the lost object or remainder (a) thereby failing to attain completeness. Consequently, this discourse endlessly repeats in an infinite variety of ways, forever striving to recoup what it loses through language. This point, the function of the remainder, will become extremely important in a moment.

---

[17] Jacques Derrida, *Writing and Difference*, (Chicago: The University of Chicago Press, 1978), 279.

Having outlined the impasse of formalization characteristic of language, I would now like to situate theological structure in terms of the masculine side of Lacan's graphs of sexuation. For Lacan, the graphs of sexuation do not refer to biological sex, nor do they refer to socially constructed gender. It is important to note that subjects that are biologically female can occupy a masculine structure of sexuation, just as subjects that are biologically male can be sexuated female. Rather than being an issue of biology, the structures of sexuation are two ways in which subjects relate to this impasse of formalization or the Real. As Žižek puts it, for Lacan,

> ...sex, sexual positions, [are] not something simply discursively constructed. But for all that, Lacan, of course, does not return to a naïve position of sex as something substantially pre-discursively given. Sex is not a symbolic discursive construction. What is it? It emerges precisely where symbolization fails. That's Lacan's point. That, in other words, we are sexed beings precisely because symbolization necessarily fails. And sexuality means two versions of this failure.[18]

My thesis is that mono-theistic structure can be comprehended in terms of the masculine side of the graph of sexuation. As a reminder, I understand mono-theistic structure to be any social formation organized around the primacy of the One or the master-signifier as a technology for totalizing language. From this mapping, we should be able to draw attention to some salient features of this type of formation.

The issue of sexuation is not about *biological sex*, but about the sort of jouissance one is able to obtain.[19] Lacan's concept of jouissance is highly polysemous, and can refer to a variety of different types of jouissance—phallic jouissance, surplus-jouissance, Other-jouissance—but the term cannot strictly be translated as "pleasure." Where pleasure is produced through a decrease in tension, according to Freud, jouissance can be thought as an increase in tension that is often experienced

---

[18] Slavoj Žižek, *Interrogating the Real*, (London: Continuum Books, 2005), 81.
[19] Bruce Fink, *Lacan to the Letter: Reading Ecrits Closely*, (Minneapolis: University of Minnesota Press, 2004), 158.

as painful. Translating the term as "enjoyment" can thus be misleading, as the term is also sometimes used to refer to any sort of affect, such as anxiety, sadness, depression, joy, etc.

Lacan presents his graph of sexuation as a formalization of two formal impasses or deadlocks in the subject's attempt to attain jouissance. The upper and lower levels of the top portion of the graphs of sexuation are to be read together such that the upper level indicates a structure of fantasy and the lower level indicates how the subject relates to jouissance. The lower portion of the graph of sexuation represents the manner in which the subject strives to surmount this real or formal impasse. The left-hand portion of the graph represents the masculine structure of sexuation, while the right-hand side represents the feminine structure of sexuation.

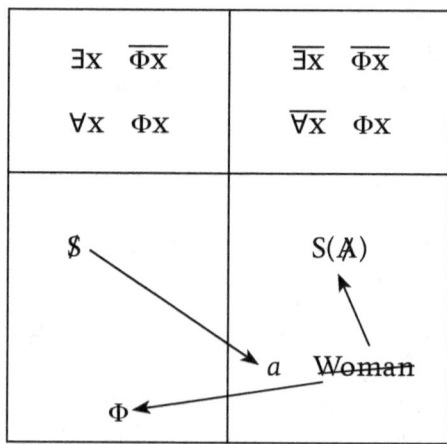

The upper portion of the masculine side of the graph of sexuation can be read as "there is a form of jouissance that is not subject to castration."[20] "Castration," here, should be taken to refer to submission to the symbolic order. In Freud's myth of the primal father in *Totem and Taboo*, the primal father exemplifies

---

[20] Fink, *Lacan to the Letter*, 160.

this proposition as he has no limits to his sexual enjoyment. That is, not only can the primal father enjoy *all* women in the tribe, he can enjoy his own mother and daughters as well. There are no limitations to his enjoyment. Whenever we say that God is omnipotent we are also saying that God exemplifies this proposition, as omnipotence implies no restriction to power and enjoyment. Similarly, some think of the extremely wealthy, rock stars, or porn stars as exemplifying this state. Roughly, whenever we imagine that there's someone who is completely satisfied, without any impediments or limitations, we're in the domain of the first line.

The lower line of the masculine side of the graph of sexuation can be read as saying "All of a man's jouissance is phallic jouissance. Every single one of his satisfactions may come up short."[21] The idea here is that all jouissance is mediated in the symbolic such that it is experienced as coming up short or lacking in some way. This is a consequence, once again, of the principle that the signifier cannot signify itself. Because the signifier is differential, no term will be immediate or complete, but will rather always embody absence or a reference to other signifiers. Every time I get a bit of recognition, every time I get a new honor, every time I get an article or a book published, every time I get a new car, buy a new book, etc., I experience this satisfaction as less than expected or as coming up short. The jouissance I actually obtain is less than the jouissance I expected. As Fink writes,

> There is no barrier between my desire for something as formulated or articulated in signifiers (S) and what can satisfy me. Thus the satisfaction I take in realizing my desire is always disappointing. This satisfaction, subject to the bar between the signifier and the signified, *fails* to fulfill me—it always leaves something more to be desired. That is phallic jouissance. Just as one cannot take the lack out of Lacan, one cannot take the failure out of the phallus.[22]

---

[21] Fink, *Lacan to the Letter*, 160.
[22] Ibid.

Fink's point here evokes Hegel's old joke about how you cannot buy "fruit." There's no such thing as "fruit," only oranges, apples, grapes, etc. Fruit is a signifier that cannot be had. The abstractness of the signifier—if that's an adequate way of putting it—is always in conflict with the concreteness of jouissance, such that each bit of jouissance we obtain is experienced as not being "it." More fundamentally, I experience myself as limited or lacking, as constitutively incomplete. This structural disappointment in the masculine side of the graph of sexuation is represented by the arrow running from the barred subject ($) to objet a, where the subject is perpetually pursuing this elusive remainder without being able to catch it. It is noteworthy that this is simply another schematization of Lacan's discourse of the master, where we saw that the totalization of the symbolic field always leaves a remainder.

Now here is the key point: *The upper level and lower level of the masculine graph of sexuation must be read together to signify a particular deadlock or antinomy within the masculine way of relating to jouissance.* Let the upper portion of the graph be a specifically masculine *fantasy* of complete or total jouissance. It is because a man believes either that A) total jouissance is possible through some action or object or social position, or B) that some other person or being has total jouissance, that he comes to find all the jouissance that is available in his day to day life insufficient. Take the following passage from Descartes' third meditation as an exemplification of this structure:

> [I]...should...[not]...think that I do not perceive the infinite by means of a true idea, but only through a negation of the finite, just as I perceive rest and darkness by means of a negation of motion and light. On the contrary, I clearly understand that there is more reality in an infinite substance than there is in a finite one. Thus the perception of the infinite is somehow prior in me to the perception of the finite, that is, my perception of God is prior to my perception of myself. For how would I understand that I doubt and that I desire, that is, that I lack something that I am not wholly perfect, unless there were some

idea in me of a more perfect being, by comparison with which I might recognize my defects?[23]

Descartes is here arguing that we cannot arrive at the idea of the infinite or perfect simply by negating the finite. Indeed, his whole point is that my very ability to see myself and entities in the world as imperfect and lacking is because I already have the idea of perfection. But since this idea of perfection is a necessary condition for seeing things as imperfect, I could not have learned this idea from experience. Therefore, says Descartes, only a perfect being could have put this idea in me. Descartes' point, then, is that the idea of God, of an uncastrated being, is the very condition of my desire insofar as I desire to move from a less perfect to a more perfect state. This passage exemplifies the structure of masculine sexuality perfectly. On the upper portion of the graph we have God, while on the lower portion of the graph we have the subject that desires to know. In between, there is always a remainder that falls away. Lacan, of course, will argue that this structure results not from God, but from our alienation in the signifier.

III. Theology and Dirt

What consequences follow from this elaboration of the theological structure of masculine sexuation? What does it allow us to discern? In order to draw these consequences, we must focus on the role that *objet a* plays in these structures. Philosophically it is difficult to know how to situate Nietzsche's proclamation that God is dead. It would be a mistake to suggest that this is an ontological thesis or a philosophical argument against the existence of God, for Nietzsche does not demonstrate to us, as an atheist might, that there is no God. Rather, Nietzsche claims that a fundamental mutation or shift has occurred in how we understand the world and

---

[23] René Descartes, *Discourse on Method and Meditations on First Philosophy* trans. Cress, (Indianapolis: Hacket Publishing Company, 1998), 76.

the nature of being. That is, Nietzsche gives us a version of the failure of symbolic efficiency. I will not here enter into a long discussion of Nietzsche's narrative as to how we came to kill God. This is not a joyous proclamation—though it may have joyous consequences—but a lament. As Lacan argues, traversing the phantasy lies not so much in coming to see how we are castrated, fissured, or non-identical, but rather coming to see how the big Other through which we organized our desire and identity does not itself exist. That is, the very co-ordinates of our world, desire, and identity collapse when we come to discern the non-existence of the big Other. This comes out most clearly in Descartes' third meditation, where we are shown how God is not simply the guarantor of the truth of clear and distinct ideas, but of our very being or existence. In this precise Lacanian sense, then, both atheist and theist can still think prior to the death of God, insofar as both rely on a guarantee of truth.

What strikes me as crucial to Nietzsche's declaration of the death of God, is the accompanying claim that we have wiped away the horizon, that we now move without direction, that we are suspended in an infinite void and cold, empty space. All of this returns us to the set theoretical paradoxes surrounding the nature of the signifier. The death of God seems to signify a world that has lost its coordinates and that the ground has disappeared beneath us. I take it that the term "God" is a generic term for any sort of transcendental signifier (the upper portion of the masculine graph of sexuation) that would fix meaning and identity. It would be a mistake to assume that "God" simply refers to the God of monotheistic religion. Rather, God is a generic term referring to a particular operator, to anything on the order of a form, essence, transcendence, identity, substance, permanence, ideal, wholeness, totality, and so on. Similar sentiments could be expressed, for instance, following the collapse of a nation or empire, where the name of the nation or empire serves this God-operation for its subjects.

While the death of God is not an ontological claim, it does present an ontological opening or challenge. This logic is deeply attached to that of identity and generates a particular sort of antagonism. In *De Ordine*, Augustine writes that,

> The soul therefore, holding fast to this order, and now devoted to philosophy, at first introspects itself; and—as soon as that mode of learning has persuaded it that reason either is the soul itself or belong to it, and that there is in reason nothing more excellent or dominant than numbers, or that reason is nothing else than number—soliloquizes thus: "By some kind of inner and hidden activity of mine, I am able to analyze and synthesize the things that ought to be learned; and this faculty of mine is called reason."...Therefore, both in analyzing and in synthesizing, it is oneness that I see, it is oneness that I love. But when I analyze, I seek a homogenous unit; and when I synthesize, I look for an integral unit. In the former case, the foreign elements are avoided; in the latter, proper elements are conjoined to form something united and perfect. In order that a stone be a stone, all its parts and its entire nature have been consolidated into one. What about a tree? Is it not true that it would not be a tree if it were not *one*? What about the members and entrails of any animate being, or any of its component parts? Of a certainty, if they undergo a severance of unity, it will no longer be an animal. And what else do friends strive for, but to be *one*? And the more they are one, so much the more they are friends. A population forms a city, and dissension is full of danger for it: to dissent—what is that, but to think diversely? An army is made up of many soldiers. And is not any multitude so much the less easily defeated in proportion as it is the more closely united? In fact, the joining is itself called a coin, a co-union, as it were. What about every kind of love? Does it not wish to become one with what it is loving? And if it reaches its object, does it not become one with it? Carnal pleasure affords ardent delight for no other reason than because the bodies of lovers are brought into union. Why is sorrow distressful? Because it tries to rend what used to be one.[24]

A central onto-theological assumption is not so much that of God—the God-function, as Descartes argues, is only a guarantor of truth and order, which cannot be guaranteed by our

---

[24] Albert Hofstadter and Richard Kuhns, eds., *Philosophies of Art & Beauty: Selected Readings in Aesthetics from Plato to Heidegger*, (Chicago: University of Chicago Press, 1964), 182-183.

senses or appearances alone—but rather the assumption of the One. Whether the One be substance remaining identical throughout change such as Descartes' wax, or the one of the transcendent form immune to the distortions of images, appearances, and sophists, or whether it be the one of personal identity, the nation, our kind of people, or a subject that is the same despite all its ever changing thoughts, or the one of a holistic universe where everything is interconnected and harmonious, or the one of a State, the one is always the avatar of theological thought. As such, the death of God signifies first and most fundamentally the end of the primacy of the One in whatever form it might take. To announce the death of the God is, as both Deleuze and Badiou have declared, to simultaneously declare that the One, the identical, the same, is only a product, a result, a term-become rather than a foundation or first.

Philosophically those ontologies premised on identity or the One as their first principle produce irresolvable set-theoretical problems. Ethically and politically such philosophies are premised on the predominance of the Imaginary, the yearning for totality, completeness and wholeness, as can be seen in Augustine's example of the army and the city, where dissension and the stranger are seen as threats. The problem is that such organizations are inherently conflictual. As Plotinus, another thinker of the One will write when describing beauty and purity,

> If a man has been immersed in filth or daubed with mud, his native comeliness disappears and all that is seen is the foul stuff besmearing him: his ugly condition is due to the *alien matter* that has encrusted him, and if he is to win back his grace it must be his business to scour and purify himself and make himself what he was.[25]

In the same passage, Plotinus draws comparisons to the besmeared man covered in mud, and the stained soul, impure gold, and the way in which the One, the Good, and the Beautiful

---

[25] Hofstadter and Kuhns, *Philosophies of Art & Beauty*, 146.

are contaminated by matter itself. In the case of both Plotinus and Augustine, there seems to be a close correlation between the primacy of the One and contamination which threatens the One. Every desire for the One—whether in the form of identity, collective unity, the holism of the universe, etc.—is always accompanied by this "foul stuff that besmears" it or the alien matter that must be *eradicated* or defended against.

IV. The One and the Extimacy of Contamination

However, while we here see a close correlation between assertions of the One and concern about the foreign, what we have not yet established is that this dialectic is *internal* to identity and the One itself. That is, it could yet be that there is the One and something comes from the *outside*, contaminating the One from without. The immigrant, as it were, invades our land. What needs to be shown is that this contamination is always already internal to the One itself. Put otherwise, it must be shown that the contamination of the One is not something that comes from the outside, sullying what would otherwise be a pure identity, but rather that organizations premised on the supremacy of the One must, by virtue of their own necessity, *produce* an outside that simultaneously marks and veils the impossibility of the One. The is, the signifier subtracted from the chain of differentiality must be veiled in its truth that it too is diacritical or differential, while simultaneously marking the place of its failure or the remainder that it produces. It is precisely this that Lacan's account of masculine sexuation, the Real, and the discourse of the master allows us to thematize.

Language is always constitutively incomplete. This is not simply a contingent accident such that we could finally rectify it by adding one more (encore!) signifier, but is an essential feature of any system or the mark of systematicity as such. From a psychoanalytic perspective, this logic is seen most clearly in *Totem and Taboo* and *Group Psychology and the Analysis of Ego*. The consistency of the social system is only made through the subtraction or addition of a particular element, a supplement—that is always provisional in its support at best—such that this element has the paradoxical status of simultaneously being a part of the system and outside the system. It is this supplementary signifier that I have referred to as the "God-function." Thus, when Lacan claims that there is no metalanguage, he is essentially claiming that there is no point of view one can adopt on language that would allow one to survey the whole from the outside.

If there is no metalanguage, then this is by virtue of the fact that language is, as we have seen, diacritical such that every "element" of language takes on its identity by virtue of its difference to the other elements. Insofar as each element only takes on its identity with respect to the other elements, no element is ever simply present, but each element is always already dispersed or "contaminated" by the other elements. Thus we encounter the formal impossibility, impasse, or Real characterizing the impossibility of ever arriving at simple identity with oneself. As many post-structuralist thinkers have observed, identity is always already contaminated by difference by virtue of the diacritical play of language. This is just another way of saying $S_1/\$$ in the discourse of the master.

Žižek gives a terrific example of this principle in his magnum opus, *For They Know Not What They Do*. As Žižek remarks in the context of a discussion of Hegel's distinction between boundary and limit,

> National identification is an exemplary case of how an external border is reflected into an internal limit. Of course, the first step towards the identity of the nation is defined through differences from other nations, via an external border: if I identify myself as an Englishman, I distinguish myself from the French, Germans, Scots, Irish, and so on. However, in the next stage, the question is raised of who among the English are "the real English," the paradigm of Englishness; who are the Englishmen who correspond in full to the notion of English...However, the final answer is of course that nobody is full English, that every empirical Englishman contains something "non-English"—Englishness thus becomes an "internal limit," an unattainable point which prevents empirical Englishmen from achieving full identity-with-themselves.[26]

---

[26] Slavoj Žižek, *For They Know Not What They Do: Enjoyment as a Political Factor*,

National identity here corresponds to the master-signifier (S_1) in the discourse of the master or the upper portion of the masculine graph of sexuation. The diacritical nature of identity is the lower portion of the masculine graph of sexuation or our inability to embody "Englishness." Žižek's point is that insofar as a nation is defined by a boundary, it's identity can only be established in its difference from other nations. We can readily observe this phenomenon at work in personal identity as well; for as Lacan shows in the second cell of the graph of desire, my identity is only arrived at differentially in relation to others.

What we have here is thus the real of identity or the way in which identity, properly speaking, is impossible. Neither a nation nor a person is able to ever arrive at identity with itself insofar as it is differentially structured with respect to other nations and identities. Thus when Žižek claims that social antagonisms are always structured around an impossible Real, one way of understanding him would be to point to this formal impossibility of achieving identity. This impossible Real is not without consequences; *for as a traumatic impossibility it turns the accomplishment of identity into an insistent demand.* Despite the fact that identity is formally impossible insofar as it is always-already contaminated by difference, identity or respite from the play of diacritics is nonetheless demanded. Just as the Real of castration produces desire in the subject, the Real of impossible identity produces a sort of collective desire or fantasy. Identity must be accomplished even if impossible. Or rather, we might say, it does not cease to write itself.

In this respect, identity is not established through a totalization of the system in question, but is instead produced by having some contingent entity stand for the totality of entities, allowing a totality to provisionally produce itself. For instance, some particular type of Englishman—perhaps the working man—comes to stand for all Englishmen. This addition to the system is simultaneously a part of the system

---

(London: Verso Books, 1991), 110.

and outside it, and functions in such a way as to grant the system a semblance of identity with itself. It is notable that the unconscious functions in exactly this way. The function of the symbol is in fact that crazy addition that allows the otherwise untotalizable unconscious to hang together as a consistent whole. The symptom is always a +1 that stands in the place of the absence lying at the center of the unconscious structured like a language. It is therefore a S($\cancel{A}$) or a signifier of the barred Other. Yet in functioning in this manner it simultaneously reveals and conceals the fact that the Other is barred.

In this respect, the symptom recreates a harmony with what would otherwise be infinite deferral. This is why the symptom can also be understood as a metaphor. By contrast, the operation of addition by which an untotalizable system takes on the semblance of totality is itself subject to the diacritical movement which effaces identity and is therefore in danger of collapsing. For this reason, the addition of one element is never enough. In addition to this +1 there must be a -1 which accounts for the failure of totalization in advance. It is here that the logic of contamination emerges in connection to those fantasies of collective wholeness. For, as we saw in the case of Plotinus and Augustine, in every semblance of totality there is always a contamination or cries of a virus corrupting the identity of the system. This contaminant is the remainder or *objet a*. This contamination is a strict corollary of the crazy identity established through the addition of that one extra signifier, and functions to account for the failure of this master-signifier or the manner in which the signifier is itself effaced by the diacritical play of difference. Just as Lacan, in Seminar 22, says that there is no subject without a symptom, it could be said that there is no social organization without a symptom. The symptom here marks the failure of the social symptom while simultaneously treating it as something external to the system that could be overcome.

The subtracted signifier or contaminant is always the immigrant, the ethnic other, women, liberals, the infidel, the terrorist, etc. However, the point not to be missed is that this subtracted term is not these entities themselves, in their substantial being, but a refracted view of the system itself as it strives to repress its own impossibility. As Žižek sometimes says, the Jew targeted by the Anti-Semite has nothing to do with real Jews, but is itself a symptom of the German social system under national socialism. It is for this reason that those discourses most characterized by the call for identity and the primacy of the One (nationalistic discourses, individualistic discourses premised on the ego, certain religious discourses, etc) are always most characterized by discussions of their Others or those supposed invaders contaminating the identity of the discourse. In fact, what the discourse encounters in these Others is its own disguised Real or the manner in which it is always already differs from itself. In short, these Others are the *objets a* that the identity has had to sacrifice in order to constitute itself in the semblance of a complete totality. For that which is repressed always returns. The question then is whether it is possible to conceive a metaphysic, ethic, and form of social organization not premised on the primacy of the One...A society, as it were, of the Real.

V. Epilogue

An amusing thing happened in the pre-publication stages of this article. One of the outside reviewers critiqued the article on the grounds that it seemed unfamiliar with the work of Levi Bryant and, in particular, the work of Bryant on sexuation and onticology[27] (my term for my variant of materialist object-oriented ontology). This is quite right. "The Other Face of God" was written in 2007 on the occasion of the *Psychoanalysis and Belief Symposium* hosted by the English and Rhetoric department at University of Texas at Arlington. At this point I had not yet made my realist turn, nor did I yet know anything about object-oriented ontology or speculative realism. At any rate, I can scarcely imagine a more delightful

---

[27] For a discussion of my current views on Lacanian sexuation cf. Levi R. Bryant, *The Democracy of Objects*, (Ann Arbor: Open Humanities Press, 2012), chapter 6, section 1.

example of withdrawal and the manner in which objects are even withdrawn from themselves.

Nonetheless, if I saw fit to attempt to publish this article despite its dated nature, then this is because the meditations on sexuation and theology I develop here are at the heart of the ethico-politico project of my onticology. These meditations would later become the groundwork of my flat ontology and critique of ontotheology in *The Democracy of Objects*. Drawn from the work of Manuel DeLanda, flat ontology is the thesis that all beings equally exist, even where they do not exist equally. While flat ontology recognizes that entities exist at different levels of scale ranging from the smallest quark to the largest galaxy, it refuses that gesture that would treat any of these entities as more ontologically *real* than others. For example, flat ontology recognizes that institutions cannot exist without people, but simultaneously argues that institutions are real entities in their own right with unique powers that cannot be reduced to the parts upon which the institution depends.

However, flat ontology above all rejects the existence of *sovereign* entities that *condition* all other entities without themselves being conditioned. Examples of sovereign entities in the philosophical tradition would be the God of theistic traditions, the Kantian and certain forms of the phenomenological subject, Platonic forms, and so on. In each of these cases, one entity conditions and organizes all of the other entities without itself being significantly conditioned by these entities. For example, Leibniz will argue that God selects each and every entity to exist thus and so in his creation of the universe. In the case of Kant's transcendental subject, while it is true that it is affected by the world apart from it in intuitions, the categories of the understanding and the forms of intuition nonetheless condition and structure all these elements given in sensibility. In the case of *vertical* ontologies, there is an entity that conditions, legislates, and organizes everything else without itself being conditioned. As in the case of Plato's Demiurge in the *Timeaus*, it is said that there is a sovereign author of all other beings. This Demiurge can take the form of the "big Demiurge" (God, force, the will to power, etc) or the form of a "little Demiurge" (the correlationist subject that organizes all being).

Initially these issues might appear to be very remote from Lacan's account of sexuation; however, if one thinks in *structural* terms, it will be noticed that the philosophical orientation of vertical ontologies share one and the same invariable structure and that this structure is that of masculine sexuation. What, then, does it mean to think in structural terms? We think structurally when we bracket the *content* of a position or artifact, instead attending to how elements are *related* as *empty placeholders* within a formation. Think here of Pythagoras's famous theorem. What Pythagoras's theorem outlines is the structure of right triangles. It doesn't articulate any *particular* right triangle, but instead presents us with the *formal* structure of a set of relationships and what follows from these relationships. In this regard, two right triangles might be quite distinct at the level of their specific content while still being *structurally identical*. They possess the same pattern. Thus, for example, the blueprints of a house and a house itself are structurally identical, and two actual houses can be structurally identical despite having different colored walls, different flooring, and one being composed of bricks while the other is composed of stone or wood. We can plug whatever content we like into the structural positions while the pattern remains the same.

The thesis of "The Other Face of God" is that ontotheology and theistic religion is structurally that of masculine sexuation. In other words, it is not the *content* that determines whether a position is theological—i.e., whether one believes in the existence of God or the supernatural—but rather the *structure*. In this regard, whether we're speaking of the God of theistic religions, the sovereign king of monarchial governments, the father of patriarchal family structures, dictators in *atheistic* governments, the nation of nationalisms, the sovereign subject that conditions all material of sensation in Kant, the structure of correlationism, certain ways in which academics relate to "master-figures" such as Lacan, Deleuze, Derrida, Heidegger, etc., and so on, these formations all have one and the same Oedipal structural pattern that is structurally identical to that of masculine sexuation. Vertical ontologies all share this same structure where one entity is posited as "uncastrated" and as capable of totalizing the heteroverse of being and all the other entities are "castrated" or subordinate to this entity.

However, this is not all. As I try to show in "The Other Face of God," it is not simply that all of these formations are structurally identical. Rather, the important point is that these structures necessarily and ineluctably generate a persecutory and paranoid structure because, due to set theoretical paradoxes internal to all attempts of totalization—Russell's paradox and Cantor's paradox—these structures necessarily generate a return of the repressed in the form of the *objet a*, the remainder that cannot be integrated into the totality, that these structures *simultaneously* attempt to both *destroy* and *recoup*. Ontotheology, masculine sexuation, is necessarily a will to mastery that requires an accursed other to *rationalize* the failure of its totalization (the immigrant, women, the queer, the heretic, Goldstein, Satan, terrorists, etc)—i.e., this remainder is misidentified as what is preventing successful harmony and totalization—and that generates the fantasy that *jouissance* can be captured and domesticated through a formation of successful totalization if this accursed share is just destroyed. Masculine sexuation or ontotheology is not simply a structure, it is a dangerous and destructive structure.

In my most recent work I have referred to this structure as "phallusophy," for phallic economies of desire are 1) premised on the fantasy that totalization is possible, 2) strive for identity and integration of all things in the heteroverse, and 3) strive to eradicate the remainder or whatever does not fit. In Lacanian psychoanalysis, phallic economies of desire are those economies that strive to totalize being and master it. Again and again we see phallusophy in what should be philosophy in the form of those idealist and correlationist positions that would capture the entire heteroverse in ideas or signifiers, that would master the world through the sovereign synthetic power of a subject, or that would postulate god or an author as the origin of all things and meaning.

It was "The Other Face of God" that first led me to recognize this structure of traditional ontological thought and that led me to begin wondering whether or not another ontological thinking—a differential ontological thinking that preserves the queer or alterity—not premised on mastery or the identification of being and thinking, might not be possible. This trajectory of thought was not completed until *The Democracy of Objects*. There I would argue that the masculine and feminine structures of sexuation mark two fundamentally different ways of thinking being and responding to the withdrawal of objects. The masculine side of sexuation premised on mastery and domination, seeks to treat the withdrawn nature of objects (castration) as an *accidental* aberration, a *fault*, in knowledge that can be surmounted for God or a sovereign subject that comes to recognize the identity of being and thinking. "Violence" is therefore inscribed in the heart of such ontological thinking as everything is to be denuded, brought into visibility, brought into mastery and control under the signifier without remainder. This is the logic of identity and identification, and it is structured around the pornographic as that which strives to master and render everything visible to the concept.

By contrast, I argue, the feminine side of the graph of sexuation begin from the premise that "there does not exist a being that is not withdrawn (castrated), but that not-all of beings are withdrawn (they manifest themselves *a bit*)." The feminine side of the graph of sexuation begins from the *constitutively* withdrawn and differential nature of entities characterized by an abyssally withdrawn core that cannot ultimately be mastered. Within this ontological thinking assemblages can be formed among entities, but they will always be assemblages of the heterogeneous where the elements of the assemblage remain heterogeneous, lively, and surprising. Here relation is a pathos of difference where entities appreciate their alterity and create on the basis of that alterity from across chasms in relating to one another. Where the masculine side strives for categorization and identification, the feminine side begins from the premise of difference. Where the masculine side proposes an ethics and politics of the same and identical, the feminine side proposes an ethics and politics appreciative of difference and generous towards difference. Where the masculine side proposes a totalitarianism of the identical, a patri-archy of obedience, the feminine side proposes a community of the different, an an-archy, a queer politics of collaboration and invention.

But, above all, reversing the traditional psychoanalytic characterization of masculinity and femininity, I argue that the masculine side represents the side of ontological *semblance*, while the feminine side is the side of ontological *truth*. If the masculine side of the graph of sexuation is the side of semblance, then this is because it obfuscates and attempts to cover over the formal deadlocks of the Real that always return to their place through the positing of a transcendent supplement whether in the form of God, Platonic forms, a sovereign, or a masculine subject. The masculine side recoils from the alterity of beings. If the feminine side of the graph of sexuation is the side of ontological truth, then it is because it inscribes these formal deadlocks at the very heart of being, facing them head on, and abjuring fantasies of completeness and totalization. Such a shift invites an ethics and politics that appreciates difference, that is generous, and that rejects the drive to master and control.

Improper Names for God
Religious Language and the "Spinoza-Effect"

Daniel Whistler

University of Liverpool

"Equality gives rise to challenging questions which are not altogether easy to answer." —First words of Frege's "On Sense and Meaning"[1]

THIS PAPER PRACTISES A *NATURPHI-losophie* of language. I treat texts as rocks to examine the linguistic forces that constitute them. In other words, this paper is born out of a hyper-realist attitude to sense that asserts: what goes on in texts should be subject to a "linguistic physics."[2] In order to bring out this linguistic physics as fully as possible, what follows is devoted to the logic of sense (or, even better, the physics of sense[3]) in *monist* philosophies. As I shall argue, monism forces the philosopher to treat words as one more class of body colliding on a surface. This is because the monist assertion that there is ultimately one thing in existence ultimately leads to the materialisation of language (at the same time as the linguistification of matter). A lacuna from the opening to Badiou's *Logic of Worlds* clarifies this point:

---

[1] Gottlieb Frege, "On Sense and Meaning" in *Collected Papers on Mathematics, Logic and Philosophy*, ed. Brian McGuinness (Oxford: Blackwell, 1984), 157.

[2] François Zourabichvili, *Spinoza: Une physique de la pensée* (Paris: PUF, 2002), 240.

[3] See Joshua Ramey and Daniel Whistler, "The Physics of Sense: Bruno, Schelling, Deleuze" in Alain Beaulieu, Edward Kazarian and Julia Sushytska (eds.), *Gilles Deleuze and Metaphysics* (Lexington, MA: Lexington, 2012 forthcoming).

> Today, natural belief [or democratic materialism] is condensed in a single statement: *There are only bodies and languages*. This statement is the axiom of contemporary conviction…It is then legitimate to counter [it] with a materialist dialectic, if by "materialist dialectic" we understand the following statement…*There are only bodies and languages, except that there are truths*.[4]

There is of course a third option: "there are only bodies."[5] According to such "monist materialism," the linguistic is reduced to the corporeal; yet, this is a radical materialism that Badiou seems loath to mention. In this paper, however, I explore the implications of such a corporeal reduction of language by focusing on two monisms—Spinoza's *Ethics* and Schelling's *Identitätsphilosophie*.

Such a *naturphilosophische* approach to monism emerges out of previous work in which I began to think through the consequences of the speculative turn for the study of language and concluded that a physics of divine names may well be a helpful way forward.[6] That is, my contention is that the speculative turn that has recently engulfed continental philosophy needs to be thought through in the realm of philosophy of language. For while this speculative turn is also an anti-linguistic turn,[7] it does not thereby foreclose philosophical investigation of language altogether. Rather,

---

[4] Alain Badiou, *The Logics of Worlds*, trans. Alberto Toscano (London: Continuum, 2010), 2-4.

[5] As well as the variant: "there is only language." However, as we shall discover by the end of the paper, "there are only bodies" and "there is only language" turn out to be synonymous.

[6] Daniel Whistler, "Language after Philosophy of Nature" in Anthony Paul Smith and Daniel Whistler (eds.), *After the Postsecular and the Postmodern: New Essays in Continental Philosophy of Religion* (Newcastle: Cambridge Scholars, 2010), 335-59.

[7] Harman speaks of "this ghetto of human discourse and language and power" to which philosophy has confined itself "for the past two hundred and twenty years" (in Brassier et al, "Speculative Realism," *Collapse* III [2007], 381) and Meillassoux is likewise concerned with the aporia to which language leads (*After Finitude*, trans. Ray Brassier [London: Continuum, 2008], 6); see further, Whistler, "Language after Philosophy of Nature," 336-9.

language must pass through the speculative epoché to be transformed from a medium that problematizes the very possibility of philosophy to a regional object of inquiry.[8] The task is to examine language not as it exists for us, but as it exists *in itself*. The route I take in the present paper—thinking through the consequences of monism for a logic of sense—is one way of attaining this end. In particular, I delineate a monist logic of sense as a means of intervening in debates over religious language. Religious language has become a paradigmatic site for anxiety over the slippage of signs. Much ink has been spilt over theorising the complex ways in which language fails to refer in religious discourse: obsessions with the metaphorical, analogic and apophatic character of such language merely name this anxiety. The present paper pursues an alternative path, teasing out a speculative philosophy of religious language by means of an analysis of the fate of names for God in monist logics of sense.[9]

My construction of a *Naturphilosophie* of monist language is organised as follows. I begin by considering precedents in the critical literature for such an enterprise in the work of Warren Montag and François Zourabichvili. Turning to Spinoza's *Ethics*, in the second section, I approach the linguistic physics it exhibits through, what I dub, the problem of improper names. That is, in dialogue with Daniel Barber's recent work on Spinoza, immanence and religion, I argue that linguistic practice in the *Ethics* is illustrated by the identification of the names "God," "substance" and "Nature." In order to make sense of this process of identification, in the third section, I take a detour through F.W.J. Schelling's philosophy of language as presented in his *Identitätssystem*, before returning to Spinoza once again to apply my Schellingian results. Spinoza's identification of names for God is, I suggest, a "Spinoza-effect" to rival the "Carroll-effect" Deleuze identifies in *The Logic of Sense*.

---

[8] See Whistler, "Language after Philosophy of Nature," 344-5.

[9] And to this extent this paper is, very literally, a working out of the project for a physics of *divine names*.

Speculations III

Part One: Spinoza's Linguistic Physics

One need not look far in either Spinoza's works or those of his circle in Amsterdam to find evidence of sustained interest in language. Balling begins *The Light Upon the Candlestick* with the following remark, "Things are not for words, but words for things"[10] and goes on to present a damning critique of language as impeding knowledge and so plunging mankind into "a sea of confusion."[11] Indeed, he remarks, "If we would better express things unto another by words and speeches, we had need find new words and consequently a whole new language: but that would be toil and labour indeed."[12] In the end, though, no such replacement language could ever be satisfactory, since language is *by nature* epistemically deficient. Spinoza shares this critical attitude. He writes, for example, "Words…can be the cause of many and great errors, unless we are wary of them…They are only signs of things as they are in the imagination, but not as they are in the intellect."[13] This is why in the *TTP* Spinoza is so critical of "superstitious veneration of the letter…adoring images and pictures, i.e. paper and ink, as the word of God."[14] Words, insofar as they attempt to designate truths, fall short.

However, this is not the aspect of Spinoza's philosophy of language on which I concentrate in this paper. My focus is not on language insofar as it represents or makes reference to truths, but language considered *in itself*—as an object existing in its own right with its representative function bracketed. This is one of the implications of a *Naturphilosophie* of

---

[10] Peter Balling, *The Light upon the Candlestick*; English translation in W. Sewel, *The History of the Rise, Increase and Progress of the Christian People called Quakers*, vol. 2, 4th ed. (London, 1800), 626.

[11] Ibid.

[12] Ibid.

[13] Benedict Spinoza, *Treatise on the Emendation of the Intellect* in *Collected Works* vol. 1, ed. and trans. Edwin Curley (Princeton: Princeton University Press, 1985), 38.

[14] Benedict Spinoza, *Theological-Political Treatise*, ed. and trans. Jonathan Israel and Michael Silverthorne (Cambridge: Cambridge University Press, 2007), 164.

language: words are considered as objects. In the Scholastic terminology that Spinoza appropriates, I am here honing in on the *formal*, not *objective*, reality of language.

That Spinoza himself makes this distinction between the formal and objective reality of language is clear from a remark he makes to Jarig Jelles:

> If I see a book containing excellent thoughts and beautifully written in the hands of a common man and I ask him whence he has such a book, and he replies that he has copied it from another book belonging to another common man who could also write beautifully, and so on to infinity, he does not satisfy me. For I am asking him not only about the form and arrangement of the letters with which alone his answer is concerned, but also the thoughts and meaning expressed in their arrangement.[15]

The point is that language exists both as a vehicle which expresses "thoughts and meanings," but also as an object of study in its own right in terms of its "form and arrangement." The former constitutes the objective existence of language (language as reference); the latter the formal existence of language (its materiality).[16] Each of these types of existence have their own causal chain: hence, "the common man" is perfectly correct to identify the cause of the book in terms of its material production; however, there is also a causal chain of *intentions*, according to which the author tries to refer to concepts or perceptions. Language exists both formally and objectively and there is a separate science (a separate causal account) for each aspect.

It could be argued that Spinoza's deployment of the image of "the common man" here is polemical: the science of the formal existence of language is trivial and hence not worth pursuing. Moreover, Spinoza's works do give the impression

---

[15] Benedict Spinoza, "Letter 40" in *Collected Works*, trans. Samuel Shirley (Indianapolis: Hackett, 2002), 865-6.

[16] The editors in the Shirley edition flag up the difference between "the objective reality of a representation" and "its formal reality" in explaining the above remark. (Ibid., 866)

that he never pursues the science of the formal reality of language either in an explicit or sustained manner. However, two recent commentators (Warren Montag and François Zourabichvili) have argued that this impression is misleading and that Spinoza does indeed engage in the science of the formal reality of language or "linguistic physics," as Zourabichvili dubs it.

Montag's reading of the *TTP* in *Bodies, Masses, Power* involves Spinoza in precisely such an endeavour. As he insists, for Spinoza texts are part of nature: "*Scriptura, sive Natura.*"[17] In other words, writing is a physical body and needs to be treated as such. *Scriptura, sive Natura* illustrates "what makes Spinoza... the first philosopher explicitly to consider Scripture, that is, writing, as a part of nature in its materiality."[18] It is primarily for this reason, according to Montag, that Spinoza intervenes in the debate over the interpretation of Scripture in the *TTP*: to persuade readers that texts are not merely vehicles for conceptual referents, but should be read as entities in their own right. Spinoza "rejects the quest for the supertextual"[19] or, as Montag puts it more fully, "Writing, whether sacred or not, is fundamentally corporeal...Writing is part of nature, a body among other bodies, and, if it is effective, 'moves' other bodies to act or to refrain from action."[20] In short, the *TTP* examines the formal reality of Scripture, ignoring for the most part its objective reality. It contributes to the Spinozist science of the formal reality of language.

Zourabichvili's *Spinoza: Une physique de la pensée* explicitly takes up the distinction between formal and objective reality as the guiding thread to Spinoza's philosophy. In particular,

---

[17] Warren Montag, *Bodies, Masses, Power: Spinoza and his Contemporaries* (London: Verso, 1999), 5. It is important to note that Montag conceives such *sive* statements as a form of dialectical identity, where the first term gives way to the second. I offer an alternative, non-dialectical reading below (ibid., 4-5).

[18] Ibid., 5.

[19] Ibid., 6.

[20] Ibid., 21. Montag defines superstition as sole concern for the objective reality of language: "The superstitious person forsakes the surface (of nature, of Scripture) in favour of the depth." (Ibid., 8)

Zourabichvili attempts to reconstruct a physics of ideas (the laws and structures of thought running parallel to a physics of bodies). His book therefore revolves around "the question of the formal being of ideas."[21] Indeed, such a "physics *cogitative*" is noticeably absent in the *Ethics* itself: the precedence Spinoza gives to the attribute of extension in Part II ensures that knowledge is discussed only in its objective existence—insofar as ideas relate to bodies. Curley, for example, takes this as a symptom of Spinoza's Hobbesian temptation to reductive materialism.[22] Ideas seem to exist to the extent that they represent bodies—and Spinoza neglects to sketch in any detail how ideas relate to each other: "The *Spinozan physics of thought* is absent."[23] This is the lack Zourabichvili addresses. He asks, "What would it be to consider the idea in its formal being and thus to relate it to an autonomous field of production analogous to that of physics, what would it be to conceive a *physics cogitative* with its own laws (not ones merely transposed from the physics of bodies)?"[24]

For our purposes, the most significant part of his answer to this question concerns the incomplete *Hebrew Grammar*. For Zourabichvili, the very idea of a grammar is a transposition of this quest for a physics of thought onto the linguistic plane: "'Grammar' is the name of a *linguistic physics*, for there is no reason not to treat a text as a natural object obeying certain laws."[25] The *Hebrew Grammar* consists in a science of the formal reality of language. It is the linguistic complement of a physics of thought. Hence, just as in a physics of extension bodies are formed and in a physics of thought ideas are formed, in grammar a text is treated as "an individual formed itself from multiple individuals."[26]

---

[21] Zourabichvili, *Spinoza*, 115.

[22] Edwin Curley, *Behind the Geometrical Method* (Princeton: Princeton University Press, 1988), 74-8; see Zourabichvili, *Spinoza*, 113-4.

[23] Zourabichvili, *Spinoza*, 10.

[24] Ibid., 115.

[25] Ibid., 240.

[26] Ibid.

Montag and Zourabichvili's work provide, then, two precursors to my argument in this paper. For them as for me, Spinoza does indeed engage in a science of the formal reality of language, a linguistic physics or (in my anachronistic expression) a *Naturphilosophie* of language. In what follows, I want to pursue this idea in the *Ethics* itself. That is, I argue that the logic underlying much of Spinoza's rhetoric in the *Ethics* can be formulated in terms of just such a linguistic physics. Taking Montag and Zourabichvili's research as my jumping off point, I attempt to fill out in more details just what such a physics would look like in detail. In particular, it is the deployment of the terms "God," "substance" and "Nature" which orients my attempt to formulate a Spinozan "grammar." As I indicated in my introduction, such an enterprise has significant consequences for philosophy of religion (as well as for philosophy of language); hence, I begin by considering a powerful interpretation of Spinoza's use of these three terms from within contemporary, continental philosophy of religion.

Part Two: Naming Immanence with Barber

What follows revolves around two concepts: improper name and proper name. Spinoza defines a proper name as follows: "By means of a proper substantive noun it is possible to indicate only a single individual, for each and every individual has a proper noun for himself only."[27] It is a noun that is sufficient for successfully naming one concept and that concept alone (in certain contexts). An improper name can therefore be defined as one name that is insufficient for successfully naming one concept and that concept alone (in any context). These definitions are significant because Spinoza deploys more than one name for God; he speaks of "God," "substance" and "Nature" indifferently, giving none priority. If the name "God" were a proper name, this rhetorical practice would be redundant: there would be little reason to provide more

---

[27] Spinoza, *Hebrew Grammar* in *Complete Works*, 600.

than one name. Therefore, "God" seems to be employed as an improper name: on its own, "God" is insufficient; it stands in need of supplementation. *Prima facie*, this is odd: "God" seems to be precisely one of the only names that successfully pick out a unique concept. My task therefore is to determine how and why "God" can be thought of as an improper name, despite all indications to the contrary.

Daniel Barber's recent essay, "Secularism, Immanence and the Philosophy of Religion," makes use of the impropriety of the Spinozan name "God" in order to reinterpret the notion of the secular. The secular has, of course, come under criticism in the last decade owing to the imperialist nature of its historical manifestations: everything particular in religious traditions has been forced, the argument goes, to be translated or mediated through the universal language of secularity. The secular is a transcendent plane that is imposed on the specificity of religions. Therefore, Barber echoes the call made by all postsecular thinkers:

> What must be expelled is what has been installed [by imperial secularity]: a transcendent, universal plane...The capacity to think without a transcendent plane must be pursued. It is in this sense, and in this sense alone, that philosophy of religion must become secular.[28]

Yet, there is an obvious difference that emerges here between Barber and postsecular thinking: while the latter calls for the elimination of the secular *tout court*, Barber demands a *reinterpretation* of the secular as an immanent, and not transcendent, plane.[29] And he achieves this end of articulating an

---

[28] Daniel Barber, "Secularism, Immanence and the Philosophy of Religion" in Smith and Whistler (eds.), *After the Postsecular and the Postmodern*, 161-2. A fuller statement of Barber's arguments can be found in *On Diaspora: Christianity, Religion and Secularity* (Eugene, OR: Cascade, 2011). Here, his affirmation of the secular is less fulsome.

[29] That such a reinterpretation is possible and that postsecular thinkers have therefore foreclosed this alternative by moving too quickly is the wager of Barber's essay: "I will argue for a secularity that is intrinsic to immanence. Only the rigour of immanence provides the possibility of a secularity that

immanent secular via Spinoza. Barber argues that there are a number of "paradoxes" in Spinoza's thought which shed light on how immanent secularity would function: they are "paradoxes that harbour the potentiality for the sort of immanent secularity and immanent affirmation of religion I am proposing."[30] The first paradox takes up Spinoza's claim: "*Deus sive Natura.*" In complete opposition to the philosophical tradition as well as common sense, Spinoza identifies God and nature—these two names refer henceforth to the same thing. In Barber's words,

> [God or Nature] is, of course, a notoriously enigmatic statement. Is it that these two terms are reversible, where they name the same thing but from different vantages? Is the distinction between these terms meant to preserve a real difference in signification, or is the distinction primarily strategic, in which only one terms designates the real (the other then being strategically preserved yet remaining ultimately derivative or epiphenomenal with respect to the real)?[31]

The problem is merely compounded when one adds "substance" to the mix, since substance is another name Spinoza employs synonymously with God and nature. Spinoza therefore has three names which each seem perfectly appropriate ways of referring to one thing (i.e. that thing which is referred to by the names "God," "nature" or "substance;" I will henceforth call it, following Barber, immanence). Immanence has three equally good names; this, then, is Barber's formulation of the problem of improper names.

2.1 *The Second Solution*

In the above quotation, Barber gives two unsuccessful solu-

---

has nothing to do with a transcendent plane. I will argue, furthermore, that an immanent secularity provides a new way of thinking about religion" (Barber, "Secularism, Immanence and the Philosophy of Religion," 162).

[30] Ibid.

[31] Ibid.

tions for justifying the impropriety of Spinozan names. These alternatives exhaust most traditional responses to the problem; however, as Barber rightly asserts, both of them ultimately fail. According to the second alternative, only one of the names is really adequate to immanence or "designates the real" (in Barber's words). The other two names are inadequate, and employed merely for *strategic* reasons. For example, "God" might be taken as a merely strategic name which Spinoza thinks is inadequate to refer to immanence, but that is still used in the *Ethics* as a cover for his atheism. In short, Spinoza could think that only one of "substance" or "Nature" is an adequate name for immanence; if this is so, the problem of improper names would be dissolved, because actually Spinoza would be committed to the claim that esoterically "substance" (for example) is *the* proper name for immanence.

However, the problem is that there is no sufficient warrant for choosing any one of the three names: Spinoza never makes clear which name he prefers. There is no evidence nor even any criterion on which to make the choice; hence, any choice would ultimately be arbitrary—deciding the undecidable, even. For example, to write off "God" as a strategic cover for Spinoza's genuine thought seems implausible considering Spinoza's strident defence of his theism in his letters.[32] At no point does Spinoza ever let his guard down to reveal himself an atheist; to call him one, then, is mere guesswork. Indeed, despite Leo Strauss' fame for jettisoning the linguistic surface of Spinoza's text in the name of a hidden meaning, even he is suspicious of writing off "God" in the *Ethics* as a strategic cover or "appeasive term."[33] There is no way of discriminating between "God," "Nature and "substance" as names for immanence. Hence, Barber speaks of "the inadequacy of a reductive interpretation of Spinoza's act of naming."[34]

---

[32] See, for example, Spinoza, "Letter 43" in *Complete Works*, 879-81.

[33] Leo Strauss, *Persecution and the Art of Writing* (Chicago: University of Chicago Press, 1988), 188-90. He insists that prior to any judgment on this matter, "one has to see whether there are not anywhere in Spinoza's writings indications, however subtle, of a strictly atheist beginning or approach" (ibid., 189).

[34] Barber, *On Diaspora*, 3. He continues, "If God is 'really' meant to signify

2.2 The First Solution

There is another option considered in the above quotation. On this alternative, each name refers to immanence, but the different connotations (or Fregean "senses") of each name means that they all add something to our idea of immanence. "Substance," "God" and "Nature," that is, all give a different perspective or "vantage" on what immanence is, and so cumulatively such perspectives define it completely. On this view, each name refers successfully but incompletely (or inadequately)—and this is why they require supplementation by each other. This is a version of the claim that each name expresses an attribute of God—an argument that Spinoza himself employs when it comes to human names (specifically, "Jacob" and "Israel").[35]

Barber concludes that this alternative cannot be correct either. This is because, for Barber, no name can successfully refer to immanence, because ultimately immanence is "nameless immanence;" it is that which forever eludes signification. If "substance," "God" and "Nature" fail to refer to immanence (which is inevitable, according to Barber), then they are unlikely to successfully connote aspects of it, however incompletely. Barber's argument thus makes use of a central concept in his essay—nameless immanence.

Another way of problematizing this supposed solution is to be found in Spinoza's definition of adequacy in Part II of the *Ethics*: "By adequate idea I understand an idea which, insofar as it is considered in itself, without relation to an object, has all the properties or intrinsic denominations of a true idea. I say intrinsic to exclude what is extrinsic, namely, the agree-

---

Nature, what does it mean that God is nonetheless invoked as sign?" (ibid., 4).

[35] "You want me to explain by example—though it is not at all necessary—how one and the same thing can be signified by two names...By 'Israel' I mean the third patriarch; by 'Jacob' I mean that same person, the latter name being given to him because he seized his brother's heel." Spinoza, "Letter 9" in *Complete Works*, 783. On the relation of God's attributes to names, see Gillian Howie, *Deleuze and Spinoza: Aura of Expressionism* (Basingstoke: Palgrave, 2002), 29-36.

ment of the idea with its object."³⁶ An adequate idea, Spinoza insists, has nothing to do with the success or failure of its reference;³⁷ rather, adequacy is the *intrinsic* aspect of truth—and this intrinsic aspect is synonymous with *completeness*.³⁸ An adequate idea is "absolute."³⁹ This distinction between intrinsic and true maps precisely onto the distinction already made between formal and objective reality: "adequacy" therefore indicates an excellence of formal reality.⁴⁰ Two further premises are required for this argument to function. First, Spinoza's presentation of his philosophy in the *Ethics* is adequate. This remains a controversial point considering Spinoza's sometimes negative views on language (discussed earlier). For example, Savan argues, "Spinoza's views on words and language make it impossible for him to hold that his writings (or anyone else's) can be a direct or literal exposition of philosophical truth." He continues, "So sharply does Spinoza separate words from adequate ideas that it is difficult to make out for language any useful philosophical function at all."⁴¹ Nevertheless, I contend the above claim must be true to some extent for Spinoza to claim to be communicating the truth, and so for present purposes I will assume that Spinoza did think his philosophical writings (somehow) expressed the truth adequately. Second, a complete idea would contain every connotation or "sense" pertaining to its referent—that is, a complete or adequate idea would include every possible perspective on its subject-matter. From these three premises, it follows that each adequate name for immanence is complete

---

36 Spinoza, *Ethics* in *Collected Works*, IID4.

37 Instead, a "true" idea "must agree with its object." (Ibid., IA6)

38 This is the presupposition behind the doctrine of *common* notions: concepts which are legitimately universal and all-encompassing. See ibid., IIP40S1.

39 Ibid., IIP34.

40 Hence, in what follows, I use "adequacy" to denote the formal excellence of names and "success" to denote the objective excellence of names, i.e. names insofar as they do refer to a concept or percept are successful.

41 David Savan, "Spinoza and Language" in S.P. Kashap (ed), *Studies in Spinoza* (Berkeley: University of California Press, 1972), 239.

and there is no necessity for it to be further supplemented by the addition of further names. And to the extent that any one of the names used in the *Ethics* is adequate, additions are redundant: each name is absolute in itself. Therefore, the problem of improper names—the problem of the seeming redundancy of Spinoza's proliferation of names for immanence—remains intact.

2.3 Barber's Answer

Barber himself claims that all three names—"God," "substance" and "Nature"—must be improper, because what they attempt to name (immanence) is ultimately unnameable. This unnameability does not, however, lead to mystic silence, but an endless proliferation of new but necessarily unsuccessful names.

At the heart of his argument stands the claim that immanence is nameless;[42] in fact, it is unnameable. The reason for this is to be found in how Barber characterises the naming process itself: to name something is always necessarily to install a transcendent plane. Barber writes, if "God" or "Nature" are considered proper names, "in each case immanence has been subjected to a transcendent plane—but immanence remains irreducible to such subjection."[43] To subject immanence to a transcendent plane is to falsify it; therefore, immanence—if it is to remain immanence—cannot be named.[44] Or, to be

---

[42] Barber, "Secularism, Immanence," 164.

[43] Ibid..

[44] *What is Philosophy?* is of course the source of this claim. Deleuze and Guattari write, "The plane of immanence is like a section of chaos and acts like a sieve…Chaos makes chaotic and undoes every consistency in the infinite. The problem of philosophy is to acquire a consistency without losing the infinite into which thought plunges" (Gilles Deleuze and Félix Guattari, *What is Philosophy?* trans. Graham Burchell and Hugh Tomlinson [London: Verso, 1994], 42). In other words, there are three types of thought: chaotic thought which is infinite but inconsistent, immanent thought which is both infinite and consistent and transcendent thought which is consistent but finite. To name immanence is to make it finite; it is to determine it and fix it in certain respects—converting an infinite plenitude into something

more precise, it cannot be named outside of a fictive register in which naming acknowledges its own inadequacy.

Yet, Barber is no less insistent that, even though it is nameless, immanence still gives rise to an endless proliferation of inadequate names. "Signification is necessary"[45]—it is part of the becoming of immanence that it is necessarily falsified by signification; or, as Barber himself puts it, "The ontological priority of immanence runs into the mediatic priority of signification."[46] Hence, though no name ever successfully refers to immanence, with immanence comes an endless proliferation of names which attempt to do so. This proliferation is, dubbed by Barber, the excessiveness or surplus of immanence: immanence goes beyond itself by generating names which endlessly fail to capture it. So, while it is impossible to name immanence, it is also "impossible not to name immanence."[47]

This is therefore Barber's solution to the problem of improper names. Spinoza employs improper names for God, because immanence always necessarily generates more and more improper names. Immanence gives rise to "the paradoxical necessity of signifying that which has no proper name."[48]

2.4 Barber and Apophaticism

At a number of points, Barber strongly distinguishes his position from apophaticism. His solution to the problem of proper names, he claims, "evade[s] the lure of apophaticism."[49] This is because, for Barber, apophaticism negates names in favour of a nameless transcendent plane. Therefore, while it

---

finite and rigid. To name is therefore to install a transcendent plane. This is why to name immanence (non-fictively) is to falsify it, and so immanence is properly nameless.

[45] Barber, "Secularism, Immanence and the Philosophy of Religion," 163.
[46] Ibid., 163.
[47] Ibid.
[48] Ibid.
[49] Ibid., 167.

may superficially appear that Barber's strategies in dealing with names are apophatic, the result of these strategies is profoundly non-apophatic: rather than indicating something beyond all immanence which cannot be named because it is so other, they indicate something so immanent it cannot be named. Thus, Barber continues, "Immanence exceeds signification not because it belongs to a plane beyond signification—this would turn immanence into yet another mode of transcendence."[50] Immanence does not exist *beyond* names, but logically *prior to* names (as their transcendental condition).

I am sceptical of this argument for a number of reasons. First, negative theologians would agree that their "God" exists prior to names, as an immanent condition productive of names. That is, Barber's characterisation of apophatic theology as installing a transcendent plane is unfair. Second, apophaticism denotes a practice, rather than a result—a practice of *apophasis* or negation: one can therefore practice apophaticism in the name of immanence, just as happily as one can practice apophaticism in the name of transcendence. Henri Bergson and Samuel Beckett, for example, are apophatic thinkers *of immanence*.[51] Therefore, I characterise Barber's solution to the problem of improper names as apophatic, and this is because it shares the defining characteristic of all apophaticism: a dissatisfaction with language as such and so an overriding concern to negate or show up the inadequacy of that language in the name of the nameless. Barber's central claim that immanence is properly nameless and so therefore

---

[50] Barber, "Secularism, Immanence and the Philosophy of Religion," Barber continues in *On Diaspora*, "The operation I am tracing here is not identifiable with the logic of negative theology. While it is the case that negative theology also grapples with the difficulty of naming the nameless, it is equally the case that negative theology addresses this difficulty by signifying that the object of signification is unsignifiable. Immanence, however, cannot permit this strategy, for such a strategy makes the unsignifiable into something that transcends signification" (8).

[51] On Beckett's non-theological apophaticism, see my comments on Sandra Wynands' *Iconic Spaces: The Dark Theology of Samuel Beckett's Drama* (Indiana: University of Notre Dame Press, 2007) in *Literature and Theology* 22.4 (2008): 494-7.

all names are inadequate is the very claim repeated by all apophatic thinkers—theologians or otherwise.[52]

It is here that I locate my fundamental disagreement with Barber's solution to the problem of improper names (at least as this problem is to be found in monistic philosophies). Barber claims that immanence is properly nameless because it exists prior to all naming: "Immanence is prior to signification," he claims—and this priority, he goes on to specify, is an "ontological priority."[53] As a reading of Spinoza's use of improper names, the disjunction between names and nameless immanence is misguided for two reasons. First, for a rigorous monist like Spinoza (and, we shall see, the same is true for Schelling), immanence *is* each name. There is no ontological priority here, but only ontological identity. In fact, the productive monisms of Spinoza and Schelling do away with the hierarchy of being altogether—and this hierarchy is of course the precondition of being able to claim that something is prior to something else.[54] For Spinoza, there is merely identity. Immanence does not exist before names, it only exists *as* names. In the second half of the paper, I am going to explore the metaphysical reasons why this is the case; for the moment, however, I merely want to claim that in asserting the priority of immanence to its names, Barber does not take Spinoza's monism seriously enough.

Second, if Spinoza wrote the *Ethics* adequately (see section 2.2), then the names he uses in the *Ethics*, like "God," "substance" and "Nature," cannot fail to refer to what they

---

[52] For example, Barber stands in the apophatic tradition when he claims that the task for philosophy of religion is to recognise the names of the secular "as fictive" (Barber, "Secularism, Immanence," 169). He writes, "It is thus imperative to inhabit that difference between immanence itself and the fictions it intrinsically produces" (ibid., 169). Apophaticism is precisely the practice by which this difference is recognised and inhabited, for this difference represents the inadequacy of all language to capture what is properly nameless. See also Barber, *On Diaspora*, 8.

[53] Barber, "Secularism, Immanence," 163.

[54] Martial Gueroult, *Spinoza* vol. 1 (Paris: Aubier Montaigne, 1968), 299; Gilles Deleuze, *Expression in Philosophy: Spinoza*, trans. Martin Joughin (New York: Zone, 1990), Chapter 11.

intend to refer to. If they were to fail, the whole of the *Ethics* would collapse and become mere wordplay with no genuine reference to reality.[55] Therefore, for Spinoza's philosophy to function as philosophy (i.e. to make claims about the truth), Barber cannot be right—Spinoza's improper names for immanence must actually *succeed* in naming immanence.

These two reasons indicate that Barber's solution to the problem of improper names cannot be correct in Spinoza's case (although it might be a perfectly good solution more generally). Barber is wrong to claim that Spinoza employs improper names because they fail to refer. Moreover, just as Barber's solution to this problem fails, so too does every apophatic solution, because apophaticism necessarily claims that all names fail in some way, shape or form. It is here that I am intervening in debates in philosophy of religion: apophaticism is not the answer here, and this is a hard pill for continental philosophy of religion to swallow. The natural inclination of most continental philosophers of religion is to resort to apophatic solutions when there is any kind of conundrum concerning language. As soon as a difficulty concerning religious language is raised, the assumption is that language is a falsification, because God is other or because God transcends human discourse or because language is structured by *différance* and so on. This is one of the reasons I am focusing on Spinoza and Schelling here, for they are the philosophers most distanced from the apophatic worldview. Their uncompromising rationalism—their concern to know everything because everything is immanent—means one cannot explain away their philosophy of religious language apophatically. One of the defining characteristics of such kataphatic thought is the excess of names they deploy—one name is insufficient for their purposes. Hence, Spinoza uses "God," "substance" and "Nature" synonymously, while Hegel speaks almost synonymously of "God," "the absolute" and "Spirit." My contention is that every apophatic solution—every solution premised on the inadequacy of names—fails to ac-

---

[55] It will be seen later in the paper that I need to qualify these claims somewhat.

count for this plurality of names. Spinoza therefore wakes us from our apophatic slumbers: he forces us to look elsewhere, re-evaluate the problem of religious language and do philosophy of religion differently. In other words, philosophers of religious language have been obsessed with the inadequacy of names to the point of ignoring kataphatic deployments of language. However, the speculative turn is kataphatic in orientation—and much work now needs to be done on analysing and unpacking the way kataphatic texts signify.

Part Three: Schelling's Metaphysics of Language

I thus need to approach anew the problem of improper names in order to work out what a metaphysics would look like in which what is referred to by "God" or "substance" or "Nature" is ontologically identical with those names. Through this metaphysical inquiry, I hope to show how monists solve the problem of improper names. To do this, I now turn to the *Identitätssystem* of F.W.J. Schelling.[56] In the *Identitätssystem*, Schelling demonstrates why, on the basis of a productive monism, God *is* the name "God" or reality *is* the name "reality." The metaphysics of Schelling's *Identitätssystem* reveals how names can be improper.

3.1 Schelling's Productive Monism Presented in Six Propositions

Proposition One: Immanence has more than one name

Unsurprisingly enough, Schelling gives a plurality of names to immanence (or what fundamentally exists in reality). He

---

[56] For a fuller account of and further justification for the reading of Schelling which follows, see Daniel Whistler, *Schelling's Theory of Symbolic Language: Forming the System of Identity* (Oxford: Oxford University Press, 2012 forthcoming). In this paper, I assume that between 1801 and 1805 Schelling's work forms a self-sufficient whole and that the major works of this period can therefore be studied in isolation from the rest of his corpus. The philosophy of this period is called, following Schelling's lead, the *Identitätssystem* (the system of identity), and all of the claims I make about Schelling in what follows are meant to apply to the *Identitätssystem* alone.

employs these names practically interchangeably throughout his *Identitätssystem*. The names include "the absolute," "identity," "indifference" and "God." It is not the case that Schelling prefers one of these names (for example, "the absolute") and uses the others derivatively or secondarily to describe certain properties or attributes of this absolute. Each name is an adequate name for what is. There is no necessity for Schelling to use more than one name, yet he does: "God," "identity," "indifference," "reality" and "the absolute" are improper names. Why, to ask once again, is Schelling so insistent on employing them all?

Proposition Two: Immanence is one

The *Identitätssystem* effectively commences with Schelling's claim, "Absolute identity is not the cause of the universe, but the universe itself."[57] Combating philosophy's "long and profound ignorance about this principle," Schelling rediscovers the "true" nature of reality—monism.[58] He writes, "All that is is, to the extent that it is, One…*There is everywhere only One Being, only One true Essence.*"[59] This is, of course, why the *Identitätssystem* is called the *Identitätssystem*, because all of reality is self-identical. Immanence is identical with itself.

Proposition Three: Immanence consists in form and essence

Schelling sees immanence as comprised of two elements—essence and form. While these two elements are utterly identical, the philosopher is able to isolate them individually. So, reality is *in essence* indeterminate identity, but it is also necessary

---

[57] F.W.J. Schelling, *Werke*, vol. 4, ed. K.F.A. Schelling (Stuttgart: Cotta, 1856-61), 129; Schelling, *Presentation of My System of Philosophy*, trans. Michael G. Vater in *Philosophical Forum* 32.4 (2001), 359.

[58] Ibid., 129, 359.

[59] Ibid., 6:156; Schelling, *System of Philosophy in General and of the Philosophy of Nature in Particular* in *Idealism and the Endgame of Theory: Three Esssays*, ed. and trans. Thomas Pfau (Albany: SUNY Press, 1994), 153.

that essence cannot exist without form. Essence always exists formed—there are no exceptions. There is therefore no such thing as unformed immanence; there is no such thing as essential identity free from formal identity. Immanence is always already determinate. There is *no ineffable "behind" or "beyond"* to what is expressed that never manifests itself; there is no hidden transcendence.

Proposition Four: Form produces essence

Form neither represents nor emanates from essence; instead, Schelling conceives of a third model for the form/essence relation. The foundation on which Schelling's alternative is built is the principle that formation is inescapable. For Schelling, this means that immanence exists by producing its own essence through a process of formation. Schellingian philosophy conceives essence as *excessive*: the produced essence is always *more than* it was prior to production. Determination is not a prison which stops us reaching what matters most; what matters most is in fact first *produced* in the very act of determination. Formation can never be a diminution, alienation, distortion or loss of essence. There is a perpetually excessive surplus of essence.

Proposition Five: Even though all forms express identity, there is more than one form

If everything is the same—if Schelling is a monist—how can formal *identity* give rise to the irreducible multiplicity of everyday life? Schelling insists that form is not singular; there is a plurality of formal identities in existence. In other words, reality is refracted into multiple instances of identity. This is how plurality arises in the Schellingian cosmos. Schelling designates these various manifestations of the law of identity *Darstellungen* (or presentations or exhibitions). Every thing and every idea is a *Darstellung*, much like it is a mode for Spinoza.

Speculations III

Proposition Six: Differentiation is quantitative

What then differentiates these forms? Schelling's answer is classically monist: there is only one substance that comprises all there is; the only differentiating attribute is therefore the degree to which this substance is instantiated. This is what Schelling means when he speaks of "amounts of being"[60] or "degrees of the absolute,"[61] or "different grades of identity."[62] It is also what Grant means when he speaks of "the quantity of identity" each entity possesses for Schelling.[63] Two claims are therefore central to Schelling's doctrine of quantitative differentiation: first, differentiation is a matter of form, and, second, it is a matter of *the degree or the excess* to which each form produces essential identity.

3.2 Schelling's Theory of Language

Every *Darstellung* is a construction of reality to a certain intensity; there is therefore a hierarchy of *Darstellungen* proceeding from those which are maximally productive of identity to those which are minimally intense. Schelling once more has numerous names for the type of form that exists at the top of this hierarchy: "idea" is one name he uses, but for our purposes the most pertinent name is "symbol."

In his Lectures on the Philosophy of Art, Schelling writes. "*Darstellung* of the absolute with absolute indifference of the universal and the particular…is possible only symbolically."[64] The symbol represents the highest, most intense form—it stands at the top of the hierarchy: "The symbolic is the

---

[60] Schelling, *Werke*, 4:123; Schelling, *Presentation*, 355.

[61] Ibid., 2:64; Schelling, *Ideas for a Philosophy of Nature*, trans. Errol E. Harris and Peter Heath (Cambridge: Cambridge University Press, 1988) 48.

[62] Schelling, *Werke*, 4:431.

[63] Iain Hamilton Grant, *Philosophy of Nature after Schelling* (London: Continuum, 2006), 174.

[64] Schelling, *Werke*, 5:406; Schelling, *Philosophy of Art*, trans. Douglas W. Stott (Minneapolis: Minnesota University Press, 1989), 45.

absolute in itself."⁶⁵ Examples of symbols for Schelling are organisms, artworks, philosophy and theology—they are all examples of maximally intense productions of reality. Yet, Schelling is equally insistent that not all symbols are equally intense, because they do not all manifest the identity *of real and ideal* (or matter and idea) to the same extent. That is, Schelling conceives the possibility of predominantly real and predominantly ideal symbols. The extent to which symbols identify real and ideal thus becomes the criterion by which to differentiate and assess them. And, in fact, Schelling claims, there is *only one symbol* which identifies the real and the ideal fully, and this is symbolic *language*.

Language, Schelling writes, "is the most appropriate symbol of the absolute or infinite affirmation of God"⁶⁶: it is an absolute *Darstellung*, so exhibits identity to the maximum possible extent. Language is not just an ordinary *Darstellung* (or form of reality), it is not merely one instance of a symbol, it is the most intense possible symbol. Schelling argues that language is the only symbol which overcomes the real/ideal binary, and so it expresses identity to an even greater extent than any other symbol. It is the symbol of symbols—the "indifference of indifference...the identity of identity."⁶⁷ In Wanning's words, "Nothing more intense is possible within the *Identitätssystem*."⁶⁸ The fact that language is the only symbolic form to fully indifferentiate real and ideal has the further consequence that *language manifests reality most*. To describe something in language is to produce it in the most intense possible manner. Entities exist most in words. Or

---

⁶⁵ Henry Crabb Robinson, "Schellings Aesthetik" in Ernst Behler, "Schellings Ästhetik in der Überlieferung von Henry Crabb Robinson," *Philosophisches Jahrbuch* 83.1 (1976), 161.

⁶⁶ Schelling, Werke, 5:483; Schelling, *Philosophy of Art*, 100.

⁶⁷ Jochen A. Bär, *Sprachreflexion der deutschen Frühromantik: Konzepte zwischen Universalpoesie und grammatischem Kosmopolitismus* (Berlin: de Gruyter, 1999), 165.

⁶⁸ Berbeli Wanning, *Konstruktion und Geschichte: Das Identitätsphilosophie als Grundlage der Kunstphilosophie bei F.W.J. Schelling* (Frankfurt am Main: Haag und Herchen, 1988), 166.

put differently, the reality of an entity is its name. Discourse, names and propositions *are* more than anything else can possible be.

Our next question is what does this mean for language—what is the structure of a Schellingian name? There is one fundamental element to Schellingian symbolic language: "Meaning is here simultaneous with being itself, passed over into the object itself and one with it."[69] Schelling is committed to an absolute identification of meaning and being in symbolic language. What a word means is nothing different from what it is. Language does not signify something outside itself. It is its own meaning. Words do not represent something in the world; in fact, there is no outside to words. In short, Schelling eliminates signification from symbolic language. Meaning does *not* (even partially) exist separate from being—and so no process or activity (including signification) is required to transfer from the latter to the former. Language remains completely immanent to itself: it is completely self-contained and self-sufficient. Signification and reference are no longer valid categories.

If reference is no longer a valid category for understanding language, what is? As we have seen, forms are characterised by the extent they produce essential identity—and the same is true for language. So, production of identity is the goal of Schellingian symbolic language; it is what remains after the elimination of reference. What matters is not the referent (for there is none), but the product. Symbolic language does not refer to reality; it *produces* reality. The rejection of reference frees language from correctly or incorrectly representing an already existing entity; what is rather at stake is how intensely entities are generated through language. *Description is replaced with production.*

There is a further important consequence: if words produce the absolute more or less intensely, then there should be ways of increasing the intensity of such production. These modes of intensification I dub *symbolic practices*. Through them, Schelling hopes to transform all language into symbolic

---

[69] Schelling, *Werke*, 5:411; Schelling, *Philosophy of Art*, 49.

language. What we have here is a version of the Romantic process of *Bildung*—what Schelling dubs, "the gradual intensification of all forms,"[70] and the symbolic practice required to make language symbolic is *eclecticism*: it is only through the eclectic accumulation of names for reality that Schelling thinks language (and so discursive practices, like philosophy) can become fully symbolic.

Returning to Schelling's metaphysics shows why: Schelling is a monist with regard to essence: there is one essence to reality, and this essence is identity. In consequence, all sciences have *essentially* the same subject matter—identity. All future scientific endeavour will repeat the same essence over and over. Scientific progress does not therefore consist in what is said, but *how* it is said. The *form of science* becomes the crucial issue. The Schellingian ideal is a form of philosophy (a language) which produces essential identity with the maximum possible intensity. This point can be turned reflexively back onto Schelling's own practice: the *Identitätssystem* merely repeats the same essence as all other philosophies. It is when it comes to *form*, Schelling claims, that it is to be set above everything else. The *Identitätssystem* is self-consciously constructed around this insight into the centrality of form to the philosophical endeavour. This is ultimately the reason why Schelling experiments with dialogue (in *Bruno*) and with the *more geometrico* (most rigorously, in the 1804 *System*); it is the reason why he adopts Spinozist vocabulary, then Platonic vocabulary, then theological vocabulary. All these various experiments in form are variations on one fundamental practice which Schelling thinks will make his system *the most* intense. According to this symbolic practice, all previous scientific discourse is reduced to the status of *materials* that can be appropriated to aid the production of identity. I designate this practice, "absolute eclecticism"—that is, the magpie-like appropriation of individual concepts and styles from various scientific discourses for the sake of producing reality.

---

[70] Schelling, *Werke*, 5:147; Schelling, *On Construction in Philosophy*, trans. Andrew A. Davis and Alexi I. Kukuljevic in *Epoché* 12.2 (2008), 285.

In other words, all forms produce identity, but some do it better than others; therefore, the task of the thinker is to locate the most productive aspects of each science and assemble them into a system; the result is a system of identity, an *Identitätssystem*. The thinker must choose anything and everything that will intensify her form of discourse and so intensify identity. In consequence, impropriety becomes the very ideal of science—and the *Identitätssystem* in particular is built on the virtue of impropriety. An improper science is one unconcerned with borders between fields, but which plunders every science (and every name) *equally* in order to intensify its productivity. It is the reason behind Schelling's appropriation of Platonic language and Spinozist method into his philosophy, and—most significantly for this paper—eclecticism is the reason behind Schelling's use of improper names. "God," "the absolute," "identity," "indifference" are names taken from various different discourses and brought into the *Identitätssystem* for the purpose of intensifying the philosophical language in which Schelling writes. Improper names for God are eclectically appropriated and deployed for the sake of a higher level of intensity in the *Identitätssystem* itself. Because Schelling employs improper names, he produces reality better.[71]

This long detour into Schelling's philosophy of language therefore helps with the problem of improper names. Two conclusions are especially crucial. First, reality is most paradigmatically a name. What is exists most intensely as a name. Second, Schelling demonstrates that a monist must do away with reference: referential relations assume some difference between word and meaning—and this cannot be the case for monists. Adding these claims together leads immediately to the conclusion: names for God are God or names for immanence are immanence. For monists, whether a name successfully refers is a redundant question: the adequacy or inadequacy of a name has nothing to do with reference. The *apophatic*

---

[71] By which I mean intensively "better" or "better" in the sense of Spinozan adequacy, rather than "better" in reference to an external model or archetype.

contention that names necessarily fail to refer to reality has no relevance to the problem of improper names as it occurs in Spinoza and Schelling's philosophy. Instead—leaving behind the way apophaticism usually frames the debate—I contend that absolute eclecticism provides the model to account for improper names: the more names given, the more intense scientific language becomes. These names are intensive productions of the absolute—and they become more intense, the more names are used. The success of the productive monism Schelling proposes in his *Identitätssystem* ultimately depends on the plurality of names he incorporates into this system. Improper names are, for Schelling, always an improvement over proper names, because plurality is an intensification. This, then, is Schelling's solution to the problem of improper names.

Part Four: Philosophy of Language for Monists

4.1 Spinoza Revisited

This Schellingian solution illuminates Spinoza's own employment of improper names. First, Spinoza's rigorous commitment to immanence means that there is no such thing as pure immanence. Any notion of immanence existing separately from its manifestations is false. Just as for Schelling there is no essence that is not formed, so too for Spinoza there is no substance outside of its modes.[72] *Immanence does not in any way stand above or outside its expressions.* Substance is "exhausted" in its modes. There is nothing behind the manifestations, for they are reality. In consequence, names for God (or substance or Nature) do not name something distinct from these names, for there is no substance as such or God as such. Immanence is fully and completely expressed in its modes—and names are modes too. Therefore, immanence is nothing outside of these names. Immanence is fully contained in the very names

---

[72] See Deleuze, *Expressionism in Philosophy*, 27; Genevieve Lloyd, *Spinoza and the Ethics* (London: Routledge, 1996), 41.

for immanence. Names are self-sufficient: they need refer to nothing outside themselves. So, just like Schelling, Spinoza—as a rigorous monist—must eliminate the referential relation from his philosophy. "God," "substance" and "Nature" are not referential, so whether they *refer* to immanence or not is just not an issue. There is no such thing as apophaticism for Spinoza, since a name cannot fail to refer.

This suggests an answer to the overriding question: if each name is a self-sufficient expression of immanence, why the need for a plurality of names? For Schelling, while all names construct immanence, some do so better than others—and the intensity of this construction ultimately depends on the number of names appropriated into philosophy (for it is *through* this plurality names are intensified). I contend that something like this must be true for Spinoza: the adequacy of the names employed in the *Ethics* depends on their interrelations with other names. The more complex the network of names, the more adequate the philosophy. So, just like Schelling, adding names intensifies philosophical discourse.

Numerous scholars have acknowledged that the *Ethics* is a text in which the meaning of traditional, philosophical names are transformed. Rocco Gangle writes, Spinoza "uses old terms in new ways such that a new subversive notion is created,"[73] continuing,

> Spinoza consistently employs philosophical terminology that has come to possess relatively precise and technical meanings across the sedimented histories of ancient philosophy and medieval Scholasticism, yet Spinoza uses these terms in ways that shift or distort their traditional senses, imposing unfamiliar meanings…[often] directly opposed to the traditional sense.[74]

Spinoza's use of "God" is a case in point: Spinoza begins with

---

[73] Rocco Gangle, "Theology of the Chimera: Spinoza, Immanence, Practice," in Smith and Whistler (eds.), *After the Postsecular and the Postmodern*, 26.

[74] Ibid. See also Zourabichvili, *Spinoza*, 111-2; Aaron Garrett, *Meaning in Spinoza's Method* (Cambridge: Cambridge University Press, 2003), Chapter 6.

a traditional-looking definition only to demonstrate over the first fourteen propositions that logical rigour necessitates a new, heterodox understanding of this name. Names are mutated by passing through the propositions.

Moreover, and this is the key claim, names are mutated by means of the relations they take up in respect to other names. Transformation occurs through the continual juxtaposition of different terms; their resulting new relations in Spinoza's philosophical system is what alters their meaning. In Gangle's words,

> [A name is a term] whose relational context becomes altered. Its new sense is generated not internally or intensively, but externally or practically through syntactical and formally deductive connections with other terms.[75]

This is what Gangle (following Zourachbivili) terms "a chimerical translation"[76]: it is a form of alchemy by which names are transmuted by mixing, dissolving and colliding with other names, in the same way as all modes mix, dissolve and collide with each other. Names (as one specific type of mode) should not be excluded from this physics (as we have seen Zourachbivili and Montag argue). A *physics of names* is just as necessary as a physics of passions.

Hence, Gangle speaks of "a new textual practice of metaphysics"[77] in regard to the *Ethics*. The results of Spinoza's philosophy are generated on the textual surface: Spinoza's propositions chart the manner in which names collide—and this mapping process is named the geometrical method. Gangle thus speaks of the geometrical method in terms of topographical maps of "peaks and valley floors…or the hubs of a transportation

---

[75] Gangle, "Theology of the Chimera," 27. Gangle's work brings out the close relation between the problem of improper names and the problem of individuation in Spinoza.

[76] Ibid., 28.

[77] Ibid., 30.

network."⁷⁸ Names collide—and the record of these collisions is Spinoza's philosophy.

In short, therefore, Spinoza employs improper names because only through putting to work a plurality of names can their mutation be guaranteed. "God" is an improper name because it needs other names ("substance" or "Nature") in order to give rise to the philosophical transformations necessary for adequate philosophy. Spinoza puts a plurality of names to work in order to intensify his philosophy: the more relations that build up between these names over the course of the *Ethics* (i.e. the different combinations and relations envisioned in the propositions), the better the philosophy.

Moreover, the type of relation that holds between different names is always, I contend, *identity*—just as for Schelling. This is another consequence of monism: everything is ultimately one, therefore the only possible form of relation between names is equality. So, the adequacy of Spinoza's system is in fact achieved by means of the successive *identifications* of a plurality of names. As these identifications proliferate, Spinozan philosophy intensifies. "God" is not only equal to "substance," it is equal to "Nature" and so "Nature" must be equal to "substance." It is implicitly in this manner that Spinoza's philosophy proceeds over the course of hundreds of propositions. And, what is more, this mode of procedure is the Spinozist solution to the problem of improper names.⁷⁹

Armed with these resources, it is time to briefly return to Barber's argument. In opposition to Barber, I maintain that immanence does not precede the name; immanence exists only as it is expressed in the name. In other words, immanence does not presuppose a nameless plane, but rather *a textual surface on which names collide*. Immanence *is* these names (such is the necessary implication of Spinoza's monism) in their

---

⁷⁸ Gangle, "Theology of the Chimera," 31.

⁷⁹ It needs to be kept in mind that I am not arguing that the Holocaust is the same as ice cream for a monist (as one critic has recently argued [Conor Cunningham, *Genealogies of Nihilism* (London: Routledge, 2002, 68)]), but that the *names* "Holocaust" and "ice cream" are ultimately identified in an *ideal* monist discourse (see Part Five). The ethical implications of this difference are substantial.

constantly complexifying interrelations and identifications. The surplus which characterises immanence is generated as more and more names are identified (for these identifications are the very surplus of immanence). The more improper names, the more intensely immanence exists. A philosophy of the secular, therefore, must name immanence as much as possible: not because we are doomed to fail again and again, but because naming intensifies immanence. Names bring immanence into being.

4.2 The Logic of Monist Sense

Improper names are involved in a process of indefinite identification, where the making identical of one name to another gradually intensifies philosophical form, making the discourse more and more adequate. This is how names function once reference is eliminated (as it must be for monists). And this is the solution to the problem of improper names: the more names are made identical, the better the philosophy.

Let us take one more look at this from a different angle, beginning from the standard Fregean picture of language, in which all names have both sense and reference. Frege defines a name as a word or sign which *expresses* its sense and *designates* its reference. As well as referring, names express—and this is the key to unlocking the problem of improper names for monists. Once reference is eliminated, what remains is *expression* or sense.[80] What is particularly pertinent here is that Frege developed this theory precisely through an examination of the sorts of cases we have been considering. What is the difference, he famously asked, between saying "the morning star is the morning star" and "the morning star is the evening star?" That is, if "morning star" and "evening star" have the same reference, why use two names—what epistemic benefit is there in using two names for the same thing rather than one? In other words, when reference is redundant, what is left of language? As one commentator puts it,

---

[80] Or what Schelling calls "production."

> If the names corefer, there is no difference in the references of the constituents of a=a and a=b...So either they cannot express different propositions, or else—and this is the inference Frege drew—what determines the proposition...cannot just have to with the structure of the [sentence] and the *references* of its constituent words and phrases.[81]

In other words, either improper names are useless, because they all mean the same thing (by picking out the same referent),[82] or there is something other than reference at stake in language which gives rise to improper names. The irreducible remainder—what is left over when reference becomes redundant—is sense. As Deleuze emphasises in *The Logic of Sense*, sense is absolutely irreducible to reference, for they work according to very different logics. The logic of sense is not the logic of truth and falsity.[83] For monists (who have eliminated reference), names *cannot* be true or false because they can neither succeed nor fail to refer to something external. Sense works on a completely different model, a model of more or less intense expression.[84]

Monist philosophical texts therefore become surfaces on which names intensify their sense. This is what is theorised

---

[81] Graeme Forbes, "Proper Names" in *The Routledge Encyclopedia of Philosophy* vol. 7, 752.

[82] "If we were to regard equality as a relation between that which the names 'a' and 'b' designate, it would seem that a=b could not differ from a=a" (Frege, "On Sense and Meaning," 157).

[83] He writes, "This is the most general problem of the logic of sense: what would be the purpose of rising from the domain of truth to the domain of sense, if it were only to find between sense and nonsense a relation analogous to the true and the false?" Gilles Deleuze, *The Logic of Sense*, trans. Mark Lester (London: Continuum, 1990), 80.

[84] If, as Gabriel has argued, Frege establishes the distinction between sense and reference in order to show that "the semantic organisation of meaning, i.e. the order of words, is not identical with the ontological order of things" (Markus Gabriel, "The Mythological Being of Reflection" in Gabriel and Slavoj Žižek, *Mythology, Madness and Laughter: Subjectivity in German Idealism* [London: Continuum, 2009], 65), then by eliminating one of the terms in this distinction (reference), Spinoza and Schelling reaffirm the identity of words and things. Significantly, Frege does consider the possibility of "a special term for signs intended to have only sense" (Frege, "On Sense and Meaning," 163)—but his choice, "representation," does not seem helpful for my purposes here.

in Deleuze's *The Logic of Sense* and practiced in Spinoza's *Ethics*. The *Ethics* as a whole is, to quote Deleuze out of context, "a machine for the production of incorporeal sense."[85] It is a surface on which names connect with each other in order to generate more and more intense—so more and more adequate—series of propositions. This is the "surface effect" which donates philosophical sense. Names "frolic on the surface of being, and constitute an endless multiplicity of incorporeal beings."[86]

Now, as Deleuze makes clear, different texts chart different surface effects: each philosophical singularity is generated from specific operations on the textual surface. Hence, in *The Logic of Sense* Deleuze describes a specific set of surface operations employed by certain philosophers which he dubs, the "Carroll effect":

> Sense is always an *effect*...or, even better, a surface effect, a position effect and a language effect...It is a product which spreads out over, or extends itself the length of, the surface...Such effect, or such a product, have usually been designated by a proper and singular name...Thus physics speaks of the "Kelvin effect," of the "Seebeck effect," of the "Zeerman effect," etc.[87]

This specific set of operations of the Carroll effect consists in paradoxes which give rise to heterogeneous series.

What I have been arguing in this paper is that there is a specific "Spinoza effect" which describes the set of operations employed by a rigorously monistic philosophy—and this "Spinoza effect" is irreducible to the "Carroll effect" described by Deleuze. There is ultimately only one operation performed on the surface of monistic philosophy—identification. Identifications proliferate indefinitely, devouring all that is different in the name of the same. There can be no contradiction, no absurdity, no excess or lack—only a continual and all-devouring

---

[85] Deleuze, *The Logic of Sense*, 82.

[86] Bréhier, quoted in Deleuze, *The Logic of Sense*, 8. In short, every name in Spinoza's philosophy falls foul of Meinong's paradox! See ibid., 41-2.

[87] Ibid., 82.

process of identification.[88] This is a "Spinoza effect"—a logic of sense without paradox, a proliferation of identifications on the textual surface of philosophy. The more names, the more identifications, the better the philosophy—this is not only true for Schellingian absolute eclecticism, it is true for all rigorous monists.

Part Five: An "Ideal" Spinoza

In the previous section, I outlined the rudiments of an "ideal" *Ethics* which would read as follows,

Proposition 1	"Substance"
Proposition 2	"Substance" = "God"
Proposition 3	"Substance" = "God" = "Nature"
Proposition 4	"Substance" = "God" = "Nature" = "Banana"
Proposition 5	"Substance" = "God" = "Nature" = "Banana" = "Harry Lime"

This structure would proceed *ad infinitum*, rather in the manner of the paratacticism analysed in *Anti-Oedipus* (substance… and God…and Nature…).[89] It exemplifies the logic of monist sense and the deployment of improper names. In this "ideal" structure of the *Ethics*, name after name is identified for the sake of philosophical amelioration. However, what becomes striking at this point is the discrepancy between this "ideal" *Ethics* and the *Ethics* Spinoza actually wrote. The *Ethics* does not look like this—and this is because the above logic of monist sense is only a partial reconstruction of Spinoza's philosophical rhetoric. There is more going on and there are more linguistic forces at play than just the identification of names. Spinoza exceeds "the Spinoza effect."

---

[88] Even if Spinoza is read in terms of parallelism, there can in the end be only one series of sense, i.e. the series of propositions of the *Ethics* itself. This is one of the meanings of Spinoza's claim that everything follows necessarily from God's essence; there are no parallel series of sense.

[89] Gilles Deleuze and Félix Guattari, *Anti-Oedipus: Capitalism and Schizophrenia*, trans. Robert Hurley *et al* (London: Continuum, 1984), 6.

Yet, the above rewriting of the *Ethics* is not only ideal to the extent that it differs from the real *Ethics*, it is also ideal in a second sense. It reconstructs the *Ethics* by means of one ideal, expansive linguistic force alone. In other words, what has been under discussion in this paper is merely one element of a Spinozist *Naturphilosophie* of language: the ideal force by which more and more names are appropriated into relations of identity.[90] It corresponds to Negri's delimitation of an "ideal phase" in Spinoza's thinking (an idealism that is not surprising considering the proximity of Spinoza to Schelling in this paper).[91] Here, we can fully realise the extent to which the transformation of language into a body has reversed itself into a transformation of bodies into language. The materialistic reduction of language into a *Naturphilosophie* leads necessarily to the anti-realistic insistence that there is nothing outside the name, that names are most real. Perhaps Badiou failed to acknowledge the radical materialism in which there are just bodies because this turns out not to be materialism at all, but linguistic idealism.

It is no surprise that the above structure comes closest to being realised at the end of Part V of the *Ethics*—the fulfilment and culmination of Spinoza's construction of philosophy where he embraces monism most fully. Here, indeed, Spinoza's propositions are often little more than a series of equations. To take one example, the human subject loves God,[92] God loves himself[93] and these two acts of love are identical: "The mind's intellectual love of God is the very love of God by which God loves himself."[94] Such a process of identification culminates

---

[90] As Žižek points out, expansion and the traversal of plurality are proper to monism: "Spinoza, the philosopher of the multitude, is, quite logically, also the ultimate monist, the philosopher of the one." *The Puppet and the Dwarf: The Perverse Core of Christianity* (Boston: MIT Press, 2003), 24.

[91] Antonio Negri, *The Savage Anomaly: The Power of Spinoza's Metaphysics and Politics*, trans. Michael Hardt, (Minneapolis: University of Minnesota Press, 1991), 33-9.

[92] Spinoza, *Ethics*, VP15D.

[93] Ibid., VP35.

[94] Ibid., VP36.

in Vp36c: "Insofar as God loves himself, he loves men, and consequently God's love of men and the mind's intellectual love of God are one and the same."[95] Here is how Matheron describes this climax to the *Ethics*:

> Subject and object are utterly confused with one another. I love myself in God, I love God, God loves himself in me, God loves me. The four affirmations are equivalent...The terms of the relation are purely and simply identified...[in] the following quadruple equation: our love for God = our love for others = God's love for men = others' love for us = others' love for God.[96]

Part V ends in a single series of equations proliferating identities.

However, the question of how Spinoza gets to this point has not been broached in this paper. This has only been a fragment of a linguistic physics: contraction, the realist force that counteracts expansion and brings it down to earth is yet to be determined. This force resists the infinite process of identifications of the ideal *Ethics*. Exposition of this element of a *Naturphilosophie* of monist language must therefore await a future occasion.

~

Acknowledgements

Thanks are due to Dan Barber for gracefully helping me articulate my worries with his work more precisely, as well as to Charlie Blake, Rocco Gangle, Philip Goodchild, Patrice Haynes, Joshua Ramey, Steve Shakespeare and Anthony Paul Smith for their discussions on this paper.

---

[95] Spinoza, *Ethics*, Vp36d.

[96] Alexandre Matheron, *Individu et communauté chez Spinoza* (Paris: Minuit, 1969), 596-7.

Namelessness and the Speculative Turn
A Response to Whistler

Daniel Colucciello Barber

Berlin Institute for Cultural Inquiry

I APPRECIATE THE ENGAGEMENT OF my work that Daniel Whistler has provided. I do not think his reading is ultimately accurate, but that is to the side, because its point of approach allows me to develop a number of ideas that are central not only to the interpretation of Spinoza and the problematic of religious language (or the naming of the divine), but also—even moreso—to the future of thought in general after the speculative turn. In what follows I will argue, first, that Whistler fails to appreciate the way the concept of namelessness functions in my theoretical construction of Spinzoa's thought. I will then address the various difficulties raised by Whistler's own account of identity, before proceeding to consider how my disagreement with Whistler runs right to the heart of arguments about the nature of the speculative turn. Indeed, my contention is that namelessness, as I articulate its immanent relation with the act of naming, is resonant with an essential tendency in the work of philosophers such as Eugene Thacker and Ray Brassier. Finally, I will look at how the concept of namelessness serves to indicate and oppose a still-effective Christian hegemony over philosophy.

Speculations III

Apophaticism's Not the Right Word

The basic point of misrecognition in Whistler's interpretation of my essay, I think, is found in the alliance he sets up between my work and apophaticism. He does, of course, note that I reject such an alliance, but he proceeds nonetheless to insist on it—and he does so by claiming that my argument "shares the defining characteristic of all apophaticism: a dissatisfaction with language as such and so an overriding concern to negate or show up the inadequacy of that language in the name of the nameless."[1] It is true, of course, that I am concerned to bring attention to the impossibility of properly naming immanence. I claim, as Whistler rightly notes, that there is a surplus of immanence, that immanence necessarily exceeds its names. This is true. But what is also true is that immanence must be named, and more precisely that it must be named in virtue of this excess. What is at stake, in other words, is the *relation* between names and namelessness. To say, then, that immanence cannot be adequately named, or that every naming of immanence must still contend, after the act of naming, with an excessive namelessness, is to utter only a partial truth. It is to attend to one side of the relation (the side with which Whistler identifies my position). The other side of the relation (the side of my position that Whistler ignores) concerns the way this excessive namelessness loops back upon names. My point is not just that namelessness exceeds names, it is that this excess necessitates the creation of new names.

What this relationality should highlight is the processual nature of my proposal. To put it somewhat simplistically, the act of naming immanence must give rise to an awareness of the excess of immanence to the enacted names—this is what I have in mind when I speak of the namelessness of immanence. But the process does not stop there. On the contrary, this awareness of excessive namelessness must give rise to

---

[1] Daniel Whistler, "Improper Names for God: Religious Language and the 'Spinoza-Effect,'" *Speculations III*: 114.

the production of new names, i.e. to a further enactment of names, at which point the process I am outlining would repeat itself. What Whistler leaves to the side, I am claiming, is the moment whereby excessive namelessness loops back to necessitate the continued act of naming. By ignoring this moment he freezes the very relay about which I am speaking. Indeed, the essence of my position is not the failure of language before nameless immanence (as Whistler implies). Neither is it the inelidable identity between names and immanence (as Whistler seems to positively argue). It is rather the irreducible nature of the relay *between* the naming of immanence and the namelessness of immanence.

The upshot of my argument, then, is not that there is something called immanence that can never be named. It is rather that immanence is intrinsically relational, it is always immanent to itself, and therefore that the naming of immanence must be situated within this process of relation, or relay. Whistler appears to attribute to me the claim that immanence, because of its namelessness, is simply beyond all names. I do not make this claim, for to do so would be to turn immanence into something transcending signification; it would also be to make the nameless into its own kind of name. My position, more precisely, is that it is proper to immanence to be improper, to exceed itself, and to do so by doubling every name—a co-constitution of namelessness and names. Namelessness is the relay of names, and names are the relay of namelessness. Thus there is a basic temporality or diachronicity to my affirmation of relay, and Whistler's oversight of this fact leads him to read me as talking about the objective inadequacy of improper names, when I would claim that what matters is the *process* of improperly naming.

In order to substantiate this interpretation of my argument, let me refer to and comment upon a passage from my essay: "signification betrays immanence when it makes immanence immanent to what is signified, but, at the same time, immanence must be signified. Only by insisting on this double necessity do we evade the lure of apophaticism."[2] It should be noted that my dissatisfaction with signification here has nothing to do with its existence as such, but rather with the position that it could possibly assume with regard to immanence. If signification betrays immanence, this is due not to its nature as signification, but rather to its tendency to transcend immanence, to foreclose immanence under the banner of a name or names (and such a tendency toward foreclosure may be resisted or avoided). To affirm the namelessness of immanence, then, is not to oppose the naming of immanence, it is to oppose the reduction of immanence to signification. It is for this reason, in fact, that I join the affirmation of namelessness with the affirmation that "immanence must be signified." This, once again, is to indicate that what is at issue here is not merely the excess of immanence to signification, but just as much the (necessary) looping back of this excess upon signification. Apophaticism focuses on the necessity of language exhausting itself in relation to the nameless, whereas my relay focuses on this necessity *as well as* the necessity of the nameless being constructively re-expressed through yet another act of naming.

It should be noted, furthermore, that my argument is for the productivity of this relay—I continue, in the same passage, by contending that immanence "exceeds signification because it produces signification, and because this signification is within immanence."[3] Whistler sees apophaticism as laboring in virtue of "the name of the nameless," and this is to attribute to it a kind of *telos* of protecting the nameless from names.[4] The direction in which I take the inadequacy of signification, however, is the production of signification. Quite importantly, this produced signification is *within* immanence. In other words, signification, even when it is

---

[2] Daniel Colucciello Barber, "Secularism, Immanence and the Philosophy of Religion," in Anthony Paul Smith and Daniel Whistler (ed.), *After the Postsecular and the Postmodern: New Essays in Continental Philosophy of Religion* (Newcastle: Cambridge Scholars' Press, 2010), 167.

[3] Ibid., 167.

[4] Whistler, "Improper Names for God," 114.

addressed in relation to the namelessness of immanence, is never severed from immanence. It is not a matter of some opposition between nameless immanence in-itself and a multitude of inadequate names, it is rather one of the relay between them. In fact, *immanence just is this relay*. To belabor the point a bit more, but also hopefully to confirm my claim that I have no stake in any opposition between immanence and names, it should be observed that I assert that the aim is "to restore signification to immanence, to signify immanently," and that my position is "less a matter of iconoclasm than a matter of polyiconicity."[5]

I want to stress this notion of polyiconicity because it is the point at which my argument becomes most difficult to reconcile with Whistler's portrayal of it as a kind of apophaticism. In fact, it is by way of polyiconicity that my position seems to advance some of the theses that Whistler sets forth in apparent contradiction to my supposed apophaticism. When he claims, for instance, that "immanence *is* each name," or that immanence "only exists *as* names," what is he affirming that I am not already affirming in terms of polyiconicity?[6] To say that immanence is polyiconic, after all, is to say that immanence is multiply named, that immanence *really is named* in a variety of manners, or modes. Accordingly, it seems quite strange that Whistler would read my argument as an apophatically-motivated denial of the claim that immanence is expressed in its names.

Interrelations Must Be External to Their Names

The fact that Whistler would read me as apophatic and iconoclastic, when I explicitly call for polyiconicity, is one that needs to be explained, and I think it can be explained by observing the narrative of continental philosophy of religion that he proposes in his own essay. There he tells us that he is "intervening" in debates about philosophy of reli-

---

[5] Barber, "Secularism, Immanence and the Philosophy of Religion," 167.
[6] Whistler, "Improper Names for God," 115.

gion precisely at the point where he opposes apophaticism. Indeed, "apophaticism is not the answer here, and this is a hard pill for continental philosophy of religion to swallow."[7] He goes on to observe that "philosophers of religious language have been obsessed with the inadequacy of names to the point of ignoring kataphatic deployments of language."[8] So Whistler's intervention, the "hard pill" he's distributing, is that continental philosophy of religion needs to end its affair with the apophatic, and that it needs to give attention to the kataphatic. I highlight this narrative because I believe it is what structures Whistler's misreading of my argument. According to this narrative, the obstacle to be overcome is apophaticism, and the way beyond this obstacle is kataphaticism. So which side is my argument on? It should be clear that it's not straightforwardly identifiable with one side or another. But if Whistler ignores the kataphatic, polyiconic tendency of my position, then it becomes much easier to ally me with the apophatic. I hope to have already demonstrated why such an alliance requires misrepresentation of my argument. Now I would like to turn, briefly, to the difficulty created by Whistler's own kataphaticism.

The approach of "absolute eclecticism," whereby it is asserted that "the more names given, the more intense scientific language becomes," is compelling, and one that I agree with in part.[9] The appeal of this approach is its ability to bring a multitude of names into relation with one another, and to affirm that such names are expressive of immanence. These, in fact, are points that my own position advances, such that my position's difference stems not from its failure to advance the kataphatic but rather from its insistence on the irreducible relation between the kataphatic and the apophatic (to continue using Whistler's terms). The necessary connection between affirmative naming and namelessness can be seen in the difficulty to which Whistler's own, sheerly affirmative position gives rise.

---

[7] Whistler, "Improper Names for God," 116.

[8] Ibid., 117.

[9] Ibid., 125.

This difficulty begins to emerge when we pose the question of how these various names relate to one another. There is nothing to protest in Whistler's claim that all names may be equally expressive of immanence, or even that "immanence exists only as it is expressed in the name."[10] The difficulty arises, however, when we begin to ask about the relations between these names. The names must be in common, they are univocal, yet this does not change the fact that the names, considered individually, do not agree. So what we face here is a univocity of disagreement. Again, thus far there is nothing off the mark, but such an account remains incomplete, for this disagreement must operate. Whistler grasps this when he speaks of immanence as "a textual surface on which names collide" and identifies immanence with the "constantly complexifying interrelations and identifications" of these names.[11] All of this is true. Yet it must be asked: if these names are not just in identification but also in interrelation, then must not such relationality be thought as such? The relations, in other words, must be in excess of the names, and so what is this excess? It will be necessary to conceive not just the names, but also the condition that enables them to relate to one another productively.

What I am here calling attention to, in Whistler, is the difficulty engendered by denying that there is anything conditioning names. Obviously that which conditions the naming of immanence cannot be something that transcends the names, but this condition (of the interrelation of names) must be otherwise conceived. Whistler does make some attempt to conceive it when he speaks of a "textual surface." But what is this surface? Does it have a name? If it does have a name, then it cannot be that on which names collide, for it would be yet another one of the colliding names. Thus it does not have a name. But if it does not have a name, then would it not be the very namelessness that I have advanced, and that he has critiqued?

---

[10] Whistler, "Improper Names for God," 128.
[11] Ibid., 128-129.

Whistler appears to displace this difficulty by attributing to my position the invocation of "a nameless plane."[12] But there is no such thing in my argument: namelessness, once again, is not something beyond names but instead that which relays them with one another. Namelessness is interstitial, it is the condition that enables names to collide and to intensify one another. To speak, as Whistler does, of an identity of all names and immanence is not exactly incorrect, but it is incomplete, for it cannot conceive the interstitial relations of these names. To write off attempts to conceive such interstitial namelessness as apophaticism is, in fact, to remain within apophaticism's frame by way of inversion. Instead of asserting the inadequacy of names, Whistler inverts the approach and asserts the adequacy of all names. My contention is that these approaches are equally flawed, and that what is exigent is an account of the relay between adequacy and inadequacy—a relay that is prior to their mutual exclusion.

The relay of namelessness and a multitude of names, in the end, has nothing to do either with an absolute failure of language or with an absolute identity of names and immanence. Its concern is the difference between a multitude of names, all of which express immanence, but each of which differs from the other. "Immanence," Whistler remarks, "is fully and completely expressed in its modes—and names are modes too."[13] In these terms, the question becomes one of the relation between modes. Gilles Deleuze's own attempt to improve Spinoza is here relevant. He transposed the relation between intensive and extensive modes into the relation, respectively, between the virtual singularities and actual individuals. In doing so, however, he broke with Spinoza's one-to-one relation between intensive and extensive. The actual individual became a resolution of a virtual difference in-itself. What Deleuze grasped, in other words, was that virtual difference must be conceived as something akin to pure disagreement. The virtual, pre-individual field of singularities was univo-

---

[12] Whistler, "Improper Names for God," 128.
[13] Ibid., 125.

cal, but this univocity was irreducible to any identity. Only in this way, I would contend, is it possible to make sense of the sort of collision of which Whistler speaks. This, then, is the condition of interrelation of modes, or names—a condition that I speak of as excessive namelessness. Such excess is therefore not beyond or separate from names, but neither is it reducible to the names, or their simple identity; it is rather the differential, nameless colliding of names.

The difficulty resulting from Whistler's failure to conceive this namelessness—the namelessness which conditions the interrelation of univocally expressive names—becomes especially evident in his statement that "Immanence is fully contained in the very names for immanence."[14] This cannot be the case, precisely because (as Whistler himself acknowledges) immanence is constituted not just by names but also by their interrelation. Immanence requires not just names, but also that which is produced by their collision—and that which is produced by the names must exceed the names, it must consist of their difference. Furthermore, it is not apt to think of immanence as something that is "contained *in*" something else. This would be to turn immanence into a name, one that is apparently both enclosed within in a multitude of other names and yet (confusingly) another one of these names. Once again, it is only by thinking of immanence not as simultaneously a name and the identity of all names, but instead as the relation of, or relay between, namelessness and names, that this difficulty can be avoided.

Namelessness and the Speculative Turn

I have already observed the presence, in Whistler's argument, of a narrative according to which continental philosophy of religion is urged to leave behind its fetishization of negativity and to reclaim "kataphatic deployments of language." His narrative adds, notably, that this demand concords with the

---

[14] Whistler, "Improper Names for God," 125-126.

speculative turn, which is "kataphatic in orientation."[15] So, if the speculative turn is bound up with Whistler's kataphatic turn, does my argument also stand against, or at least outside of, the host of philosophical developments associated with speculative realism? Not at all. In fact, what I would like to observe, as a way of troubling Whistler's narrative, is the possibility of espying, within the speculative turn, a tendency that is not at all kataphatic. Of course, the tendency I have in mind is not exactly apophatic either—hence my dissatisfaction with the mutual exclusion inherent in Whistler's narrative. What is compelling about the speculative turn, when viewed in relation to the question of how immanence is named, is its ability both to critique the human pretension to delimit access to the real and to affirm the capacity to name the real through an encounter with that which exceeds pre-existing articulations. It is this sort of tendency, rather than a more traditional apophaticism, and rather than Whistler's emergent kataphaticism, that is indicated by the namelessness of immanence.

As an instance of the tendency I have in mind, we might refer to Thacker's discussion of a "non-human" or "unhuman" mysticism, one which would no longer be theological in a traditional sense, but which would make use of this theological material in a radically ungrounded manner. As he puts it:

> If the supernatural in a conventional sense is no longer possible, what remains after the "death of God" is an occulted, hidden world. Philosophically speaking, the enigma we face is how to confront this world, without immediately presuming that it is identical to the world-for-us (the world of science *and* religion), and without simply disparaging it as an irretrievable and inaccessible world-in-itself.[16]

The emphases that emerge in Thacker's prescription are those of the enigmatic and the hidden, and—importantly

---

[15] Whistler, "Improper Names for God," 117.
[16] Thacker, *In the Dust of This Planet: Horror of Philosophy, Vol. 1* (Alresford, UK: Zero Books, 2011), 97.

for my purposes—they are positioned neither in terms of the kataphatic (which would repress the enigmatic character of the real) nor in terms of the apophatic (which would abandon the real to the simple beyond). Thacker's interest, to translate it—surely with too much bluntness—into the terms of my debate with Whistler, is to focus on a real that is simultaneously non-manifest (at least in any direct manner) and non-inaccessible. We have to do, then, with something that is accessible yet hidden. If we take this as an instance of thought that emerges after the speculative turn, then we see that there is no need to adopt a narrative in which the kataphatic overcomes the apophatic. An awareness of the immanent relay of namelessness and names is much more to the point. Indeed, we see something precisely like a conception of this relay in Thacker's remark that "mysticism today—after the death of God—would be about the impossibility of experience, it would be about that which in shadows withdraws from any possible experience, and yet still makes its presence felt, through the periodic upheavals of weather, land, and matter."[17]

While I agree with Whistler's critique of continental philosophy's overdependence on apophaticism, I do not accept that namelessness, as I develop it, falls under this critique. Nor do I accept that namelessness need be seen as mutually exclusive with the speculative turn. On the contrary, as I hope to have indicated with this brief mention of Thacker's work, it is possible to see namelessness as a novel and speculatively-driven account of what it means to think under the condition of an encounter with the enigmatic real. There is no need to see this encounter in terms of Whistler's definition of identity. In fact, even when identity plays a key role in speculative thought, such as it does for François Laruelle, it is encountered only through a radical displacement, through a bracketing of normative philosophical practice by way of the "non-." Here, it could be said, namelessness functions as a condition for the performance of thought—of non-philosophy.

---

[17] Thacker, *In the Dust of This Planet*, 158.

Speculations III

Namelessness and Decontraction Against Biotheology

I thus contend that namelessness, far from involving a defensive apophaticism that doubles-down on the limits of the human before an inaccessible beyond, bears an essential affinity with the speculative turn. It belongs to the attempt to conceive of negativity or unknowability in terms of active voiding or annihilating.[18] Spinozist namelessness, as I have developed it, has a particularly strong resonance with the thesis of Brassier's *Nihil Unbound*, especially its concluding remarks. There Brassier puts his account of the inorganic's priority over organic life in terms of decontraction: "Although life diverges from the inorganic in ever more circuitous detours, these are no more than temporary extensions of the latter, which will eventually contract back to their original inorganic condition, understood as the zero-degree of contraction, or *decontraction*."[19] If we understand namelessness in terms of the inorganic, and names as so many divergent circuits of life, then we can find yet another resonance between the relay I am advancing and the possibilities of thought made available by the speculative turn.

In fact, Brassier's logic of the relation between the inorganic and organic life, like that of the relation between excessive namelessness and the multitude of names, articulates an unthinkability that, without being traditionally apophatic, calls for the voiding or annihilation of every desire for full identity, or for a plentitudinous containment of immanence. The identity that is here advanced is not the one proposed by Whistler, whereby all names would be identical with immanence. It is instead the identity that is unthinkable by human life. It is the identity of namelessness and every name, an identity much like that found in decontraction's

---

[18] Along these lines, another vector of thought with which my concept of namelessness of resonates is that of Nicola Masciandaro. See, for instance, his "Unknowng Animals," *Speculations II*: 228-44, or "The Sorrow of Being," *Qui Parle: Critical Humanities and Social Sciences* 19: 9-35.

[19] Brassier, *Nihil Unbound: Enlightenment and Extinction* (London: Palgrave MacMillan, 2007), 360.

"being-nothing," where we find "the identity of entropic indifference and negentropic difference."[20] Every name is made possible by an indifferent namelessness, and every name, in its construction of this indifference, differs from every other name, thus constructing namelessness collisionally and differentially. The identity that is ultimate, then, cannot finally be named—not even as identity—precisely because it is that of every name *and* namelessness; namelessness cannot be integrated (nor *contained*) within identity, for identity is ultimately that of namelessness and every act of naming.

The implications of all this are not just philosophical, they are also political—or, more precisely, theologico-political. The desire to remove every obstacle to identity...from whence does it arise? Or, what makes it so powerful, so difficult to resist? There are, of course, a number of ways one might answer this question, and without claiming to have found the only possible answer, I would like to call our attention to one possibility: Christianity. This is obviously not the only source motivating the tendency towards absolute identity, but it is certainly one of the major sources—historically and materially speaking—of this tendency's support, maintenance, and normalization. For far too long we have treated philosophy as something clearly and distinctly differentiated from religion, when in fact these two domains (or concepts) have overlapped and interwoven everywhere, especially when their distinction is insisted upon. And this overlapping and intertwining of philosophy and religion has a history, a hegemonically *Christian* history.[21]

There are several implications and lines of research that stem from an insistence on this point, but for the moment I want to observe a single consequence—and this is that the

---

[20] Brassier, *Nihil Unbound*, 364.

[21] I have developed the genealogical and conceptual implications of this thesis in my recent book, *On Diaspora: Christianity, Religion, and Secularity* (Eugene, OR: Cascade Press, 2011). For more on the still-determinative influence of Christianity within our purportedly secular and post-Christian epoch, see the work of Gil Anidjar, especially *Semites: Race, Religion, Literature* (Stanford: Stanford UP, 2008).

Christian desire for the identity of all is very much still in play as we interpret and respond to the speculative turn. I would propose that Brassier's antagonism towards "life" should be simultaneously understood as an antagonism towards the history of Christianity. Indeed, the philosophical concept of life—especially when we highlight its connotations of integration into the one true life, of all life in one, beyond its differences—cannot be disentangled from the theological concept of life. As Gil Anidjar has perceptively argued, the contemporary problem of the biopolitical is really a problem of the biotheological.[22] On the interpretation I am advancing, then, when Brassier poses the inorganic against organic life, his basic orientation is not eliminativist, not nihilist, and not even anti-correlationist. It is anti-Christian, and precisely because it exerts violence on the ultimately violent instinct to integrate everything, including nothingness, into life (or "Life"). Before life, after life, always haunting life…there is death. Nothingness, we might say, is the alpha and the omega—or, even better, it is before the alpha and after the omega.

Along these lines, I do not find it surprising that *Nihil Unbound* concludes with a discussion of two Jewish thinkers, i.e. Levinas and Freud, for Jewish thought has always defined itself in relation to (and more or less in opposition to) Christian thought. We should not presume that this Christian-Jewish difference passed away with the dawn of supposedly post-Christian, secular thought. Indeed, both Levinas and Freud paid essential attention to the way being Jewish affected thought, which is to say not only that they knew the pressures of integration and identification, but also that—understanding how normative accounts of the thinking subject depended on a denial of this subject's conditionality—they directed thought at the pre-cognitive. They understood that thought should be given not to what the human is defined as able to think, not to the world as it correlates with the human subject, but instead to what affects the subject prior to its self-identification, to

---

[22] See Anidjar, "The Meaning of Life," *Critical Inquiry* 37: 697-723. My argument in this section is significantly indebted to the work Anidjar does in this essay.

what the subject disavows in the name of its being-subject. Brassier, I am proposing, should be read as part of this anti-normative, anti-Life, anti-Christian tradition. What he has in common with Levinas and Freud is an awareness of the way that every attempt at integration disavows its identity with that which makes it impossible—in this sense, Brassier's entropic indifference belongs to the same lineage as Levinas' alterity and Freud's unconscious.

And all of these, I might add, could be connected to the kabbalistic rendering of Genesis 1:1, which reads, "With Beginning, _____ created Elohim."[23] What this Jewish mystical text claims—against Christian orthodoxy's belief that the life of God can be identified with the divine-human life of the Son of God, and that all human life can and/or should be identified with the concrete-universal of Jesus—is that even God (Elohim) is conditioned. Furthermore, the conditions of God cannot be correlated with God's being. That which created God, or conditions God's existence, is _____. It is nameless, and yet not beyond. Even God (or Nature) is haunted by this namelessness.

---

[23] *Zohar: The Book of Enlightenment*, trans. Daniel Matt (Ramsey, NJ: Paulist Press, 1983), 50.

Diagonals
Truth-Procedures in Derrida and Badiou

Christopher Norris

School of English Communication and Philosophy
University of Cardiff

I

BADIOU'S RELATIONSHIP TO DERRIDA is complex, ambivalent, at times distinctly fraught, and often—despite an impeccable politeness of phrasing—somewhat impatient in tone. All the same it doesn't exhibit anything like the pattern of routine inter-generational conflict that has characterised so many episodes of post-war French intellectual history. Thus it bears no resemblance to those acts of barely concealed parricidal intent by which Sartre ousted the dominant currencies of pre-war (whether rationalist or Bergson-influenced) thought, or the structuralism of Lévi-Strauss, Althusser and company purported to consign Sartrean existentialism to the dustbin of outworn humanist ideas, or structuralism in turn gave way to the combined assaults of post-structuralists, postmodernists and other such reactive movements. Indeed there is something decidedly majestic about the way that Badiou rises above such manifestations of the short-term *Zeitgeist* or sad displays of the *odium scholasticum* that all too often substitutes for serious debate. His attitude toward Derrida—as evidenced by the brief but revealing encomium collected in the volume *Pocket Pantheon*—is one of admiration mixed with a certain ironic reserve and some shrewdly aimed though far from hostile remarks about the lack of any direct activist involvement on Derrida's part in the events of May 1968.[1] Even here Badiou is keen to make allowance for the highly mediated character of "deconstructive politics" or the need to approach that topic with a due regard for Derrida's immensely patient, meticulous and painstaking way with texts, among them (if belatedly) the texts of Marx.[2] More than that: he puts the case for Derrida as a political thinker of the first importance, just so long as we read his work with the kind of extreme attentiveness and rigour that he brings to the work of others.

So Badiou is unencumbered by any desire to stake his claim as a replacement *maître à penser* or as one who has seen through the kind of "textualist" mystification that has often been laid at Derrida's door by Marxists, activists, and—from a different through related angle—by Foucault in his early polemical rejoinder.[3] Nevertheless, I shall argue, it is a complex relationship and one that brings out some salient tensions not only between the two thinkers but also within their respective projects. Badiou's answer in the *Pocket Pantheon* essay might well be characterised as a case of interpretative "strong revisionism" as Harold Bloom describes it, that is, a mode of commentary that aims not so much to establish a relationship of fidelity and subservience to the text in hand but rather to transform or trans-value that text in keeping with the commentator's own priorities.[4] Of course this is Badiou's regular practice in the many exegetical chapters of *Being and Event* where he takes a whole roster of the great philosophers from Parmenides, Plato, and Aristotle to Descartes, Spinoza, Leibniz, Kant, Hegel, and their modern progeny—along with

---

[1] Alain Badiou, *Pocket Pantheon: figures of postwar philosophy*, trans. David Macey (London: Verso, 2009).

[2] Jacques Derrida, *Spectres of Marx: the state of the debt, the work of mourning, and the New International*, trans. Peggy Kamuf (London: Routledge, 1994).

[3] Michel Foucault, "My Body, This Paper, This Fire," *Oxford Literary Review*, Vol. IV, No. 1 (1979), 9-28.

[4] See for instance Harold Bloom, *The Anxiety of Influence: a theory of poetry* (New York: Oxford University Press, 1973).

poets such as Mallarmé and Hölderlin—and subjects them to a reading (mostly in the critical-diagnostic mode) accordant with the book's general thesis.[5] Such reading goes against the intentional grain so as to bring out those symptoms of conflict, internal contradictions, or conceptual stress-points that indicate the workings of a transverse or "diagonal" logic at odds with the overt gist. This is often a matter of showing how the argument turns back against itself and can be seen to undermine its overt commitment to a plenist ontology that would, in effect, preclude any real possibility of change whether in states of mathematical-scientific knowledge, conditions of the body politic, or modes of artistic practice. It involves an alertness to certain symptomatic blind-spots of repression whose existence, once detected, opens the way to a radically different "subtractive" ontology wherein that possibility not only exists but becomes the chief motor or driving force of progress in those various domains.

My reference to Bloom on the process of creative misprision—the way that "strong misreaders" (poets for the most part) absorb and then transform the work of their great dead precursors—needs to be qualified in one major respect. That is to say, Badiou's is a distinctively *philosophical* approach where intellectual creativity goes along with a high degree of conceptual and argumentative rigour and can therefore claim something more in the way of exegetical warrant or justification. I must defer any detailed commentary on the crucial significance of mathematics (more specifically, of developments in set-theory after Cantor) for his thinking about the dialectic of being and event, or the process whereby a given ontology or conceptual scheme comes up against that which radically challenges and eventually transforms its operative scope and limits.[6] What interests me here is the difference between Badiou's deployment of this basically dialectical (or

---

[5] Alain Badiou, *Being and Event*, trans. Oliver Feltham (London: Continuum, 2006).

[6] See Badiou, *Being and Event*; also *Number and Numbers*, trans. Robin Mackay (London: Polity Press, 2008).

immanent-critical) approach as applied to thinkers in the mainstream Western philosophical tradition and his particular take on Derrida's project, involving as it does a more nuanced and delicate negotiation of the differences between them. At one level this has to do mainly with the question of political activism and with Derrida's (as Badiou sees it) very marked disinclination to advance from the stage of intensive engagement with complications in the texts of Western logocentric tradition to the stage of engagement with issues of direct or urgent political concern. At another—though closely related to that—it has to do with Badiou's ambivalent relation to just those practices of textual close-reading, surely epitomised by deconstruction, that offer what he sees as an all too handy pretext for evading or endlessly deferring issues of political commitment.

One would not expect Badiou to single Derrida out for exemption from this particular line of attack. After all, the charge of political evasiveness has very often been laid at Derrida's door by Marxists especially but also by thinkers of a broadly leftist or social-activist persuasion.[7] Moreover, it would fit readily enough with Badiou's emphatic opposition to the "linguistic turn" in its many and varied showings over the past century.[8] These range from the Frege-Russell mode of analytic philosophy or its "ordinary-language" (e.g., Wittgensteinian or Austinian) variants to Heideggerian hermeneutics, poststructuralism, Richard Rorty's "strong" descriptivist brand of neo-pragmatism, Foucault's archaeologies or genealogies of discourse, and postmodernism as theorised—with snippety reference to most of the above—by a thinker like Lyotard.[9] For Badiou, what marks them all out (though some more

---

[7] See especially Michael Sprinker (ed.), *Ghostly Demarcations: a symposium on Jacques Derrida's* Spectres of Marx (London: Verso, 1999).

[8] For his most forceful statement of this view, see Alain Badiou, *Manifesto for Philosophy*, trans. Norman Madarasz (Albany, NY: State University of New York Press, 1999).

[9] For further discussion of these and allied developments, see Christopher Norris, *The Truth About Postmodernism* (Oxford: Blackwell, 1993) and *On Truth and Meaning: language, logic and the grounds of belief* (London: Continuum, 2006).

than others) as involving a sheer dereliction of philosophy's proper role is their way of falling back on an appeal to language, discourse, or representation as the ultimate horizon of intelligibility or the end-point of ontological enquiry. However, as I have said, he appears to exempt Derrida from the general charge and to do so for reasons closely connected with his own project. Although these emerge plain to view only in the *Pocket Pantheon* essay—after what must seem a remarkably long period of abstention from anything like a serious or sustained engagement with Derrida—they are likely to possess a revelatory force for suitably attuned readers, and moreover to strike them as casting a powerful retrospective light on crucial aspects of Badiou's work.

At any rate he does his utmost to deflect that blanket charge of Derrida's having raised subtleties of verbal exegesis to a high point of "textualist" mystification which in turn provides a standing excuse for the avoidance of any definite, i.e., any non-deconstrucible commitment in matters of politics. Nor does he subscribe to the other, more specific version of it which holds that the deconstructionist obsession with logical-rhetorical figures like aporia, paradox, undecidability, and so forth, is just what might be expected of a movement so determined to block any process of constructive or problem-solving thought and—beyond that—any prospect of its application to the sorts of problem confronted by theoretically minded political activists. If indeed there is a certain unwillingness to lay that commitment on the line then this should rather be attributed, as Badiou says in the passage already cited in my Introduction, to the kind of "diagonal obstinacy" that typifies Derrida's thought, along with his clearly evinced "dislike of abrupt metaphysically derived divisions" and the fact that his way of brooding productively on fine points of textual interpretation gives rise to a mindset "clearly not suited to stormy times when everything comes under the law of decisiveness, here and now."[10] Of course these phrases carry more than a hint of irony, coming as they do from

---

[10] Badiou, *Pocket Pantheon*, 138.

one who has unceasingly upheld the good old cause of May 1968 along with the undying political significance of other "failed" or abortive revolutions such as (pre-eminently) the 1871 Paris Commune, and addressed as they are to a thinker whose revolutionary commitments were, to say the least, a great deal more guarded and circumspect.[11] Still the irony is by no means so heavy or censorious as to cancel what is clearly Badiou's genuine appreciation of a thinker whose intellectual temperament, though very different from his own, nevertheless has a fair claim to represent one possible way that a radical intelligence might come to terms with the conflicting pressures of its own time and place.

One should also note, in that phrase "diagonal obstinacy," a more than casual allusion to the role of set-theoretical concepts in Badiou's re-thinking of the relationship between being and event, i.e., the Cantor-derived technique of "diagonalisation" as that which enables thought to conceive and then work with multiple orders or "sizes" of infinity.[12] I shall have more to say in this connection at a later stage but will here just remark on its singular effect when drawn into a discussion of Derrida's work in relation to politics, on the one hand, and to mathematics, logic and the formal sciences on the other. Thus it opens the way for Badiou to enlist Derrida as having arrived at something closely analogous to the formal procedure that Badiou sets out in *Being and Event* and elsewhere, albeit a procedure (that of deconstruction) that makes no explicit appeal to set-theoretical concepts and which operates more through the close-reading of philosophical and other texts. So we should, I think, take Badiou very much at his word—and not (or not merely) as conforming to the old

---

[11] On this and associated themes, see especially Alain Badiou, *Metapolitics*, trans. Jason Barker (London: Verso, 2005); *Polemics*, trans. Steve Corcoran (London: Verso, 2007); *The Century*, trans. Alberto Toscano (London: Polity Press, 2007).

[12] Badiou, *Being and Event*; also *Infinite Thought: truth and the return to philosophy*, trans. Oliver Feltham and Justin Clemens (London: Continuum, 2003); *Theoretical Writings*, ed. and trans. Ray Brassier and Alberto Toscano (London: Continuum, 2004).

French custom of high-toned testamentary tributes—when he declares that he will henceforth emulate Derrida's famous punning neologism *différance* (= difference/deferral/deference) by likewise substituting an anomalous *a* for the "correct" letter *e* in the final syllable of his own key-word *inexistence*.[13] Just as *différance* functions in Derrida's texts as a signifier of that which eludes any possibility of conceptual closure or univocal definition so *inexistance* will function in Badiou's texts as a pointedly apt designation of that which eludes the mathematical, scientific, or socio-political count-as-one. It is the term for whatever "inexists" or finds no place within some given situation or state of knowledge, whether through being denied any form of effective political representation (like the "paperless" North African immigrant workers in France) or through figuring nowhere in the currently accredited tally of beliefs, propositions, or truth-claims.[14] Thus, for Badiou, "the wager of Derrida's work, of his infinite work, ... is to *inscribe the inexistent*." If that word has acquired its deviant spelling by the end of Badiou's short essay then this is no mere linguistic *jeu d'esprit*—any more than with Derrida's numerous inventive yet philosophically load-bearing neologisms—but a shift brought about strictly in consequence of certain precise and far-reaching analogies between their two projects.

There is further evidence of this when the passage just cited brings together a markedly Derridean inscriptionalist or textual idiom with a thoroughly Badiouan appeal to the range of conceptual resources opened up by Cantor's exemplary passage through and beyond the paradoxes of traditional thinking about the infinite. Thus the reference to Derrida's "infinite work" of inscribing the inexistent is no idle compliment or piece of neatly turned phraseology but rather a precisely gauged evocation of the link between Badiou's set-theoretically inspired re-thinking of ontologi-

---

[13] See Jacques Derrida, "Différance," in *Margins of Philosophy*, trans. Alan Bass (Chicago: University of Chicago Press, 1982), 3-27.

[14] For his full-scale philosophical treatment of this theme, see Alain Badiou, *Logics of Worlds*, trans. Alberto Toscano (London: Continuum, 2009).

cal issues and Derrida's less formally explicit but, in their own way, just as rigorous deconstructive procedures. This is most likely why Badiou exempts Derrida from his otherwise sweeping condemnation of the linguistic turn in its sundry current guises as merely an update on old sophistical or cultural-relativist themes. What is crucially different about Derrida's commentaries on canonical texts from Plato to Husserl is his relentless teasing-out of aporetic or contradictory chains of logical implication which can then be seen to pose a large problem to any orthodox or fideist account.[15] Such are those conflicts that arise between the *vouloir-dire* of authorial intent and that which a text is logically constrained to signify when examined with a readiness to track certain discrepant details that challenge or subvert more conventional protocols of reading. The result may very well go against not only our best evidence of what the writer expressly, consciously or knowingly meant to say but also the weight of received exegetical wisdom as well as, very often, our intuitive sense of interpretative validity or truth. Hence the elusive yet marked affinity between Derrida's way with texts—his "patient deconstruction of oppositions" as Badiou puts it, not without a certain muted irony—and Badiou's approach to the various thinkers (philosophers and poets) whose work he subjects to a form of immanent dialectical critique. Where they differ is chiefly in Derrida's far greater emphasis on textual close-reading or exegesis as the means to locate those tensions, aporias, or moments of undecidability when classical (bivalent or true/false) logic is forced up against its limits. In Badiou, the procedure is pursued to broadly similar ends—with a view to exposing the covert implications, the suppressed premises or (in Derrida's phrase) the "unthought

---

[15] For some classic examples, see Jacques Derrida, *Speech and Phenomena and Other Essays on Husserl's Theory of Signs*, trans. David B. Allison (Evanston, IL: Northwestern University Press, 1973); *Of Grammatology*, trans. Gayatri. C. Spivak (Baltimore, MD: Johns Hopkins University Press, 1974); *Writing and Difference*, trans. Alan Bass (London: Routledge & Kegan Paul, 1978); *Dissemination*, trans. Barbara Johnson (London: Athlone Press, 1981); *Margins of Philosophy*, trans. Alan Bass (Chicago: University of Chicago Press, 1982).

axiomatics" of a dominant tradition—but more by way of conceptual analysis than through a sedulous attention to details of the text.

II

In this respect Badiou may be said to stand closer to Adorno, or negative dialectics in its first-generation Frankfurt mode, than to any version of the well-nigh ubiquitous linguistic turn that has undeniably left a strong imprint on Derrida's work.[16] (Although Badiou is notably out of sympathy with Adorno as regards the latter's critique of Wagnerian music-drama this is in a highly specific context of debate and scarcely indicative of any deeper-lying or principled opposition to that mode of thought.[17]) And yet, as emerges to striking (even moving) effect, Badiou is attracted not only by the rigour of Derrida's work but also—what might seem at odds with that—by its quest for alternative, less sharply polarised terms of address or some means to shift argumentative ground from a downright clash of contradictory logics (within the text or amongst its commentators) to a "space of flight," as Badiou describes it, beyond all those vexing antinomies.

> You take, for example, the great metaphysical oppositions. We shall have to diagonalize them. Because restricting discursive space means leaving no massivity, no linear massivity. Binary oppositions cannot possibly locate the hors-lieu in any lieu. So, we will have to deconstruct them. We will have to cut across them. That is what deconstruction is. Deconstruction is, basically, the set of operations that can bring about a certain restriction of the space of flight, or of the space of the vanishing point.[18]

---

[16] See especially Theodor W. Adorno, *Negative Dialectics*, trans. E.B. Ashton (New York: Seabury Press, 1973).

[17] Alain Badiou, *Five Lessons on Wagner*, trans. Susan Spitzer (London: Verso, 2010); Theodor W. Adorno, *In Search of Wagner*, trans. Rodney Livingstone (Verso, 2005).

[18] Badiou, *Pocket Pantheon*, 136.

"Restriction," that is, in so far as it places certain definite limits on the space for manoeuvre as concerns this or that particular text, or again—more precisely—on what should count as a warranted claim with regard to those specific complications of sense, reference and logic that result from a properly deconstructive reading. Hence the well-known passages (in *Of Grammatology* and elsewhere) that find Derrida emphatically asserting the need to respect indications of authorial intent so far as possible while none the less remaining maximally alert to those symptoms of conceptual stress that signal the presence of a counter-logic at odds with the text's overt (intentional) purport.[19] Indeed, as Badiou very pointedly remarks, it is just this Derridean preference for re-inscribing (that is, first inverting then displacing) certain kinds of binary opposition that is most characteristic not only of deconstruction as a formal procedure or practice of textual close-reading but also of Derrida's mode of address to political and ethical themes. So we should not take it as a cunning backhander—or a case of praising with faint damns—when Badiou refers to Derrida's having been "kept apart from the truth of the red years between 1968 and 1976," and when he further explains that the truth in question "spoke its name with the words: One divides into two."[20]

No doubt Badiou is here staking his own militant distance from any such conflict-avoidance strategy, as well as signalling for those in the know that this political difference goes along with an equally decisive difference in terms of their respective commitments with regard to certain aspects of the relation between language, truth and logic. Of course it is not the case that these two utterly distinctive thinkers are at bottom saying the same thing, the one (Derrida) in linguistically oriented or "textualist" and the other (Badiou) in mathematically derived or formalist terms. Yet one should, I think, take Badiou at his word in the *Pocket Pantheon* essay when he allows that some thinkers—those, like Derrida, with

---

[19] See especially Derrida, *Of Grammatology*, 157-8.

[20] Badiou, *Pocket Pantheon*, 138.

sufficient exegetical as well as political patience—can and should pursue the other, basically non-confrontational path. Moreover one can see how this way of thinking, or something very like it, played a role in the development of Badiou's ideas from the binary-dominated concepts and categories of *Being and Event* to the more nuanced, differential understanding of the relationship between being and existence that typifies *Logics of Worlds*.

> When Derrida outlines the concept of "différance" he wants to suggest a single term that can activate the being/existence distinction in its vanishing point. Derrida *puts to flight* what remains of a metaphysical opposition in the being/existence difference in such a way that we can grasp difference as such, *in its act*. And différance in action is obviously that which stands at the vanishing point of any opposition between being and existent, that which cannot in any sense be reduced to the figure of that opposition. And then we have to examine the democracy/totalitarianism opposition in the same way. Or the real impact of the Jew/Arab opposition on the Palestinian conflict. When he takes a stance on the Jew/Arab opposition in the Palestinian conflict, he once again deconstructs its duality.[21]

This makes it very clear how close are the links, as Badiou perceives them, on the one hand between Derrida's early and his later (more overtly political) writings, and on the other between Derrida's work as a whole and Badiou's critical ontology—his conception of the being/event dialectic—as it moved toward the more stratified or nuanced account laid out in *Logics of Worlds*.

So we shouldn't too easily fall in with the idea that these two thinkers stand squarely apart as regards the single most divisive issue in present-day philosophy of language and logic. It is not just a matter of situating each of them at some point on a scale that runs from the language-first proposition, i.e., that any critique of prevalent ("logocentric") ideas must always take account of its own embeddedness in a certain

---

[21] Badiou, *Pocket Pantheon*, 137-8.

cultural-linguistic milieu or tradition, to the logicist claim that such critique has to start with a strenuous rejection of the turn toward language as—supposedly—the ultimate limit or horizon of intelligibility. This is basically the same issue that divides continental thinkers of a strongly hermeneutic or language-centred orientation such as Heidegger and Gadamer from those, like Adorno or Habermas, who whatever their otherwise sharp differences agree on the need for a critical approach that holds out against received ideas and their customary modes of expression. From the latter viewpoint it is a *sine qua non* of enlightened or progressive thought that it should always maintain the utmost vigilance with regard to those ingrained habits of belief that may always turn out to have been kept in place by the inertial force of communal usage or linguistically encoded prejudice. On this account the true dividing-line falls not, as the textbook story would have it, between (so-called) continental and (so-called) analytic philosophy but rather between those thinkers on either side who pretty much go along with the linguistic turn for all practical purposes and those others who reject it on philosophical, political, or ethical grounds.[22] Nobody who has read Badiou's *Manifesto for Philosophy* or registered the impact of his forceful reflections on the prevalence of latter-day "sophistry"—especially where influenced by Wittgenstein—could be in any doubt as regards his deep and principled aversion to this whole movement of thought. Worst of all, in his view, is the way that it precludes any substantive critique of existing beliefs, values, or truth-claims by declaring that such criticism has to make sense by the lights of some communal consensus or cultural life-form which would otherwise find it unacceptable or downright unintelligible.

One can therefore see why Badiou's readings of (among others) Plato, Aristotle, Descartes, Spinoza, Leibniz, Hegel, and Heidegger proceed more directly through a critical engagement with the conceptual and argumentative structures

---

[22] For further discussion see Christopher Norris, *Minding the Gap: epistemology and philosophy of science in the two traditions* (Amherst, MA: University of Massachusetts Press, 2000).

of their thought and not, as in Derrida, through a practice of meticulous textual close-reading. Of course it is then open for any Derridean to ask how Badiou could possibly advance his strong-revisionist claims—for instance, his subversion of the plenist ontology or the static and immobile concept of being endorsed by a thinkers from Parmenides to Spinoza—unless through a rigorous textual analysis that locates and deconstructs those specific passages where the doctrine in question can be shown to encounter certain problems unresolvable on its own express terms.[23] And indeed it is the case that Badiou arrives at his unsettling conclusions through some careful and detailed as well as critically acute and markedly heterodox readings. Still there is a difference between, on the one hand, Derridean close-reading where the problems emerge in and through a process of direct engagement with the text and, on the other, Badiou's mode of dialectical critique which takes for granted the text's having been read with adequate attention to detail and which thus—on the strength of that previous engagement—presumes the entitlement to argue its case at a certain level of abstraction from the kinds of exegetical detail required of an *echt*-deconstructive approach. One motivating factor here, as I have said, is Badiou's opposition to anything—any argument, theory, or school of thought—that goes along with the linguistic turn or the notion of language as an end-point of critical enquiry. This helps to explain his ambivalence toward Derrida's work despite their both being centrally concerned to expose the symptomatic blind-spots, aporias, or conflicts between manifest and latent sense which reveal the limits of a certain restrictive ontology (Badiou) or a certain logocentric "metaphysics of presence" (Derrida) whose liability to such disruptive effects is an index of its deeply ideological character.

This kinship emerges with unmistakeable force if one compares, say, Badiou's strongly heterodox yet rigorously consequent readings of Plato, Aristotle, Descartes, Rousseau, Kant, Hegel, or Heidegger with Derrida's no less strenu-

---

[23] Badiou, *Being and Event*, 112-20.

ously argued deconstructive commentaries on those same thinkers.[24] In Derrida it is chiefly a matter of revealing the various deviant, non-classical, or paraconsistent logics that can be shown to inhabit their texts and produce those moments of undecidability—aporias, in the strict sense of the term—which call into question certain of the author's leading premises or presuppositions.[25] If the *modus operandi* is that of textual close-reading then this should not be seen as consigning Derrida's work to the realm of literary criticism or applied rhetoric but rather as offering the means to make that case with a high degree of demonstrative force and with reference to certain highly specific contexts of argument. In Badiou, it is a chiefly a matter of showing how certain overt ontological commitments—those that endorse some version of a plenist or changeless, timeless, and wholly determinate ontology—are fissured by the need to introduce an anomalous term that implicitly concedes the problematical status of any such doctrine and its covert reliance on that which it has striven to keep off bounds. This is why Badiou devotes a large portion of his commentary in the early sections of *Being and Event* to a detailed rehearsal of the issue of the one and the many as raised to intensely thought-provoking though somewhat baffled effect in Plato's dialogue *Parmenides*.[26] What emerges here is the conceptual impossibility of thinking an absolute plenitude of being—an absolute dominion of the one over the many, or of the timeless and unchanging over everything subject to time and change—and hence the need (so deeply repugnant to Plato's idealist mind-set) to reckon with this in any workable theory of truth and knowledge.

---

[24] Badiou, *Being and Event*; also entries for Derrida under Note 15, above.

[25] See Graham Priest, "Derrida and Self-Reference," *Australasian Journal of Philosophy*, Vol. 72 (1994), 103-111 and *Beyond the Limits of Thought* (Cambridge: Cambridge University Press, 1995); also Christopher Norris, "Derrida on Rousseau: deconstruction as philosophy of logic," in *Language, Logic and Epistemology: a modal-realist approach* (London: Palgrave-Macmillan, 2004), 16-65.

[26] Badiou, "Being: Multiple and Void. Plato/Cantor," in *Being and Event*, 21-77; also "The Subtraction of Truth," in *Theoretical Writings*, 95-160.

Thus Badiou sees a strong proleptic link between Plato's reflections on that topic and the subsequent history of more or less bewildered attempts, on the part of philosophers and mathematicians, to get a grip on the concept of the infinite as something more than a merely notional, virtual, or placeholder term.[27] His reading of intellectual history is premised on the claim that what Cantor eventually achieved—an operational grasp of the infinite and its multiple "sizes" or cardinalities—was there already as a readable subtext to the vexing antinomies of Plato's dialogue and was then worked out through numerous episodes in the long history of subsequent attempts to resolve them. Only with Cantor did these dilemmas, supposedly endemic to any thinking about the infinite, at last give way to a conception that would "turn paradox into concept" or transform what had so far been a cause of intellectual anxiety into a source of knowledge-transformative insights not only in mathematics but (so Badiou maintains) with respect to basic ontological questions across the whole range of scientific, social, and humanistic disciplines. What Cantor's discovery made it possible to think was the concept (not merely the idea) that there existed multiple orders of the infinite—such as the infinity of integers and even numbers, or integers and fractions thereof, or rational and real numbers—and, moreover, that these could be reckoned with or subject to calculation in rigorous and perfectly intelligible ways. The effect was to open up a vast new region of transfinite operations that David Hilbert famously described as "a mathematician's paradise," and which finally laid to rest those deep misgivings about the topic that had typified the response of many thinkers from Plato and Aristotle down to Cantor's more orthodox-minded contemporaries.[28] So it was that his breakthrough soon gave rise to a whole range of pow-

---

[27] Plato, *Parmenides*, trans. Mary L Gill and Paul Ryan (Indianapolis: Hackett, 1966).

[28] On the often heated debate around Cantor's claims concerning the multiple "sizes" of infinity and Hilbert's enthusiastic endorsement, see especially Marcus Giaquinto, *The Search for Certainty: a philosophical account of the foundations of mathematics* (Oxford: Oxford University Press, 2002).

erful techniques for creating (or discovering, as mathematical realists would say) new possibilities of further extending the set-theoretical domain.

Plato's worry is conveyed in the dialogue through Socrates' encounter with his senior and mentor Parmenides. It has to do with the way that reflection on the infinite tends to generate problems, dilemmas, aporias, or instances of limit-point paradox which pose a real threat to the kind of thinking—the pursuit of a well-defined systematic structure for the conduct of rational enquiry—that philosophers have typically espoused. The result of this encounter is to force Socrates and his admiring, ever-faithful, yet at this point discernibly independent-minded student and chronicler Plato into a sequence of hard-pressed dialectical manoeuvres on the theme of the one and the many that leads both thinkers, like many others after them, right up to and (arguably) just beyond the point of conceptual deadlock. Thus the dialogue, at least as Plato reconstructs it, brings Socrates out decidedly at odds with Parmenides' doctrine that only the one can truly be said to exist while the multiple is merely a product of delusory phenomenal or sensuous experience. Instead it is seen to manifest an incipient grasp of the contrary truth according to which multiplicity precedes and outruns any limit arbitrarily placed upon it by this or that particular state of knowledge, ontological scheme, discursive regime, or appearance of consistency brought about by some local operation of the merely stipulative count-as-one. This the dialogue achieves despite and against Plato's well-known predilection for the transcendent unifying power of that which participates in the abstract realm of the forms, or ideas, such as justice, beauty, and (ultimately) goodness. In short, "[w]hat Plato is endeavouring to think here, in a magnificent, dense text, is evidently inconsistent multiplicity, which is to say, pure presentation, anterior to any one-effect, or to any structure."[29] And again, in a pithy formulation by Badiou that very clearly credits Plato with a precocious (perhaps preconscious) attempt to make

---

[29] Badiou, *Being and Event*, 33.

sense of that thesis: "in the absence of any being of the one, the multiple in-consists in the presentation of a multiple of multiples without any foundational stopping-point."[30]

"In-consists" is here used in the pointedly technical sense developed throughout *Being and Event*. What the neologism nicely and compactly denotes is that absolute precedence of the multiple over the one—or the inconsistent over the consistent—which plays a central role in Badiou's thinking not only about mathematics but also on other topics central to his work, among them most importantly politics. This he conceives as elementally a matter of the count-as-one and its exclusionary effect when deployed to distinguish some socially dominant fraction of the populace as members in good standing and to marginalise or negate some other fraction (for instance, that of the *sans papiers* or "economic migrants") as lacking such status.[31] Nevertheless, just as Plato's "official" (Parmenidean) doctrine of transcendental monism encountered resistance from certain inbuilt necessities of thought—a resistance that would finally give rise to Cantor's conceptual breakthrough—so likewise those oppressed or victimised minorities exert a counter-pressure at certain points in the existing body politic which at critical times may become the sites of protest, struggle, and (potentially) social transformation. Thus, in terms of the more-than-analogical relation that Badiou posits between set theory and politics, any such change is likeliest to start at "evental sites" where conditions exist for the emergence of an aberrant or "uncounted" multiple, that is, a collectivity—something like Sartre's "group-in-fusion"—with a shared interest in bringing it about.[32] These are subject-multiples who "belong" but are not "included," or owing to whose conspicuous absence from

---

[30] Badiou, *Being and Event*, 33.

[31] See Note 11, above.

[32] Jean-Paul Sartre, *A Critique of Dialectical Reason*, Vol. 1, *Theory of Practical Ensembles*, trans. A. Sheridan-Smith (London: New Left Books, 1976) and Vol. 2, trans. Quintin Hoare (London: Verso, 2006); also Badiou, "Jean-Paul Sartre (1905-1980)," in *Pocket Pantheon*, 14-35.

the count-as-one the extant social structure can be known to "inconsist," i.e., to harbour absences (defects of adequate representation or shortfalls of accountability) that call its legitimacy into question.

This is all worked out with great precision and care for detail in Badiou's writings on the course of set-theoretical investigation after Cantor. It is expounded chiefly with reference to the work of Paul Cohen who devised (or discovered) a formal means of explaining how certain as-yet unknowable or unprovable truths in mathematics might none the less be implicit through their absence from the present state of knowledge and the power of that absence to generate certain specific problems and aporias.[33] Here again, as so often with Badiou, the Sartre comparison—famously exemplified by Pierre's absence from the café—is one that fairly leaps to mind.[34]

I hope that by now it will be clear what I am suggesting with regard to the relationship between Badiou and Derrida. There is no doubt that Badiou is the more overtly formal thinker, or the one whose work has drawn more heavily on developments in mathematics, logic, and the formal sciences. There is also no doubt that Derrida is the more language-oriented or text-conscious thinker of the two, a difference that might seem to set them apart on basic philosophical grounds. However, to repeat, this impression ought to be checked by considering the well-nigh ubiquitous character of the "linguistic turn" across numerous schools of post-1920 "analytic" and "continental" thought. One effect of this—for thinkers not overly in hock to that typecast dichotomy—has been to question the very idea that an extreme sensitivity to linguistic nuance cannot go along with (must indeed be inimical to) an adequate power of conceptual grasp. Nor should it be forgotten, as so often it has by admiring and hostile commentators alike, that

---

[33] Paul J. Cohen, *Set Theory and the Continuum Hypothesis* (New York: W.A. Benjamin, 1966). See also Michael Potter, *Set Theory and Its Philosophy: a critical history* (Oxford: Oxford University Press, 2004).

[34] Jean-Paul Sartre, *Being and Nothingness*, trans. Hazel Barnes (London: Routledge, 2003), 9.

Derrida more than once invokes formal arguments such as Gödel's undecidability-theorem in order to explain what is involved in the deconstructive reading of a text.[35] This is not just a vaguely analogical or downright opportunist appeal to the presumed authority of mathematics and logic but a reference-point that precisely captures the movement—the logico-syntactic-semantic procedure—of Derrida's classic readings.

III

My point is that Derrida's meditations on the logics of the *pharmakon* in Plato, of supplementarity in Rousseau, of parergonality in Kant, or of *différance* in Husserl along with his later, more generic reflections on the aporetic logics of the gift, hospitality, and auto-immunity are all of them essentially formal despite (or more accurately just on account of) their often starting out from some localised evidence of textual complication.[36] That is, they have to do with the scope and limits of classical (bivalent) logic—its coming up against strictly unresolvable instances of self-contradiction or aporia—and are therefore dependent on textual exegesis *only though crucially* in order to present this case with the maximum degree of evidential warrant and demonstrative (logical) rigour.

Indeed, one could plausibly interpret the development of Derrida's thought over five decades of intense activity as a

---

[35] See Note 27, above; also Paul Livingston, "Derrida and Formal Logic: formalizing the undecidable," *Derrida Today*, Vol. 3, No. 2 (2010), 221-39 and Norris, "Deconstruction, Science and the Logic of Enquiry," 178-200.

[36] See entries under Note 15, above, and Jacques Derrida, "The Parergon," in *The Truth in Painting*, trans. Geoff Bennington and Ian McLeod (Chicago: University of Chicago Press), 15-147; also—for the more obviously "topical" turn in his later work—Jacques Derrida, *Of Hospitality*, trans. Rachel Bowlby (Stanford, CA: Stanford University Press, 2000); *On Cosmopolitanism and Forgiveness*, trans. Mark Dooley and Michael Hughes (London: Routledge, 2001); *Rogues: two essays on reason*, trans Pascale-Anne Brault and Michael Naas (Stanford U.P., 2005); *Beast and the Sovereign*, Vol. 1, ed. Michel Lisse, Marie-Louise Mallet, and Ginette Michaud, trans. G. Bennington (Chicago: University of Chicago Press, 2009).

shift of focus from textual close-reading as the *sine qua non* of interpretative truth or validity to a somewhat more generalised or less context-specific mode of conceptual analysis. I have ventured this claim in somewhat cautious and tentative style because it is misleading in one respect at least, namely its failure to acknowledge the wider (referential or real-world) contexts to which those later writings are very specifically addressed and to which they often respond in strongly marked ethico-political terms.[37] Here again, as with the (putative) issue concerning "formal" *versus* "textualist" modes of thought, if one takes due account of this dimension—always present in Derrida's work but latterly more overt and emphatic—there will seem fewer problems about finding significant points of contact between that work and various aspects of Badiou's project. It will then become clearer that their thinking converges on certain shared objectives, among them the concern to articulate a formally adequate account of the contradictions that they both find implicit across a great range of discourses, concepts, institutions, socio-political orders, and practices. Moreover, they can then be seen as holding the shared belief that those contradictions have their locus of emergence only in the various specific contexts—from mathematics, logic and the physical sciences to politics, ethics, and art—where thinkers and practitioners must henceforth discover the relevant validity-conditions as well as an anticipatory grasp of what would truthfully count as an advance on the present state of knowledge or current ideas of justificatory warrant.

All this was implicit in the well-known aphorism of Roland Barthes when he sought some common ground between structuralists and their Marxist or socialist-realist opponents by remarking that "a little formalism turns one away from history, but a lot brings one back to it."[38] What I think he had more specifically in mind—and what bears directly on our current

---

[37] See Notes 2 and 38, above; also Cathy Caruth and Deborah Esch (eds.), *Critical Encounters: reference and responsibility in deconstructive writing* (New Jersey: Rutgers University Press, 1995).

[38] Roland Barthes, "Myth Today," in *Mythologies*, trans. Annette Lavers (London: Granada, 1973), 112.

discussion—is the difference between a wholesale version of the "linguistic turn" (whether post-structuralist, Wittgensteinian, late-Heideggerian, or Rortian neo-pragmatist) and a version that concedes the centrality of language to human thought and cognition yet also acknowledges the constraints imposed by logic on the one hand and referential ties or commitments on the other. Thus a formalist approach is one that preserves at least this much of the classical *trivium* model with its three major disciplines of logic, grammar, and rhetoric. The model was devised so as to allow rhetoric its appointed place as the study of language in its suasive or performative aspect but always within the order of priority laid down by a due regard for logic and, next to that, for grammar as the structural component of language that serves to articulate its proper relation to the correspondent structures of truth, fact, or veridical knowledge and experience. It was subject to drastic revision through various programmes of reform from Ramus down, and is nowadays either consigned to the intellectual history-books or resurrected by boa-deconstructors like Paul de Man in order to advance a radically extended conception of rhetoric that would claim to undo—subvert or undermine—the priority of logic and grammar.[39]

Whatever one's assessment of de Man's somewhat wire-drawn arguments to this effect it is clear that the *trivium* conception suffers from an overly literal understanding of the correspondence-relation between logic, language and reality and a failure to conceive how that relation might be subject to disturbance by factors beyond the remit of logical or grammatical analysis. Still it is the model that looms over Wittgenstein's early Tractarian account of these matters, and also—of course—the model that he roundly rejected in the *Philosophical Investigations* and other "late"-period writings.[40]

---

[39] For further discussion (albeit from a decidedly idiosyncratic angle) see Paul de Man, *The Resistance to Theory* (Manchester: Manchester University Press, 1986); also Christopher Norris, *Paul de Man and the Critique of Aesthetic Ideology* (New York: Routledge, 1988).

[40] Ludwig Wittgenstein, *Tractatus Logico-Philosophicus*, trans. David Pears and Brian McGuiness (London: Routledge, 1961) and *Philosophical Investigations*,

Wittgenstein's was the most extreme—arguably the most naïve and literal-minded—of those doctrines that typified analytic philosophy in its early, predominantly logicist period. His subsequent turnaround was likewise the most extreme of those sundry reactive movements of thought which swung right across to a notion of language (language-games, discourses, phrase-regimes, descriptive paradigms, worldviews, conceptual schemes, etc.) as the furthest we can get toward a better understanding of the relation between thought and world.[41] It is in this context that Badiou and Derrida can be seen to hold out against the limiting conditions imposed on philosophy by a cyclic swinging back and forth between opposite and equally disabling doctrinal poles. Both thinkers maintain a steady commitment to standards of logical consistency and analytic-conceptual rigour along with an acute critical awareness of the ways in which certain problematic or anomalous instances—"events" for Badiou, aporias or moments of undecidability for Derrida—may on occasion require a suspension and consequent redefinition of those same standards.

Badiou focuses on the effect of some crucial intervention in mathematics, science, politics, or art which establishes a novel truth-procedure whose longer-term consequences are then worked out by "militants of truth"—or those with the requisite degree of post-evental fidelity—and brought to the point where there occurs a decisive transformation in the existing order of knowledge, society, or artistic expression. Derrida is more apt to describe such events in textual terms, that is to say, as likewise transformative occurrences but of the sort best exemplified by what happens when a deconstructive reading of (say) Plato, Rousseau, Kant, Hegel, Marx, Nietzsche, Husserl or Heidegger controverts not only the received understanding of those thinkers but also its bearing on issues in the sphere of general and regional ontology. Indeed there

---

trans. G.E.M. Anscombe (Oxford: Blackwell, 1954).

[41] See entries under Note 9, above, for more extended analysis and critique of these various (as I see them) closely related developments.

are some major misconceptions about Derrida that might be dispelled by noting the salient points of convergence between his project and Badiou's more explicitly ontological approach to the ongoing dialectic of being and event. One is the old canard, still much bandied about amongst Derrida's detractors, that in making his notorious claim to the effect that "there is nothing outside the text" ("*il n'y a pas de hors-texte;*" better rendered "there is no 'outside' to the text") he should be taken to espouse a textualist variant of absolute or transcendental idealism according to which, quite literally, written marks on the page are all that can be known to exist.[42] Another is the notion often advanced by critics on the left that when Derrida claims to deconstruct the Western logocentric "metaphysics of presence" from Plato to Heidegger he must have in mind some timeless and seamless structure of false consciousness—or mode of self-perpetuating error and delusion—that has remained perfectly unaffected by even the most radical interim changes of socio-political life.[43] My comparison with Badiou may help to make the contrary point, i.e., that each of those textual engagements raises a historically specific range of issues which in turn have to do with a particular form of ideological misrecognition or a distinct, politically inflected way that the logocentric prejudice has taken hold under given material and cultural conditions. In short the main task of critical reading, as Derrida conceives it, is precisely to articulate those fault-lines in the structure of metaphysical presupposition that are normally concealed by our placid assurance of knowing our way around language and the world but which show up to most striking effect when placed under deconstructive scrutiny.

Nor should this for one moment be taken to suggest that Derrida is proposing linguistic therapy in the Wittgensteinian mode, i.e., seeking to talk us down from the giddy heights of metaphysical abstraction and restore us to a communally

---

[42] Derrida, *Of Grammatology*, 158; also Note 38, above.

[43] See Note 7, above.

sanctioned sense of what constitutes apt or proper usage.[44] One additional benefit of viewing his work in relation to Badiou's is that it shows just how far they share a decidedly anti-Wittgensteinian emphasis on the power of critical thought to question, challenge, unsettle and subvert the complacent habits of belief typically enshrined in (so-called) ordinary language. This in turn allows both thinkers to locate a certain very specific role for the subject—the human subject of choice, agency, knowledge, and commitment albeit here defined in terms far removed from those of traditional humanism—as that which alone brings about the possibility of any such critical advance. Such is Badiou's concept of the subject as itself brought about or summoned into being through its faithful adherence to a truth-procedure in the wake of some particular breakthrough event in mathematics, the sciences, politics, or art.[45] Beyond that, it suggests perhaps the most promising solution to those long-running and by now somewhat dead-end debates over whether or not Derridean deconstruction goes so far in its (supposed) rejection of all such (supposed) humanist residues as to leave no room for the subject as locus of truth-seeking and activist engagement.[46] That is to say, it gets over the false antinomy—one very pointedly deconstructed in Derrida's early writings on Husserl—between truth as a matter of absolute ideal objectivity and truth as that which has to be conceived as discovered or at any rate discoverable by human enquirers at a certain stage of intellectual advance, political progress, or artistic achievement.[47]

---

[44] Wittgenstein, *Philosophical Investigations*.

[45] See especially Alain Badiou, *Theory of the Subject*, trans. Bruno Bosteels (London: Continuum, 2009) and Bruno Bosteels, *Badiou and Politics* (Durham, NC: Duke University Press, 2011).

[46] See for instance Eduardo Cadava, Peter Connor and Jean-Luc Nancy (eds.), *Who Comes After the Subject?* (London: Routledge, 1991).

[47] See especially Derrida, *Speech and Phenomena and Other Essays on Husserl's Theory of Signs* (Note 15, above); also *Edmund Husserl's "Origin of Geometry": an introduction*, trans. John P. Leavey (Pittsburgh: Duquesne University Press, 1978) and "'Genesis and Structure' and Phenomenology," in *Writing and Dif-*

This is I think the key to resolving what would otherwise constitute an insuperable problem for any attempt to find common ground between Badiou's insistence on mathematics as ontology, i.e., as that which always potentially exceeds the compass of human epistemic grasp and Derrida's undoubted starting-point in the project of Husserlian phenomenology, no matter how deep and far-reaching his critique of its basic suppositions. It is here that both thinkers stake their claim to have moved decisively beyond the whole range of typecast dilemmas—ultimately those between subject and object, mind and world, or truth within the bounds of human cognition and truth as recognition—or verification-transcendent—that have vexed the discourse of Western philosophy since its ancient Greek origins, and all the more so in the wake of Kant's self-professed "Copernican Revolution."[48] Hence Badiou's highly qualified version of mathematical Platonism, one that unlike the classical (and inherently dilemma-prone) version makes due allowance for the truth-revealing powers of actively engaged exploratory thought. Hence also, in a different register, Derrida's meticulous analysis of the constant alternating movement in Husserl between a transcendental phenomenology premised on the existence of absolute ideal objectivities and a more historically grounded and lifeworld-oriented approach that instead takes account of the various temporal factors that can now be seen to have impinged on the process of discovery.[49] It is in this way that a better understanding of Badiou's claims with regard to mathematics, ontology and truth can help toward a better—since again less dilemma-prone—grasp of how subjectivity figures in Derrida's readings of Husserl and other thinkers.

As we have seen, Badiou offers numerous examples of the process or procedure whereby some given state of knowledge,

---

ference, trans. Alan Bass (London: Routledge & Kegan Paul, 1978), 154-68, 160.

[48] On the dubious warrant for Kant's claims in this regard, see Quentin Meillassoux, *After Finitude: an essay on the necessity of contingency*, trans. Ray Brassier (London: Continuum, 2008); also Norris, *Re-Thinking the Cogito: naturalism, reason and the venture of thought* (Continuum, 2009).

[49] See entries under Note 49, above.

political situation, or stage of artistic advance—along with the ontology that underwrites it—is thrown into doubt or forced to the point of crisis and transformation through various strictly consequent though strictly unforeseeable turns in the logic of events. Indeed that phrase, "logic of events," is one that neatly encapsulates the nature of this process as Badiou describes it, since the logic (or intelligible sequence of developments) emerges fully formed only "after the event" yet with no less a sense of rigorous necessity given the new advance in knowledge, the new access to political power on the part of a hitherto oppressed group, or the new possibilities of expression opened up by some breakthrough artistic achievement. In mathematical terms—always his ultimate point of reference—it involves that quintessentially set-theoretical operation of "turning paradox into concept," or finding the resources for a radical re-thinking of some presently insoluble problem which then becomes the springboard for a full-scale conceptual revolution. Such were prototypically the advances achieved by Cantor with his grasp of the multiple orders of infinity and by Cohen with his account of "forcing" as that which made possible all such advances, itself included.[50] If one asks what relevance this might have to Derrida's (on the face of it) very different body of work then the answer has to with that jointly logical and referential dimension which, as I have argued, sets it decidedly apart from most developments in sceptically-inclined philosophy of language or critical theory over the past half-century.

Thus Derridean deconstruction, as distinct from its various spin-offs or derivatives, necessarily maintains a due respect for those axioms or precepts of classical logic (such as bivalence and excluded middle) that have to be applied right up to the limit—the point where they encounter some instance of strictly irresolvable aporia—if such reading is to muster any kind of demonstrative force. The same goes for those basic referential constraints on language that are built into its very nature as a mode of informative-communicative discourse

---

[50] See Notes 28, 30 and 35 above.

and which Derrida doesn't for one moment deny even though he shows how they are subject to certain complicating factors when approached with a sufficiently nuanced sense of their involvement in larger chains of contextual and logico-semantic entailment. Moreover the two considerations are closely intertwined since, as can be seen from debates on the topic from Frege down, there is simply no separating issues of reference from issues of truth, issues of truth from issues of (Fregean) sense, and these in turn from issues concerning the logical structure of the sentences, propositions, or other such larger units of discourse within which alone terms can properly be said to refer or to possess a determinate (referentially warranted) truth-value.[51] Of course that set of claims has been subject to much debate, with some—Quine among them—criticising Frege on radically holistic grounds for not having pressed right through with the contextualist argument and extended it beyond the sentence to the entire "web" or "fabric" of discourse (or currently accredited knowledge) at any given time.[52] However this contention has been challenged in turn by those, like Michael Dummett, who object that we could never get a purchase on language—never learn to use it in the first place or manifest a grasp of its working principles—unless (*contra* Quine) we had a prior grasp of its compositional structure, i.e., the dependence of language-as-a-whole on those sentential structures that define the conditions of assertoric warrant for this or that statement or truth-claim.[53] Quite simply, we should then be at a loss to understand the most basic elements of linguistic intelligibility or to figure out other people's meanings, intentions, or communicative gist on the basis of a rationally informed conjecture as to the sense (and the truth-conditions) that they are likeliest to have

---

[51] For further discussion see Norris, *Language, Logic and Epistemology*.

[52] See especially W.V. Quine, *Ontological Relativity and Other Essays* (New York: Columbia University Press, 1969) and "Two Dogmas of Empiricism," in *From a Logical Point of View*, 2nd ed. (Cambridge, MA: Harvard University Press, 1961), 20-46.

[53] Michael Dummett, *Frege and Other Philosophers* (Oxford: Oxford University Press, 1996).

in mind for their discourse from one sentence to the next.

What most needs stressing against the common currency of pro- and anti-Derrida commentaries alike is that Dummett's argument is fully borne out in the case of those classical deconstructive readings that constitute the heart of Derrida's project. To be sure there are passages, much cited in the secondary literature, where he does give every appearance of endorsing a wholesale contextualist position *à la* Quine. On this account it must be the aim of such readings to subvert or undermine every last appeal to the "transcendental signified," whether this be conceived in idealist terms as the ultimate reality behind sensory-phenomenal appearances or—in realist terms—as the referential point of anchorage between language and reality or word and world. However it will soon strike any attentive reader that when Derrida writes about the logic of the *pharmakon* in Plato, or supplementarity in Rousseau, or the *parergon* in Kant, or *différance* in Husserl (etc.) he is certainly out to discredit the former (idealist) conception but by no means seeking to undermine the very notions of truth and reference. Indeed, if one wanted to characterise "deconstruction" in philosophical (as distinct from literary-theoretical or cultural-critical) terms then its specific *differentia* would lie precisely in the tension—or the constant possibility of conflict—between an adherence to those "classical" values and the kinds of anomalous or discrepant evidence that may be encountered in the course of a sufficiently intelligent, sensitive, and rigorous deconstructive reading. My point, to repeat, is that Derrida shares with Badiou this desire not only to detect and locate but, so far as possible, to *analyse and formalise* whatever creates such an obstacle or challenge to existing modes of belief. More than that, it gives rise to a truth-procedure that may for some time—like Cantor's proposals—come up against strong doxastic or institutional resistance, but which thereafter acts as a periodic spur to the activity of thought by which paradox is turned into concept.

IV

I would therefore suggest that Derrida's protocols of reading, early and late, can best be understood as closely analogous to those transformative events that Badiou describes across a range of disciplines, domains or practices from mathematics to politics and which find their most rigorous formal specification in the set-theoretical procedure of forcing developed in the work of Cohen. Thus when Badiou offers his against-the-grain readings of canonical philosophers from Plato and Aristotle to Descartes, Spinoza, Leibniz, Hegel, or Heidegger it is through a formal procedure—not merely an interpretative option—devised in order to explain how set-theoretical theorems or conjectures can be truth-tracking or sensitive to future discovery even though they exceed the utmost compass of current provability or present-best knowledge. That is to say, those thinkers can be held to have thought truer than they knew just on condition (1) that their texts are read with sufficient care, and (2) that this care is directed more toward structures of conflictual logico-semantic implication than toward whatever the author may have declared with regard to their express, conscious, programmatic, or manifest purport. For Derrida likewise, as explained in a famous passage from *Of Grammatology*, it is a matter of bringing out the often complex and contradictory relationship between that which an author knows or acknowledges concerning his/her writerly intentions and that which eludes their grasp precisely on account of its resisting or subverting any straightforward intentionalist approach.

This point is worth more detailed treatment since it has often been ignored or subject to misunderstanding among a sizeable number of Derrida's commentators. On the one hand, he declares, it is vital to take stock of an author's manifest intent since "[w]ithout this recognition and this respect, critical production would risk developing in any direction at all and authorize itself to say almost anything."[54] Nevertheless—the point of departure for a deconstructive reading—

---

[54] Derrida, *Of Grammatology*, 158.

"this indispensable guardrail has always only *protected*, it has never *opened* a reading." To suppose otherwise would be to confine criticism or philosophy to the subaltern and wholly uncritical task of "reproducing, by the effaced and respectful doubling of commentary, the conscious, voluntary, intentional relationship that the writer institutes in his exchanges with the history to which he belongs thanks to the element of language."[55] What deconstruction seeks to reveal, conversely, is "a certain relationship, unperceived by the writer, between what he commands and what he does not command of the patterns of the language that he uses." And again—as should be emphasised in view of its distorted reception-history to date—deconstruction in the proper sense of that term, i.e., as exemplified by Derrida's classic essays must involve not only a keen awareness of these intra-linguistic complications but also a strong analytical grasp of the logical or logico-semantic structures that are thereby subject to a dislocating torsion beyond their power to contain or control. After all, this could be the case—or register as such—only on condition that the reader is able and willing to apply the most rigorous standards of logical accountability (including the axioms of classical or bivalent true/false reasoning) and thereby locate those moments of aporia or logico-semantic breakdown that signal the limits of any such reckoning.

Hence Derrida's doubtless mischievous but by no means disingenuous expression of outrage when John Searle upbraids him for thinking to deconstruct Austin's categorical distinctions—e.g., between proper and improper speech-acts, or apt and non-apt contexts, or good-faith and insincere, deceptive, or imitation speech-acts—by applying a strict bivalent logic that is simply out of place (Searle claims) in the context of everyday, ordinary, non-regimented linguistic usage.[56] The passage is worth quoting at length since it goes clean against—and helps to discredit—such a range of prejudicial ideas on the topic of Derridean deconstruction. Thus:

---

[55] Derrida, *Of Grammatology*, 158.
[56] Ibid., 158.

> [f]rom the moment that Searle entrusts himself to an oppositional logic, to the "distinction" of concepts by "contrast" or "opposition" (a legitimate demand that I share with him, even if I do not at all elicit the same consequences from it), I have difficulty seeing how he is nevertheless able to write [that] phrase ... in which he credits me with the "assumption," "oddly enough derived from logical positivism," "that unless a distinction can be made rigorous and precise, it is not really a distinction at all."[57]

Derrida's point is not so much to cock a snook at logical positivism but rather to bring home the unwitting irony of Searle's setting up as the appointed guardian of "analytic" values and priorities while blithely recommending that they be relaxed, suspended, or held in abeyance whenever (as in the context of speech-act theory) they encounter problems or anomalous instances. Here again he agrees with Badiou that thought can make progress—whether in mathematics, the physical sciences, politics, art, or ethics—only so long as it persists in the effort to work its way *through and beyond* those dilemmas that periodically emerge in the course of enquiry and can later be seen to have supplied the stimulus to some otherwise (quite literally) unthinkable stage of advance. There is no direct equivalent in Derrida to the set-theoretical procedure of "forcing" as formalized by Cohen and extended by Badiou to fields that would normally be seen as altogether resistant to any such approach. Nevertheless, as I have said, there is a more than suggestive analogy between Badiou's meticulous working-out of that procedure in its various contexts of application through a stage-by-stage sequence of mathematically-based demonstrative reasoning and Derrida's likewise meticulous attention to those deviant or non-classical logics—of supplementarity, *différance*,

---

[57] Jacques Derrida, "Afterword: toward an ethic of conversation," in Gerald Graff (ed.), *Limited Inc* (Evanston, IL: Northwestern University Press, 1989), 111-54, 123. For the background to this rejoinder see also Derrida, "Signature Event Context," *Glyph*, Vol. 1 (Baltimore: Johns Hopkins University Press, 1975), 172-97; John R. Searle, "Reiterating the Differences," ibid, 198-208; Derrida, "Limited Inc abc," *Glyph*, Vol. 2 (1977), 75-176.

parergonality, autoimmunity, and so forth—which he finds at work in the texts of a culture that has consistently striven to conceal or efface them.

Moreover, the analogy is greatly strengthened by his telling invocations of Gödel's incompleteness-theorem at just those cardinal points—notably in his treatment of Mallarmé's paradoxical reflections on language, logic, reference, and truth—where deconstruction is most deeply engaged in exposing the extent of that same concealment.[58] In Badiou's essay of tribute to Derrida he elects to pass over the Gödelian connection and to focus instead on the link with Cantor's technique of diagonalization, that is, his proof that there exist infinite sets (like that of the real numbers) that cannot be placed in a one-for-one order of correspondence with the infinite set of integers or natural numbers, just as the power-set of any given set (the set of all its subsets) must always numerically and exponentially exceed the set itself. However that technique was taken over and put to various other mathematical and logical purposes, among them most notably Gödel's incompleteness theorem.[59] At any rate these various connections help to explain not only Badiou's (as it might seem) curious take on Derrida in the *Pocket Pantheon* piece but also the development in his thinking—some would say the outright transformation—between the two master-texts *Being and Event* and *Logics of Worlds*. After all, it is in the latter that Badiou offers his full-scale exposition of the themes that dominate his later work and which also find cryptic though eloquent expression in the tribute to Derrida. Chief among them are the ideas of *existence* (as distinct from being), *inexistence* (with its proximate source in the subtractive ontology of *Being and Event*), *degrees of existence* (these

---

[58] See Note 37, above; also Derrida, "The Double Session," in *Dissemination*, 173-286.

[59] Kurt Gödel, "On Formally Undecidable Propositions of *Principia Mathematica* and Related Systems," trans. B. Meltzer (New York: Basic Books, 1962); see also Ernest Nagel and James Newman, *Gödel's Theorem* (London: Routledge & Kegan Paul, 1971) and S.G. Shanker (ed.), *Gödel's Theorem in Focus* (London: Routledge, 1987).

taken to vary for any given being or entity across different worlds), and the likewise differing *transcendentals* that exert their existence-bestowing effect on or in each of those worlds. "Given a multiplicity that exists in a world, there will always be an element in that multiplicity that is a non-existent in that world. A non-existent cannot be characterised in ontological terms, but only in existential terms; it is a minimal degree of existence in any determinate world."[60] To be sure, this conception has its ultimate source in the set-theoretical terms and procedures laid out in *Being and Event*. But they have now undergone a major shift of emphasis with the turn to a scalar (differential) account of the way that existence supervenes on being, or the process by which certain beings make the passage from existing only in that "minimal" degree to existing in a world that allows full scope to their diverse powers of thought, imagination, scientific inventiveness, political activism, or artistic creativity.

It is here that Badiou locates the point of convergence between his own and Derrida's work, i.e., in the latter's kindred desire to articulate those various kinds and degrees of inexistence that mark the subordinate term of any binary pair, or whatever finds itself excluded or marginalised by prevalent social, political, cultural, or conceptual structures. The greatest error, according to Derrida as Badiou reads him, is to confuse the order of being with that of existence, and—by the same token—to confuse inexistence with nothingness. This leads to the wholly mistaken presumption that there is no need to reckon with multiples (e.g. ethnic, social or political groups) that occupy a world wherein their existence is restricted to a bare minimum by a transcendental that rules against their enjoying a more active or effective mode of involvement. Thus "any multiplicity is assigned a degree of existence in the world, a degree of appearance. The fact of existing, qua appearing in a determinate world, is inevitably associated with a certain degree of appearance in that world, with an intensity of appearance, which we can also call intensity of

---

[60] Badiou, *Pocket Pantheon*, 130.

existence."⁶¹ Hence Badiou's recognition of Derrida as having raised this topic to a high point of critical visibility despite doing so in a "textualist" register that he (Badiou) clearly finds less than appealing. Indeed, within the short compass of this *Pocket Pantheon* text he manages to link up the major concerns of "early" and "late" Derrida with a force of logical (as opposed to merely suggestive or associative) argument that has so far eluded most of Derrida's commentators. In particular, he brings out the marked though elusive continuity between a mode of deconstruction primarily focused on issues of textual exegesis (albeit with large epistemological and ontological implications) and a mode of deconstruction that engages more directly with real-world problems and dilemmas.

Badiou offers a way of reading Derrida that has no problem in negotiating the passage from texts like *Of Grammatology*, *Margins of Philosophy* or *Writing and Difference* to later works where his approach is for the most part conceptual-thematic and therefore, as I have said, takes the work of textual close-reading very largely for granted. Most striking here is Badiou's brief but pregnant commentary on Derrida's *Spectres of Marx*, a text that many critics have found brilliantly inventive, passionate, and ethically stirring yet oddly devoid of substantive political or theoretical content.⁶² Derrida's refusal to meet those demands—to deliver some programme, formula, or theory that might be cashed out in the present—is itself a sure mark of the desire to make room for that which currently lacks any adequate means of representation, or any acknowledged right to exist (in Badiou's distinctive sense of that term) under currently prevailing cultural, political, or socio-economic conditions. Badiou's reading does much to redeem *Spectres* from the charge brought against it by left-activist detractors who deplore what they see as its merely gestural Marxist "commitment" and failure to achieve any real depth of political or philosophic thought.⁶³ On the other

---

⁶¹ Badiou, *Pocket Pantheon*, 128.

⁶² Derrida, *Spectres of Marx* (Note 2, above).

⁶³ See Note 7, above.

hand his reading strikes a cautionary note for those Derridean adepts overly enthused by the notion of "hauntology," that is, the idea that Marxism ought to embrace a "spectral" conception of political justice which accepts its endless deferral to a future of indefinite or unspecifiable since ontologically fugitive possibility. Although Derrida works this conception out with his usual inventive brilliance—and, be it said, with a charge of ethico-political passion undiminished by the book's highly speculative character—there is no doubt that it can easily serve, for others more impressed by the brilliance than inspired by the passion, as a pretext for the failure or refusal to engage with practical issues in the world outside the text. Thus to read Marx through Derrida, or with an eye to those aspects of Derrida's Marx so adroitly drawn out by Badiou, is to see how and why these (seemingly) opposite responses both fall short of an adequate reckoning. Let me quote the most relevant passage at length since it makes this point with the inseparable mixture of passion and precision that typifies all three thinkers.

> In Marx's analysis of bourgeois or capitalist societies, the proletariat is truly the non-existent characteristic of political multiplicities. It is "that which does not exist." That does not mean that it has no being .... The social and economic being of the proletariat is not in doubt. What is in doubt, always has been, and is now so more than ever, is its political *existence*. The proletariat is that which has been completely removed from political representation. The multiplicity that it is can be analysed but, if we take the rules of appearance in the political world, it does not appear there .... That is obviously what the *Internationale* sings: "We are nothing, let us be all." ... From the point of view of their political appearance, they are nothing. And becoming "all" presupposes a change of world, or in other words a change of transcendental. The transcendental must change if the ascription of an existence, and therefore a non-existence or the point of a multiplicity's non-appearance in a world, is to change in its turn.[64]

---

[64] Badiou, *Pocket Pantheon*, 130-31.

This is clearly a "creative" or revisionist reading of *Spectres* in so far as it attributes to Derrida words, phrases, concepts, ontological concerns, and certain "technical" (mainly mathematical) thought-procedures that are not to be found in Derrida's work, at least on the literal face of it. However it can fairly be said to respect what Derrida calls the "classical exigencies" of interpretation, that is, the conditions incumbent upon any reading that wishes to avoid the familiar charge—one often brought against Derrida himself although, I would argue, without adequate warrant—of treating the text in hand as merely a pretext for some ingenious display of self-willed "strong" misprision. Those conditions include (though it might surprise some of Derrida's "literary" disciples) an attitude of qualified regard for the claims of authorial intent and also—what entails that qualification—a demand that texts be read with the utmost attentiveness to their complex and sometimes contradictory structures of logical implication. Such is the requirement even, or especially, where this leads up to an aporetic juncture or moment of strictly unresolvable impasse so that the *logical* necessity arises to deploy a non-classical, i.e., a deviant, paraconsistent, non-bivalent, or (in Derrida's parlance) a "supplementary" logic.[65]

However, crucially, this is not the kind of readiness to switch or revise logics at the drop of a speculative hat that has characterised a good deal of Anglo-American "analytical" discussion in the wake of Quine's "Two Dogmas of Empiricism" and Hilary Putnam's kindred reflections.[66] Rather it is revisionism only under pressure, that is, as the upshot of a logically meticulous reading that must be undertaken if deconstruction is not to take refuge in irrationality or even—as with certain of its US literary variants—in some specially (often theologically) sanctioned realm of supra-rational ambiguity or paradox.[67]

---

[65] See Notes 27 and 37, above.

[66] For classic statements of the "strong" logical-revisionist case, see Willard Van Orman Quine, "Two Dogmas of Empiricism," and Hilary Putnam, *Mathematics, Matter and Method* (Cambridge: Cambridge University Press, 1975); also Christopher Norris, *Hilary Putnam: realism, reason and the uses of uncertainty* (Manchester: Manchester University Press, 2002).

[67] See for instance Mark C, Taylor, *Erring: a postmodern a/theology* (Chicago:

V

This is the aspect of Derrida's work that has made the greatest impression on Badiou, as witness his striking re-assessment of *Spectres of Marx*. Above all, it offers a needful corrective to the widespread idea—one that Badiou, given his antipathy toward the "linguistic turn" in its sundry manifestations, might well be expected to endorse—that Marxism "after Derrida" is a merely textual or rhetorical affair with no purchase on issues of real-world history and politics. What counts so strongly against that charge is Derrida's sheer analytic acuity, a virtue that places him more in the company of an *echt*-analytical philosopher like Russell than exponents of the language-first, conventionalist, social-constructivist, or communitarian outlook. Or again, it is Derrida's temperamental as well as intellectual affinity with a thinker like Austin who managed to combine a Wittgensteinian attentiveness to "ordinary language" with an undiminished power of analytic thought and—owing to that—a very un-Wittgensteinian precision of conceptual grasp as applied to the finest nuances of linguistic usage.[68] Thus despite his ill fame amongst analytic philosophers as the *ne plus ultra* of "textualist" (i.e., post-structuralist, postmodernist, or more broadly "continental") thinking, Derrida is much better understood as an immensely gifted close-reader of numerous philosophical texts who has also—by way of that same close-reading activity—put forward some remarkably original theses concerning the structural and historical genealogy of certain crucially load-bearing philosophical concepts. This is why Badiou can advance a speculative reading which itself goes beyond the letter of Derrida's text—beyond any "straight" interpretation—and yet finds adequate probative

---

University of Chicago Press, 1984) and John D. Caputo, *Prayers and Tears of Jacques Derrida: religion without religion* (Bloomington: Indiana University Press, 1997); also Arthur Bradley, "Derrida's God: a genealogy of the theological turn," *Paragraph*, Vol. 29, No. 3 (2006), 21-42. For a powerful and timely antidote to such thinking, see Martin Hägglund, *Radical Atheism: Derrida and the time of life* (Stanford, CA: Stanford University Press, 2008).

[68] See entries under Note 59, above.

warrant in aspects, features, or logical dimensions of that text that lack (and may even turn out to controvert) the supposed self-evidence of direct or express authorial intent.

It is therefore a reading very much in line with Badiou's repeated demonstrations, both in and outside the set-theoretical context, of the way that thought typically achieves its most radical or world-transformative advances through a process either identical with or closely analogous to the formal operation of "forcing" as defined by Cohen. The truth-procedure set to work in this particular instance of Badiou's practice as a textual analyst-commentator is the same as that brought to bear in those passages of strong-revisionist yet closely reasoned and intensely critical commentary on philosophers from Plato to Heidegger that punctuate *Being and Event*. Such, to repeat, is the process of enquiry by which certain truths can be shown to have been latent within some earlier state of knowledge and yet, at the time in question, to have exceeded any currently available means of proof, discovery, or verification. This leaves Badiou flatly opposed to the strain of logico-semantic-metaphysical anti-realism that was first introduced to analytic philosophy of mathematics, logic and language by Michael Dummett and which denies on principle the objectivist (alethic realist) claim that truth might always exceed or transcend our best intellectual or cognitive powers.[69] Indeed, it is on account of their shared resistance to this and other doctrines of epistemic, linguistic, or discursive constraint—doctrines which make truth coterminous with the scope and limits of human knowledge and/or linguistic expression—that Badiou can propose his heterodox reading of Derrida as nothing less than what Derrida's work requires if that work is to be read in keeping with its own critical practice. Or again, the great virtue of Badiou's brief yet piercing traversal of Derrida's *oeuvre* is that it brings out

---

[69] See especially Michael Dummett, *Truth and Other Enigmas* (London: Duckworth, 1978) and *The Logical Basis of Metaphysics* (Duckworth, 1991); also Christopher Norris, *Truth Matters: realism, anti-realism and response-dependence* (Edinburgh: Edinburgh University Press, 2002) and Neil Tennant, *The Taming of the True* (Oxford: Clarendon Press, 2002).

the crucial though less than obvious relationship between textual close-reading, political engagement, and a formal dimension none the less rigorous for going by way of those essential formative and motivating "conditions" that Badiou considers indispensable to any philosophical project meriting the name.

For it is just his point that the approach to these issues *via* mathematics—as the discourse of ontology *par excellence*—is uniquely revealing even when applied to thinkers who make no explicit use of it just so long *as* their thought is sufficiently disciplined to register the pressures and counter-pressures of a truth-oriented discourse capable of pointing beyond their present-best state of knowledge. That Derrida would accept this characterisation of his own work is, I think, strongly attested by the fact that he makes such careful allowance for the constant imbrication of blindness and insight—or ideology and critical acumen—in so many texts of the Western logocentric canon from Plato to Husserl. What gives Badiou's reading of Derrida a special interest is its clear demonstration of the fact—to adapt Barthes' aphorism once more—that while "a little formalism" may lead thought away from a sense of its larger historical and social responsibilities the effect of adopting a more consistent and rigorously formalised approach may well be to restore that missing dimension.[70]

---

[70] See Note 40, above.

Synchronicity and Correlationism
Carl Jung as Speculative Realist

Michael Haworth

Goldsmiths, University of London

The name of Carl Gustav Jung tends not to be associated with a concern for philosophical realism, seen, as he is, as one of the worst apologists for obscurantism, mysticism and spiritualism of the modern age. Yet the thesis I try to defend here is that Jung's work can be read as an elaborate attempt to escape the "correlationist circle" and the impasse of finitude every bit as rigorous and compelling as that undertaken by Quentin Meillassoux in *After Finitude*. I propose to advance this argument via a reading of that work of his which is considered perhaps the *least* defensible in terms of philosophical or scientific realism, namely the short treatise entitled *Synchronicity: An Acausal Connecting Principle*. It is here that the monist or "psychoid" ontology underpinning all of Jung's psychological work on the archetypes of the collective unconscious is given its most extensive treatment. This, I will argue, rather than being a pre-critical metaphysical curio is a remarkably sophisticated philosophical concept, consistent with Kant's transcendental conditions while transgressing them from within in order to undermine the gap of finitude between thought and being.

Speculations III
Intellectual Intuition

In the letter to Marcus Herz of February 1772, in which he famously announces his readiness to embark on the critical project, Kant interrogates the correspondence between the object of our representation and the representation itself. What, he asks, guarantees the reference of the internal sense-image to the external object? If the former is merely the result of the subject's being affected by the latter then it can be explained as of cause to effect, otherwise:

> if that in us which is called representation was *active* with regard to the object, i.e., *if the object were produced by the representation itself* [my italics] (as one thinks of divine cognitions as the archetypes of things) then the conformity of the representations with the objects would also be understood. And so one can at least understand the possibility of both an *archetypal* intellect, upon whose intuition the things themselves are grounded, as well as an *ectypal* intellect, which attains the data of its logical activity from the sensuous intuition of things.[1]

In finite sensuous intuition the object is the cause of the representation, while in the divine intellectual intuition it is the other way around: its "objects" spring forth from the cognition itself. So while our intuition is dependent upon the object being given to it, the infinite mind of God could not conceivably be so dependent upon an object to which it has to conform because this would amount to a limitation and the Supreme Being, as infinite, could have no such limitations. Intellectual intuition is thus a limit concept, like the noumenon, invoked in order to ground our finite cognition and root it in the senses. It acts to demonstrate that if we were to step outside of the Kantian system we would immediately involve ourselves in contradictions and absurdities.

This distinction is at the heart of the transcendental turn

---

[1] Immanuel Kant, *Prolegomena to Any Future Metaphysics and the Letter to Marcus Herz, February 1772*, trans. James W. Ellington (Indianapolis: Hackett), AA 130.

and plays a key role in Kant's critique of dogmatic pre-critical metaphysics, the latter tacitly assuming that the things as they appear to us are the same as they are outside of any reference to our faculties of cognition. Such a doctrine assumes an eternal God's-eye perspective as the normative, ideal archetype, of which our human perspective is but a less perfect, confused, although strictly homogeneous version. The belief is that the further we extend our understanding of the way things are—the structure of being—the closer we come to absolute knowledge. The move Kant instigates, however, is to radically separate finite human cognition from infinite divine cognition and this is at the root of the division into appearances and things in themselves, this dichotomy being the difference between things as they appear from our human standpoint and the same things as seen in their intrinsic being by God. Due to its reliance upon receptivity there is thus an insuperable limit in place upon our knowledge: we can know the object only as it appears to us, which structurally obscures the thing as it is in itself.

So fundamental and far-reaching is this schism that any philosophy that makes a claim to positive knowledge of a truth beyond sensibility must reckon with this question of correspondence and give an account of how it purports to have come by this knowledge. So when Quentin Meillassoux boldly asserts that through the knowledge of the necessity of facticity we gain access to a purely intelligible absolute, the question must be raised as to just what kind of knowledge this is. It cannot be gathered through sensible intuition because it is precisely our senses that impose upon us the belief in the necessity of natural laws, through habit and superstition, while from a rational point of view nothing at all supports such an inference. It is here that Meillassoux, somewhat surprisingly, resorts to the Kantian concept of intellectual intuition:

> [We] discover in our grasp of facticity the veritable *intellectual intuition* of the absolute. "Intuition," because it is actually in what is that we discover a contingency with no limit other than itself; "intellectual"

because this contingency is neither visible nor perceptible in things and only thought is capable of accessing it, just as it accesses the chaos that underlies the apparent continuity of phenomena.[2]

Evidently it is not being employed in a faithful Kantian sense because here thought accesses absolute being while by no means creating it, but it is nothing less than *noumenal insight*, as described by Kant in a memorable passage in the second *Critique* bearing the grandiose subheading "On the Wisely Commensurate Proportion of the Human Being's Cognitive Power to His Practical Vocation." However, in a move exactly counter to Kant's, such a knowledge does not impress upon us a vision of "God and eternity, with their dreadful majesty," but rather the complete absence of any necessity, whether divine or otherwise.[3] Knowledge is thus radically separated from the senses, indeed on this point is shown to be in direct conflict with the senses.

Now we are entitled to ask, as Kant does in the letter to Herz, how we are to guarantee the necessary reference of this intellectual intuition to the nature of being itself. The two alternatives Kant presents us with surely still apply: either the innately mathematical essence of being gives itself to thought or thought projects its logical reasoning into being. However, neither option is available to Meillassoux, since taking the former would commit him to an untenable Pythagorean ontology, which he has already explicitly ruled out, and the latter, of course, is intellectual intuition in the Kantian sense. This is why for Kant intellectual intuition could never be *receptive*, because it is impossible to conceive of how its object would be transmitted to thought. The very bedrock of Meillassoux's enterprise is the thesis that mathematics allows us access to a reality independent of thought, but if this is merely thought's projection onto reality then we are not yet free of

---

[2] Quentin Meillassoux, *After Finitude: An Essay on the Necessity of Contingency*, trans. Ray Brassier (London: Continuum, 2008), 82.

[3] Immanuel Kant, *Critique of Practical Reason*, trans. Werner S. Pluhar (Indianapolis: Hackett, 2002), AA 146.

the correlationist circle. Ray Brassier makes a similar point, writing that if reality is "neither inherently mathematical nor *necessarily* intelligible," why should we assume that being is susceptible to intellectual intuition?[4] If this reference is itself also intuited intellectually then too much is conceded to thought and correlationism creeps back in.

In the face of Brassier's objections, Meillassoux clarified his position somewhat, implicitly acknowledging that his somewhat impish use of such a problematic term from German Idealism conspired to undermine his project, and had to be jettisoned. Thus he proposes instead to employ the oxymoronic term "dianoetic intuition," meaning "the essential intertwining of a simple intuition and of a discursivity, a demonstration—both being entailed by the access to factuality."[5] As he goes on to explain, if in order to break out of the correlationist circle we were to merely posit an autonomous real axiomatically, the correlationist will always have the rejoinder that this supposedly autonomous real is still *posited* by thought. The only remaining strategy, Meillassoux says, is the one taken by *After Finitude,* namely to start from *within* the circle of correlationism and demonstrate how, in order to maintain its consistency, it must itself appeal to an absolute—facticity:

> Hence, the only way to the Real, according to me, is through a proof, a *demonstration*: a demonstration unveils that facticity is not an *ignorance* of the hidden reasons of all things but a *knowledge* of the absolute contingency of all things. The simple intuition of facticity is transmuted by a *dianoia*, by a demonstration, into an intuition of a radical exteriority...We have a *nous* unveiled by a *dianoia,* an intuition unveiled by a demonstration. This is why I called it an intellectual intuition: not, of course, because it is an intuition which creates its object, as Kant defined it, but because it is an intuition discovered by reasoning.[6]

---

[4] Ray Brassier, "The Enigma of Realism: On Quentin Meillassoux's *After Finitude,*" Collapse II, (2007): 46.

[5] Quentin Meillassoux, "Speculative Realism," *Collapse* III (2007): 433

[6] Ibid., 433-4.

A direct intuition could never give us access to the Real, because, as the correlationist would remind us, we only ever intuit our own phenomenal presentations. But a simple logical positing of the Real from which we then draw conclusions will not satisfy the correlationist either. So intellectual (or dianoetic) intuition in Meillassoux's sense is not an immediate, all-at-once revelation of the way things are but is the logical explication of a prior intuition. Through rational demonstration, this intuition (of facticity) is shown to be not what we thought it was. What had seemed to be the insurmountable limit to thought and the essence of finitude is, through dianoetic intuition, revealed to be the key to the very overcoming of finitude.

So methodologically speaking, any philosophy that attempts to break free of the correlationist circle must of necessity start from within it. In other words, a philosophy which seeks to transgress the Kantian limits of possible experience must nevertheless remain consistent with Kant in order to avoid charges of indulging in groundless metaphysical speculation. These two critical moments in Meillassoux's procedure—the immanent point of departure and the subsequent transgression through logical reasoning—I will argue, describe equally Jung's approach to the circle of correlation and his comparable endeavour to secure a "primary absolute" in order to guarantee further, derived speculative theses.

Archetypes and Noumena

As has often been noted by Jungian scholars, one understands nothing of Jung's concept of the archetypes, the prepersonal ideas, motifs and symbols recurrent throughout human history, if one takes it to be a doctrine asserting that every man is born with a set of innate fully-formed psychic images. Rather, in spite of occasional terminological inconsistencies which can lead to confusion, Jung draws a clear and unequivocal distinction between the archetypal *ideas* and the archetypes themselves, corresponding very closely to the Kantian division between phenomena and noumena. The term archetype applies exclusively to "those psychic contents which have not yet been submitted to conscious elaboration and are therefore an immediate datum of psychic experience."[7] The archetypes *stricto sensu* are hypothetical and irrepresentable deep-structure psychic patterns leading to certain types of universal mental experience, and we must only assume their existence from their effects and the way they are expressed in fantasmatic forms. Therefore the name archetype does not designate the myths, fables, fairytales or religious stories that are their conscious derivatives, and which already bear the trace of critical evaluation and distance. Nor does it refer to their "immediate manifestation, as we encounter it in dreams and visions," which "is much more individual, less understandable and more naïve than in myths."[8] Their appearance in dreams, hallucinations or fantasy is a truer representation than in myths and religious stories, which have become hardened into dogma over time, but they are still manifestations, and as such not the archetypes *themselves*:

> The archetype is essentially an unconscious content that is altered by becoming conscious and by being perceived, and it takes its colour from the individual consciousness in which it happens to appear.[9]

The archetypes in themselves are the same in every subject but the form or manner in which they appear is constituted and shaped by the personal history and circumstances of the subject, although generally proceeding according to familiar patterns. So rather than images sitting there deep within the unconscious of every person's psyche, they are patterns of behaviour making their appearance "only in the course of amplification."[10] The therapeutic process Jung calls

---

[7] Carl G. Jung, "Archetypes of the Collective Unconscious," in *The Collected Works of Carl Jung*, 9.1, trans. R.F.C. Hull (London: Routledge and Kegan Paul, 1973), 5.

[8] Ibid., 5.

[9] Ibid., 5.

[10] Carl G. Jung, "On the Nature of the Psyche," in *The Collected Works of Carl Jung*, 8, trans. R.F.C. Hull (London : Routledge and Kegan Paul, 1969), 205.

active imagination is the forcing or helping on its way of this course of amplification, delving into the unconscious psyche by way of active, spontaneous fantasy. On following these fantasmatic inventions where they lead of their own volition they invariably follow certain 'grooves' or psychic imprints, where archaic or mythological figures and motifs appear which betray their archetypal character. So they are not so much inborn, inherited ideas but rather the predisposition or propensity towards those ideas.

There is thus a clear, although implicit, correspondence between the archetypes and the Kantian rational ideas which govern our moral behaviour. These latter are not subject to temporal conditions, but are fixed and unchanging; all that is variable are the particular circumstances in which they make their appearance. They determine our actions only indirectly, via the categorical imperative, since immediate, direct access is constitutively denied to us. Likewise, the archetypes are timeless, inborn and sensuously unconditioned, however unlike the ideas of reason they are dynamic rather than fixed and *non-rational*. But just as we have practical but not theoretical proof of freedom and the other supersensible ideas, we have pragmatic proof of the archetypes without our being able to encounter them directly. Indeed were we to do so the consequences would no doubt be as catastrophic for our psyche as immediate access to the noumenal dimension is said to be. Gazing straight into this abyss would overwhelm and engulf our individual ego, obliterating us as a result.

Perhaps the closest Kantian parallel is with the early parodical work *Dreams of a Spirit-Seer*, in which Kant allows himself, in an ironic fashion, to speculate upon that which is beyond the bounds of human experience and knowledge. Here, through a satirical reading of the work of Swedish mystic Emmanuel Swedenborg (more of whom later), Kant posits in addition to the material world of sense an *immaterial*, or spirit world, which is a whole self-subsisting realm, "its parts in mutual conjunction and intercourse without the instrumentality of anything corporeal."[11] The human soul is said to be conjoined

---

[11] Immanuel Kant, *Dreams of a Spirit-Seer, Illustrated by Dreams of Metaphysics*,

in the two worlds at the same time, but so long as it is incarnated in a body it only *clearly* perceives the material world, having but a hazy intimation of the other side. As soon as the material body dies this link between the two territories is severed but the soul continues to exist in the spirit realm, unencumbered by materiality.

This spirit world bears an obvious resemblance to the collective unconscious, which we likewise inhabit alongside our personal psyche without being clearly aware of it. Furthermore, Kant (still in a satirical register) suggests that there can be communion between the two worlds and spiritual ideas can

> pass over into the personal consciousness of man, indeed, not immediately, but still in such a way that, according to the law of the association of ideas, they stir up those pictures which are related to them and awake analogous ideas of our senses. These, it is true, would not be spiritual conceptions themselves, but yet their symbols.[12]

What else is the archetypal idea other than a mediated, "analogous idea of the senses" that acts as a symbol for the archetype itself. Since these archetypes cannot be presented immediately but only indirectly evoked, this account corresponds very closely with the model of "aesthetic ideas" Kant develops in the *Critique of Judgement*. These are artistic presentations of the imagination which strive to give sensuous form to that which transgresses the limits of all possible experience, evoking something universal and absolute while manifesting it in an original and singular expression.

Not only is the collective unconscious "the repository of man's experience" but "at the same time the *prior condition of this experience*."[13] So archetypes are not merely the effect and deposits of ancestral events but at the same time they are significant determinants of such events. They are there-

---

trans. E.F. Goerwitz, Reprint Ed. (Indianapolis: Kessinger, 2003) 56.

[12] Kant, *Dreams of a Spirit-Seer*, 69.

[13] Carl G. Jung, "Two Essays on Analytical Psychology," in *The Collected Works of Carl Jung*, 7, trans. R.F.C. Hull (London : Routledge and Kegan Paul, 1966), 93.

fore both cause and effect, the snake eating its own tail. As Jung often notes, the constellating of archetypal ideas in the unconscious takes place as compensation for neglected parts of the subject's psyche, so that when they build up an irresistible force they impose themselves on the life of the subject, forcing them in a certain direction so as to reorient their psychic balance. "Perhaps—who knows?—these eternal images are what we mean by fate."[14]

Unus Mundus

Jung equates the irrepresentable nature of the archetypes with the smallest particles that physics deals with, whose nature can only be known by their effects. In both cases the physicist or psychologist is attempting to define an objective order of nature whose behaviour is altered by the fact of its being observed and can at best build up a probable model or construction of how these quantities behave based on their observable effects. In a situation where we have two entities or properties whose existence must be assumed but which cannot be represented or shown in person,

> there is always the possibility—which we tend to overlook—that it may not be a question of two or more factors but of one only. The identity or non-identity of two irrepresentable quantities is something that cannot be proved....Since psyche and matter are contained in one and the same world, and moreover are in continuous contact with one another and ultimately rest on irrepresentable, transcendental factors, it is not only possible but fairly probable, even, that psyche and matter are two different aspects of one and the same thing.[15]

Jung uses the term *"psychoid"* (always as an adjective, never a substantive) to describe these irrepresentable psychophysical

---

[14] Jung, "Two Essays on Analytical Psychology," 107.
[15] Carl G. Jung, "Synchronicity: An Acausal Connecting Principle," in *The Collected Works of Carl Jung*, 8, trans. R.F.C. Hull (London : Routledge and Kegan Paul, 1969), 214-5.

processes and this "one and the same thing" which is neither psychic nor material in nature but prior to both, antecedent to their differentiation, is named, using the terminology of alchemy and Medieval philosophy, *unus mundus*, meaning "one unitary world." Jung felt this hypothesis to be far from the obscure mysticism it can appear to be at first sight, but to be a legitimate response to empirical data, informed by developments in particle physics. Indeed, as is well known, Jung developed this concept in collaboration with the Nobel Prize winning physicist and quantum pioneer Wolfgang Pauli (a relationship generally passed over in silence in physics circles, or excused as the individual eccentricities of a great man that has no bearing on his work.)

For Jung there are certain privileged events or experiences which manifest this irrepresentable unity of psyche and world and which carry profound and far-reaching implications. Such events are those statistical anomalies attributed to chance or coincidence which seem to fall outside of any known causality and so elude rational explanation. A classic example is the well-documented case of the above-mentioned spiritualist Emanuel Swedenborg's dramatic vision of the great fire of Stockholm in 1759 while he was dining in Gothenburg, 250 miles away. It was only two days later that reports from Stockholm confirming Swedenborg's vision, down to the smallest detail, reached them in Gothenburg. Another famous example is one of Jung's own, from his analytic experience. A young patient of his was describing a dream she had had in which she was given a golden scarab. In the middle of her account Jung noticed a tapping against the window of his practice and opened the window, through which flew a rose-chafer beetle, "the nearest analogy to a golden scarab that one finds in our latitudes...which contrary to its usual habits had evidently felt an urge to get into a dark room at this particular moment."[16]

Although the two cases are very different in nature—for one thing the patient was not presenting her dream as if it were

---

[16] Jung, "Synchronicity," 438.

a prophetic vision—both are examples of the phenomenon Jung calls *synchronicity*, defined as the "coincidence of a psychic state with a corresponding objective process."[17] More everyday, commonly experienced instances are unlikely meaningful coincidences, such as thinking of a friend from whom you haven't heard in a long time immediately before receiving a telephone call from that same friend, or successions of chance events such as a number or word recurring again and again throughout the course of a day or number of days.

Jung does not try to explain away such occurrences with rational accounts, which we are all well versed in providing, but takes them at face value, wishing to account for them on their own merits. However, since these are singular, anomalous occurrences they are on principle incapable of being premeditated and examined in controlled conditions, for the experimental method by nature aims at establishing regular, repeatable events and thus ruling out of consideration the unique or rare results which are put down to chance deviations. Causality, says Jung, anticipating Meillassoux, is a *statistical* truth, not an absolute truth, and is only *generally* valid, when operating on the macrocosmic scale: "In the realm of very small quantities *prediction* becomes uncertain, if not impossible, because very small quantities no longer behave in accordance with the known natural laws."[18] So broadly speaking the course of nature can be unfailingly expected to follow the laws of cause and effect, but when we are dealing with particular events on a micro scale we can never predict the outcome with complete certainty. Jung also asserts, repeating an often-voiced limitation of the scientific procedure, that the answers given by nature in experimental practices are influenced by the questions asked, thus giving only a partial, statistical or average view of the natural world. So far, so relatively uncontroversial, but Jung draws from this the contentious conclusion that since causality is not an absolute there must be connections of events which are

---

[17] Jung, "Synchronicity," 480.
[18] Ibid., 421.

acausal, and thus demanding another connecting principle to account for them.

However, discovering such a principle poses considerable problems, for how can one base a theory on "[a]bsolutely unique or ephemeral events whose existence we have no means of either denying or proving?"[19] We can only rely on anecdotal evidence, which is inherently unreliable. Furthermore, how are we to distinguish genuinely synchronistic or acausal events from mere chance? Much of Jung's evidential foundations rest on J.B. Rhine's famous parapsychic experiments (later used by Bill Murray in *Ghostbusters*) which involve the experimenter turning up a series of cards with different geometrical patterns on them while the subject, who is separated by a screen, guesses the sign as each card is turned. In a significant number of cases the quantity of correct guesses exceeded to a highly improbable degree that which would be expected by chance. After the first set of experiments the distance between experimenter and subject was increased, even up to hundreds of miles, and much the same results were achieved. Yet more tests were done in which the subjects were told to predict the series of shapes in a set of cards that were only to be turned over at some point in the future, and still the amount of correct guesses exceeded chance probability. Since evidently neither time nor space is an inhibitory factor over the results Jung stresses that such phenomena can have nothing to do with the transmission of force, as the distance to be overcome would diminish its effects. What it points to in fact, Jung suggests, is a psychic relativity of time and space, and a "psychic function or psychic condition" which is capable of abolishing the time factor and the spatial factor.[20]

What these experiments, as well as the events referred to above, demonstrate according to Jung, is that "there are events which are related to one another…*meaningfully*, without there being any possibility of proving that this relation is a causal

---

[19] Jung, "Synchronicity," 422-3.
[20] Ibid., 433.

one."²¹ So we are not dealing with a relation of cause and effect, but rather a "falling together in time, a kind of simultaneity. Because of this factor of simultaneity, I have picked on the term 'synchronicity' to designate a hypothetical factor equal in rank to causality as a principle of explanation."²² It is important to note the term *hypothetical*, and the sense that synchronicity does not constitute a positive addition to knowledge but rather a regulative model to help guide an explanation of seemingly unaccountable phenomena.

Like Freud before him, Jung refers to Kant's conditions of sensibility and suggests, albeit in a very different way to Freud, that these conditions do not hold in the unconscious. They are "postulated" by the conscious mind, only becoming fixed concepts "in the course of [man's] mental development, thanks largely to the introduction of measurement."²³ This strongly recalls Heidegger's account of the genesis of our vulgar concepts of time and space, and the covering over of our primordial existential experience:

> They [time and space] are hypostatised concepts born of the discriminating activity of the conscious mind, and they form the indispensable coordinates for describing the behaviour of bodies in motion. They are, therefore, essentially psychic in origin, which is probably the reason that impelled Kant to regard them as *a priori* categories. But if space and time are only apparently properties of bodies in motion and are created by the intellectual needs of the observer, then their relativisation by psychic conditions is no longer a matter for astonishment but is brought within the bounds of possibility. This possibility presents itself when the psyche observes, not external bodies, but *itself*.²⁴

In the case of the parapsychic experiments, the subjects do not "see" the shapes on the cards through some magical power of clairvoyance, for the information does not reach

---

[21] Jung, "Synchronicity,", 435.
[22] Ibid., 435.
[23] Ibid., 436.
[24] Ibid., 436.

them from the outside but from the *inside*. Thus for Jung the distinction between inner and outer is not as clear-cut as it is for Freud and what the latter calls "reality testing"—assessing whether an internal perception corresponds to an external object—is not such a straightforward matter.[25] These inner processes can become drawn to the subject's attention by the seeming "impossibility" of the task, for as we saw above archetypal contents emerge in a state of impasse or hopelessness and it is generally with the archetypes that we are dealing in synchronistic phenomena. The dream of the golden scarab, for instance, occurred at a critical moment of deadlock in the patient's treatment, and the scarab is supposedly a familiar archetypal symbol of rebirth. Since the collective unconscious is universal and unlocalisable, and by nature the same across every case, there is the ever-present possibility that what is taking place at any one time in the collective psyche of an individual is "also happening in other individuals or organisms or things or situations."[26] This is what apparently seems to have occurred in the scarab dream; it was a conscious representation deriving from the causally inexplicable unconscious knowledge of the events of the following day's session with her doctor.

What this points to, according to Jung, is a form of "'knowledge,' or 'immediacy' of psychic images" which does not derive from sense perception.[27] The conscious interpretation of this unconscious knowledge comes upon the subject like any other spontaneous thought and can only be verified as a synchronistic occurrence after the physical event has been noted. This suggests that there may be many such examples of this inexplicable knowledge which are never recognised as such because the physical event with which it corresponds is not witnessed by the person to whom it has appeared. Many of

---

[25] Cf. Sigmund Freud, "A Metapsychological Supplement to the Theory of Dreams," in *Standard Edition of the Complete Psychological Works of Sigmund Freud*, 14, trans. James Strachey (London: Hogarth, 1957), 231-4.

[26] Jung, "Synchronicity," 481.

[27] Ibid., 446.

us must have experienced at some time or another that uneasy sensation of ominous precognition, and there are numerous stories, an example of which is given by Jung, where a person claims to have "sensed" or known when a loved one has died. What happens in such cases "is a kind of *creatio ex nihilo*, an act of creation that is not causally explicable," something ruled out as inconceivable by any finitist philosophy.[28] The two seemingly immovable impediments to such a notion are, firstly, that every psychical image or impression derives from sensibly given material, and so any exercising of the imagination amounts only to a reorganisation of this material, and secondly, that the necessary consistency of the time-series precludes it. As Kant argues, if something were to arrive out of nothing there would have had to have been a point of time in which it was *not*, but "to what will you fasten this point of time, if not to what is already there?"[29] Both objections, however, are overcome in the light of synchronistic phenomena: the first by the inexplicable non-sensible knowledge such experiences exhibit and the second by the "psychic relativity" of time and its abolition in the unconscious.

So what Jung is "finally compelled to assume" is that "there is in the unconscious something like an *a priori* knowledge or immediate presence of events which lacks any causal basis."[30] If such events were a case of causality then either the dream or vision which foresees a future or simultaneous event "caused" the event to take place in some telekinetic way or the physical event "caused" the psychical process, retroactively positing itself somehow. "In either case," says Jung, "we come up against the unanswerable question of transmission."[31] This question of transmission is, of course, that of the two possible relationships explaining the correspondence between object and representation that Kant gives in the letter to Marcus

---

[28] Jung, "Synchronicity," 480.

[29] Immanuel Kant, *Critique of Pure Reason*, trans. Werner S. Pluhar (Indianapolis: Hackett, 1996), A188 / B231.

[30] Jung, "Synchronicity," 447.

[31] Ibid., 483.

Herz. What Jung does, however, is to displace the terms of the question by presenting a *third* alternative that Kant did not, and indeed could not, have considered.

This third alternative relies on the *unus mundus* hypothesis, suggesting that the two related terms—the psychical experience and the physical event—take place on another plane prior to their differentiation, and both the knowledge and the event itself could be said to be its respective manifestations. In other words, "the same living reality [is] expressing itself in the psychic state as in the physical."[32] So with regard to the two alternatives Kant poses, this would be neither a receptive nor a productive intuition, but still nevertheless a form of intelligible correspondence between thought and object, one that is not mediated through the senses. As such the problem of transmission is overcome, but what exactly forms the correspondence between the two states if it is not a case of causation? Jung's answer to this question postulates an *a priori* "meaning" or equivalence, which exists independently of the psyche:

> If—and it seems plausible—the meaningful coincidence or "cross-connection" of events cannot be explained causally, then the connecting principle must lie in the *equal significance* of parallel events; in other words, their *tertium comparationis* is *meaning*. We are so accustomed to regard meaning as a psychic process or content that it never enters our heads to suppose that it could also exist outside the psyche. But we do know at least enough about the psyche not to attribute to it any magical power, and still less can we attribute any magical power to the conscious mind. If, therefore, we entertain the hypothesis that one and the same (transcendental) meaning might manifest itself simultaneously in the human psyche and in the arrangement of an external and independent event, we at once come into conflict with the conventional scientific and epistemological views.[33]

So for Jung this is the *least* mystical, most scientifically rig-

---

[32] Jung, "Synchronicity," 452.
[33] Ibid., 482.

orous explanation that does justice to the empirical data without ascribing to the psyche "a power that far exceeds its empirical range of action," namely intellectual intuition.[34] However, by avoiding attributing *this* particular supernatural power to the psyche Jung risks ascribing to it another, equally extravagant faculty. For when the threshold of consciousness is sufficiently lowered so that unconscious, archetypal contents can penetrate into our conscious mind this can grant us access to what Jung calls, in quotation marks for caution, "absolute knowledge," pointing to "the presence in the microcosm of macrocosmic events."[35] The microcosm here, which like the Leibnizian monad reflects the whole of reality, is the collective unconscious.

This is speculative language which must necessarily sound somewhat fantastic because it aims to render intelligible to consciousness something which is essentially inconceivable to it. So in the case of Swedenborg's prophetic vision, for instance, we are not dealing with paranormal foreknowledge, or still less psychokinesis, but with two distinct manifestations of the *same event* that are connected by "meaning" or significance. Since in the unconscious psyche time and space no longer apply and "knowledge finds itself in a space-time continuum in which space is no longer space, nor time time," then if the unconscious should "develop or maintain a potential in the direction of consciousness, it is then possible for parallel events to be perceived or 'known.'"[36] Such a knowledge cannot be deliberately utilised, however, since such events are by their nature rare and incapable of being premeditated.

Towards a Neutral Language

For Jung, the psyche is not exclusively localised to cognitive activity, it rests also on "a nervous substrate like the sympathetic system, which is absolutely different from the

---

[34] Jung, "Synchronicity," 482.

[35] Ibid., 489.

[36] Ibid., 481.

cerebrospinal system in point of origin and function, [and which] can evidently produce thoughts and perceptions just as easily as the latter."[37] Jung illustrates this with anecdotal accounts of people in comas "seeing" or "knowing" what is going on around them and giving detailed reports of what they saw upon regaining consciousness, as well as the behaviour of lower organisms such as bees, which in their much-discussed communicative movements (or dances) display "transcerebral thought and perception."[38] This non-cerebral, bodily form of knowledge is, for Jung, an exemplar of the psychoid property inherent in matter so that "thought," broadly conceived, is not confined to the human mind but pervades that which is its "object." But this is not a *simple* panpsychism, suggesting that water, plants or rocks possess a rudimentary form of conscious perception, although it is undoubtedly redolent of it. For such a notion could still be considered a dualism, extending the capacity for thought to inanimate objects while upholding its exceptional status.[39] Rather, Jung's ontology levels down the disjunction between "mere thought" and positive being, since it is only for a system which strictly upholds such a distinction that the synchronicity phenomena remain inconceivable. These latter do not erect a miraculous bridge across two properties, establishing a momentary sympathetic connection between thought and external reality while forever keeping them separated by an irreducible chasm, but point to a way of re-conceiving the relationship itself. For a bridge would merely be a means of passage or communication between isolated territories, and this correspondence can only be conceived according to the relation of causality. Rather, Jung offers us a way of escaping the problem, appearing to show "that there is some possibility of getting rid of the incommensurability between the

---

[37] Jung, "Synchronicity," 510-11.

[38] Ibid., 511.

[39] As a caveat it should be noted that panpsychism is a far from homogeneous concept and the charge of dualism would not necessarily apply to all of its variants.

observed and the observer. The result, in that case would be a unity of being which would have to be expressed in terms of a new conceptual language—'neutral language,' as W. Pauli once called it."[40] Neutral because it does not distinguish or discriminate between what is inner and what is outer, the knower and the known.

Just as in Jung's analytic treatment the archetypes are constellated at a point of impasse to disclose a hitherto unthinkable means of escape, so Jung himself shows us a line of advance out of the impasse of finitude. As long as thought is considered as an ontological exception we will be forever barred access to the in-itself. The postulate of psychophysical synchronisation, then, simultaneously accomplishes two seemingly contradictory demands: Firstly, by redrawing the ontological lines of demarcation it abolishes the special status of thought, bringing it down from its lonely tower and is thus consistent with cognitive science's insistence on treating consciousness as fundamentally no different from any other physical phenomenon. But secondly, in doing so, thought is not *reduced* but greatly enhanced and set free from finite limits and its enslavement to receptivity. In passing it could be noted that this thesis proposes a new reading of the Parmenidean dictum that thinking and being are the same, without resorting to an idealist privileging of the former over the latter.

The obvious objection presents itself that this is merely a variation on the procedure Meillassoux calls "*absolutising the correlation*."[41] What I have tried to show here however, is that far from an absolutised reciprocity of thinking and being, Jung's psychoid absolute takes place *prior* to the correlation and names a stratum of being antecedent to the differentiation into subject and object, thought and the given. Neither side of the relationship can be conceived in such terms—thought is not yet thought, being is not yet *given* to thought; this is why a new "neutral language" is required. To return to those two founding

---

[40] Jung, "Synchronicity," 512.
[41] Meillassoux, *After Finitude*, 37.

moments of Meillassoux's discourse, it can now be seen that his procedure could be quite comfortably mapped onto that of Jung. As we have shown, Jung too recognises the necessity of remaining consistent with Kantian limits to avoid charges of dogmatism, while breaking free of them to allow thought to exceed itself and access an absolute independent of and prior to thought. Or in Meillassoux's terms, Jung escapes the correlationist circle from within rather than merely positing an autonomous real. Secondly, just as Meillassoux proceeds to access an absolute truth via the logical explication of an intuition (of facticity), so Jung's absolute is approached via rational demonstration following the intuition of causally inexplicable phenomena. In both cases we run up against the "unanswerable question of transmission" but it is boldly and convincingly sidestepped through an imaginative "speculative solution."[42] And finally, is the thesis of *unus mundus* really any more outlandish or counter-intuitive than Meillassoux's hyper-chaos or Graham Harman's vicarious causation? It is perhaps time for Jung to be re-claimed for philosophy and rescued from his most fervent New Age admirers as much as his fiercest rationalist detractors.

---

[42] The name of a piece of music by Florian Hecker composed in collaboration with Urbanomic, released on Editions Mego, 2011.

Über stellvertretende Verursachung[1]

Graham Harman

übersetzt von Sergey Sistiaga

Trotz der anhaltenden Unbeliebtheit der Metaphysik, sowie des Realismus innerhalb der kontinentalen Tradition, entwirft dieser Artikel den Umriss einer realistischen Metaphysik. Anstelle eines trüben Materialismus geistloser Atome und Billardkugeln, der üblicherweise heraufbeschworen wird, um den Spaß in der Philosophie zu verderben, werde ich einen seltsamen Realismus *verteidigen*. Dieses Modell beinhaltet eine Welt, vollgepackt mit gespenstigen, realen Objekten, die sich gegenseitig aus unerforschlicher Tiefe Signale senden und unfähig sind sich einander ganz zu berühren. Hier besteht eine offenkundige Beziehung zur Tradition, die als Okkasionalismus bekannt ist und die als Erste nahelegte, dass eine direkte Wechselwirkung zwischen Entitäten unmöglich sei. Eine andere klare Verbindung besteht zur verwandten skeptischen Tradition, die Objekte als nebeneinanderliegend und ohne direkte Verbindung betrachtet, obwohl die betreffenden Objekte hier eher menschliche Wahrnehmungen, denn reale unabhängige Objekte sind. Dennoch wird dieser Artikel die Lösung des Problems durch eine einsame, magische Superentität,

---

[1] Übersetzung von Graham Harmans Aufsatz: *On Vicarious Causation*. Dieser wurde zuerst publiziert in: *Collapse II* (March 2007), S.171-205 (A.d.Ü.).

Graham Harman – Über stellvertretende Verursachung

die verantwortlich für jede Relation ist (sei es Gott für Malebranche und seine irakischen Vorläufer oder der menschliche Geist für Skeptiker, Empiristen und Idealisten), zugunsten einer stellvertretenden Verursachung verwerfen, welche lokal über jeden Teil des Kosmos verteilt ist. Obwohl ihre Seltsamkeit eher zu Verwunderung als zu Widerstand führen mag, ist stellvertretende Verursachung nicht irgendein autistischer Mondstrahl, der durch das Fenster eines Asyls eindringt. Stattdessen ist sie die Startrampe für eine rigoros post-heideggerianische Philosophie einerseits, wie die angemessene Rückkehr zum ehrwürdigen Problem der Kommunikation zwischen Substanzen andererseits.

~

Der Begriff der „stellvertretenden Verursachung"[2] besteht aus zwei Teilen, die beide gegen den Strich der heutigen Philosophie gehen.[3] Kausalität war seit dem 17. Jahrhundert selten ein eigenständiges Thema der Forschung. Die vermeintlich große Debatte zwischen skeptischen und transzendentalen Philosophen über Kausalität ist bestenfalls ein Streit über das Ja oder Nein der Frage, ob kausale Notwendigkeit existiere oder nicht und in der Praxis nur eine Auseinandersetzung, ob diese erkannt werden könne oder nicht. Was fehlte, war eine aktive Auseinandersetzung über die eigentliche Natur der Kausalität als solcher. Folgendes wird heute für selbstverständlich gehalten: Ein Objekt übt Kraft auf ein anderes aus und bewirkt eine Änderung seiner physikalischen Lage oder anderer Eigenschaften. Niemand sieht auch nur die Möglichkeit über die Interaktion zwischen Feuer und Baumwolle zu sprechen, da sich die Philosophie ausschließlich mit der alleinigen Kluft zwischen Mensch und Welt beschäftigt, sei es auch nur um diese zu verneinen. Unbelebte Beziehungen wurden den Laboratorien zur Erforschung überlassen,

---

[2] Übersetzung von *vicarious causation*: Das englische *vicarious*, vom lateinischen *vicarius* = stellvertretend stammend, wurde mit „stellvertretend" übersetzt (A.d.Ü.).

[3] Dieses Konzept wurde zuerst in meinem Buch; *Guerrilla Metaphysics. Phenomenology and the Carpentry of Things*, Chicago, Open Court 2005, eingeführt.

wo deren metaphysischer Charakter offen verworfen wird. Das Thema der Verursachung in der Philosophie wieder zu beleben, bedeutet die Dominanz Kants kopernikanischer Revolution mitsamt ihrem einzigen und einsamen Graben zwischen Menschen und allem anderen zurückzuweisen. Obwohl ich behaupten werde, dass reale Objekte jenseits des sinnlichen Zugangs der Menschen existieren, sollte dies nicht mit Kants Unterscheidung zwischen Phaenomena und Noumena verwechselt werden. Während Kants Unterscheidung nur für Menschen alleine besteht, behaupte ich, dass sich eine Billardkugel vor einer anderen nicht weniger verbirgt, wie die Billardkugel an sich sich vor Menschen verbirgt. Wenn ein Hagelsturm Weinhänge verwüstet oder Wellen in einem Teich schlägt, dann sind diese Relationen[4] der Philosophie genauso würdig, wie der endlose Disput über die Kluft oder Nicht-Kluft zwischen Sein und Denken. Weder Kant noch Hegel oder deren heutige Cousins haben etwas über die Kollision von Billardkugeln an sich zu sagen. Im vergangenen Jahrhundert wurde Parmenides' Doktrin, dass Sein und Denken dasselbe seien, von Husserl impliziert, von Heidegger explizit gemacht und nachdrücklich von Badiou wieder betont. Aber diese Gleichsetzung von Sein und Denken muss abgelehnt werden, da sie uns in einer Mensch-Welt-Kupplung stranden lässt, die die Erfolge vergangener Jahre bloß nachstellt. Das Problem der Kausalität wiederzubeleben bedeutet aus einer epistemologischen Sackgasse auszubrechen und die metaphysische Frage, was Relation bedeutet, wieder zu beleben. Neben der Verursachung gibt es auch noch den „stellvertretenden" Teil des Begriffs, der anklingen lässt, dass Relationen niemals direkt auf die autonome Realität ihrer Komponenten stoßen. Auch nach tausend Jahren ist „Substanz" der beste Name für eine solche Realität. Die weitverbreitete Zurückhaltung gegenüber der Substanz ist nichts anderes als die Abscheu vor gewissen unzutreffenden Substanzmodellen und solche Modelle können ersetzt werden. Neben Substanz

---

[4] Die Worte „Relation" und „Beziehung" werden synonym für das englische *relation* verwendet (A.d.Ü.).

wird der Begriff der „Objekte"[5] benutzt, um auf unabhängige Realitäten aller Art zu verweisen. Mit dem Vorteil, dass dieser Begriff Platz für zeitliche und künstliche Objekte schafft, die zu oft vom Rang der Substanz ausgeschlossen wurden.

Indem dieser Artikel jedes Privileg menschlichen Zugangs zur Welt zurückweist und die Frage des menschlichen Bewusstseins auf genau die gleiche Grundlage stellt, wie ein Duell zwischen Kanarienvögeln, Mikroben, Erdbeben, Atomen und Teer, könnte man meinen er höre sich an wie eine Verteidigung des wissenschaftlichen Naturalismus, der alles auf physikalische Ereignisse reduziert. Aber der Begriff „stellvertretend" wurde dazu entworfen, allen Formen des Naturalismus entgegenzuwirken, indem er darauf hinweist, dass wir immer noch keine Ahnung haben, wie physische Relationen (oder jeder anderen Art) an erster Stelle möglich sind. Denn wie ich behaupten werde, verbergen sich Objekte endlos voreinander und fügen sich ihre Stöße nur über einen Vikar[6] oder Mittelsmann zu. Die Philosophie befindet sich seit einigen Jahrhunderten in der Defensive gegenüber den Naturwissenschaften und genießt nun weniger gesellschaftliches Prestige und hat überraschenderweise einen engeren Gegenstandsbereich. Ein kurzer Blick auf die Geschichte zeigt, dass dies nicht immer der Fall gewesen ist. Um die Offensive wieder aufzunehmen, müssen wir nur den lange bestehenden Trend umkehren, der besagt auf alle Spekulation über Objekte zu verzichten. Und freiwillig für eine Ausgangsperre für immer kleinere Gettos rein menschlicher Wirklichkeiten eintreten: Sprache, Text, politische Macht. Stellvertretende Verursachung befreit uns von einer solchen Gefangennahme, indem sie uns ins Herz der unbelebten Welt, ob künstlich oder natürlich, zurückführt. Die Einzigartigkeit

---

[5] Im Folgendem werden die Wörter „Objekt" und „Gegenstand" synonym für das englische *object* verwendet (A.d.Ü.).

[6] Im Original handelt es sich um ein Wortspiel bestehend aus der Kombination des Adjektivs *vicarious* und dem Substantiv *vicar*. Ein Vikar ist ein Stellvertreter. Üblicherweise ein ständiger oder zeitweiliger Stellvertreter einer anderen Amtsperson innerhalb der kath. Kirche. In der Schweiz kann ein Vikar auch Stellvertreter eines Lehrers sein (A.d.Ü.).

der Philosophie wird nicht durch die Abschottung einer erlesenen Zone menschlicher Wirklichkeit, die durch die Wissenschaft unantastbar bleibt, gewonnen, sondern durch die Behandlung derselben Welt, nur auf andere Art und Weise. In klassischen Worten ausgedrückt müssen wir einmal mehr über Verursachung spekulieren und zugleich deren Reduktion auf effiziente Verursachung verbieten. Stellvertretende Verursachung, von der die Wissenschaft momentan nichts weiß, ist dem, was man formale Ursache nennt näher. Zu sagen, dass die formale Ursache stellvertretend operiert, heißt, dass Formen einander nicht direkt berühren, sich aber irgendwie verschmelzen, fusionieren und in einen gemeinsamen Raum dekomprimieren, von dem alle teilweise abwesend sind. Meine Behauptung ist, dass sich zwei Entitäten gegenseitig nur beeinflussen, wenn sie sich im Inneren einer Dritten treffen, wo sie nebeneinander existieren, bis etwas passiert, das ihnen erlaubt in Wechselwirkung zu treten. In diesem Sinne ist die Theorie der stellvertretenden Verursachung eine Theorie der geschmolzenen Innenkerne von Objekten—eine Art Plattentektonik der Ontologie.

1. Zwei Arten von Objekten

Während die phänomenologische Bewegung Husserls und Heideggers zu wenig unternahm den Idealismus des vorangegangenen Clusters großer Philosophen zu überwinden, zeigen sie und ihre Nachfolger oftmals ein neuartiges Interesse an spezifischen und konkreten Entitäten. Briefkästen, Hämmer, Zigaretten und Seidenkleidung sind in der Phänomenologie auf eine Weise zu Hause, wie sie es niemals für die früheren klassischen Figuren des deutschen Denkens waren. Auch wenn Husserl und Heidegger dem menschlichen Dasein als dem Mittelpunkt der Philosophie zu verhaftet bleiben, so heben doch beide, leise und jeder in unterschiedlicher Manier, Objekte in die Hauptrolle. Während Husserl sein System auf intentionalen oder ideellen Objekten basiert (welche ich in sinnliche Objekte umtaufen werde), stellt

Graham Harman – *Über stellvertretende Verursachung*

Heidegger mithilfe seiner berühmten Zeug-Untersuchung[7] reale Objekte wieder für die Philosophie her. Es wird selten erkannt, dass diese zwei Objekttypen beide unterschiedlich und ergänzend sind. Wird das Zusammenspiel zwischen realen und sinnlichen Objekten ernst genommen, liefert es der Ontologie ein radikal neues Thema.

In Heideggers Zeug-Untersuchung, die seine Gegner nicht weniger fasziniert wie seine Verbündete, finden wir vielleicht die beständigste Einsicht der Philosophie des 20. Jahrhunderts. Unser ursprüngliches Verhältnis zu Objekten liegt nicht in der Wahrnehmung oder unserem theoretisieren über sie, sondern einfach in unserem sich auf sie Verlassen für ein tiefer liegendes Ziel. Dieser erste Schritt ist zwar nützlich genug, verfehlt aber das Wesen des heideggerschen Durchbruchs, den selbst er nie ganz begreift. Bleiben wir auf dieser Stufe stehen, könnte es den Anschein haben, dass Heidegger bloß behauptet, alle Theorie sei in der Praxis begründet und wir bräuchten eine alltägliche Beziehung zu Leoparden oder Säuren, bevor wir sie anstarrten oder eine Wissenschaft über sie entwickelten. Man halte fest, dass selbst unsere praktische Bezugnahme zu diesen Objekten es versäumt diese vollständig zu erfassen. Der Stammesangehörige, der mit dem gottgleichen Leopard lebt oder der Gefangene, der geheime Nachrichten mit Zitronensaft schreibt, sind der dunklen

---

[7] „Zeug-Untersuchung" ist lediglich die Übersetzung des vom Verfasser dieses Artikels als *tool-analysis* bezeichneten Konzepts. Dieses ist so bei Heidegger oder in der Heideggerforschung nicht zu finden, stellt aber den zentralen Interpretationszugang des Verfassers zu Heidegger dar. Die *tool-analysis* bezieht sich auf die Unterscheidung zwischen der „Vorhandenheit" und „Zuhandenheit" von Gegenständen oder Zeug, wie dem berühmten Hammer Heideggers. Für Harman ist Heideggers Untersuchung des Zeugs nicht als Sieg der Praxis über die Theorie oder sprachlicher Zeichen über die „Dinge an sich" zu deuten, sondern im Gegenteil, als Weg zu den Gegenständen ansich zurück. „Zuhandenheit" bezieht sich für Harman nicht auf Gegenstände, insofern diese menschlichen Zwecken dienen, sondern auf Objekte, die sich theoretischem wie praktischem Zugang der Menschen entziehen und die eine eigene, nie fassbare, Realität besitzen, die auf keinem Weg vollständig erschöpft oder gekannt werden kann. Siehe dazu: Harman, G., *Tool-Being: Heidegger and the Metaphysics of Objects*, Open Court Publishing Company 2002, hier: S.1-2. (A.d.Ü.).

Realität dieser Objekte nicht weniger weit entfernt, als der Wissenschaftler, der sie anstarrt. Wenn beide—Wahrnehmung und Theorie—Entitäten objektivieren und sie zu einseitigen Karikaturen ihrer tosenden Tiefe reduzieren, dann ist dasselbe für praktische Manipulation wahr. Wir verzerren, wenn wir sehen und wir verzerren, wenn wir benutzen. Auch ist die Sünde der Karikatur kein rein menschliches Laster. Hunde haben keinen Kontakt mit der vollen Realität des Knochens, genauso wenig wie Heuschrecken mit Getreidestängeln, Viren mit Zellen, Steine mit Fensterscheiben oder Planeten mit Monden. Es ist nicht das menschliche Bewusstsein, das die Realität verzerrt, sondern Relationalität *per se*. Heideggers Zeug-Untersuchung gibt uns unbewussterweise die tiefstmögliche Darstellung des klassischen Risses zwischen Substanz und Relation. Wenn etwas „vorhanden" ist, bedeutet dies schlicht, dass es durch irgendeine Art der Relation registriert wird: ob sinnlich, theoretisch, praktisch oder rein kausal. „Zuhanden" zu sein bedeutet nicht im engeren Sinne nützlich zu sein, sondern sich in unterirdische Tiefen zu entziehen, auf die sich andere Objekte stützen, ohne diese jemals voll zu sondieren oder auszuloten.[8] Wenn Objekte uns verfehlen erfahren wir eine Negation ihrer zugänglichen Konturen und werden uns gewahr, dass sich das Objekt all dem was wir von ihm erfassen entzieht. Dieses Dilemma gibt den Anlass zum Thema der stellvertretenden Verursachung. Denn wenn Objekte sich allen Relationen entziehen, könnten wir uns wundern, wie sie überhaupt Kontakt herstellen. Heideggers Zeug-Untersuchung öffnet die Tore für einen neuen seltsamen Realismus, in dem Entitäten vage vom Meeresgrund aufflimmern: die unfähig sind Kontakt herzustellen, aber es trotzdem irgendwie schaffen.

Eine andere Art Objekt bildet die Basis für Husserls Philosophie. Trotz komplizierter Anstrengungen Husserl von Anschuldigungen des Idealismus freizusprechen, grenzt er die Philosophie zu einem Raum purer Idealität ein. Die Phän-

---

[8] Für eine detaillierte Interpretation von Heiderggers „Zeug-Untersuchung," siehe mein erstes Buch: *Tool-Being: Heidegger and the Metaphysics of* Objects, Chicago, Open Court 2002.

omenologie kann nicht darüber sprechen, wie ein Gegenstand einen anderen zerbricht oder verbrennt, da dies die Welt der Macht wissenschaftlicher Erklärungen ausliefern würde, die ausschließlich naturalistische Theorien verwendet. Die einzige rigorose Methode besteht für Husserl darin, zu beschreiben, wie die Welt dem Bewusstsein vor aller solcher Theorie gegeben ist. Philosophie wird zur Studie von Phänomenen, nicht von realen Objekten. Nichtsdestoweniger sind Phänomene Objekte: in einem neuen idealen Sinne. Denn was wir in der Wahrnehmung erfahren sind keine körperlosen Eigenschaften, wie der Empirist meint; stattdessen begegnen wir einer in Stücke zerbrochenen Welt. Bäume, Briefkästen, Flugzeuge oder Skelette liegen vor uns ausgebreitet, von denen jedes spezifische Stimmungen herbeiführt und mit verschiedenen untergeordneten Eigenschaften funkelt. Da wir nur über den phänomenalen Bereich sprechen, macht es nichts aus, ob es sich bei diesen Dingen um Halluzinationen handelt; selbst Illusionen leisten die ehrliche Arbeit, unsere Wahrnehmung in diskrete Zonen zu organisieren. Es ist bereits anzumerken, dass sinnliche Objekte ein anderes Schicksal als reale Objekte teilen. Während echte Zebras und Leuchttürme sich direktem Zugang entziehen, entziehen sich ihre sinnlichen Gegenstücke nicht im geringsten. Denn hier ist ein Zebra vor mir. Zugegebenermaßen kann ich es aus einer unendlichen Vielfalt von Winkeln und Abständen betrachten, in Trauer oder Begeisterung, während eines Sonnenuntergangs oder im peitschenden Regen und keiner dieser Momente erschöpft alle möglichen Wahrnehmungen davon. Trotzdem ist das Zebra als Ganzes in allen möglichen partiellen Profilen für mich da; ich sehe direkt durch diese hindurch und schaue auf es, als ein vereinigtes Objekt. Obwohl gewisse spezifische visuelle oder konzeptuelle Profile des Zebras für uns nötig sind, um es zu erfahren, liegt das vereinigte sinnliche Zebra auf einer tieferen Ebene der Wahrnehmung, als diese vorübergehenden und veränderbaren Bilder. Jedes sinnliche Profil ist auf dem vereinigten Zebra-Objekt verkrustet, wie ein Überzug aus Salzlake. Während sich reale Objekte entziehen, liegen sinnliche Objekte direkt vor uns, über und über vereist mit einer wirbelnden und überflüssigen äußeren Schale. Dieser Unterschied aber scheint den sinnlichen Objekten den entgegengesetzten kausalen Status von realen Objekten zu geben. Vorausgesetzt, dass reale Objekte sich niemals direkt berühren, können deren Kausalbeziehungen nur stellvertretend sein. Sinnliche Objekte dagegen, weit davon entfernt sich zu entziehen, existieren von Beginn an nebeneinander in demselben Wahrnehmungsraum, da wir zahlreichen Phänomenen gleichzeitig begegnen. Dies stellt das gegenteilige Problem zur stellvertretenden Verursachung dar: namentlich, warum nicht alle Erscheinungen sofort in einem einzigen Klumpen verschmelzen? Hier muss es ein unbekanntes Blockadeprinzip zwischen ihnen geben. Wenn reale Objekte stellvertretende Verursachung verlangen, dann sind sinnliche Objekte einer gepufferten Verursachung ausgesetzt, in der ihre Interaktionen teilweise gedämmt und nicht voll entwickelt sind.

Die Lage ist verworren, dennoch sollte der allgemeine Pfad dieses Artikels bereits klar sein. Reale Objekte entziehen sich, kausaler Verbindungen beraubt, in dunkle gähnende Unterwelten zurück. Im Kontrast dazu neigen sinnliche Objekte derart dazu mit ihren Nachbarn zu interagieren, dass wir uns wundern, warum sie dies nicht jeden Augenblick tun. Der einzige Ort im Kosmos, wo Wechselwirkungen auftreten, ist in anderen Worten der sinnliche, phänomenale Bereich. Gegen Philosophien, die die Oberfläche als formal oder steril betrachten und kausale Kraft nur schattigen Tiefen gewähren, müssen wir die gegenteilige Ansicht verteidigen: Diskrete, autonome Form liegt nur in der Tiefe, während dramatische Kraft und Wechselwirkung entlang der Oberfläche fließen. Alle Beziehungen sind oberflächlich. Aus diesem Grund müssen wir herausfinden, wie reale Objekte in den Bereich der Erscheinungen durchstoßen, dem einzigen Ort, an dem man Verbindungen eingeht. Die vielfältigen Eruptionen realer Objekte in die Sinnlichkeit liegen Seite an Seite vor sofortiger Wechselwirkung gepuffert. Irgendetwas muss auf der sinnlichen Ebene passieren, das ihnen erlaubt in Kontakt zu treten, genauso wie bei korrosiven, Seite an Seite in einer

Bombe liegenden Chemikalien, die nur durch einen dünnen Film getrennt werden, der über die Zeit hinweggefressen wird oder von entfernten Signalen durchbrochen wird.

2. Ein Puzzlespiel

Es ist bekannt, dass Husserl Wert auf die Intentionalität des Bewusstseins legt. Wir sind uns immer etwas bewusst, immer auf ein bestimmtes Haus fokussiert, eine Kiefer, einen Wasserball oder einen Stern und in der Tat auf viele solche Objekte zugleich. Es ist nicht weithin bekannt, dass Husserl auch über das schicksalhafte Paradox stolpert, wonach Intentionalität beides sei, eines und zwei. In einem ersten Sinne ist meine Begegnung mit einer Kiefer eine vereinigte Relation. Wir können von der Begegnung als Ganzem sprechen und dieses Ganze widerstrebt einer erschöpfenden Beschreibung. Aber in einem anderen Sinne fusioniere ich klarerweise nicht mit dem Baum in einen einzigen massiven Klumpen; er bleibt in der Wahrnehmung von mir unterschieden. Daraus ergibt sich das seltsame Resultat, dass wir beide in meiner Intention des Baumes das Innere der gesamten intentionalen Relation bewohnen. Diese scheinbar trockene Beobachtung Husserls hat nicht viel Interesse bei seinen Lesern entfacht. Sogar dann, wenn sie kombiniert mit Heideggers Einsicht in den Entzug realer Objekte hinter jede Relation alle Teile für eine neue Philosophie liefert.

Um es zu wiederholen, die Kiefer und ich sind separate Gegenstände im Innern eines Dritten liegend: der Intention als Ganzem. Es gibt aber eine faszinierende Asymmetrie unter den Mitgliedern dieses Trios. Wir kommen nicht umhin zu bemerken, dass von den zwei Objekten im Inneren eines Dritten lebend, ich ein reales Objekt bin, die Kiefer aber ein bloß sinnliches. Das Ich, aufrichtig vertieft in die Dinge, die es wahrnimmt, ist nicht das Ich von anderen aus gesehen, sondern eher das reale Ich, da mein Leben in diesem Moment tatsächlich darin besteht von diesen Erscheinungen beschäftig zu werden und nicht darin ein sinnliches Objekt für den Blick anderer oder sogar für meinen eigenen zu sein. Im Gegensatz dazu bewohnt die reale Kiefer nicht die Intention, da der echte Baum (angenommen es gibt so ein Ding) außerhalb jeder Relation zu ihr steht und sich in Tiefen zurückzieht, in die niemals Außenstehende eindringen. Schließlich muss die Intention als Ganzes eher als reales Objekt klassifiziert werden, denn als sinnliches Objekt: Denn selbst wenn meine Intention des Baumes die verkommenste Halluzination darstellen sollte, so ist die Intention selbst tatsächlich im Gange, völlig unabhängig davon, ob sie sich mit etwas Außenstehendem in Beziehung setzt. Um zusammenzufassen; wir haben eine reale Intention, deren Kern von einem realen Ich und einer sinnlichen Kiefer bewohnt wird. Zusätzlich ist da auch ein entzogener realer, außerhalb der Intention liegender Baum (oder etwas, das wir dafürhalten), der aber fähig ist, diese Intention auf noch unbekannten Wegen zu affizieren. Zu guter Letzt erscheint der sinnliche Baum niemals in der Form eines nackten Wesens, sondern immer mit verschiedenen Sorten von Lärm verkrustet. Woanders habe ich es „schwarzes Rauschen" genannt, um hervorzuheben, dass es stark strukturiert ist und keine Art formloses Chaos, nahegelegt vom „weißen Rauschen" des Fernsehers oder Radios.[9] Schwarzes Rauschen scheint anfänglich in drei Varianten vorzukommen. Erstens besitzt der sinnliche Baum zentrale oder essenzielle Qualitäten[10], die immer zu ihm gehören müssen, unter Androhung der Strafe, dass das intentionale Agens es nicht länger als dasselbe Ding ansieht. Zweitens hat der Baum akzidentelle Eigenschaften, die von Moment zu Moment an seiner Oberfläche schimmern, ohne unsere Identifikation von ihm als ein und demselben zu beeinträchtigen. Schließlich steht die Kiefer in Beziehung zu unzähligen peripheren Objekten, die dieselbe Intention bevölkern (benachbarte Bäume, Berge, Wild, Hasen, Nebelwolken).

Wir sollten fünf verschiedene Relationsarten zwischen all diesen Objekten festhalten:

---

[9] *Guerrilla Metaphysics*, S. 183ff.

[10] Die Wörter „Eigenschaft" und „Qualität" werden synonym für das englische *quality* benutzt (A.d.Ü.).

Graham Harman – *Über stellvertretende Verursachung*

1. Enthaltensein. Die Intention als Ganzes enthält beides, das reale Ich und den sinnlichen Baum.

2. Nachbarschaft. Die verschieden sinnlichen Objekte in einer Intention liegen Seite an Seite, ohne sich einander zu beinträchtigen. Nur manchmal verschmelzen oder vermischen sie sich. Innerhalb gewisser Grenzen kann jeder Nachbar des sinnlichen Objektes vermischt und variiert werden, ohne die Identität dieses Objekts zu beschädigen, genauso wie wenn wabernde Nebelschwaden nicht mit meinem Blickpunkt auf den Baum interferieren.

3. Aufrichtigkeit. Genau in diesem Augenblick bin ich in den sinnlichen Baum vertieft oder von ihm fasziniert, selbst wenn meine Haltung zu ihm völlig zynisch und manipulativ sein sollte. Ich beinhalte nicht den sinnlichen Baum, denn das ist die Rolle der vereinigten Intention, die die Bühne meiner Aufrichtigkeit liefert, ohne mit ihr identisch zu sein. Und ich bin nicht bloß mit dem Baum benachbart, da er mich in der Tat auf eine Weise berührt, die mein ganzes Leben ausfüllt. Ich gebe meine Energie aus, um den Baum ernst zu nehmen, wohingegen der sinnliche Baum mir diesen Gefallen nicht erwidern kann, da er nicht real ist.

4. Verbindung. Die Intention als Ganze muss aus einer realen Verbindung realer Objekte erwachsen, wenngleich einer indirekten Verbindung. Immerhin liefern die anderen möglichen Verbindungen komplett verschiedene Resultate. Zwei sinnliche Objekte sitzen schlicht Seite an Seite. Und mein aufrichtiges Vertieftsein in Bäume oder Windmühlen ist bloß das Innere der Intention, nicht die vereinigte Intention selbst. Daher wird aus der Verbindung zweier anderer realer Gegenstände, durch unbekannte stellvertretende Mittel, selbst ein reales Objekt geboren.

5. Überhaupt keine Relation. Das ist der gewöhnliche Zustand der Dinge, verneint nur von fanatischen Holisten, jenen Extremisten, die Spiegel wie Zucker in der Straße an jedes Objekt verteilen, das die Straße herunterstolpert. Reale Objekte sind zu direktem Kontakt unfähig und viele üben in der Tat überhaupt keine Wirkung aufeinander aus. Selbst das allgemeine Gesetz der Gravitation trifft nur auf eine kleine

Speculations III

Klasse physikalischer Objekte zu und betrifft selbst dann nur einen kleinen Teil ihrer Realität.

Und in einem unterschiedlichen Fall hat der sinnliche Baum keinerlei Beziehung zu mir, selbst wenn ich aufrichtig in ihn vertieft bin. Der Sauerstoff, den ich einatme, kommt vom realen Baum, nicht von meiner Wahrnehmung desselben. Der sinnliche Baum ist ein Phantasma, das nur im Kern irgendeiner Intention überlebt und nicht einmal unabhängige Relationen mit seinen phantomartigen Nachbarn unterhält. Diese werden nur stellvertretend durch mich zueinander in Beziehung gesetzt, insofern ich aufrichtig in beide vertieft bin.

Die diese Welt bevölkernden Objekte stehen immer in einer dieser fünf Beziehungen zueinander. In *Guerilla Metaphysics* schlug ich vor, dass Verursachung immer stellvertretend, asymmetrisch und gepuffert ist. „Stellvertretend" bedeutet, dass sich Objekte durch einen Stellvertreter begegnen. Über sinnliche Profile, die ausschließlich im Inneren einer anderen Entität gefunden werden. „Asymmetrisch" bedeutet, dass sich die anfängliche Konfrontation jedes Mal zwischen einem realen Objekt und einem sinnlichen entfaltet. Und „gepuffert" bedeutet, dass weder ich mit dem Baum verschmelze, noch der Baum mit seinen sinnlichen Nachbarn, da alle durch unbekannte Firewalls in Schach gehalten werden, welche die Privatsphäre eines jeden aufrechterhalten. Aus dem asymmetrischen und gepufferten Innenleben eines Objekts entstehen gelegentlich stellvertretende Verbindungen (im zweifachen Sinne), die neuen Objekten mit eigenem Innenraum das Leben schenken. Es besteht ein beständiges sich Treffen von asymmetrischen Partnern im Inneren eines vereinigten Objektes: Ein Reales trifft den sinnlichen Vikar oder Stellvertreter eines anderen. Verursachung selbst ereignet sich, wenn diese Hindernisse irgendwie aufgehoben oder durchbrochen werden. In den Begriffen des 17. Jahrhunderts ist die unmittelbare Nähe von realen und sinnlichen Objekten bloß die *Okkasion* für eine Verbindung zwischen einem realen Objekt innerhalb der Intention und einem anderen, außerhalb von ihr liegendem realen Objekt. Auf diesem Weg werden Schächte und Frachttunnel zwischen Objekten konstruiert, die andernfalls in privaten Vakua in Quarantäne gehalten würden.

Wir haben jetzt fünf Objektarten (reale Intention, reales Ich, realer Baum, sinnlicher Baum, sinnliches Rauschen) und fünf verschiedene Relationstypen (Enthaltensein, Nachbarschaft, Aufrichtigkeit, Verbindung, und keine). Des Weiteren haben wir drei Adjektive für das, was sich in einem Objekt entfaltet (stellvertretend, asymmetrisch, gepuffert) und drei verschiedene Arten des Rauschens (Qualitäten, Akzidentien, Relationen), welche das sinnliche Objekt umgeben. Während dies nicht unbedingt einen vollständigen Zensus der Wirklichkeit darstellt und eventuell aufpoliert werden muss oder einer Erweiterung bedarf, so bietet es doch ein gutes Anfangsmodell, dessen bloße Strenge helfen wird, jene Elemente auszuräuchern, die es vielleicht übersehen haben könnte. Was abzuwarten bleibt, ist, wie diese Elemente interagieren, wie eine Relationsart sich in eine andere umwandelt und wie neue reale Objekte paradoxerweise aus der Interaktion zwischen realen und sinnlichen Objekten entstehen und sogar wie sinnliche Gegenstände es schaffen sich zu verkuppeln und zu entkuppeln wie Waggons eines Geisterzuges. Diese Art von Problemen stellt den Inhalt Objekt-orientierter Philosophie[11] dar; dem unvermeidlichen Mutanten aus Husserls intentionalen Objekten und Heideggers realen. Diese wiederum sind nur die derzeitigen Erben von Humes benachbarten Impressionen und Ideen (Husserl) und den unzusammenhängenden Objekten Malebranches und dessen asch'aritischen Vorläufern (Heidegger).

---

[11] Das Label „Objekt-orientierte-Philosophie" wurde vom Autor Graham Harman selbst geprägt. *Object-oriented philosophy* kann diesem zufolge als Unterart des „Spekulativen Realismus" (*speculative realism*) gesehen werden. Die zwei zentralen Pfeiler dieser auf Objekte zentrierten Philosophie sehen wie folgt aus: 1. Verschiedene Entitäten unterschiedlichen Maßstabs (nicht nur Quarks oder Neutrinos) sind der ultimative Stoff, aus dem das Universum besteht. 2. Diese Entitäten werden niemals durch ihre Relationen oder die Summe all ihrer Relation erschöpft, sie sind mehr als das. Im Gegenteil, Objekte entziehen sich geradezu jeder Relation. Vgl.: Graham Harman, *brief SR/OOO tutorial*, in: (http://doctorzamalek2.wordpress.com/2010/07/23/brief-srooo-tutorial/) (A.d.Ü.).

Das Problem der Philosophie ähnelt nun einem Puzzlespiel. Wir haben die Teile so vorsichtig wie möglich ausgemacht und keines scheint in aller Deutlichkeit zu fehlen. Auch haben wir ein Bild davon, wie die ultimative Lösung aussehen sollte: die Welt, so wie wir sie kennen, mit ihren verschiedenen Objekten und Wechselwirkungen. Ungleich einem Puzzlespiel entfaltet sich diese in mindestens drei Dimensionen, die sich unablässig von Augenblick zu Augenblick verändern: Aber wie ein solches Puzzle ist es, statt das Originalbild nachzuahmen, mit Spalten und strategischen Überschneidungen übersät, die alles in einem neuen Licht erscheinen lassen. Genauso wie Fünfjährige gegenüber einem riesigen tausendteiligen Puzzlespiel, liegt unsere größte Bedrohung darin, den Mut zu verlieren. Aber während frustrierte Kinder wütend die Stücke auf den Boden werfen und ihre Betätigung wechseln, bleiben wir von Beginn an in unserem Puzzle gefangen, da es das Rätsel unserer Welt selbst ist. Philosophen können nur mittels Wahnsinn, mithilfe eines Strickes oder Revolvers daraus entkommen.

3. Ontologie und Metaphysik

Neulinge in der Philosophie fragen oft nach dem genauen Unterschied zwischen Ontologie und Metaphysik. Fakt ist, dass es hier keine konsistente Unterscheidung gibt, da jeder Philosoph diese Begriffe für individuelle Zwecke redefiniert. Für Heidegger ist Ontologie die Darstellung, wie den Menschen das Sein enthüllt wird, während Metaphysik ein beleidigender Begriff für Philosophien bleibt, die alles Seiende in Begriffen irgendeiner privilegierten Entität erklären. Für Levinas gehört Ontologie zum globalen Krieg zwischen Seienden, während Metaphysik vom unendlichen Anderssein, das jenseits eines solchen Konfliktes liegt, spricht. Ich für meinen Teil habe diese Begriffe generell austauschbar für eine realistische Position benutzt, die allen menschenzentrierten Philosophien entgegengesetzt ist; manchmal, wie im Eröffnungsteil dieses Artikels, bleibt eine solche Beweglichkeit nützlich. Dennoch würde ich gerne eine exaktere Unterscheidung

Graham Harman – *Über stellvertretende Verursachung*

vorschlagen—eine die nicht ohne Bezug auf ihre klassische Abgrenzung ist. Von nun an soll sich „Ontologie" auf die Beschreibung der basalen strukturalen Eigenschaften—die von allen Objekten geteilt werden—beziehen und „Metaphysik" soll die Diskussion fundamentaler Charakteristiken spezifischer Entitätstypen bedeuten. In diesem Sinne gehören die vorher erwähnten Puzzleteile alleinig der Ontologie an, da kein Objekt von ihrer Herrschaft befreit ist. Diese schließen die basalen Gegensätze zwischen realen und sinnlichen Objekten, die fünf Relationstypen zwischen ihnen und die Bindung der sinnlichen Objekte an ihre unterschiedlichen Qualitäten, Akzidentien und Relationen ein. Raum und Zeit gehören ebenfalls zur Ontologie, da selbst ewige und nichträumliche Objekte dem engen raumzeitlichen Bereich entweichen, aber keineswegs Raum und Zeit in einem breiteren Sinne entkommen. Die Frage der Universalien scheint auch ein globales Thema der Ontologie zu sein und hier könnte es noch andere geben. Was die Metaphysik betrifft, die sich abgrenzt und die inneren Organe jeder spezifischen Entität analysiert, so sind offensichtlicherweise Menschen, Sprache, Kunstwerke und sogar Gott mögliche Themen. Jede Art voneinander verschiedener Objekte, wie verschwommen auch immer ihre Grenzen sein mögen, kann zum Gegenstand einer Metaphysik werden. Es könnte eine Metaphysik der Kunstwerke, der Psyche oder der Sprache geben und sogar über Restaurants, Säugetiere, Planeten, Teehäuser oder Sportligen. Insofern sich die Philosophie klar von anderen Aktivitäten wie Singen oder dem Glückspiel unterscheidet, könnte es eine Metaphysik der Philosophie selbst geben, welche die ausschlaggebenden Eigenschaften dieser Disziplin aufdeckt, egal wie ihre unzähligen Variationen und degenerierten und ausgeklügelten Formen auch aussehen mögen.

Die Unterscheidung zwischen Ontologie und Metaphysik wird hier aus einem besonderen Grund vorgeschlagen. Entlang realer Objekte haben wir auch sinnliche Objekte beschrieben, die nur im Inneren irgendeines intentionalen Ganzen existieren. Dennoch wird Intentionalität von fast allen als eine aufs Menschliche beschränkte Eigenschaft angesehen. Sollte diese Schilderung wahr sein, dann würden sinnliche Objekte auf eine Metaphysik der menschlichen Wahrnehmung beschränkt werden, ohne Platz in einer Ontologie, die dafür entworfen wurde, um sich an Plastik und Sanddünen nicht weniger zu richten, wie an Menschen. Diese Beschränkung der Sinnlichkeit auf das menschliche Reich muss abgewiesen werden. Intentionalität ist überhaupt keine speziell menschliche Eigenschaft, sondern eine ontologische Eigenschaft von Gegenständen im Allgemeinen. Für unsere Zwecke bedeutet Intentionalität Aufrichtigkeit. Mein Leben wird immer zu einem begrenzten Umfang von Gedanken und Wahrnehmungen in Anspruch genommen. Während es verlockend ist solch ein Vertieftsein mit Bewusstsein zu verwechseln, müssen wir uns auf die rudimentärste Bedeutung der Aufrichtigkeit konzentrieren: dem Kontakt zwischen einem realen und einem sinnlichen Objekt. Zum Beispiel könnte ich aufrichtig in die Kontemplation auf der Tischoberfläche angeordneter Glasmurmeln vertieft sein. Das ist meine Aufrichtigkeit in diesem Moment, da ich auf andere Möglichkeiten größerer oder geringerer Wichtigkeit verzichte, um dieses asketische Zen-Spektakel zu erleben. Man bemerke, dass die Glasmurmeln selbst aufrichtig in ihr Auf-dem-Tisch-Liegen vertieft sind, statt in einem Hochofen zu schmelzen oder durch einen Minenschacht zu rollen. (Auch wenn sie „Murmeln" für niemand sonst außer Menschen oder verspielte Kätzchen sein mögen, brauchen wir einen Spitznamen für das vereinigte Objekt, dass wir in unsere Spiele einbeziehen.) Die Frage für uns ist nicht die Fragestellung des Panpsychisten, ob diese Murmeln irgendwelche rudimentären Denk- und Fühlfähigkeiten besitzen, sondern ob sie als reale Objekte der Tischoberfläche als sinnlichem Objekt begegnen.

Die Antwort lautet Ja. Wir müssen die üblichen Bedeutungen der Sinnlichkeit ignorieren und unseren Blick auf eine primitivere kosmische Schicht richten. Es ist klar, dass die Murmeln irgendwo in der Realität in Kontakt mit gewissen anderen Entitäten stehen müssen, die sie kurzzeitig in dem einen oder anderem Zustand stabilisieren. Die Entitäten, die sie konfrontieren, können keine realen Objekte sein, da diese sich dem Kontakt entziehen. Noch können die Murmeln gegen ungebundene sinnliche Qualitäten anrennen, da Eigenschaften im sinnlichen Bereich immer an Gegenstände gebunden sind. Es bleibt nur eine Alternative übrig: Die Murmeln sind aufrichtig in sinnliche Objekte vertieft. Dieses indirekte Argument wird noch überzeugender, wenn wir die von Murmeln bewohnte Landschaft überprüfen, von der sich herausstellt, dass sie die grundlegenden strukturellen Eigenschaften der menschlichen Intentionalität teilt. Man nehme zunächst Notiz davon, dass diese Murmeln absolut dazu fähig sind, zwischen dem Tisch und der benachbarten relationalen Umgebung zu unterscheiden, wenn auch nicht mit einer primitiven Urteilsfähigkeit im Sinne des Panpsychismus. Gegenwärtig liegen die Murmeln auf dem Tisch, sind aber andererseits von Luft umgeben; weswegen Luft und Tischoberfläche im Leben der Murmeln benachbart sind. Selbst wenn wir die Murmeln vorsichtig mit Büchern oder geschmolzenem Wachs einrahmen, bleibt der Tisch, unberührt von unseren ausgefallenen Manipulationen, dasselbe intentionale Objekt. Zweitens konfrontiert die Murmel die Tischoberfläche gänzlich abseits ihrer akzidentiellen Kälte und Glattheit, obwohl es diese Eigenschaften womöglich genauso auf eine Weise registriert. Erhitzen wir die Oberseite des Tisches oder machen sie klebrig oder körnig, indem wir verschiedene Materialien auf sie gießen, so bleibt der Tisch als intentionales Objekt der gleiche. Die letzte Frage ist, ob die Murmeln einen Unterschied zwischen dem Tisch und seinen wesentlicheren Eigenschaften, wie seiner Härte, Ebenheit, Stabilität oder dem Mangel an Perforation machen können. Selbst Menschen können diese Unterscheidung zwischen Objekten und deren Qualitäten nur in sehr speziellen Fällen treffen; da ich diese Fälle bald unter der Überschrift „Verlockung" beschreiben werde, sollten wir mit der Frage warten, ob Glasmurmeln fähig sind, dem zu gehorchen. Was schon offensichtlich geworden ist, ist, dass alle realen Objekte eine Landschaft sinnlicher Objekte bewohnen—eine Spielwiese—deren Fluktuationen das Entstehen neuer realer Verbindungen ermöglicht. Einige dieser Fluktuationen sind ein bloß häusliches Drama, während andere neue Relationen mit der Außenwelt hervorrufen. Alles aber was an der menschlichen Kognition besonders ist, gehört zu einer komplizierteren Ebene der Philosophie als derjenigen der sinnlichen Gegenstände, obwohl sie in den Begriffen dieser ausgedrückt werden können muss.

Woanders habe ich die Wendung „jede Relation ist selbst ein Objekt" gebraucht und ich halte diese Behauptung immer noch für wahr. Aber da dieser Artikel Relationen redefiniert hat und diese jetzt Enthaltensein, Aufrichtigkeit und Nachbarschaft mit einschließen, muss der Slogan wie folgt umformuliert werden: „Jede Verbindung ist selbst ein Objekt." Mein Enthaltensein im intentionalen Akt macht uns beide nicht zu einem neuen Objekt und genauso wenig machen (meistens) zwei oder drei nahe gelegene Wahrnehmungen von Autos kein vereinigtes Objekt. Zwei stellvertretend verbundene reale Gegenstände aber formen ein neues Objekt, da sie einen neuen Innenraum kreieren. Wenn zwei Objekte ein neues durch stellvertretende Verbindung verursachen, erschaffen sie ein neues vereinigtes Ganzes, das nicht nur von außen unerschöpflich ist, sondern auch im Inneren mit einem realen Objekt gefüllt ist, das aufrichtig in sinnliche vertieft ist. Und genauso wie jede Verbindung ein Objekt ist, ist jedes Objekt das Resultat einer Verbindung. Die Geschichte dieser Verbindung bleibt in dessen Herz eingemeißelt, wo seine Bestandteile in einer Art kaleidoskopischem Duell eingesperrt sind. Verbindungen entstehen aber nur zwischen realen Objekten und keinen anderen Kombinationen. Dies zieht nach sich, dass meine Beziehung zur sinnlichen Kiefer selbst kein Objekt darstellt, sondern einfach nur eine Konfrontation zwischen zwei Objekten völlig unterschiedlicher Art. Daher ist Intentionalität, obwohl sie eine Relation zwischen mir und der sinnlichen Kiefer zu sein scheint, bloß ihr Inneres. Die Intention selbst resultiert nur aus der ungeklärten stellvertretenden Fusion zwischen mir und der realen Kiefer oder mit was auch immer, das meinen irregeleiteten Glauben erzeugt, ich würde eine wahrnehmen.

Graham Harman – *Über stellvertretende Verursachung*

Um es zu wiederholen; meine Relation mit der sinnlichen Kiefer ist keine ausgewachsene Verbindung, sondern nur eine Aufrichtigkeit. Diese Aufrichtigkeit kann in der Tat in ein Objekt konvertiert werden, wie es in der Analyse unserer eigenen Intentionen oder der anderer geschieht. Wenn ich meine Beziehung zur sinnlichen Kiefer analysiere, habe ich diese Relation zum ersten Mal in ein Objekt umgewandelt. Sie wurde zu einem realen Objekt, insofern ihre exakte Natur der Sicht entweicht, da diese egal wie oft analysiert unerschöpflich bleibt. Wir stehen nun einer bloß sinnlichen Erscheinung der ursprünglich aufrichtigen Beziehung gegenüber, die sich jeder Analyse entzieht, genauso wie Hämmer sich ihrer Handhabung entziehen. Ein zweiter und noch gelangweilterer Beobachter könnte sich nun dazu entschließen eine Analyse meiner Analyse durchzuführen und sie damit in einen Gegenstand zu konvertieren, dessen Natur niemals erfasst werden kann und so weiter bis ins Unendliche. Aber man sollte registrieren, dass es sich nicht um einen infiniten Regress handelt: all diese Objekte sind nicht von Beginn an unbegrenzt in der Situation enthalten, sondern werden abfolgend *ad nauseam* von einer immer verdrehteren und pedantischeren Reihe an Analysten produziert. Zurück zur ersten Ebene, wo sogar meine Beziehung zur sinnlichen Kiefer kein reales Objekt darstellt, sondern einfach eine aufrichtige Relation zweier verschiedener Elemente innerhalb eines größeren Elements. Vereinigte Objekte können beliebig aus diesem tonartigem Inneren geformt werden. Dies zeigt bereits einen Weg für aufrichtige Relationen auf, in reale Verbindungen konvertiert zu werden. Ob dies der einzige Weg ist und ob diese Methode alleine den Menschen gehört ist noch unklar.

Ein anderer Punkt ist nun an der Reihe, bevor zum letzten Abschnitt übergegangen wird. Zu sagen, dass sich jedes Objekt auf dem geschmolzenen sinnlichen Kern eines anderen Objektes befindet, unterminiert einige von Heideggers Schlüsselannahmen. Für ihn transzendiert das menschliche Dasein teilweise anderes Seiendes, indem es sich erhebend einen Blick auf dieses, vor dem Hintergrund der Nichtigkeit erhascht. Aber das Innere eines Objektes lässt weder Raum für Transzendenz noch für Distanz zu: ein in einem einige Meilen entfernten Tal gesehenes Pferd berührt mich immer noch direkt, insofern ich es sehe. Entfernung liegt nicht in der Sphäre der Wahrnehmung, wo mich alles direkt mit größerer oder geringerer Intensität streift, sondern nur in den sich gegenseitig ausschließenden, hinter der Wahrnehmung liegenden, realen Gegenständen. Wir schreiten nicht über irgendetwas hinaus, sondern sind eher wie Maulwürfe, die sich durch Wind, Wasser und Ideen, nicht weniger wie durch Sprechakte, Texte, Sorgen, Staunen und Dreck tunneln. Wir transzendieren die Welt nicht, stattdessen steigen oder buddeln wir uns hinab in Richtung ihrer zahllosen unterirdischen Hohlräume—jeder eine Art Kaleidoskop, wo sinnliche Objekte ihre Farben und Flügel ausbreiten. Weder Endlichkeit noch Negativität befinden sich im Herz der Objekte. Und jeder Fall menschlicher Sterblichkeit ist nur ein tragisches Ereignis unter Trillionen von anderen, den Tod von Haustieren, Insekten, Sternen, Zivilisationen und schlecht geführten Läden oder Universitäten eingeschlossen. Der Heidegger-Blanchot Todeskult muss aus der Ontologie verbannt werden und gegebenenfalls sogar aus der Metaphysik.

4. Verlockung und Verursachung

Manche mögen es störend finden an eine Welt, bestehend aus vakuumversiegelten Objekten zu denken, jedes mit einem funkelnden phänomenalen Inneren, in welches nur von Zeit zu Zeit benachbarte Gegenstände eindringen. Ein wahrscheinlicheres Problem jedoch ist Gleichgültigkeit. Es scheint kein Bedarf an einer solch sonderbaren Sicht der Wirklichkeit zu geben, da es leicht genug ist an eine Welt bestehend aus rohen Stücken unabänderlicher fester Materie zu denken: wo „primäre Qualitäten" die flüchtigen und dynamischen Serien menschlicher Projektionen stützen. Meiner Ansicht nach, jedoch hat Heidegger dieses Weltbild obsolet gemacht. Obwohl seine Zeug-Untersuchung nur auf eine Beschreibung des Entzogenseins der Objekte vor dem menschlichen Bewusstsein zielt, ist auch praktische Tätigkeit unfähig die Tiefe der Objekte zu erschöpfen und selbst Kausalrelationen scheitern darin einander vollständig zu begegnen.[12] Schließlich wird auch das Konzept der schieren physikalischen Präsenz im Raum von der Zeug-Untersuchung in seinen Grundfesten erschüttert: Eine Position innerhalb des Raumes einzunehmen heißt immerhin auf Relationen einzugehen und auch wenn Gegenstände Raum einnehmen, ihre Realität ist etwas Tieferes. Die Welt ist weder einer graue Matrix objektiver Elemente, noch Rohmaterial für die Projektion eines sexy menschlichen Dramas auf Schotter und Schlamm. Stattdessen ist sie mit nur lose zusammengewobenen Realitätspunkten gefüllt: Ein Archipel aus Orakeln oder Bomben, die nur aus der Verborgenheit hervorgesprengt werden, um neue abgeschiedene Tempel hervorzubringen. Die Sprache hier ist metaphorisch, weil sie es sein muss. Während die analytische Philosophie darauf Stolz ist, nie mehr zu unterstellen, als sie tatsächlich sagt, wird dieses Verfahren einer Welt nicht gerecht, wo Gegenstände immer mehr sind, als sie buchstäblich ausdrücken. Diejenigen, die nur Wert darauf legen Argumente zu erzeugen, erzeugen fast nie Objekte. Neue Gegenstände jedoch sind die einzig heiligen Früchte für Schriftsteller, Denker, Politiker, Reisende, Liebende und Erfinder.

Entlang der Unterscheidung zwischen realen und sinnlichen Objekten gab es fünf verschiedene Beziehungsweisen zwischen diesen: Enthaltensein, Nachbarschaft, Aufrichtigkeit, Verbindung und keine. Unser Ziel ist es etwas Licht auf den Ursprung der Verbindung zu werfen, der einen der fünf Relationen, die am meisten Ärger für eine Theorie geisterhafter und entweichender Objekte zu bereiten scheint. Eine Verbindung existiert einfach oder scheitert zu existieren; es handelt sich schlicht um eine binäre Frage. Des Weiteren muss eine Verbindung stellvertretend sein, da ein bloß nacktes Objekt dem anderen immer entweicht. Ein Gegenstand existiert

---

[12] Die Idee, dass physikalische Relationen auch eine intentionale Struktur haben, ist eine Minderheitsansicht, aber keineswegs meine eigene Erfindung. Siehe zum Beispiel George Molnars faszinierendes *Powers: A Study in Metaphysics*, Oxford, Oxford University Press 2003, S. 60 ff.

einfach und diese Existenz kann niemals vollständig im Herzen eines anderen gespiegelt werden. Was wir suchen, ist ein fruchtbarer Boden für Relationen, aus dem Verbindungen in die Existenz hervorquellen: eine Art Relation, die fähig ist, als Motor der Veränderung im Kosmos zu dienen. „Verbindung" selbst kann nicht die Lösung liefern, da sie genau das ist, was wir versuchen zu erklären; wenn zwei Objekte verbunden sind, dann ist die Arbeit, die wir zu beobachten wünschen bereits getan. Die Option „überhaupt keine Relation" hilft auch nicht, denn wenn Dinge nicht aufeinander bezogen sind, dann bleiben sie es, solange wie der gesuchte Vermittler fehlt. „Enthaltensein" ist uns genauso wenig behilflich. Auch hier haben wir bloß eine binäre Frage: Entweder sind die sinnliche Kiefer und ich zusammen innerhalb einer gegebenen Intention oder wir sind es nicht. Letztlich gibt uns auch „Nachbarschaft" nicht, was wir brauchen: Bestenfalls verteilt das Wechselspiel der sinnlichen Objekte nur die Grenzen unter ihnen neu, ohne aber zu echten Veränderungen außerhalb ihres geschmolzenen inneren Heimatlandes zu führen. Die einzig verbliebene Option ist „Aufrichtigkeit." Dies muss die Stätte des Wandels in der Welt sein. Ein reales Objekt wohnt, gegen zahlreiche sinnliche gedrückt, dem Kern einer Intention inne. Irgendwie durchbohrt es den farbigen Beschlag und verbindet sich mit dem bereits in der Nähe liegenden, aber vom direkten Kontakt gepuffertem realen Objekt. Wenn Licht auf diesen Mechanismus geworfen werden kann, könnte sich die Natur der vier anderen Relationstypen ebenfalls aufklären.

Es läuft alles auf eine Dynamik der Aufrichtigkeit hinaus, egal ob für ein menschliches oder andersgeartetes reales Objekt. Aufrichtigkeit hat mit sinnlichen Objekten zu tun, die über ihre Qualitäten definiert werden und in periphere Akzidentien und Relationen eingehüllt sind. Was wir suchen, ist die Weise, auf der die aufrichtige Beziehung mit einem sinnlichen Objekt in eine direkte Verbindung mit einem realen Objekt umgewandelt wird. Das Kuppeln und Entkuppeln realer und sinnlicher Objekte ist jetzt unser zentrales Thema. Wir wissen, dass ein sinnlicher Gegenstand von seinen

Graham Harman – *Über stellvertretende Verursachung*

Akzidentien und Relationen abtrennbar ist. Die interessante Frage ist, ob er auch von seinen Qualitäten abkoppelbar ist, die auf intimere Weise zu ihm zu gehören scheinen. Mit Qualitäten meine ich die wesentlichen Qualitäten, ohne die man ein Objekt nicht mehr länger als dasselbe Ding betrachten würde. Man erinnere sich, dass es hier keine händeringende Krise der Objektivität gibt, da wir von Eigenschaften sprechen, die nicht zum Wesen eines realen Objektes gehören, sondern ausschließlich zu den sinnlichen Dingen, die unsere Aufmerksamkeit verlangen—einem Bereich, indem wir selbst die höchsten Richter im Land sind. Jetzt kann man sich vorstellen, dass wir die Eigenschaften der Murmeln dadurch befreien können, indem wir offen alle bedeutenden Eigenschaften der Murmeln entdecken und auflisten, ohne die sie nicht sein könnten. Dies war die große Hoffnung Husserls Methode der eidetischen Variation. Aber der Effekt dieser Prozedur ist oberflächlich und kann die sinnlichen Murmeln nicht in ihrer Wesenheit erfassen. Es gilt einzufangen, dass sogar während unsere Analyse dieser Objekte fortschreitet, wir diese weiterhin als Einheiten ansehen, selbst wenn wir sie auf bestechende Weise in Tausende separater Merkmale zerschneiden. Sogar im Falle eines sinnlichen Objektes können die wesentlichen Eigenschaften nicht angegeben und analysiert werden, ohne zu etwas wie Akzidentien zu werden: ungebundene vom Objekt als Ganzem losgelöste Merkmale. Unsere Aufrichtigkeit beschäftigt sich nicht wirklich mit einer Liste solcher losgelöster Merkmale, wie Husserl es einsieht, wenn er dem vereinigtem sinnlichen Objekt Priorität über die Myriaden seiner Facetten gewährt. Die Einheit solcher Objekte deutet sogar darauf hin, dass da nur eine Eigenschaft infrage kommt: dieses Murmel-Wesen oder diese Kieferessenz. Die vereinigte Dingqualität ist überhaupt kein Rauschen, sondern das sinnliche Objekt selbst. Was Aristoteles Frage betrifft, ob ein Ding mit seinem Wesen identisch sei, so lautet die Antwort für sinnliche Objekte Ja. Obwohl Eigenschaften weiter oben im Artikel als eine Form des Rauschens beschrieben wurden, ist dies nur insofern wahr, falls diese in Richtung eines akzidentellen Status abschweifen, sie ausgebrochen sind und einzeln angeführt werden. Aber die Existenz einer vereinigten Dingqualität bedeutet, dass dem sinnlichen Bereich ein gewisses „ich weiß nicht was" innewohnt, welches die Murmel zu einem stetigen Fokus meiner Aufmerksamkeit macht. Anders als die Anhänger von Locke sagen wir nicht *je ne sais quoi* in einem Geist leichten Spottes, sondern als wahre Aussage über sinnliche Gegenstände. Das sinnliche Ding selbst hat einen vereinigten und im Grunde unaussprechlichen Effekt auf uns—einen, der nicht zu irgendeiner Auflistung von Merkmalen reduziert werden kann. Aber wenn so eine Aufzählung der Merkmale ein Ding nicht von seinen Qualitäten abtrennt, dann könnte es einen anderen Weg geben, der dies ermöglicht. Wir haben schon gesehen, dass die stellvertretende Verursachung—das verzauberte Einhorn, welches wir suchen—den Kontakt mit den wesentlichen Qualitäten eines Dinges erfordert, ohne den Kontakt zum Ding als Ganzem. In diesem Sinne könnte die Entdeckung, wie das sinnliche Objekt sich von seinen Eigenschaften abspaltet, ein Sprungbrett dafür sein ein analoges Ereignis unter realen Objekten zu finden.

Die Trennung eines sinnlichen Objekts von seinen Eigenschaften kann als „Verlockung"[13] bezeichnet werden.[14] Diese Bezeichnung zeigt genau den bezaubernden Effekt an, der dieses Ereignis häufig für Menschen begleitet und zudem deutet er auf den verwandten Begriff der „Anspielung" hin, da die Verlockung nur auf das Objekt anspielt, ohne dessen Innenleben direkt zu vergegenwärtigen. Im sinnlichen Bereich begegnen wir mit rauschenden Akzidentien und Relationen verkrusteten Gegenständen. Mögen wir uns auch ausdrücklich einiger ihrer wesentlichen Qualitäten bewusst sein, auch wenn so eine Liste die Qualitäten bloß in etwas

---

[13] Im Original spricht der Autor von *allure*, das mit „Verlockung" übersetzt wurde, um den Aspekt des Köderns auszudrücken, der sich aus dem französischen *leurre* herleitet. Das Wort Ködern selbst gibt aber die ästhetische Dimension des Reizes nicht adäquat wieder und da beide Dimensionen (ködern, reizen) im Begriff der „Verlockung" enthalten sind habe ich dafür optiert (A.d.Ü.).

[14] Siehe auch *Guerrilla Metaphysics*, S. 142-4.

Graham Harman – *Über stellvertretende Verursachung*

Akzidentielles umwandelt und es verfehlt uns die vereinigte Bindung zu geben, die das sinnliche Ding zu einem einzelnen Ding macht. Wir benötigen stattdessen eine Erfahrung, in welcher das sinnliche Objekt von seinen vereinigten und zusammengefügten Eigenschaften abgetrennt ist, denn dies wird zum ersten Mal auf ein reales, hinter einer einzelnen Oberflächenqualität liegendes Objekt, hindeuten. Für Menschen ist die Metapher eine solche Erfahrung. Wenn der Dichter, „mein Herz ist ein Hochofen" schreibt, dann fängt das sinnliche Objekt, bekannt als Herz, vage bestimmte Hochofeneigenschaften ein und zieht diese stockend in seine Umlaufbahn. Die Unfähigkeit des Herzens leicht mit Hochofenmerkmalen zu verschmelzen (im Gegensatz zu wörtlichen Aussagen wie „mein Herz ist der stärkste Muskel meines Körpers"), bringt eine Anspielung auf ein gespenstiges, hinter der familiären und alltäglichen Bekanntschaft mit einem sinnlichen Herz, liegendes Herzobjekt zuwege. Man nehme Notiz, dass die umgekehrte Metapher gegenüber der Ersten vollständig asymmetrisch ist: „Der Hochofen ist ein Herz" zieht kardiale Züge in die Umlaufbahn eines sinnlichen Hochofens, welches befreit von den Bindungen zu seinen gewöhnlichen Eigenschaften als versteckte Hochofenseele evoziert wird, eine deren *animus* jetzt rhythmisches Klopfen und einen Kreislauf antreibt. Humor tut etwas Ähnliches: Wir können Bergsons *Das Lachen* folgen und die Spannungen zwischen einem komisch Düpiertem und den Charakterzügen bemerken, die er nicht mehr frei an sich ändernde Gegebenheiten anpasst. Diese Eigenschaften werden nun als diskret sichtbare Hülle zur Schau gestellt, unter welcher der Akteur glücklos daran scheitert diese zu kontrollieren. Es gibt unzählbare Beispiele für Verlockung. In Momenten der Schönheit ist ein Objekt nicht die totale Summe seiner schönen Farben und Proportionen an der Oberfläche, sondern eine Art Seele, die Eigenschaften von innen heraus beseelend zu Schwindel oder sogar Hypnose beim Betrachter führen kann. Wenn Heideggers Hammer versagt, scheint sich ein verborgenes Hammerobjekt in einiger Distanz zu seinen einstmals familiären Eigenschaften aus dem Dunkeln abzuzeichnen. In der Sprache rufen Namen nach Objekten, die tiefer liegen als ihre Qualitäten; in der Liebe hat die geliebte Entität eine gewisse unter den Konturen und Mängeln der zugänglichen Oberfläche schwebende Magie. Die Liste der Möglichkeiten ist so umfassend, dass sie es verdienen in einer Enzyklopädie der Ästhetik kategorisiert zu werden. Bis jetzt hat die Ästhetik der Philosophie im Allgemeinen als verarmte Tänzerin gedient—bewundert für ihren Charme, kein Gentleman jedoch würde sie heiraten. Doch in Anbetracht des scheinbar überwältigenden Ausmaßes der Verlockung könnte die Ästhetik eine eher große Rolle in der Ontologie verdienen. Verschiedene sinnliche Objekte innerhalb der gleichen Intention werden als benachbart beschrieben, sie verschmelzen nicht miteinander, sondern werden vom intentionalen Agens als unterschiedlich angesehen und dieses Agens ist das letzte Berufungsgericht im Reich des Sinnlichen. Dies trifft auf das zu, was Relationen der sinnlichen Objekte genannt wurde. Akzidenzien aber stellen einen anderen Fall dar. Die Oberfläche eines sinnlichen Objekts liegt nicht bloß Seite an Seite mit ihnen. Selbst wenn wir direkt durch diese Akzidenzien hindurchschauen, um das zugrundeliegende sinnliche Ding zu fixieren, werden die Akzidenzien nicht als vom Ding abgetrennt, sondern als auf seiner Oberfläche verkrustet aufgefasst. Dieses Vereisen mit peripheren Qualitäten kommt auf interessante Weise daher. Man erinnere sich daran, dass der sinnliche Baum als Ganzes nur aus einer Eigenschaft besteht (derjenigen von der er in der Verlockung getrennt wird). Man beachte, dass diese vereinigte Baumerscheinung immer noch Teile besitzt. Beginnen wir Zweige und Blätter zu entfernen, dann kommen wir zu einem Punkt, an dem wir ihn nicht mehr als denselben Baum ansehen; der Baum hängt von seinen Teilen ab. Dennoch sind diese Teile nur entlang eines eigentümlichen Pfades im Baum vereinigt. Er verschlingt diese nie vollständig, verwendet aber nur eine begrenzte Portion ihrer Realität. Was wir als die Akzidenzien des sinnlichen Baumes kennen, sind einfach die Überbleibsel seiner Teile, die im neuen Objekt nicht eingesetzten Überreste. Jedes dieser Teile ist kompliziert, weil es aus weiteren Teilen besteht und so weiter bis ins Unendliche. Wie weit auch immer wir in Richtung dieser Unendlichkeit vordringen, wir finden weiterhin Objekte, keine rohen Sinnesdaten. Es wäre falsch zu denken wir würden einem Feld von Farbpixeln gegenüberstehen und dieses dann in objektive Abschnitte formen. Zuerst ist es willkürlich zu denken, dass Punkte von Grün qualitativ basaler seien als eine vereinigte Baum- oder Zweigeigenschaft; alle sind dazu fähig meine Aufrichtigkeit auszufüllen und alle haben einen spezifisch persönlichen Stil. Zweitens nimmt auch ein angenommenes Grünpixel mindestens die räumliche Ausprägung eines Punktes ein und ist deshalb selbst ein kompliziertes Objekt. Im Reich des Sinnlichen gibt es immer größte Objekte: nämlich jene, die in der Aufrichtigkeit jeden Moment erkannt werden. Aber man kann kein Kleinstes finden, da es immer ein Überbleibsel vom Rest der Teile gibt und Teile von Teilen, wie die endlosen Obertöne angeschlagener Klaviernoten. Diese Akzidenzien sind die einzig mögliche Quelle des Wandels, da sie alleine die potenzielle Brücke zwischen einem sinnlichen Objekt und einem anderen sind. Denn in einem sinnlichen Objekt selbst, welches immer als ein *fait accompli* erkannt wird, kann es keine Veränderung geben, es kann höchstens vernichtet oder durch ein Neues ersetzt werden. Akzidenzien besitzen den dualen Status der Zugehörigkeit und Nicht-Zugehörigkeit zu einem Objekt, wie Wimpel an einem Maibaum oder Juwelen auf einer Wasserpfeife. Akzidenzien sind verführerische Haken, die aus dem sinnlichen Objekt hervorragen und ihm die Chance geben sich mit anderen zu verbinden und dadurch zwei in eines zu fusionieren.

Aber die Teil-Ganzes Relation taucht nicht nur im sinnlichen Bereich auf. Auch ein reales Objekt wird aus Teilen gebildet, deren Verschwinden geradezu dessen Existenz bedroht.

Der Unterschied liegt darin, dass die Teile eines sinnlichen Objekts eingekrustet an seiner Oberfläche liegen: Eher noch fusionieren gewisse Aspekte dieser Teile, um es zu erschaffen, während der Rest dieser Teile als Rauschen von der Oberfläche ausströmt. Im Gegensatz dazu sind die Teile eines realen Objekts im Inneren dieses Objekts enthalten und nicht auf dessen äußere Kruste gepflastert. In beiden Fällen gibt es jedoch eine stellvertretende Ursache, die es den Teilen ermöglicht sich zu verbinden. Das kann durch die historische Unterscheidung zwischen Skeptizismus und Okkasionalismus, die auf dieselbe Weise komplementär sind, wie Verkrustung und Verbindung, verdeutlicht werden. Hume und Malebranche stehen gegensätzlichen Versionen desselben Problems gegenüber. Obwohl Hume vermeintlich die Möglichkeit einer Verbindung anzweifelt, sollte man Notiz nehmen, dass sich für ihn bereits eine Verbindung ergeben hat: Er ist niemals überrascht, dass zwei Billardkugeln gleichzeitig in seinem Geist liegen, er zweifelt nur daran, ob diese unabhängige Kräfte besitzen, um sich gegenseitig Stöße zu versetzen. In diesem Sinne beginnt Hume mit der Verbindung innerhalb der Erfahrung und zweifelt bloß an der Trennung außerhalb dieser. Malebranche beginnt, die Existenz getrennter Substanzen voraussetzend, auf die umgekehrte Weise, zweifelt aber daran, dass diese denselben Raum auf solch eine Weise einnehmen können, um ihre Kräfte auszutauschen—was ihn dazu führt, die Macht Gottes als ultimativen Verbindungsraum aller Entitäten zu postulieren. Wie Hume können wir das intentionale Agens als stellvertretende Ursache anderenfalls getrennter Erscheinungen betrachten. Der Baum und sein bergiger Hintergrund sind tatsächlich verschieden, dennoch sind sie in sofern vereinigt, wie ich aufrichtig in beide vertieft bin. Aber mehr als das: Wenn die Teile des Baumes fusionieren, um den Baum mit seiner einzelnen Baumqualität hervorzubringen, dann bin auch ich die stellvertretende Ursache für die Verbindung dieser sinnlichen Gegenstände. Selbst wenn ich bloß passiv herumsitze ohne auf übertriebene Weise meine Augen oder meinen Geist zu überanstrengen, haben sich diese Teile immer noch für mich verbunden. Hier dient ein reales Objekt (ich selbst) als stellvertretende Ursache für zwei oder mehr sinnliche. Im umgekehrten Falle Malebranches können wir den Pistolenschuss einer Gottheit nicht als unsere vermittelnde Ursache akzeptieren, da nicht erklärt wird, wie Gott als ein reales Objekt andere reale Objekte berühren könnte: Angst vor Blasphemie ist der

Graham Harman – *Über stellvertretende Verursachung*

einzige Schutz für diese unvollständige Theorie. Stattdessen müssen, genau wie zwei sinnliche Objekte von einem realen stellvertretend verbunden werden, zwei reale Objekte stellvertretend durch ein sinnliches verbunden werden. Ich trete mit einem andern Objekt nicht durch den unmöglichen Kontakt mit seiner Innenwelt in Beziehung, sondern nur indem ich seine Oberfläche in einer Weise streife, die sein Innenleben ins Spiel bringt. Genauso wie nur die gegenteiligen Pole von Magneten Kontakt aufnehmen und wie auch nur gegensätzliche Geschlechter allein fruchtbar sind, ist es auch der Fall, das zwei Objekte desselben Typs sich nicht gegenseitig berühren. Direkter Kontakt zwischen sinnlichen Objekten ist ohne ein intentionales Agens unmöglich und eine Verbindung zwischen zwei realen ereignet sich nicht, außer durch einen sinnlichen Vermittler.

Daraus folgt, dass jeder Kontakt asymmetrisch sein muss. Egal wie tief ich mich in die Welt hinein grabe—ich begegne nur sinnlichen Gegenständen und genauso wenig begegnen reale Gegenstände jemals etwas anderem als meiner eigenen sinnlichen Fassade. Der Schlüssel zur stellvertretenden Verursachung liegt darin, dass sich zwei Objekte irgendwie berühren müssen ohne sich zu berühren. Im Falle des sinnlichen Bereichs passiert dies, wenn das intentionale Agens als stellvertretende Ursache für die Fusion multipler sinnlicher Objekte dient: Eine Fusion, die nur unvollständig verbleibt, verkrustet mit zurückbleibenden Akzidenzien. Aber im Falle realer Objekte ist der einzige Weg eines zu berühren ohne es zu berühren nur durch Verlockung beschreitbar. Nur hier entkommen wir dem toten Punkt eines bloßen Herumwälzens in den Düften der sinnlichen Dinge und begegnen Qualitäten, die eher zu einem entfernten signalisierendem Ding gehören als zu einem fleischlich Präsentem. Die einzige Möglichkeit reale Objekte in die sinnliche Sphäre zu bringen, ist sinnliche Objekte auf so eine Weise zu rekonfigurieren, dass sie nicht mehr nur länger in ein Neues fusionieren, wie Teile in ein Ganzes, sondern vielmehr durch die Anspielung auf eine dahinterliegende, tiefe Kraft animiert werden: einem realen Objekt. Das Gravitationsfeld eines realen Gegenstandes muss irgendwie in das existierende sinnliche Feld einfallen. So wie ich der stellvertretende Link zwischen zwei sinnlichen Objekten bin, ist der verlockende Baum die stellvertretende Verbindung zwischen mir und dem realen Baum. Die genaue Dynamik dieses Prozesses verdient eine ausgedehntere Behandlung, aber dennoch ist etwas Ungewöhnliches offensichtlich geworden. Die Trennung eines Dinges von seinen Eigenschaften ist nicht länger ein lokales Phänomen der menschlichen Erfahrung, stattdessen aber die Wurzel aller Beziehungen zwischen allen realen Objekten, Kausalrelationen eingeschlossen. Verlockung, in anderen Worten, gehört zur Ontologie als ganzer und nicht zur speziellen Metaphysik der tierischen Wahrnehmung. Relationen zwischen allen realen Objekten, inklusive geistloser Dreckklumpen, ereignen sich nur durch eine Form der Anspielung. Aber insofern wir Verlockung mit einem ästhetischen Effekt identifiziert haben, bedeutet dies, dass die Ästhetik zur ersten Philosophie wird.

Speculative Realism
After finitude, and beyond?
A vade mecum

Louis Morelle

Translated by Leah Orth with the assistance of Mark Allan Ohm, Jon Cogburn, and Emily Beck Cogburn

Introduction: Does speculative realism even exist?

PRESENTED AS THE FIRST SIGNIFI-cant movement in continental philosophy since structuralism, speculative realism (SR) vociferously announces the end of correlationism and anthropocentrism in philosophy in favor of a "speculative turn." By accommodating things, matter, science, and the real *qua* objects as important as (if not more so than) language, thought, the phenomenal, and the social, SR has garnered attention and criticism from all sides these past few years. "Speculative Realism" was originally the title of a conference in 2007 that brought together four lesser-known but promising philosophers, and then it subsequently spread like wildfire via the Internet through blogs and open-access publishers, in addition to the traditional journal articles, books, colloquia, conferences and other official channels of academia. It has now become a "legitimate" subject of scholarship, taught in certain departments of contemporary philosophy and aesthetics and acquiring a section on the website Philpapers.[1] And yet, what is SR? For SR seems to have become, in

---

[1] http://philpapers.org/browse/speculative-realism

Anglo-Saxon "continental" circles, a buzzword, one of these fashionable terms whose meaning is obscured the more it spreads. Originally naming a philosophically diverse core of young philosophers seeking to emphasize themes that have become relatively marginal in continental philosophy such as metaphysical speculation, the inorganic, or the absolute, and united by a common refusal to attend solely to textual objects or phenomenal experience, this vague designation has sparked a diffuse desire among continental intellectuals to break with some presuppositions inherited from previous generations. Crystallizing a Zeitgeist, the term has lost its specificity, becoming the generic name for all those among the philosophical "young guard" who are laying claim to a "new metaphysics."

The undertaking of this exposé is therefore risky on several accounts, since it concerns the state of a current of thought with a conceptual solidity and durability that may appear uncertain at first glance. I will certainly not strive to regulate the correct or incorrect use of the term "speculative realism," nor make it strictly historical, but rather attempt to offer a concise list of the positions, arguments, and concepts at work among the founding practitioners of SR, beginning from what they have in common.

My preliminary hypothesis is therefore the following: it is possible to discover a nontrivial philosophical core of SR. The verification or refutation of this hypothesis will settle one way or the other all related questions about SR, its future, its actual importance, and its ephemeral or fashionable character.

∼

With these preliminary precautions in mind, we can begin by studying the central question: what are the common characteristics of SR? Evidently, this cohesiveness must first be sought in the only agreed upon reference point for these philosophers: *correlationism*. If we refer to Quentin Meillassoux's original definition:

Louis Morelle – *Speculative Realism*

> By "correlation" we mean the idea according to which we only ever have access to the correlation between thinking and being, and never to either term considered apart from the other. We will henceforth call *correlationism* any current of thought which maintains the unsurpassable character of the correlation so defined.[2]

The term refers to the tendency of Western philosophy since Kant to base all philosophical discourse on conditions of knowledge and to reject metaphysical propositions since they involve freedom from reference to experience, particularly phenomenal experience. More precisely, it seeks to point out the refinement that correlationism brings to idealism, namely, that we do not reduce everything to a single origin, but to a dual relation (subject-object, *Dasein*-Being, etc.) from which escape is impossible. This improvement is intended to provide philosophy with a foolproof protection from any realist or metaphysical illusion. It does not change the thrust of the thesis, to reduce every real being to being dependent on the relation to an originary ground, which is itself invariably reduced to an anthropological determination (whether of experience or language).

This condensed description of the most criticized aspects of correlationism (it is, after all, an intrinsically polemical concept) is more or less common to all the philosophers identified with "speculative realism." None of them, however, solely subscribe to this general characterization; by studying them closely one can distinguish extremely acute deviations. In fact, the problem is understanding which element, which assumption the correlation is based on ("the correlationist two-step," as Meillassoux calls it) and how correlationism should be characterized. We can say that the challenge is to give substantial meaning, proper content, to the undetermined form of correlationism outlined by Meillassoux in *After Finitude* by linking it to a fundamental source or error. However, according to the nature of the diagnosed error, the

---

[2] Quentin Meillassoux, *After Finitude: An Essay on the Necessity of Contingency*, trans. Ray Brassier (London: Continuum, 2008), 5.

excesses of correlationism accepted as symptomatic reveal diseases of a very different sort.

For two of these philosophers, the problem resides in the relation between ontology and epistemology, between being and knowledge.

- For Ray Brassier, the problem of correlationism is found in the dissolution of the barrier between metaphysics and epistemology. Indeed, by reducing all possible knowledge to a singular apprehension determined by the nature of a fundamental correlation, correlationism contributes to the reduction of every factual proposition, every meaning, to a particular standpoint cut off from any universality. It is therefore impossible to single out a solid epistemological criterion—this impossibility, which Brassier most strongly opposes, is due to misconstruing a contingent relation as a fundamental feature of reality, typically, but not exclusively, subjective or phenomenal experience.[3]
- In contrast, for Graham Harman, the problem is the reduction of every statement to its epistemological preconditions, that is to say, to human knowledge; the original sin of correlationism is the implicit presupposition of the superiority of the epistemological relation of knowledge over all other relations.[4]

---

[3] "Correlationism is subtle: it never denies that our thoughts or utterances *aim at* or *intend* mind-independent or language-independent realities; it merely stipulates that this apparently independent dimension remains internally related to thought and language. Thus contemporary correlationism dismisses the problematic of skepticism, and of epistemology more generally, as an antiquated Cartesian hang-up." Ray Brassier, *Nihil Unbound: Enlightenment and Extinction* (New York: Palgrave Macmillan, 2007), 53.

[4] Graham Harman, *The Quadruple Object* (Washington: Zero Books, 2011), chapter 3. Also: "Correlationism arbitrarily treats the human/world relation as philosophically more important than any object/object relation." "In correlationism, human and world are the sole realities and are mutually determined by their permanent rapport." Graham Harman, *Prince of Networks* (Melbourne: re.press, 2009), 176, 185.

The other two philosophers believe it is essential to search for a solution in the relation between thought and *the absolute*.

- Iain Hamilton Grant sees the correlationist error in the confusion between the structure of knowledge (the Kantian transcendental) and its dynamic preconditions, which can be reconstructed from the structure, but are not found within it.[5]
- Finally, for Quentin Meillassoux, correlationism errs by ignoring the intrinsic possibility of a relation between thought and the absolute, which is revealed to be the absolute character of contingency.

We are thus dealing with versions of the same concept that are, if not opposed, at the very least clearly distinct. Moreover, it is possible to articulate the differences by demonstrating that the speculative realists recapitulate certain elements of correlationism, while at the same time rejecting a central element of it. In other words, we can identify, *in each of their positions*, elements that partially validate the correlationist position. While keeping this in mind in each of the following sections, it will be necessary to elucidate precisely how each position is anti-correlationist, and, perhaps more importantly, how some of their theses are implicitly drawn from correlationism.

Nevertheless, one may certainly be tempted to think that this diversity seems to clearly constitute evidence against a cohesiveness of SR, since nobody seems to even agree on the nature of the problem to be tackled. Does it still make sense, then, to discuss a cohesiveness based on a mere rejection of an idea? I think so, insofar as this denial and the disagreements that it entails make significant philosophical debate between theorists possible, although it is clear that the

---

[5] "The Idea is external to the thought that has it, the thought is external to the thinker that has it, the thinker is external to the nature that produces both the thinker and the thought and the Idea." Ray Brassier, Iain Hamilton Grant, Graham Harman, and Quentin Meillassoux, "Speculative Realism," in *Collapse*, Vol. III, 340.

unity thereby produced is a weakened one. One can make an historical analogy here: just as the rejection of Kantian and Hegelian idealism gave rise to currents as diverse as Peirce's and James' pragmatism,[6] the logical positivism of the Vienna Circle, ordinary language philosophy, and phenomenology; in the same way the rejection of correlationism enables the birth of heterogeneous philosophical currents capable of communicating with one another. This is due to the fact that the rejection of correlationism remains a topic of discussion and a project common to all these currents, even though disagreement reigns over the effective content of the project.

Despite the vagueness of the positive content, it can be formulated. Rejection of correlationism implies the truth of at least parts of modern naturalism as exemplified by Meillassoux's concept of ancestrality. The problem then becomes the same as with correlationism: what is the truth that naturalism superficially manifests? For Brassier, "naturalism" means complete materialism; for Harman, one must go beyond naturalism to reach an ontology where all levels of the world would be equally real; for Grant, nature as a power of creation and irreducible transformation becomes the absolute.

It is thus apparent that the rejection of correlationism is full of consequences, and this allows one to say quite seriously that speculative realism signs the birth certificate of a possible *continental metaphysics*.

A *metaphysics* first, because introducing the term "correlationism" into philosophy shifts the presuppositions correlationism rests on from the status of obvious facts to questionable and debatable points. Thus, correlationism is no longer a rejection of metaphysics, but one metaphysics among others, an additional metaphysics. As such, all attempts (for example, along the lines of Heidegger and Derrida) of an "overcoming of metaphysics"[7] are rejected as obsolete,

---

[6] Jean Wahl, *The Pluralist Philosophies of England and America*, trans. Fred Rothwell (London: Open Court, 1925).

[7] Pierre Aubenque, *Faut-il déconstruire la métaphysique?* (Paris: Presses Universitaires de France, 2009).

not so much because they are false, but because they rely on a disavowed metaphysics. Bypassing certain usual precautions, we can then reinterpret certain theses with uncertain status in continental philosophy as properly metaphysical propositions. For instance, when, at the end of "The Earth Does Not Move," Husserl postulates the transcendental ego that precedes and remains independent of the existence of every living being,[8] or when Heidegger asserts that the historicity of Being involves literal metamorphoses of it, transforming from ancient Greece and medieval theology to modernity,[9] are we not thus dealing with propositions supported by "metaphysical" entities every bit as speculative as Spinozist substance or Leibnizian monads? The speculative realists abandon the suspicion associated with metaphysical activity: rather than being required to *justify* its metaphysical approach, or examine its endless possibility, we must simply tackle the problem, since we cannot escape it[10]

There is room then for metaphysics, and rational discussion between conflicting positions, where argumentation and refutation cannot be evaded. Every metaphysical attempt is *prima facie* legitimate, because of the mere fact that no absolute prohibition can be put in place prior to discussion. It is true that the form metaphysics must take still remains vague, especially with respect to what it must abandon and what it can keep, precisely because it must first be discussed,

---

[8] See also his affirmation, in the *Ideas*, that God would perceive not the things in themselves, but a thing's adumbrative perception. Edmund Husserl, *Ideas Pertaining to a Pure Phenomenology and to a Phenomenological Philosophy: First Book, General Introduction to a Pure Phenomenology*, trans. F. Kersten (The Hague: Marinus Nijhoff, 1982), §43.

[9] Lee Braver, *A Thing of this World: A History of Continental Anti-Realism* (Evanston: Northwestern University Press, 2007), 270-272.

[10] "Heidegger seeks a way out of metaphysics. He endeavors to clear a space where he can evade its grasp. But Whitehead doesn't yearn for a return before, or for a leap beyond, metaphysics. Much more subversively, I think, he simply does metaphysics in his own way, inventing his own categories and working through his own problems." Steven Shaviro, *Without Critera: Kant, Whitehead, Deleuze, and Aesthetics* (Cambridge MA: MIT Press, 2009), x.

proven.[11] In this way SR has been hailed as a "liberation" by those who rejoiced in seeing the possibility reestablished of discussing a thing as something other than a constitutive impasse of thought, this famous "finitude." To paraphrase Harman, a pleasing aspect of this metaphysical revival is that while SR's followers may run the risk of uttering falsities or nonsense, at least they are saying *something*, that is, they maintain precise theses and defend them through considerations and argument, rather than cloaking themselves in the *pathos* of a principle of undecidability.

Continental, then, for three reasons. The first reason, which is not insignificant, is that most of SR's participants come out of Anglo-Saxon academia, where continental philosophy constitutes a specific and autonomous field in the margins of mainstream, analytical philosophy, which most people see as "philosophy tout court," while in France for example the situation is exactly reversed. For this reason, we should not be surprised that they choose to identify themselves as continentals.

Second, because correlationism can be presented as the unifying characteristic of the quasi-totality of what had been coupled with the term "continental philosophy," Bergson, Whitehead, and Deleuze, the only notable (although this is certainly a subject of discussion) exceptions to this unity, can be considered the precursors of SR. The almost completely "definitive" character of the Kantian turn in the eyes of classic continental philosophers (i.e., the endorsement of correlationism) provides evidence for this historical argument. This is developed in detail in Lee Braver's *A Thing of this World: A History of Continental Anti-Realism*, which has became a collective reference SR supporters use in interpreting the philosophical tradition. In this text, Braver identifies a continuous line of thought from Kant to Derrida through other major figures (Hegel, Nietzsche, Heidegger, Foucault), where anti-realism[12] develops in a more and more radical manner, from

---

[11] Meillassoux, *After Finitude*, 109-110.

[12] Composed of six possible cumulative theses: rejection of the truth-

a common conceptual scheme that serves as the foundation for the various options adopted. This extremely ambitious reconstruction is interesting in that it provides a common framework for the evolution of continental philosophy,[13] presenting it as a coherent project, which is precisely what SR seeks to reject.

Finally, the metaphysics that SR produces is certainly a continental metaphysics to the extent that it does not depart from another central point in the continental tradition, namely, the problematic status given to rationality, in particular discursive rationality. It is for this reason that "typically continental" philosophers such as Heidegger, Laruelle, Deleuze, or even Derrida (according to Martin Hägglund), far from being dismissed, are quite acceptable references in these metaphysical debates. The paradoxical idea of a metaphysics that does not seek to ignore objections to it but to incorporate their contributions, makes the "realism" in question "speculative," since it tries to develop specific modes of thought and foundation, taking seriously the inevitable intertwining of reason with other forms of thought, apprehension, and existence. Of course, this last point is highly problematic for the justification of doctrines resulting from such a process (we will have the opportunity to return to this), but it is crucial to understand how SR is very much a continuation of the continental line of thought.

In this text, I will attempt to present the main threads of SR. I will not concentrate as much on the proposed renewal of *subjects* of philosophical inquiry (thus leaving aside the insistent call to "return to the real," to focus on material objects or the contributions of natural science or the social sciences), but rather on the various metaphysical and ontological alternatives that underlie this "turn" (the central anthology of SR is titled *The Speculative Turn*, echoing the

---

correspondence, of independence from the mind, ontological pluralism, rejection of bivalence, active role of the subject relative to its knowledge, plurality of the subject.

[13] As well as a framework for communication between analytics and continentals.

"linguistic turn"). I will also consider the arguments, concepts, and points of debate that emerge, as this is the heart of the subject. I will successively present Harman's *object-oriented ontology*, Brassier's "nihilism", and finally Grant's variety of neo-vitalism.[14]

I. Object-Oriented Ontology: Graham Harman (Latour / Heidegger)

Variants: Levi Bryant, Bruno Latour

CORRELATIONISM: Every apprehension and every relation is essentially different from the object it aims at (the tree that I think is by definition different from the tree itself).

ANTI-CORRELATIONISM: there is no fundamental ontological difference in the relations between subject and object and the relations between objects.

∾

Object-oriented ontology (OOO)[15] asserts the reality and fundamentality of singular individuals, baptized *objects*. An object is defined as *a substantial singularity endowed with*

---

[14] I leave aside Quentin Meillassoux, firstly because Martin Fortier has more than adequately introduced his work in the seminar in which this paper was initially presented (now archived at http://www.atmoc.fr/seances/; scroll down to the seventh presentation in the series for Fortier's talk), secondly, because, unlike other currents, Meillassoux does not "make a school," at least to my knowledge, for reasons due to human contingency (non-appearance of *L'Inexistence divine*), and probably, also to the very singular character of his thought.

[15] [In Morelle's translation, *l'ontologie objectuelle*, literally, "philosophy oriented towards the object" (Tristan Garcia translates this literally in French as *philosophie-orientée-objet*). The term dates from 1999, and its variant (OOO) from 2008. The "official" translation [in French] is *philosophie centrée sur l'objet* ["philosophy centered on the object"]. Graham Harman, *L'Objet quadruple*, trans. Olivier Dubouclez (Paris: Presses Universitaires de France, 2010). The term adopted [by Morelle, i.e., *ontologie objectuelle*] is personal, and responds to criteria of simplicity and euphony.]

unity and irreducible to the whole of relations that relate to it (what Harman summarizes by the expression "unified and autonomous"[16]). OOO is therefore an attempt to argue that the concept of substance is still as indispensible to metaphysics as it is to every other theory and discourse. The domain of objects includes: physical objects (a quark) and theoretical objects (concepts), natural objects (a dog) and artificial objects (a computer), intangible objects (a multinational) and concrete objects, real objects and imaginary objects. The central claim of OOO is that these are all on equal footing. And the concept of object has the concept of relation as its correlate, either determining the object independently, or on the interior of another object (the car that I observe and the car that the road supports are one and the same object, but apprehended through two distinct relations: vision and spatial copresence). Yet these relations are not dealing with the car itself, in its proper being, but with a *version* of this: the "visible car" and the "heavy car." The real car itself is inaccessible to every relation. To be real, it must exist by itself, from itself, and not by another thing: the reality of a thing, whatever it may be, is its withdrawal (and for this reason relations only deal with second-order objects, equivalent to Husserlian intentional objects, distinct from real objects: Harman baptizes them "sensual objects").

The concept of withdrawal is directly inherited from Heidegger. But whereas the German philosopher attributed withdrawal to Being alone, denying it to beings "immediately accessible," present at hand entities, OOO claims that withdrawal is the essential characteristic of every reality *qua* individual reality. In fact, because it equates reality with withdrawal, every negation of the fundamental feature of objects is, in effect, the negation of their reality. If objects were in some way effects in an order of things distinct from themselves, they would quite simply not exist. Consequently, a "radical" position, that denies the reality of objects,[17] is equivalent in the end to a

---

[16] Harman, *Prince of Networks*, 154.

[17] Harman, *Prince of Networks*; Harman, *The Quadruple Object*, chapter I:

more or less well-disguised monism, essentially returning to a form of correlationism. And yet correlationism only consists in elevating a specific type of relation above all others: the relation between human being and world. In order to maintain a reality full of individual objects, it is necessary to assert that there is no ontological difference between subject/object relations and object/object relations.

Thus experience and thought are restricted to a particular case of the universal category of relation: their emergence can only be envisioned as one leap among others, purely "ontic," and never ontological.[18] The problem that remains is knowing how each relation—of causality, of subjectivity, or of mereological composition—is metaphysically possible, which leads to the renewal of the ancient problem of occasionalism.[19] What is essential, however, is that the mystery is not limited to the sphere of humanity or sentience.

In addition, perception, *qua* relation, is necessarily a caricature, but a legitimate caricature, present on all levels of the cosmos; from there perceptual realism dissolves, since no object is present in any relation, but always in the reduced, intelligible form given to experience. We are faced with a paradox: objects are precisely as they are given (*qua* sensual objects) and precisely other than they are given (*qua* real objects). OOO is presented as an ontological realism and an epistemological anti-realism, a position that sparks a number of internal difficulties.

Indeed, as we have said, since there is no difference between subject/object relations and object/object relations, in Husserlian language they are both "intentional" (because they take place between singular objects).[20] To contest this thesis

---

"Undermining and Overmining."

[18] Harman, *The Quadruple Object*, chapter VIII: "Levels and Psyche." See also Graham Harman, *Guerrilla Metaphysics: Phenomenology and the Carpentry of Things* (Chicago: Open Court, 2005), chapter XII: "Some Implications;" the emergence of perception is presented there as a simple case among other "gradations" composing the history of the universe.

[19] Harman, *The Quadruple Object*, chapter V: "Indirect Causation."

[20] Graham Harman, *Tool-Being: Heidegger and the Metaphysics of Objects* (Chi-

would mean denying the *specific* character of each interaction, namely, that it depends upon the nature of the objects in play. For example, obviously a table does not enter into a similar relation with a feather falling on it as it does with a heavy stone that is capable of smashing it. We notice, however, that it is through Husserl that Harman defends this thesis; in fact, his refutation of empiricism in the *Logical Investigations* uses an interpretation of the sensible as composed of immanent or intentional objects.[21] But such a theoretical gesture is not made without raising a number of difficulties.

Indeed, activating a distinctive category of experience, intentionality, in order to attribute it to every relation *qua relation*, is double-edged; on one hand, it seems to exhaust the logic of the decentering of ontology by attributing what seems to only be a privilege of human perception to every interaction between objects of all sorts; on the other, the specter of what one can call *the sophism of the projection*, that is, the idea of covertly reducing what is called ontology to only human subjectivity, becomes a looming danger. The type of position defended by OOO is at times called a *flat ontology*,[22] and the metaphor is here quite meaningful: by "flattening" the ontological terrain, and as a result forcing the rethinking of every type of existence and relation "on the same level," the problem immediately arises of knowing *which* level this is, how to succeed in determining its essence, and above all, whether it constitutes a form more or less disguised by projection in the way we just introduced.

Therefore, we are again confronted with a particular version of the absolute like "the night in which all cows are black." Such a difficulty was already present in a precursor of SR such as Whitehead, who admits to identifying his concept

---

cago: Open Court, 2002), 121, 220; Graham Harman, "Intentional Objects for Non-Humans," Lecture given at the Université de Toulouse le Mirail, France, November 18 2008.

[21] Harman, *Guerrilla Metaphysics*, chapter II and 154-158; Harman, *The Quadruple Object*, chapter II.

[22] Term borrowed from Manuel De Landa, *Intensive Science and Virtual Philosophy* (London: Continuum, 2002), 47.

of *prehension* (that is to say, every relation between entities) with the concept of thought or of idea:

> With the purpose of obtaining a one-substance cosmology, "prehensions" are a generalization from Descartes' mental "cogitations," and from Locke's "ideas," to express the most concrete mode of analysis applicable to every grade of individual actuality.[23]

This question, which can be called the "problem of decentering," is especially troublesome with respect to OOO, because it cannot itself be *envisioned*, since the will to abolish all ontological privilege connected to human subjectivity precludes any conceptual account of the modalities of human subjectivity, and therefore cannot avoid making its central idea unclear. It thus fails to conceive of subjectivity as a "mere" particularization of ontology, that is to say, as something other than a hidden model that would dissolve the decentering. For this reason, it is not satisfying to conceive of alterity solely via a fundamental withdrawal, despite Harman's call for "polypsychism" as a remedy to "panpsychist" excesses, claiming that only the latter falls prey to the "sophism of projection." This is because, in both cases, the relational variations begin from the model of human subjectivity.[24] This problem of decentering would involve an incapacity, in the end, to distinguish "flat" ontologies from their correlationist adversaries (see, for example, the literature on the rapprochements between Whitehead and phenomenology, and Pierre Cassou-Noguès' recent book, *Le bord de l'expérience* [PUF, 2010], dealing explicitly with such a project).

---

[23] Alfred North Whitehead, *Process and Reality: An Essay in Cosmology* corr. and ed. David Ray Griffin and Donald W. Sherburne (New York: Free Press, 1978), 19.

[24] Despite the exciting possibility that this opens. On the description of the interior of objects: "I would even propose a new philosophical discipline called 'speculative psychology' dedicated to ferreting out the specific psychic reality of earthworms, dust, armies, chalk, and stone" (Harman, *Prince of Networks*, 213). This project is taken seriously by Ian Bogost, who concentrates on technological objects in his *Alien Phenomenology, or What It's Like to Be a Thing* (Minneapolis: University of Minnesota Press, 2012).

The discussion within SR focuses on the possibility of a valid epistemology starting from the presuppositions of OOO. In order to summarize this debate, it is useful for us to focus on Bruno Latour, and more precisely on his explicitly ontological work, *Irreductions*, which can be used as a smaller model of OOO's essential propositions on this terrain. Ray Brassier targets it in his article "Concept and Objects," with the same goal. In short, Latour is criticized for the complete dissolution of the limits separating real objects from representations; that is, he is guilty of endorsing the impossibility of every notion of the true and false by way of a collapsing of all things into a neutral monism of "actants" and their mutual "trials of strength."

Indeed, Latour redraws the epistemological relations of knowledge in *pragmatic* terms, envisaging representations and concepts, not as detached modes of contemplating established facts, but as relations between actants. As beings of the world these actants not only demand an exercise of force and a material effort in order to be realized, but *are* an exercise of force themselves: "Nothing is known—only realized" (*Irreductions*, 1.1.5.4). For example, in order to know the chemical properties of a liquid, it is necessary to subject it to diverse *trials* of composition and decomposition, as in some sort of torture where the liquid actant reveals its characteristics through resistance to confronting forces. "A sentence does not hold together because it is true, but *because it holds together* we say that it is 'true.'"[25] If concepts have truth, it is because they are things among others and are subject to the same rules of efficacy as any other relation. The reading of *Irreductions* is extremely disturbing in this regard, because it forces one to consider ideas from a completely desecrated view, yet within the framework of a fully coherent line of reasoning.

Yet for Brassier, this "actualist" conception of ontology only serves to destroy every limit which might allow the separation of valid discourse from fabrication. He accuses

---

[25] Bruno Latour, "Irreductions," in *The Pasteurization of France* (Cambridge MA: Harvard University Press, 1988), 2.4.8.

Latour of reductionism with regard to epistemology, forming a metaphysics liberated from any demand for justification and argumentation:

> the difference between "words" and "things" turns out to be no more than a functional difference subsumed by the concept of "actant"—that is to say, it is a merely nominal difference encompassed by the metaphysical function now ascribed to the metaphor "actant."[26]

Brassier's critique proves problematic, both because it rests on a rather heavy set of presuppositions (see the following section), and because it does not give an account of the finer points of Latour's ontology. However, it certainly helps make the problem of Latour's "flat ontology," as well as OOO, very acute as they fail to offer an *internal* epistemological criterion: why qualify ontological unities as actants rather than as passive subjects of external forces? Thus, the confusion produced by ontological decentering proves to be difficult to eliminate without the risk of falling into a metaphysics with a foundation that would prove, ultimately, irrational. The fundamental problem then consists in noticing how difficult it is to supply it with a true epistemological foundation *with the proper tools* of OOO. Such a foundation would be the complete loss of OOO's project, hopelessly engulfing it in a theory of sense and representation as the point of departure for philosophy. Effectively, the responses of OOO's followers to the objections born from epistemological preoccupations such as Brassier's,

---

[26] Ray Brassier, "Concepts and Objects," in *The Speculative Turn: Continental Materialism and Realism*, ed. Levi Bryant, Nick Srnicek, and Graham Harman (Melbourne: re.press, 2011), 52. See also: "It is instructive to note how many reductions must be carried out in order for irreductionism to get off the ground: reason, science, knowledge, truth—all must be eliminated. Of course, Latour has no qualms about reducing reason to arbitration, science to custom, knowledge to manipulation, or truth to force: the veritable object of his irreductionist afflatus is not reduction per se, in which he wantonly indulges, but explanation, and the cognitive privilege accorded to scientific explanation in particular." Thus, it is impossible, according to Brassier, to philosophically recontextualize the category of explanation without putting a radical attack in its place, since epistemology is, irrevocably, first philosophy.

or from the relation between the sophism of projection and ontologies of decentering are something like denial, or, in the best case scenario, accusing opposing positions of being victims of idealism.[27] On this account, the problem remains unresolved, even if it is not necessarily insoluble.

II. "Normative nihilism," or transcendental nihilism: Ray Brassier (Churchland/Brandom/Laruelle)

Variants: Peter Wolfendale, Martin Hägglund

CORRELATIONISM: There can only be knowledge and meaning within the limits specified by rationality.

ANTI-CORRELATIONISM: Rationality is independent from any origin situated in subjective experience.

∼

The second theoretical side of SR is clearly less unified than the first since as it does not boast of a distinct conceptual invention theorists could be reunited around. Rather, we are dealing with a current of thought with diverse aspirations and variable forms: transcendental nihilism (Brassier), non-philosophy (Laruelle), radical atheist materialism (Hägglund), transcendental realism (Brassier, Wolfendale), methodological naturalism, normativism, inferentialism, anti-vitalism...This is not about enumerating labels, and I would not do it if this diversity were not significant. In fact, the unification of the viewpoint is less about a particular concept or original thesis than allowing the possibility of linking together a number of separate and individually discussed theses. It consists of the following positions:

---

[27] Graham Harman, "And I am also of the opinion that materialism must be destroyed," in *Environment and Society D: Society and Space*, 28 (2010), 772-790; Harman, *The Quadruple Object*, chapter VIII.

(a) Ordinary realism (independence of the world from the mind)
(b) Inferentialism (formal autonomy of reason)
(c) Scientific realism (the propositions produced by scientific and mathematical method genuinely inform us about the world)
(d) Eliminativism concerning experience (the contents of experience do not literally represent any real determination)
(e) Materialism (ontological priority of inorganic over organic, of matter over the living)

Not only are these compatible, but they also mutually entail one another based on concepts of a reality independent of the mind and reason being tied to truth. The conclusion of nihilism, that is, the inexistence of any "meaning" inherent to things thus emerges, as the essential truth of the Enlightenment project (the emancipation of Reason).[28] In other words, if for Continentals the truth (or, in its stead, what philosophy produces) is supposed to be exciting or grand, and if, for the analytics, to discover it involves making it tedious,[29] for

---

[28] An attempt, which I am not entirely satisfied with, at connecting these theses: Reason, impersonal and formal, is the condition of possibility of all thought and speculation (inferentialism). It compellingly makes possible the rational knowledge of reality (transcendental realism). This knowledge is based on the idea of a reality absolutely independent of thought, and postulated by the already established concept of reason. In turn, this allows a set of substantial deductions about the world, devoid of meaning and harmony between human being and the world, thought and being, facts and values (nihilism).

[29] "Any effort in philosophy to make the obscure obvious is likely to be unappealing, for the penalty of failure is confusion while the reward of success is banality." Nelson Goodman, *The Structure of Appearance* (Boston: R. Reidel, 1977). On the continental side, see the concept of image of thought defended by Gilles Deleuze in *Difference and Repetition* (New York: Columbia University Press, 1994). "As long as we're content with criticizing the 'false,' we're not bothering anyone (true critique is the criticism of true forms, not false contents. You don't criticize capitalism or imperialism by denouncing their 'mistakes')." Gilles Deleuze, *Desert Islands and Other Texts, 1953-1974* (Cambridge MA: MIT Press, 2004), 138, or the more systematic defense of rhetoric by Harman in *Prince of Networks*, 168-174. Let us add ("of course") that these characterizations do not constitute value judgments. Here I es-

Brassier, the truth proves to be despairing, (even must be, according to the interpretation that we will form) or, more rigorously, violently demystifying.

It is the link between these fundamental theses, rather than these theses themselves, that give an identity to this current. It would be largely inaccurate, except for the sake of exposition, to discuss this position only through its eliminativist or scientist aspects, as is often done, since the conceptual framework of the theory is actually much larger.[30] That also complicates the task of summarizing this underlying philosophical project in an intelligible way, since one could dedicate (and some indeed have) entire books to each individual thesis.

One can quickly give an adequate idea of Brassier's position by contrasting it with another "materialist" of SR, Quentin Meillassoux. As we have seen with Meillassoux, the discovery of the absence of an ultimate reason for things is that of an absolute:

> Instead of laughing or smiling at questions like "Where do we come from?" or "Why do we exist?," we should ponder instead the remarkable fact that the replies "From nothing. For nothing" really *are* answers, thereby realizing that these really were questions—and excellent ones at that.[31]

But if, for Meillassoux, this absence of reason (or principle of unreason) is an absolute fact, in an even more audacious way for Brassier, it is a fact which carries a substantial thesis: the absolute ontological primacy of matter over mind, of death over life.[32] Philosophy then becomes the discipline charged with bringing to light the insurmountable truth of extinction.

---

sentially refer to the differences in attitude concerning language, rhetoric, and the nature of knowledge produced by philosophy in the two traditions.

[30] It would be difficult for "standard" eliminitavists, à la Churchland, not only to refer to, but to admit as acceptable, the philosophical methods drawn from Laruelle, Badiou, or Heidegger...

[31] Meillassoux, *After Finitude*, 110.

[32] Brassier, *Nihil Unbound*, preface.

For instance, coming back to the eliminativist thesis, if one supposes its literal truth,[33] then one infers from it that the ultimate meaning of this truth is that thought and experience allow access to no real determination. Therefore, it passes from "grass is not really, *in itself*, green," to "our experience of grass is only a secondary effect and foreign to grass itself." Ultimately Brassier's anti-correlationism consists in its literal inversion: the correlate of thought is not being, but non-being.

This project, and the theses that it proposes, can seem excessively heavy, arbitrary, or absurd (a sort of philosophical Houellebecq). This would be the case indeed if there were no method to support this ambition. And yet one of them exists, found principally by Brassier, in the French philosopher François Laruelle.[34] I will certainly not venture to summarize the thoughts of this rather arduous author, but will quickly present the part which concerns us here: Laruelle's project involves replacing philosophy with "non-philosophy," i.e., the systematic opposition to every philosophical attempt to use thought to add anything to the "flat" discoveries of scientificity and the "radically immanent" presence of the Real. The Real is always present, always accessible, but, since it is not an idea or a concept, the nature of philosophy is to perpetually miss it. Indeed, the sin of philosophy is its inaugural *Decision* to understand the Real (or the One) by something other than it (by idea, intuition, language, etc.), to divide itself from it in order to understand it. Philosophy does nothing except develop this circular Decision. All the subsequent work of philosophy involves the desperate attempt to rejoin what has been separated, forming a synthesis from an always-arbitrary control-point.[35] This negative thesis, which corresponds to a formal and generalized version of denunciations of meta-

---

[33] We understand what we suppose to be true, if demonstrated philosophically to be true. I will return to this. That is, if we suppose it philosophically demonstrated to be true.

[34] Hägglund makes use of Derrida in his approach, seeking to unearth the constructive tools of a "radical atheist materialism" within deconstruction.

[35] What Laurelle calls the method of "transcendental deduction" Brassier, *Nihil Unbound*, 123.

physics by Heidegger or Derrida,[36] permits abolishing every attempt to think about the world apart from the insurmountable *facts* of the real that are proposed to us.[37] To think of the Real as separate from thought requires a "non-Decisional" philosophy that, with one of the most painful lexical choices of the twentieth century, Laruelle baptizes "non-philosophy."

We now return to eliminativism (which is not the only thesis of Brassier's nihilism, but is rather useful for us as a guiding thread here): the most contemporary opposition against eliminativism involves categorizing it as nonsense, either through self-contradiction, or because it is incapable of giving a ground for itself, and must resort to a form of, at the very least, insufficient pragmatism.[38] Laruelle's method, reviewed by Brassier, accepts philosophical irreducibility from the *fact* of the absence of correlation between being and thought—not only the empirical, but the ontological truth of the consequences of eliminativism: "We gain access to the structure of reality via a machinery of conception which extracts intelligible indices *from a world that is not designed to be intelligible and is not originarily infused with meaning.*"[39]

---

[36] "[Laruelle's] innovation is fundamentally formal," Brassier, *Nihil Unbound*, 148.

[37] "Metaphysics conceived of the autonomy of the object in terms of the model of substance. But successive critiques of the hypostatization of substance from Kant to Heidegger have undermined the plausibility of metaphysical (substance based) realism, thereby securing the triumph of correlationism. Laruelle's work challenges this correlationist consensus by proposing a version of transcendental realism wherein the object is no longer conceived of as a substance but rather as a discontinuous cut in the fabric of ontological synthesis. It is no longer thought that determines the object, whether through representation or intuition, but rather the object that seizes thought and forces it to think it, or better, *according* to it." Ibid., 149.

[38] Teed Rockwell, "Beyond Eliminative Materialism: Some Unnoticed Implications of Churchland's Pragmatic Pluralism," Revised version, October 1998, unpublished article. Accessed May 31 2011: http://users.sfo.com/~mcmf/beyondem.html

[39] Ray Brassier, "Concepts and Objects," §4 (Our emphasis). Compare this with Churchland's declaration: "it is far from obvious that truth is either the primary or the principal product of [cognitive] activity. Rather, its function would appear to be the ever more finely tuned administration of the organism's behaviour." Paul M. Churchland, *A Neurocomputational Perspective: The*

Brassier's other method of supporting his position consists in maintaining that every attempt to deny the objectivity-nihilism correlation, through vitalism or an overturning of the category of objectivity, is based on an illegitimate concept of reason or thought that exceeds what can be defended *by* reason. The paradigmatic example here would be that of Bergson, whose philosophy of life celebrates novelty and relies heavily on a limited conception of reason, the latter being marginalized in favor of intuition. Against such a current of thought (which brings together Deleuze, Whitehead, Heidegger, Hegel, and all the metaphysicians of SR), Brassier resorts to a deconstruction inspired by Wilfrid Sellars and his critique of the "myth of the given." The myth of the given is "the idea that there is a certain *stratum* of experience which is somehow making a truth claim and which is somehow more basic than any acquired conceptual system."[40] For Brassier, all the vitalist or phenomenological claims of conceptual priority for lived experience and the non-conceptual over conceptual reason are reduced to nothingness, either through critique of the myth of the given,[41] or through a prior reduction to a form of correlationism undermined by this critique: "In the absence of any physicalist corrective to vitalist hubris, biocentrism leads infallibly to noocentrism."[42] Thus, every appeal to intellectual or sensual intuition is humiliated and rejected in favor of an irreducible attachment to an "impersonal" concept of reason borrowed from Robert Brandom (*Making It Explicit*). This rejection is not only formal, but also implies a substantial conclusion, namely the priority of death over

---

Nature of Mind and the Structure of Science (Cambridge MA: MIT Press, 1989), 150, cited in Brassier, *Nihil Unbound*, 19.

[40] Wilfrid Sellars, Notre Dame Lectures, 1969-1986, transcr. Pedro Amaral, 249. Accessed July 1 2012: http://zimmer.csufresno.edu/~pedroa/Wilfrid%20Sellars%20Notre%20Dame%20Lectures.pdf

[41] Ray Brassier, "Bergson, Lived Experience, and the Myth of the Given," Lecture given at colloquium in Zagreb, June 18 2011.

[42] Brassier, *Nihil Unbound*, 200.

life: "The living is only a form of what is dead, and a very rare form" (Nietzsche).[43] The omnipresence of extinction in the very heart of life and thought is the highest truth.

How, then, can this conception be critiqued? The most obvious problem resides in its very specific usage of philosophical rationality that claims to discover some "subtractionist" truths—both substantial and negative truths (namely, nihilism)—by a formal method. It is uncertain whether such a position is tenable, at least according to the precision with which Brassier guards himself. So, more generally, his position is based on an emphatic interpretation of the nature of the ideas of objectivity and rationality, which in their proper form would have profound substantial content;[44] yet this method, though proving definitively powerful when it comes to refutation, appears much weaker when it comes to defending its own theses. Moreover, the arguments against him, incidentally, are less concerned with the extremely technical metaphysical presuppositions borrowed from Badiou and Laruelle, than his reprise of scientific realism (and his eliminativist conclusions) via inferentialism, titled "transcendental realism." The metaphysical tit-for-tat response (from Harman to Brassier) consisted in showing how attempts to identify scientific rationality with ontology were doomed to failure because they themselves rely on an extremely unsophisticated metaphysics equivalent to a "naïve" process-relationalism (cf. the next section). On a broader level, Harman objects to Brassier because he absolutizes scientific methods and results. This, argues Harman, does not constitute the deeper message of the Enlightenment, but simply underwrites a form of correlationism, since this affirms that the conditions of possibility of knowledge delimit the framework of ontology.[45]

---

[43] Friedrich Nietzsche, *The Gay Science*, ed. Bernard Williams (Cambridge: Cambridge University Press, 2001), III, §109.

[44] As Brassier summarizes it: "I am a nihilist because I believe in truth."

[45] Cf. Brassier, "Concepts and Objects," §1, and Harman, "I am also of the opinion that materialism must be destroyed."

It seems that the question remains open since the rejection of the position (normative nihilism) involves an ontology close to OOO (and inversely), because the two tend to mutually refute each other. We will therefore examine what makes up the last type of position.

III. Neo-Vitalisms: Iain Hamilton Grant (Schelling/Deleuze/Whitehead)

Variants: Manuel De Landa, Steven Shaviro

CORRELATIONISM: No essential difference exists between the material and the ideal.

ANTI-CORRELATIONISM: It is impossible to reduce the origin of existence to properties or determinations that are individually identifiable or can be apprehended by an experience.

~

The last current of SR is not the easiest to approach, on the one hand, because alternate versions abound (especially inspired by Deleuze and Whitehead[46]), and, on the other hand, because its "original" representative, Iain Hamilton Grant, expresses his thought in a way that is difficult to access, by confining it to the narrow space of Schellingian studies. In fact, for Grant, the abandonment of active nature, which characterizes modern philosophy in general and correlationism in particular (its *aphysia*, or forgetting of Nature), found a worthy adversary in F. W. J. Schelling's *Naturphilosophie*. His essentially historical work demonstrates the existence of nontrivial thought about nature in Schelling, and he argues that it is irreducible to any other philosophical alternative. In doing so, he arrives at a vitalist version of idealism. By "idealism," he means:

---

[46] I will not linger here on the Whiteheadians, such as Steven Shaviro, in order to simplify this introduction somewhat.

(a) Platonist realism (the Idea exists just as much as thought and things),
(b) a concept of matter as active and substantial rather than as a mere negation of form,[47] and
(c) relativity of the existence of singular things, commensurate with a dynamism more profound than the things themselves (Nature).

Idealism is the condition, (a) of every metaphysics, (b) of every true materialism, and (c) of a realism that is not naïve and essentialist. We obtain the only tenable realism by reuniting these three aspects: a speculative realism, in the sense Schelling gave to speculative physics. What matters for Grant is to be opposed to contemporary negations of these three fundamental theses. e Idea within correlation to the thinking subject, endorsing the incessant survival of a neo-Fichteanism against the Schellingianism he defends. Against (b), the Aristotelian privilege accorded to form, resulting in a negative conception of matter against Plato's active matter. The other forms of speculative realism do not literally subscribe to (a), but, are not, strictly speaking, opposed to it (above all object-oriented ontology, which accepts the reality of concepts as objects); by contrast, it is with (b) and (c) that the difference is the clearest. First, concerning (b), there is no doubt that OOO and transcendental nihilism are clearly devoted to the autonomy of form over matter.

For Brassier, the negation of (b) is twofold: there is a reality of form, since its autonomy with respect to every determination is the condition of existence of reason and thought, uprooted from every "intuition;" but there is also a primary reality of inert matter, since Brassier completely adopts the concept of inert matter that Grant rejects and makes the ultimate truth of ontology from it.

---

[47] Iain Hamilton Grant, *Philosophies of Nature after Schelling* (London: Continuum, 2006), 47.

For Harman, who does not hide his Aristotelian heritage on this point,[48] the presence of formalism is rather patent: the world is structured in terms of objects, and, since we cannot know the full reality of objects, then strictly speaking only their generic form is accessible to ontology. Yet this form is universal and identical for all objects. Harman would completely agree with Grant on the fact that it is necessary to reject the concept of physical matter as the fundamental category of ontology (i.e., physicalism), because such a concept is only the pretext for a hidden idealism.[49] However, he does not support the concept of active matter, but only the idea of objects being active.

The last point is, in reality, the true grounds for opposition between the various neo-vitalisms, (whether they are inherited from Schelling, as in Grant, from Deleuze, or from Bergson) and OOO. Active matter is rejected by OOO not because of a taste for an inert conception of matter, but because active matter deprives singular objects of their reality by situating activity, novelty, and, in the end, reality, outside of objects in a mysterious substrate. Critiquing Jane Bennett's "vital materialism," Harman thus declares:

> Ultimately, what is real in her new Nicene Creed is a pluriverse not of many things, but of "one matter-energy" that is "traversed by heterogeneities." The danger for Bennett, as for Deleuze and Deleuze's Spinoza, is that objects are liberated from slavery to the human gaze only to fall into a new slavery to a single "matter-energy" that allows for no strife between autonomous individual things.[50]

---

[48] Graham Harman, "Aristotle With a Twist," in *Speculative Medievalisms: A Laboratory-Atelier*. Edited by Nicola Masciandro and Eileen A. Joy. (Brooklyn, NY: punctum books, forthcoming 2012)

[49] "To define a thing as material stuff that occupies space is to reduce it to a system of coordinates and measurable properties. Though it may seem that matter is autonomous, it is only autonomous insofar as humans define it according to certain properties, not in its own right." Harman, *Prince of Networks*, 141. See also 107-112, as well as Harman, "I am also of the opinion that materialism must be destroyed."

[50] Graham Harman, "Autonomous objects: a review of Jane Bennett's Vibrant Matter: a political ecology of things," *New Formations* 71 (Spring 2011), 125-130.

Thus, it is because (b) and (c) are closely linked in Grant's idealism and contemporary neo-vitalisms that OOO is opposed to the idea of matter defined as active. On the other side, the neo-vitalists are opposed to the existence of individual things and prefer a form of non-individuated monism, because these things would be inextricably tied to a concept of a manipulable and calculable thing: "[we] view the world as if it consisted not of an ever-changing flow of time but of a calculable set of things," laments Bennett.[51] Such a flow, a "process," is at the center of vitalist ontologies,[52] and is criticized very insistently by the other SR participants.[53] Either we are literally dealing with a unique "dynamism" (or the beyond of unity) that produces the individuality of things, in which case it becomes difficult to see how things have ever been able to be individuated from an entirely indeterminate *apeiron*); or, we assert that only non-individual dynamism is real, and that separate things are only a product of a human sensation,[54] in which case we are dealing with an idealism that privileges subjectivity over the real being of things. Or, finally, we take recourse to hybrid concepts such as Gilbert Simondon's "preindividual singularities" or De Landa's

---

[51] Jane Bennett, *Vibrant Matter: A Political Ecology of Things* (Durham: Duke University Press, 2010), 77.

[52] "To take the most obvious example, in some realist approaches the world is thought to be composed of fully formed objects whose identity is guaranteed by their possession of an essence, a core set of properties that defines what these objects are. Deleuze is not a realist about essences, or any other transcendent entity, so in his philosophy something else is needed to explain what gives objects their identity and what preserves this identity through time. Briefly, this something else is dynamical processes. Some of these processes are material and energetic, some are not, but even the latter remain immanent to the world of matter and energy." De Landa, *Intensive Science and Virtual Philosophy*, 2-3.

[53] Harman, *Prince of Networks*, 160-161; Tristan Garcia, *Forme et objet: un traité des choses* (Paris: Presses Universitaires de France, 2011), 46.

[54] "The distinct outlines which we see in an object, and which give it its individuality, are only the design of a certain kind of influence that we might exert on a certain point of space: it is the plan of our eventual actions that is sent back to our eyes, as though by a mirror, when we see the surfaces and edges of things." Henri Bergson, *Creative Evolution*, 12.

"heterogeneous continuum" in order to explain such a passage, although the consistency of such concepts is greatly diminished by their synthetic nature and they simply name a problem, rather than solving it. This is the main challenge that all vitalist, and, more broadly, panpsychist, positions must face, and that emerges in contemporary continental metaphysics: to show how their concepts are both sound and capable of overcoming "poor" materialism.

∽

How to conclude after multiple back and forths, tentative philosophical hypotheses, and their repeated rebuttals? Ultimately, what can be said about speculative realism as such, which appears so divided and dispersed? The best response I have at my disposal to these two questions consists in maintaining that, despite the incomplete or problematic nature of the theories proposed, they all contain a philosophical, and perhaps an even larger existential, core. This seems to be the essential contribution of speculative realism: namely, that realism cannot be a trivial or obvious position, but conversely, a reality that is not a pragmatic expedient requires important ontological commitments in order to retain the specificity of the real in relation to every representation. In a word, that realism has a price.

Bibliography of Speculative Realism

General Introduction

The order of these texts is a suggested reading order.

Bryant, Levi, Nick Srnicek, and Graham Harman, "Towards a Speculative Philosophy," in *The Speculative Turn: Continental Materialism and Realism* (Melbourne: re.press, 2011).

Saldanha, Arun, "Back to the Great Outdoors: Speculative Realism as Philosophy of Science," in *Cosmos and History* 5.2 (2009), 304-321.

Brassier, Ray, Iain Hamilton Grant, Graham Harman, and Quentin Meillas-

soux, "Speculative Realism," in *Collapse* 3 (2007): 306-449.
Ennis, Paul, *Post-Continental Voices: Selected Interviews* (Winchester: Zero Books, 2010).

Major Works

Brassier, Ray, *Nihil Unbound: Enlightenment and Extinction* (New York: Palgrave Macmillan, 2007).

Braver, Lee, *A Thing of this World: A History of Continental Anti-Realism* (Evanston: Northwestern University Press, 2007).

Bryant, Levi, Nick Srnicek, and Graham Harman, ed., *The Speculative Turn: Continental Materialism and Realism* (Melbourne: re.press, 2010).

De Landa, Manuel, *Intensive Science and Virtual Philosophy* (London: Continuum, 2002).

Garcia, Tristan, *Forme et objet: un traité des choses* (Paris: Presses Universitaires de France, 2011).

Grant, Iain Hamilton, *Philosophies of Nature after Schelling* (London: Continuum, 2008).

Hägglund, Martin, *Radical Atheism: Derrida and the Time of Life* (Stanford: Stanford University Press, 2008).

Harman, Graham, *Prince of Networks: Bruno Latour and Metaphysics* (Melbourne: re.press, 2009).

—, *The Quadruple Object* (Winchester: Zero Books, 2011).

—, *Quentin Meillassoux: Philosophy in the Making* (Edinburgh: Edinburgh University Press, 2011).

Laruelle, François, *Philosophies of Difference: A Critical Introduction to Non-Philosophy*, trans. Rocco Gangle (London: Continuum, 2010).

Latour, Bruno, "Irreductions," in *The Pasteurization of France* (Cambridge MA: Harvard University Press, 1988).

—, Graham Harman, and Peter Erdélyi, *The Prince and the Wolf: Latour and Harman at the LSE* (Winchester: Zero Books, 2011).

Meillassoux, Quentin, *After Finitude: An Essay on the Necessity of Contingency*, trans. Ray Brassier (London: Continuum, 2007).

Shaviro, Steven, *Without Critera: Kant, Whitehead, Deleuze, and Aesthetics* (Cambridge MA: MIT Press, 2009).

Wolfendale, Pete, "Transcendental Realism," 20 May 2010, Available at: http://deontologistics.wordpress.com/2010/05/20/transcendental-realism/

Speculations III

Journals

Collapse: http://urbanomic.com/publications.php
Cosmos and History: http://cosmosandhistory.org/index.php/journal
Speculations: Journal of Speculative Realism: http://www.speculations-journal.org/
Pli: Warwick Journal of Philosophy: http://www.warwick.ac.uk/philosophy/pli_journal
Ozone: A Journal of Object-Oriented Studies: http://ozone-journal.org/

Blogs

Speculative Heresy: http://speculativeheresy.wordpress.com/
Anthem: http://anthem-group.net/
Levi Bryant: http://larvalsubjects.wordpress.com/
Graham Harman: http://doctorzamalek2.wordpress.com/
Adrian Ivakhiv: http://blog.uvm.edu/aivakhiv/
Tim Morton: http://www.ecologywithoutnature.blogspot.com/
Paul Ennis: http://www.anotherheideggerblog.blogspot.com/
Pete Wolfendale: http://deontologistics.wordpress.com/

Other Texts

Badiou, Alain, *Being and Event* (London: Continuum, 2005).
Bennett, Jane, *Vibrant Matter: A Political Ecology of Things* (Durham: Duke University Press, 2010).
Bergson, Henri, *Creative Evolution* (London: Macmillan and Co, 1922)
Bogost, Ian, *Unit Operations: An Introduction to Videogame Criticism* (Cambridge: MIT Press, 2006).
—, "Process vs. Procedure," from the Fourth International Conference of the Whitehead Research Project, "Metaphysics and Things: New Forms of Speculative Thought," (2010).
—, *Alien Phenomenology, or, What It's Like to Be a Thing* (Minneapolis: University of Minnesota Press, 2012).
Brassier, Ray, "Concepts and Objects," in *The Speculative Turn: Continental Materialism and Realism* (Melbourne: re.press, 2011).
—, *Alien Theory: The Decline of Materialism in the Name of Matter*, Doctoral thesis, University of Warwick (2001).

—, "Bergson, Lived Experience, and the Myth of the Given," Colloquium in Zagreb 18 June 2011.
Bryant, Levi, "The Ontic Principle: Outline of an Object-Oriented Ontology," in *The Speculative Turn: Continental Materialism and Realism* (Melbourne: re.press, 2011).
Cassou-Noguès, Pierre, *Le bord de l'expérience: Essai de cosmologie* (Paris: Presses Universitaires de France, 2010).
Debaise, Didier, *Vocabulaire de Whitehead* (Paris: Ellipse, 2007).
Deleuze, Gilles, *Difference and Repetition* (New York: Columbia University Press, 2004).
Ennis, Paul. *Post-Continental Voices: Selected Interviews* (Winchester: Zero Books, 2010).
Grant, Iain Hamilton, "The Eternal and Necessary Link Between Philosophy and Physics: A Repetition of the Difference Between the Fichtean and Schellingian Systems of Philosophy," in *Angelaki* 10.1 (2005).
—, "Schellingianism and Postmodernity: Towards and Materialist *Naturphilosophie*," 2000, Available at: http://www.bu.edu/wcp/Papers/Cult/CultGran.htm
—, "Mining Conditions: A Response to Harman," in *The Speculative Turn: Continental Materialism and Realism* (Melbourne: re.press, 2011).
—, "Does Nature stay what-it-is?" in *The Speculative Turn: Continental Materialism and Realism* (Melbourne: re.press, 2011).
Harman, Graham, *Tool-Being: Heidegger and the Metaphysics of Objects* (Chicago: Open Court, 2002).
—, *Guerrilla Metaphysics: Phenomenology and the Carpentry of Things* (Chicago: Open Court, 2005).
—, "On Vicarious Causation," in *Collapse* II (2006).
—, "On the Horror of Phenomenology: Lovecraft and Husserl," in *Collapse* IV (2008).
—, "Intentional Objects for Non-Humans," Conference at the Université de Toulouse le Mirail, France, 18 November 2008.
—, *Prince of Networks: Bruno Latour and Metaphysics* (Melbourne: re.press, 2009).
—, "I am also of the opinion that materialism must be destroyed," in *Environment and Planning D: Society and Space* 28 (2010), 772-790.
—, "On the Undermining of Objects," in *The Speculative Turn: Continental Materialism and Realism* (Melbourne: re.press, 2011).
—, "Response to Nathan Coombs," *Speculations* I (2010).
—, "Response to Shaviro," in *The Speculative Turn: Continental Materialism and Realism* (Melbourne: re.press, 2011).

—, *Towards Speculative Realism: Essays and Lectures* (Winchester: Zero Books, 2010).
—, *Circus Philosophicus* (Winchester: Zero Books, 2010).
Ladyman, James and Don Ross, with David Spurrett and John Collier. *Every Thing Must Go: Metaphysics Naturalized* (Oxford: Oxford University Press, 2007).
Lozano, Benjamin, "A Contested Revolution," in *Cosmos and History: The Journal of Natural and Social Philosophy* 6.1 (2010).
Meillassoux, Quentin, *After Finitude: An Essay on the Necessity of Contingency* trans. Ray Brassier (London: Continuum, 2008).
—, "Temps et surgissement *ex nihilo*," Lecture at the École Normale Supérieure, 24 April 2006.
—, "Potentiality and Virutality," in *Collapse* II (2006).
—, "Subtraction and Contraction," in *Collapse* III (2006).
—, "Répétition, itération, réitération : une analyse spéculative du signe dépourvu de sens," Lecture at the École Normale Supérieure, 21 February 2011.
Metzinger, Thomas, *Being No One: The Self-Model Theory of Subjectivity* (Cambridge: MIT Press, 2004).
Molnar, George, *Powers: A Study in Metaphysics* (Oxford: Oxford University Press, 2007).
Shaviro, Steven, "The Actual Volcano: Whitehead, Harman, and the Problem of Relations," in *The Speculative Turn: Continental Materialism and Realism* (Melbourne: re.press, 2011).
Skrbina, David, *Panpsychism in the West* (Cambridge: MIT Press, 2005).
—, ed. *Mind That Abides: Panpsychism in the New Millenium* (Amsterdam: John Benjamins, 2009).
Stengers, Isabelle, *Thinking with Whitehead: A Free and Wild Creation of Concepts* trans. Michael Chase (Cambridge MA: Harvard University Press, 2011).
Whitehead, Alfred North, *The Concept of Nature* (Cambridge: Cambridge University Press, 1920).
—, *Process and Reality: An Essay in Cosmology* corr. ed. (New York: Free Press, 1978).
Zizek, Slavoj, *The Ticklish Subject: The Absent Centre of Political Ontology* (London: Verso, 1999).
—, *The Parallax View* (Cambridge MA: MIT Press, 2006).

Outward Bound
On Quentin Meillassoux's *After Finitude*
Christian Thorne
Williams College

*I*L N'Y A PAS DE HORS-TEXTE. IF POST-structuralism has had a motto—a proverb and quotable provocation—then surely it is this, from Derrida's *Of Grammatology*.[1] *Text has no outside. There is nothing outside the text.* It is tempting to put a conventionally Kantian construction on these words—to see them, I mean, as bumping up against an old epistemological barrier: *Our thinking is intrinsically verbal—in that sense, textual—and it is therefore impossible for our minds to get past themselves, to leave themselves behind, to shed words and in that shedding to encounter objects as they really are, in their own skins, even when we're not thinking them, plastering them with language, generating little mind-texts about them.* But this is not, in fact, what the sentence says. Derrida's claim would seem to be rather stronger than that: not *There are unknowable objects outside of text*, but *There are outside of text no objects for us to know*. So we reach for another gloss—*There is only text...ain't nothing but text*—except the sentence isn't really saying that either, since to say that there is nothing outside text points to

---

[1] Jacques Derrida, *Of Grammatology*, trans. Gayatri Spivak (Baltimore: Johns Hopkins University Press, 1976), 158.

the possibility that there is, in a manner yet to be explained, something *inside* text, and this something would not itself have to be text, any more than caramels in a carrying bag have to be made out of cellophane.

So we look for another way into the sentence. An alternate angle of approach would be to consider the claim's implications in institutional or disciplinary terms. *The text has no outside* is the sentence via which English professors get to tell everyone else in the university how righteously important they are. No academic discipline can just dispense with language. Sooner or later, archives and labs and deserts will all have to be exited. The historians will have to write up their findings; so will the anthropologists; so will the biochemists. And if that's true, then it will be in everyone's interest to have around colleagues who are capable of reflecting on writing—literary critics, philosophers of language, the people we used to call rhetoricians—not just to proofread the manuscripts of their fellows and supply these with their missing commas, but to think hard about whether the language typically adopted by a given discipline can actually do what the discipline needs it to do. If the text has no outside, then literature professors will always have jobs; the idea is itself a kind of tenure, since it means that writerly types can never safely be removed from the interdisciplinary mix. The idea might even establish—or seek to establish—the institutional primacy of literature programs. *Il n'y a pas de hors-texte*. There is nothing outside the English department, since every other department is itself engaged in a more or less literary endeavor, just one more attempt to make the world intelligible in language.

Such, then, is the interest of Quentin Meillassoux's *After Finitude*, first published in French in 2006.[2] It is the book that, more than any other of its generation, means to tell the literature professors that their jobs are not, in fact, safe. Against Derrida it banners a counter-slogan of its own: "it could be that contemporary philosophers have lost the *great outdoors*,

---

[2] Quentin Meillassoux, *After Finitude: An Essay on the Necessity of Contingency*, trans. Ray Brassier (New York: Continuum, 2008).

the *absolute* outside."[3] It is Meillassoux's task to restore to us what he is careful not to call nature, to lead post-structuralists out into the open country, to make sure that we are all getting enough fresh air. Meillassoux means, in other words, to wean us from text, and for anyone beginning to experience a certain eye-strain, a certain cramp of the thigh from not having moved all day from out his favorite chair, this is bound to be an appealing prospect, though if you end up unconvinced by its arguments—and there are good reasons for doubt, as the book amounts to a tissue of misunderstanding and turns, finally, on one genuinely arbitrary prohibition—then it's all going to end up sounding like a bullying father enrolling his pansy son in the Boy Scouts against his will: *Get your head out of that book! Why don't you go in the yard and play?!*

Of course, Meillassoux's way of getting the post-structuralists to go hiking with him is by telling them which books to read first. If you start scanning *After Finitude's* bibliography, what will immediately stand out is its programmatic borrowing from seventeenth and early eighteenth-century philosophers. Meillassoux regularly cites Descartes[4] and poses anew the question that once led to the *cogito*, but will here lead someplace else: What is the one thing I as a thinking person cannot disbelieve even from the stance of radical doubt? He christens one chapter after Hume and proposes, as a knowing radicalization of the latter's arguments, that we think of the cosmos as "acausal."[5] In the final pages, Galileo steps forward as modern philosophy's forgotten hero.[6] His followers are given to saying that Meillassoux's thinking marks out a totally new direction in the history of philosophy, but I don't think anyone gets to make that kind of claim until they have first drawn up an exhaustive inventory of debts. At one point, he praises a philosopher publishing in the 1980s for having "written with a concision worthy of the philosophers of the

---

[3] Quentin Meillassoux, *After Finitude*, 17.

[4] Ibid., 3.

[5] Ibid., 92.

[6] Ibid., 113.

seventeenth century."⁷ That's one way to get a bead on this book—that it resurrects the *Grand Siècle* as a term of praise. The movement now coalescing around Meillassoux—the one calling itself speculative realism—is a bid to get past post-structuralism by resurrecting an ante-Kantian, more or less baroque ontology, on the understanding that nearly all of European philosophy since the first *Critique* can be denounced as one long prelude to Derrida. There never was a "structuralism," but only "pre-post-structuralism."

Meillassoux, in sum, is trying to recover the Scientific Revolution and early Enlightenment, which wouldn't be all that unusual, except he is trying to do this on radical philosophy's behalf—trying, that is, to get intellectuals of the Left to make their peace with science again, as the better path to some of post-structuralism's signature positions. His argument's reliance on early science is to that extent instructive. One of the most appealing features of Meillassoux's writing is that it restages something of the madness of natural philosophy before the age of positivism and the research grant; it retrieves, paragraph-wise, the sublimity and wonder of an immoderate knowledge. In 1712, Richard Blackmore published an epic called *Creation*, which you've almost certainly never heard of but which remained popular in Britain for several decades. That poem tells the story of the world's awful making, before humanity's arrival, and if you read even just its opening lines, you'll see that this conception is premised on a rather pungent refusal of Virgil and hence on a wholesale refurbishing of the epic as genre: "No more of arms I sing." Blackmore reclassifies what poets had only just recently been calling "heroic verse" as "vulgar;" the epic, it would seem, has degenerated into bellowing stage plays and popular romances and will have to learn from the astrophysicists if it is to regain its loft and dignity. Poets will have to accompany the natural philosophers as they set out "to see the full extent of nature" and to tally "unnumbered worlds."⁸

---

⁷ Meillassoux, *After Finitude*, 95.

⁸ Richard Blackmore, *Creation: A Philosophical Poem* (Unknown: London,

The point is that there was lots of writing like this in the eighteenth century, and that it was aligned for the most part with the period's republicans and pseudo-republicans and whatever else England had in those years instead of a Left. This means that the cosmic epic was to some extent a mutation of an early Puritan culture, a way of carrying into the eighteenth century earlier trends in radical Protestant writing, and especially the latter's Judaizing or philo-Semitic strains. The idea here was that Hebrew poetry provided an alternative model to Greek and Roman poetry: a sublime, direct poetry of high emotion, of inspiration, ecstasy, and astonishment. *The Creation* is one of the things you could read if you wanted to figure out how ordinary people ever came to care about science—how science was made into something that could turn a person on—and what you'll find in its pages is a then new aesthetic that is equal parts Longinus and Milton, or rather Longinus plus Moses plus Milton plus Newton, and not a Weberian or Purito-rationalist Newton, but a Newton supernal and thunder-charged, in which the *Principia* is made to yield science fiction. It is, finally, *this* writing that Meillassoux is channeling when he asks us—routinely—to contemplate the planet's earliest, not-yet-human eons; when, like a boy-intellectual collecting philosophical trilobites, he demands that our minds be arrested by the fossil record or that all of modern European philosophy reconfigure itself to accommodate the dinosaurs. And it is the eighteenth-century epic's penchant for firebolt apocalyptic that echoes in his descriptions of a cosmos beyond law:

> Everything could actually collapse: from trees to stars, from stars to laws, from physical laws to logical laws; and this not by virtue of some superior law whereby everything is destined to perish, but by virtue of the absence of any superior law capable of preserve anything, no matter what, from perishing.[9]

1712), 1 (all quotations).

[9] Meillassoux, *After Finitude*, 53.

Meillassoux's followers call this an idea that no-one has ever had before. The epic poets once called it Strife.

That so many readers have discovered new political energies in Meillassoux's argument is perhaps hard to see, since the book contains absolutely nothing that would count, in any of the ordinary senses, as political thought. There are, it's true, a few passages in which Meillassoux lets you know he thinks of himself as a committed intellectual: a (badly underdeveloped) account of ideology critique;[10] the faint chiming, in one sentence, of *The Communist Manifesto*;[11] a few pages in tribute to Badiou.[12] With a little effort, though, the political openings can be teased out, and they are basically twofold: 1) Meillassoux says that thought's most pressing task is to do justice to the possibility—or, indeed, to the archaic historical reality—of a planet stripped of its humans. On at least one occasion, he even uses, in English translation, the phrase "world without us."[13] For anyone looking to devise a deep ecology by non-Heideggerian means—and there are permanent incentives to reach positions with as little Heidegger as possible—Meillassoux's thinking is bound to be attractive. The book is an entry, among many other such, in the competition to design the most attractive anti-humanism. 2) The antinomian language in the sentence last quoted—*laws could collapse; there is no superior law*—or, indeed, the very notion of a cosmos structured only by unnecessary laws—is no doubt what has drawn to this book those who would otherwise be reading Deleuze, since Meillassoux, like this other, has designed an ontology to anarchist specifications, though he has done so, rather surprisingly, without Spinoza. Still, there may be good reasons for going back Kant and Hegel. *Another world is possible* wasn't Marx's slogan—it was Leibniz's—except at this level, it has to be said, the book's politics remain for all intents and purposes allegorical. Meillassoux's argument operates at most as a peculiar, quasi-theological reassurance

---

[10] Meillassoux, *After Finitude*, 33-34.

[11] Ibid., 92.

[12] Ibid., 103-104.

[13] Ibid., 114.

that if we set out to change the political and legal order of our nation-states, the universe will *like it*.[14]

Maybe this is already enough information for us to see that *After Finitude*'s relationship to post-structuralism is actually quite complicated. Any brief description of the book is going to have to say that it is out to demolish German Idealism and post-structuralism and any other philosophy of discourse or mind. But if we take a second pass over *After Finitude*, we will have to conclude that far from flattening these latter, its chosen task is precisely to shore them up, to move anti-foundationalism itself onto sturdy ontological foundations. Meillassoux's niftiest trick, the one that having mastered he compulsively performs, is the translating of post-structuralism's over-familiar epistemological claims into fresh-sounding ontological ones. What readers of Foucault and Lyotard took to be claims about knowledge turn out to have been claims about Being all along, and it is through this device that Meillassoux will preserve what he finds most valuable in the radical philosophy of his parents' generation: its anti-Hegelianism, its hard-Left anti-totalitarianism, its attack on doctrines of necessity, its counter-doctrine of contingency, its exploding of ideology.

Adorno was arguing as early as the mid-'60s that thought needed to figure out some impossible way to think its other, which is the unthought, "objects open and naked," the world out of our clutches. "The concept takes as it most pressing business everything it cannot reach." Is it possible to devise "cognition on behalf of the non-conceptual?"[15] This is the

---

[14] Leibniz's position, of course, was that other words were possible *but undesirable*, and the political consequences of that idea have never been lost on anyone. It was left to Leibniz's students in the late twentieth century to retain the possible worlds and ditch the theodicy. See Deleuze's *The Fold: Leibniz and the Baroque* (Minneapolis: University of Minnesota Press, 1992) or, in a very different idiom, David Lewis's *On the Plurality of Worlds* (Oxford: Wiley-Blackwell, 1986), or, for that matter, some of string theory's more occult byways, such as brane cosmology and M-theory.

[15] Theodor Adorno, *Negative Dialektik* (Frankfurt am Main: Suhrkamp, 1997), translations mine, from "With Regard to System" and "The Interest of Philosophy."

sense in which Meillassoux, far from breaking with poststructuralism and its cousins, is simply answering one of its central questions. It's just that he does so in a way that any convinced Adornian or Left Heideggerian is going to find baffling. Cognition on behalf of the non-conceptual turns out to have been right in front of us all along—it is called science and math. Celestial mechanics has always been the better anti-humanism. A philosophical anarchism that has thrown its lot in with the geologists and not with the Situationists—that is the possibility for thought that *After Finitude* opens up. The book, indeed, sometimes seems to be borrowing some of Heidegger's idiom of cosmic awe, but it separates this from the latter's critique of science—such that biology and chemistry and physics can henceforth function as vehicles of ontological wonder, astonishment at the world made manifest. And with that idea there comes to an end almost a century's worth of radical struggle against domination-through-knowledge, against bureaucracy, rule by experts, the New Class, technocracy, instrumental reason, and epistemological regimes. On the back cover of *After Finitude*, Bruno Latour says that Meillassoux promises to "liberate us from discourse," but that's not exactly right and may be exactly wrong. He wants rather to free us from having to think of discourse as a problem—precisely not to rally us against it, in the manner of Adorno and Foucault—but to license us to make our peace with, and so sink back into, it.

Lots of people will find good reasons to take this book seriously. It is, nonetheless, unconvincing on five or six fronts at once.

1) *It is philosophically conniving*. There are almost no empirical constraints placed on the argumentative enterprise of ontology. Nothing in everyday experience is ever going to suggest that one generalized account of all Being is right and another wrong, and this situation will inevitably grant the philosopher latitude. Ontologies will always be tailored to extra-philosophical considerations, any one of them elected only because a given thinker *wants* something to be true about the cosmos. Explanations of existence are all speculative and

in that sense opportunistic. It is this opportunism we sense when we discover Meillassoux baldly massaging his sources. Here he is on p. 38: "Kant maintains that we can only describe the *a priori* forms of knowledge..., whereas Hegel insists that it is possible to *deduce* them." Kant, we are being told, doesn't think the categories are deducible. And then here's Meillassoux on pp. 88 and 89: "the third type of response to Hume's problem is Kant's...objective deduction of the categories as elaborated in the *Critique of Pure Reason*."

2) *The leap from epistemology to ontology sometimes falls short*. At one point, Meillassoux thinks he can get the better of post-structuralists like so: Imagine, he says, that an anti-foundationalist is talking to a Christian (about the afterlife, say). The Christian says: "After we die, the righteous among us will sit at the right hand of the Lord." And the anti-foundationalist responds the way anti-foundationalists *always* respond: "Well, you could be right, but it could also be different." For Meillassoux, that last clause is the ontologist's opening. His task is now to convince the skeptic that "it could also be different" is not just a skeptical claim about what we can't know—it is not an ignorance, but rather *already* an ontological position in its own right. What we know about the real cosmos, existing apart from thought, is that everything in it could also be different. And now suppose that the anti-foundationalist responds to the ontologist by just repeating the same sentence—again, because it's really all the skeptic knows how to say: "Well, you could be right, but it could also be different." Meillassoux at this point begins his end-zone dance. He has just claimed that *Everything could be different*, and the skeptic obviously can't disagree with this by objecting that *Everything could be different*.[16] The skeptic has been maneuvered round to agreeing with the ontologist's position. But Meillassoux doesn't yet have good reasons to triumph, because, quite simply, he is using "could be different" in two contrary senses, and he rather bafflingly thinks that their shared phrasing is enough to render them identical. He has simply routed

---

[16] Meillassoux, *After Finitude*, 57-58.

his argument through a rigged formulation, one in which ontological claims and epistemological claims *seem* briefly to coincide. The skeptical, epistemological version of that sentence says: "Everything could be different from how I am thinking it." And the ontological version says: "Everything could be different from how it really is now." There may, in fact, occur real-word instances in which skeptics string words into ambiguous sentences that could mean either, and yet this will never indicate that they unwittingly or via logical compulsion mean the latter.

3) *Meillassoux's theory of language is lunatic.* Another way of getting a bead on *After Finitude* would be to say that it is trying to shut down science studies; it wants to stop literary (and anthropological) types from reading the complicated utterances produced by science as writing (or discourse or culture). Meillassoux is bugged by anyone who reads scientific papers and gets interested in what is least scientific in them—anyone, that is, who attributes to astronomy or kinetics a political unconscious, as when one examines the great new systems devised during the seventeenth century and realizes that they all turned on new ways of understanding "laws" and "forces" (or, depending on the language, "powers"). Meillassoux's own philosophy requires, as he puts it, "the belief that the realist meaning of [any utterance about the early history of the planet] is its *ultimate meaning*—that there is *no* other regime of meaning capable of deepening our understanding of it."[17] The problem is, of course, that it's really easy to show that science writing does, in fact, contain an ideological-conceptual surcharge; that, like any other verbally intricate undertaking, it can't help but borrow from several linguistic registers at once; and that there is always going to be some other "order of meaning" at play in statements about strontium or the Mesozoic. Science studies, after all, possesses lots of evidence of a more or less empirical kind, and Meillassoux's response is to object that this evidence concerns nothing "ultimate." But then what would it mean for a sentence to have an "ulti-

---

[17] Meillassoux, *After Finitude*, 14.

mate meaning" anyway? A meaning that outlasts its rivals? Or that defeats them in televised battle? What, then, is the time that governs meanings, such that some count as final even while the others are still around? And at what point do secondary meanings just *disappear*? What are the periods of a meaning's rise and fall?

Meillassoux doesn't possess the resources to answer any of those questions; nor, as best as I can tell, does he mean to try. The phrase "ultimate meaning" is not philosophically serious. It does little more than commit us to a blatant reductionism, commanding us to disregard any complexities and ambiguities that a linguistically attentive person would, upon reading Galileo, discover. We can even watch Meillassoux's own language drift, such that "ultimate meaning" becomes, over the course of three pages, exclusive meaning. "Either [a scientific] statement has a realist sense, and *only* a realist sense, or it has no sense at all."[18] It exasperates Meillassoux that an unscientific language would so regularly worm its way into science writing; and it exasperates him, further, that English professors would take the trouble to point this language out. His response is to install a prohibition, the wholly unscientific injunction to treat scientific language as simpler than it is even when the data show otherwise. It is perhaps a special problem for Meillassoux that the ideological character of science writing is especially pronounced in the very period to which he is looking for intellectual salvation—the generations on either side of Newton, which were crammed with ontologies explicitly modeled on the political theology of the late Middle Ages—new scientific cosmologies, I mean, whose political dimensions were quite overt. And it is definitely a problem for Meillassoux that he has himself written a political ontology of roughly this kind—a cosmology made-to-order for the punks and the Bakuninites—since one of his opening moves is to disallow the very idea of such ontologies. *After Finitude* only has the implications its anarchist readership takes it to have if its language means more

---

[18] Meillassoux, *After Finitude*, 17.

than it literally says, and Meillassoux himself insists that it can have no such meaning.[19]

4) *He poses as secular but is actually a kind of theologian.* It is not just that Meillassoux is secular. He is *pugnaciously* secular or, if you prefer, actively anti-religious. He casually links Levinas with fanaticism and Muslim terror.[20] He sticks up for what Adorno once called the totalitarianism of enlightenment, marveling at philosophy's now vanished willingness to tell religious people that they're stupid or at its determination to make even non-philosophers fight on its terms. And against our accustomed sense that liberalism is the spontaneous ideology of secular modernity, Meillassoux sees freedom of opinion instead as an outgrowth of the Counter-Reformation and Counter-Enlightenment. Liberalism, in other words, is how religion gets readmitted to the public sphere even once everyone involved has been forced to concede that it's bunk.[21] And yet for all that, Meillassoux has entirely underestimated how hard it is going to be to craft a consequent anti-humanism without taking recourse to religious language. At the heart of *After Finitude* is a simple restatement of the religious mystic's ecstatic demand that we "get out of ourselves"[22] and thereby learn to "grasp the in-itself;" the book aches for an "outside which thought could explore with the legitimate feeling of being on foreign territory—of being entirely elsewhere."[23] In the place of God, Meillassoux has installed a principle he calls "hyper-Chaos," to which, however, he then attaches all manner of conventional theological language, right down to the capital-C-of-adoration. Hyper-Chaos is an entity...

...for which nothing is or would seem to be impossible...capable of

---

[19] One good walkthrough of seventeenth-century political ontology is provided by Francis Oakley's *Omnipotence, Covenant, & Order: An Excursion in the History of Ideas from Abelard to Leibniz*, (Ithaca: Cornell University Press, 1984).

[20] Meillassoux, *After Finitude*, 43, 47, 48.

[21] Ibid., 46-47.

[22] Ibid., 3.

[23] Ibid., 7.

destroying both things and worlds, of bringing forth monstrous absurdities, yet also of never doing anything, of realizing every dream, but also every nightmare, of engendering random and frenetic transformations, or conversely, of producing a universe that remains motionless down to its ultimate recess, like a cloud bearing the fiercest storms, than the eeriest bright spells.[24]

No-one reading that passage—even casually, even for the first time—is going to miss the predictable omnipotence language with which it begins: Chaos is the God of Might. Meillassoux himself acknowledges as much. What may be less apparent, though, is that this entire line of argument simply extends into the present the late medieval debate over whether God was constrained to create this particular universe, or whether he could have, at will, created another, and Meillassoux's position in this sense resembles nothing so much as the orthodox Christian defense of miracles, theorizing a power that can, in defiance of its own quotidian regularities, "bring forth absurdities, engender transformations, cast bright spells." There have been many different theories of contingency over the last generation, especially among philosophers of history. As a philosopheme, it has, in fact, become rather commonplace. Meillassoux is unusual in this regard *only* in that he has elevated contingency to the position of demiurge and so returned a full portion of metaphysics to a position that had until now been trying to get by without it. Such is the penalty after all for going back behind Kant, that you'll have to stop your ears again against the singing of angels.

Two generations before the three *Critiques* there stood Christian Wolff, whom Meillassoux does not name, but on whose system his metaphysics is modeled and who wrote, in the 1720s and '30s, that philosophy was "the study of the possible as possible." Philosophy, in other words, is the one all-important branch of knowledge that does not study actuality. Each more circumscribed intellectual endeavor—biology,

---

[24] Meillassoux, *After Finitude*, 64.

history, philology—studies what-now-is, but philosophy studies events and objects in our world only as a subset of the much vaster category of what-could-be. It tries, like some kind of interplanetary structuralism, to work out the entire system of possibilities—every hypothetical aggregate of objects or particles or substances that could combine without contradiction—and thereby reclassifies the universe we currently inhabit as just one unfolding outcome among many unseen others. Meillassoux, in this same spirit, asks us to imagine a cosmos of "open possibility, wherein no eventuality has any more reason to be realized than any other."[25] And this way of approaching actuality is what Wolff calls theology, which in this instance means not knowledge of God but God's knowledge. Philosophy, for Wolff—as, by extension, for Meillassoux—is a way of transcending human knowledge in the direction of divine knowledge, when the latter is the science not just of our world but of all things that could ever be, what Hegel called "the thoughts had by God before the Creation"—sheer could-ness, vast and indistinct.[26]

5) *He misdescribes recent European philosophy and is thus unclear about his own place in it.* Maybe this point is better made with reference to his supporters than to Meillassoux himself. Here's how one of his closest allies explains his contribution:

> With his term "correlationism," Meillassoux has already made a permanent contribution to the philosophical lexicon. The rapid adoption of this word, to the point that an intellectual movement has already assembled to combat the menace it describes suggests that "correlationism" describes a pre-existent reality that was badly in need of a name. Whenever disputes arise in philosophy concerning realism and idealism, we immediately note the appearance of a third personage who dismisses both of these alternatives as solutions to a pseudo-problem. This figure is the correlationist, who holds that we can never think of

---

[25] Meillassoux, *After Finitude*, 58.

[26] On Wolff (and Hegel), see Werner Schneiders' "Deus est philosophus absolute summus: Über Christian Wolffs Philosophie und Philosophiebegriff," in *Christian Wolff, 1679-1754: Interpretationen zu seiner Philosophie und deren Wirkung*, (Hamburg: Felix Meiner, 1983), 9-30.

the world without humans nor of humans without the world, but only of a primal correlation or rapport between the two.[27]

As intellectual history, this is almost illiterate. We weren't in need of a name, because the people who argue in terms of the-rapport-between-humans-and-world or subject-and-object were already called "Hegelians," and the movement opposing them hasn't just "sprung up," because philosophers have been battling the Hegelians as long as there have been Hegelians to fight. Worse still is the notion, projected by Meillassoux himself, that all of European philosophy since Kant must be opposed for leading inexorably, shunt-like, to post-structuralism. This is just the melodrama to which radical philosophy is congenitally prone; the entire history of Western thought has to become a single, uninterrupted exercise in the one perhaps quite local error you would like to correct, the cost of which, in this instance, is that Meillassoux and Company have to turn every major European thinker into a second-rate idealist or vulgar Derridean and so end up glossing Wittgenstein and Heidegger and Sartre and various Marxists in ways that are tendentious to the point of unrecognizability. There are central components of Meillassoux's project that philosophers have been attempting since the 1790s, and he occasionally gives the impression of not knowing that European philosophy has been trying for generations to get past dialectics or humanism or the philosophy of the subject or whatever else it is for which "correlationism" is simply a new term. Perhaps Meillassoux thinks that his contribution has been to show that Wittgenstein and Heidegger were more Hegelian than they themselves realized. But then this, too, seems more like a repetition than a new direction, since European philosophy has always had a propensity for auto-critique of precisely this kind. Auto-critique is in lots of ways its most fundamental move: One anti-humanist philosopher accuses another of having snuck in some humanist premise or another. One

---

[27] Harman, Graham, *Quentin Meillassoux: Philosophy in the Making*, (Edinburgh: Edinburgh University Press, 2011), 7-8.

philosopher-against-the-subject accuses another of being secretly attached to theories of subjectivity. And so on. For Meillassoux to come around now and say that there are residues of Kant and Hegel all over the place in contemporary thought—well, sure: That's just the sort of thing that European philosophers are *always* saying.

6) *He is wrong about German idealism.* Kant, Meillassoux says, is the one who deprived us all of the Great Outdoors, which accusation seems plausible…until you remember that bit about "the starry sky above me." This is one more indication that Meillassoux is punching air, though the point matters more with reference to Hegel than to Kant. Hegel's philosophy, after all, turns on a particular way of relating the history of the world: At first, human beings were just pinpricks of consciousness in a world not of their own making, mobile smudges of mind on an alien planet. But human activity gradually remade the world—it refashioned every glade and river valley—worked all the materials—to the point where there now remains nothing in the world that hasn't to some degree been made subject to human desire and planning. The world has, in this sense, been all but comprehensively humanized; it is saturated with mind. What are we to say, then, when Meillassoux claims that no modern philosopher since Kant can even begin to deal with the existence of the world before humans; that they can't even take up the question; that they have to duck it; that it is what will blow holes in their systems? Hegel not only has no trouble speaking of the pre-human planet; his historical philosophy downright presupposes it. The world didn't used to be human; it is now thorough-goingly so; the task of philosophy is to account for that change. And it is the great failing of Meillassoux's book that, having elevated paleontology to the paradigmatic science, he can't even begin to explain the transformation.

You might ask yourself again whether Meillassoux's account of science is more plausible than a Hegelian one. What, after all, happened when Europeans began devising modern science? What did science actually start *doing*? Was it or wasn't it a rather important part of the ongoing process by which human beings subjected the non-human world to mind? Meillassoux urges us to think of science as the philosophy of the non-human, positing as it does a world separable from thought, a planet independent of humanity, laws that don't require our enforcing. But does science, in fact, bring that world about? Meillassoux hasn't even begun to respond to those philosophers, like Adorno and Heidegger, who wanted to pry philosophy away from science, not because they were complacently encased in the thought-bubbles of discourse and subjectivity, but more nearly the opposite—because they thought science *was* the philosophy of the subject, or one important version of it, the very techno-thinking by which human being secures its final dominion over the non-human. Meillassoux, in this sense, is trying to theorize, not the science that actually entered into the world in the seventeenth century, but something else, an alternate modernity, one in which *aletheia* and science went hand in hand, a fully non-human science or science that humans didn't control: *gelassene Wissenschaft*. But the genuinely materialist position is always going to be the one that takes seriously the effects of thought and discourse upon the world; the one that knows science itself to be a practice; the one that faces up to the realization that the concept of "the non-human" can only ever be a device by which human beings do things to themselves and their surroundings. There is nothing real about a realism that offers itself only as a utopian counter-science, a communication from the pluriverse, a knowledge that presumes our non-existence and so requires, as bearer, some alternate cosmic intelligence that it would be simplest to call divinity.

The Noumenon's New Clothes[1]
(Part 1)

Peter Wolfendale

Independent Researcher

A SPECTRE IS HAUNTING CONTInental philosophy—the spectre of **Object-Oriented Ontology** (**OOO**). All the disciplines and groupings that have traditionally allied themselves with continental theory in the anglophone world are poised to greet its manifestation: aesthetic theory and artistic practice, political philosophy and heterodox geography, Francophile post-post-structuralists and Germanist neo-romantics. Who among them has not heard the siren song of OOO's litanies of inhuman objects (menageries of stock markets and stock cubes, quarks and clerks, etc.)?

---

[1] This paper has been a long time in development. It was initiated at the suggestion of Graham Harman, after previous attempts at informal engagement with his ideas (which can be found in the commentary section of my blog here: http://deontologistics.wordpress.com/commentary) became too extensive for him to easily respond to. In its long gestation it has benefited immeasurably from my discussions with Ray Brassier, Damian Veal, Robin Mackay, Daniel Sacilotto, Dustin McWherter, Nick Srnicek and Jon Cogburn, some of whom were gracious enough to provide comments on early drafts of the material that has come to make up this paper. It has also benefited from the comments of numerous more or less anonymous individuals who have read and responded to the informal engagements already mentioned. Finally, I owe an immense debt to Fabio Gironi, without whose incredible patience and careful encouragement this piece never would have appeared.

Who among them has not begun to shrug off the oppressive, anthropocentric legacy of Post-Kantian philosophy, bravely railing against the tyrannical correlationists of the continental academy, the dreary technicians of the analytic mainstream, and even the scientific fury of its Neo-Kantian heirs?

I will plead forgiveness for my bombast, but there is a certain grandeur to the pronouncements regarding the emergence of OOO as a philosophical movement that demands parody, and I hope this can be taken in good spirit, as a sort of gesture to clear the air. I have every intention of taking these pronouncements as seriously as possible, and perhaps even more seriously than they are intended. Graham Harman, the erstwhile leader of this most vocal faction of what was once, fleetingly, called **Speculative Realism** (**SR**), has often expressed a preference for what he calls **hyperbolic readings** of philosophies.[2] The idea here is to imagine the relevant philosophy in a position of nigh-unassailable strength, so as to tease out what would be missing from a world in which it had become dominant. To imagine a given philosophical tendency actually *winning* the discursive battles in which it is engaged is to treat it with the utmost seriousness. It is to treat it as a genuine *contender* for truth, whose claims to truth are *sincere* enough to be taken at face value. This is the kind of *respect* that any serious philosophical position should be treated with, and this goes double for nascent philosophical movements that claim to have both wide ranging implications and applications. The aim of this paper is to take OOO seriously, and to treat it with at least this level of respect (my initial parody aside).

However, the hyperbolic method is surprisingly difficult to apply to OOO itself, given both the diversity and tentativeness of the commitments of its principal practitioners (canonically: Graham Harman, Levi Bryant, Ian Bogost, and Tim Morton). There is most definitely a common rhetoric binding these fig-

---

[2] "Delanda's Ontology: Assemblage and Realism" in *Continental Philosophy Review* (2008) 41:3, 367-383; *Prince of Networks*, 121-122; Graham Harman, *Quentin Meillassoux: Philosophy in the Making* (Edinburgh: Edinburgh University Press, 2011), 152-158.

ures together—an insistence upon **ontological egalitarianism**, a rehabilitation of the concept of **substance**, and a pervasive metaphorics of **withdrawal**—but a deeper examination of each of these raises serious questions regarding the content of the shared commitments they purport to name. There are disagreements regarding just *how* egalitarian we must be (e.g., what it is to say that *everything* is an object), just what it means to return to a metaphysics of substance (e.g., whether it is permissible to conceive it in *processual* terms), and precisely *what it is* to say objects are withdrawn and thereby what we can *know* about them. There are obviously a number of common issues to which these ideas are addressed, but it's not clear that they represent *genera* of common solutions that could be neatly broken up into variant *species*. It is quite possible that this problem will be alleviated by time, but for now, at least, we must pursue another strategy.[3]

Given this problem, the aim of the current paper is to lay the groundwork for a proper engagement with OOO by focusing upon the philosophical system of its progenitor: Graham Harman's own **Object-Oriented Philosophy (OOP)**. As the oldest and most well-defined variant of OOO, this provides us with the best starting point for any wider engagement with the movement. However, to treat OOP with proper respect means to deal with it in its specificity, which in turn means outside of the context of the overarching rhetoric which binds together the different strands of OOO. This is particularly important, insofar as although it is often clear *what* the proponents of OOO think, it is often far less clear *why* they think it, which only exacerbates the problem of divergences between them. The first step of my approach will thus be to present as complete and concise a summary of the "what" of OOP as I can, breaking the metaphysical system down into three distinct aspects: **withdrawal**, **the fourfold**, and **vicarious causation**. The second step will then be to present

---

[3] Some may think that this is a hasty conclusion. I would direct them to my more informal (but nonetheless extensive) attempts to engage with and understand the differences between Harman's and Bryant's variants of OOO, which can also be found in the commentary section of my blog (see fn. 1).

as charitable an interpretation of the "why" of OOP as I can, teasing out and reconstructing the possible arguments for each of these three aspects in as much detail as is feasible, before assessing them on their merits. The third step will be to make a number of overarching criticisms of the project of OOP on the basis of this assessment, pinpointing several key problems that run throughout it. The final step will then be to present the hyperbolic projection of OOP initially promised, and to draw some conclusions about precisely what OOP (and perhaps OOO) has to offer on these grounds. Carrying out these steps will be a lengthy process, and so the paper will be split in two: the first two steps will be carried out here, and the second two will be published subsequently.[4]

Before delving into the details (and wrestling with the Devil who hides in them), it's also worthwhile to explain the title of this paper, the meaning of which may not yet be evident. Although he is willing to admit that his philosophy amounts to a radicalisation of a certain kind of **correlationism** (the **weak** form), in similar fashion to Meillassoux's philosophy (in relation to the **strong** form), Harman nevertheless presents his work as both a trenchant critique and an important step beyond the menace of correlationism in contemporary philosophy. I do not intend to dispute the idea that there is such a correlationist menace (though I do take it to be more complicated than it is sometimes thought to be), but I will take issue with Harman's presentation of his own relationship to it. When it is properly understood, Harman's work should be seen not as a *critique* of correlationism, but a *consolidation* of its central tenets.

Harman essentially attempts to overcome the inconsistencies inherent within correlationism by sacrificing one of its core features—the prohibition on **metaphysics**—in order to construct a metaphysical prop whose purpose is nothing less than to bolster the rest of the calamitous edifice. He revives and transforms Kant's **noumenal** realm in order to preserve

---

[4] This will of course appear in the next issue of *Speculations*. I must once again express my gratitude to Fabio, and the whole *Speculations* team, for making possible something as unusual as this piece.

the most disastrous prejudices of the correlationist tradition he claims to break with. Far from being a truly "weird" realism, OOP is no more than the eccentric uncle of the correlationist family. The metaphysical spoils it claims to have liberated from the Kantian stronghold are so much ashes and rust. After all is said and done, it returns to us naked, claiming to be wreathed in the finest vestments. The only proper gesture of respect in this circumstance is to point out its immodesty.[5]

1. The Lava that Dares not Speak its Name

Before performing exploratory surgery on the beating heart of OOP, it is first necessary to present the customary compliments regarding the overall shape and style of its vascular architecture. Whatever else can be said about Harman's presentation of OOP, it is certainly *compelling*. On the one hand, it attempts to reveal the inherent *oddness* of the world we live in, by painting us a landscape of a reality in which everything is radically individual, cut off from everything else in almost every respect, connected only by fleeting glimmers of phenomenal appearance. On the other, it attempts to *humble* humanity by seeing humans as just one more disparate association of objects within the universal diaspora, and the intentional terms through which they relate to one another as merely an expression of a more fundamental sensual connectivity in which everything may partake. We must applaud such willingness to countenance counter-intuitive metaphysical conclusions and to embrace ontological humil-

---

[5] As this indicates, this paper is indeed a polemic of sorts. I will not pre-empt this polemic by endeavouring to outline its scope in advance, but I will attempt to pre-empt objections based on the idea that I violate my own principle of respect simply by adopting a polemical *tone*. Harman's own words on this topic are eminently suited for this purpose: "Polemical writing in philosophy no longer enjoys its previous level of acceptance, and is now often dismissed as the product of incivility, aggression, even jealousy. Against this attitude, we should appreciate the clarifying tendencies of polemic—always the favored genre of authors frustrated by the continued clouding of an important decision, whether through fashionable cliché or dubious conceptual manoeuvres." Graham Harman, *Guerilla Metaphysics*, (Open Court, 2005), 11.

ity wherever we find it.

Moving on, the central axis around which Harman's metaphysical system turns is the distinction between the **real** and **sensual**. He is fond of describing this by appealing to a volcanic metaphor: the reality of things consists in their "molten cores," the liquid specificities of which withdraw behind a "sensual crust" of visible features. On this view, the substantial *magma* at the heart of every entity is forever trapped beneath a rocky outer surface whose stillness is only occasionally interrupted by the tectonic forces it unleashes. However, these occasional eruptions always catch us unawares. We never glimpse the molten essence as it leaks through the fault lines in its phenomenal facade, but only catch it as it cools, already crystallising into new sensual continents. The metaphorical *lava* is nowhere to be found. To twist this metaphorical register for the purposes of summary: Harman's is a world of disconnected volcanic island nations floating in a cool sensual sea. A world in which you can travel as much as you like, but you'll always be a tourist. No matter how hard you try, you'll never see the *real* island, only beaches full of German holidaymakers and chintzy gift shops. You might get the occasional *taste* of it—a wiff of the exotic food the real islanders eat as you pass by, or a stolen glimpse of the real lives of the inhabitants over a whitewashed wall—but that's all you'll ever get.

In order to provide an adequate exposition of Harman's noumenal cosmology, I'm going to divide my discussion of the ways in which he develops and expands upon the split between the real and the sensual in three. I will tackle the relation between the real and the sensual under the heading of **withdrawal**, which is the most famous aspect of Harman's position. I will then tackle the way this is complicated by the introduction of a second axis—the distinction between **objects** and **qualities**—under the heading of the **fourfold**, which is the name of the structure Harman derives from their intersection. Finally, I will address the most prominent metaphysical problem that emerges from Harman's system under the heading of **vicarious causation**, which names its corresponding solution.

Speculations III

a) Withdrawal

It is all too easy to say that Harman's world is divided in two: a celestial plane of intentional facades masking a hellish realm of machinic forces, an open space of sensual contact concealing the endlessly churning reality that makes it possible. The truth is that these two sides of his cosmos are folded into one another at every opportunity: there is no straight line from one sensual point to another that does not pass through a real one, nor vice-versa. What we have instead is a pluriverse of infernal engines that present themselves to one another so as to hide their internal machinations, each a realm unto itself, like the many hells of Buddhist lore, composed out of further layers of tortuous machinery, each part of which is available to its fellows only in outline, containing its own inexplicable depths, concealing further strange and sulphurous landscapes, evermore intricate and malicious economies of action, yet to be explored. This is the world of **real objects**. It is a world to which we ourselves belong, along with everything that has any real *effect* upon us—or indeed, upon anything at all. This is the site of everything that really *happens* in the world.

It's important to distinguish between two kinds of happening though: **execution** and **causation**. For Harman, a real object just is its execution, which is to say it's *being-whatever-it-is*, or rather, *doing-whatever-it-does*. This is to say that each real object is defined by some inscrutable **end** for which it is the corresponding **act**. The relation between every real thing taken as a whole and the parts that compose it is to be understood in terms of **functional relations**, like the relation between a machine and its components. The real object *consists* in the unitary action of its parts deployed towards the given end: it is its execution insofar as it is a *function in action*. There is more that could be said about this, but it's important to recognise that although this action is certainly a happening of sorts, it is the occurrence of *sameness*, or simple **persistence**. The various machinic arrangements of parts and wholes that compose the real are essentially *synchronic*. For Harman, causation is the occurrence of *difference*, or **change**, and it emerges from *diachronic* relations of interaction between real objects. The paradox with which he closes his first book, *Tool-Being*, is that his characterisation of such objects as persisting unities seems to preclude the possibility that they could effect change in one another, implying an essentially static cosmic order, in opposition to the seeming reality of change that constantly assails our senses.

The reason for this is that the reality of persistence *qua* execution implies that real objects **withdraw** from one another, unable to affect one another by default. This withdrawal has two facets: the **excess** of everything over its presentations, and the **independence** of everything from everything else. Excess follows from the inscrutability of the end governing each object, insofar as it occludes its *internal economy* of action (execution) and thereby the *external capacities* for action (causation) that emerge from it. Execution is a pure act of persistence underlying every actual interaction, and a pure actuality underlying every possible interaction. This means that it *transcends* both interaction and possibility. We can never *know* the sheer execution of the thing that lies behind every possible encounter. Insofar as **ontological humility** demands that we treat the way we grasp the capabilities of objects, through either *theoretical* or *practical* engagement with them, as just one more instance of an encounter between any two real objects, we must conclude that our inability to grasp an object's veiled execution through any particular possible interaction is a deeper fact about the metaphysics of encounters. This is the fact that the world also contains **sensual objects**. Our own experience of the world is *phenomenologically* constituted by intentional relations directed at *unitary objects*, and this implies that objects' experience of one another is *metaphysically* constituted by something similar. If objects encounter one another as unities, and yet fail to encounter one another *directly*, then encounters must be mediated by unitary intentional facades or caricatures entirely *distinct* from the executant realities that project them. Independence follows from this, insofar as every real object is protected from every other by an honour guard of distinct sensual objects, forever precluding access to it, at least by default.

Finally, it must be emphasised that withdrawal does not merely occur *between* isolated real objects, like a non-aggression pact between the many hells, but also occurs *within* them, in the form of **mereological isolation**. It is easy to see how this involves the mutual withdrawal of the **parts** of an object from one another, insofar as they are real objects in their own right, but it also consists in the withdrawal of parts from the **wholes** they *compose*, and wholes from the parts they *contain*. Of course, the whole is dependent upon its parts, insofar as it cannot subsist without them, but it is equally independent of them in two senses: A) it is entirely possible for its parts to be replaced without significantly altering its internal economy, and B) this economy produces capacities which exceed the capacities of the parts taken in isolation. Similarly, although the parts may be reciprocally dependent upon one another to some extent, insofar as they require certain conditions in which to function, they are equally independent of their context in two senses: A) it is entirely possible for them to be transplanted into a different whole without dissolving their own distinct unity, and B) new contexts may reveal hitherto unexpressed capacities that were previously suppressed. A real object considered as a whole is a specific arrangement of parts that both transcends and fails to exhaust their specificity. Despite the fact that the real object consists in transcending this excess of specificity, it nevertheless plays an additional role, insofar as the whole draws upon it in generating the sensual objects it hides behind. The various inessential features of a real object's parts become resources for producing the phenomenal **accidents** that cloak its executant reality.

b) The Fourfold

Once we begin to talk about the features and capacities of objects as distinct from the objects themselves, we are stumbling upon the second fundamental axis around which Harman's system turns: the distinction between *objects* and their *qualities*.

Things are not just torn between their subterranean execution and its phenomenal effects, but between their persistent **unity** and its constituent **plurality**. This does not concern how a singular whole is *composed* by a multiple parts (e.g., the composition of an ice cube out of molecules), though this is a related issue, but how a single entity is *determined* in a various ways (e.g., the coldness, hardness, or translucency of the ice cube). The mutual withdrawal between parts and whole we've already seen consists in wholes having qualities their parts lack (e.g., the molecules are neither translucent nor hard), and parts having qualities their wholes ignore (e.g., the unique chemical properties of the trace amount of minerals in the water is usually entirely irrelevant to the ice cube). Qualities are not objects, even if the qualities a thing possesses somehow bubble up from the objects that compose it.[6]

These two distinctions are not merely parallel, but cut across one another. This produces a fourfold of terms: in addition to the distinction between sensual objects (**SO**) and real objects (**RO**), there is a distinction between **sensual qualities** (**SQ**) and **real qualities** (**RQ**). The objects that appear in our phenomenal experience are **encrusted** with sensible features that may vary from moment to moment, but the latter are entirely distinct from the real features **submerged** in the silent execution they conceal. Here we begin to see the way the four poles interact with one another to form Harman's ten **categories**. The relation between a sensual object and its sensual qualities (SO-SQ) is the condition of the variation of its encrusted accidents, or **time** itself, whereas the relation between a sensual object and its real qualities (SO-RQ) is the submerged anchor around which this variation is fixed, or what Husserl calls **eidos**. These two categories are the first of what Harman calls the **tensions** between object and quality. The emergence of sensual objects in our experience is dependent upon the sensible features the corresponding real objects allow them to present from perspective to perspective, and the distinctness of these underlying real objects is in

---

[6] We will complicate this claim to some extent in section 2(A)(iii) and 2(B)(i).

turn dependent upon differences between the features they can never present. This gives us the remaining two tensions. The relation between a real object and its sensual qualities (RO-SQ) is the condition under which it can relate to another object through a sensuous facade, or **space**, whereas the relation between a real object and its real qualities (RO-RQ) is its principle of uniqueness, or what Zubiri calls **essence**. Taken together, these four tensions provide the schema of *sameness* and *difference* between objects, both real and apparent, along with their *constancy* and *variation*.

Harman calls the changes that emerge within this schema **fissions** and **fusions**. This is because two tensions (time and eidos) have a persistent state of **connection** between object and quality for two of the tensions—so that change demands fission of this connection—and two (space and essence) have a persistent state of **separation**—so that change demands fusion of what is separated. It's important to recognise that the fissions take place within the sensual realm, insofar as they involve breaks in the connections between the sensual objects we experience and their qualities. In **confrontation**, it gets broken from its sensual qualities (time), such that its accidental features are somehow revealed *as* accidental. This occurs when we recognise something *as* something (e.g., a tree *as* a gallows), thereby separating those qualities irrelevant to this characterisation (e.g., height, branch structure, etc.) from those that aren't (e.g., colour, foliage, etc.). In **theory**, it gets broken from its real qualities (eidos), such that its eidetic features are somehow contrasted to its accidental ones. This occurs when we strive to grasp the constants that underlie the shifting surface variations all things are subject to (e.g., to analyse the tree's morphology, or its genetic structure). By contrast, only one of the fusions marks the emergence of the real object within the phenomenal sphere, so as to redraw its boundaries from within, whereas the other is entirely withdrawn, and so is only apparent in the ways it redraws these boundaries from without. The former is **allure**, where it interacts with the features of the sensible facades it projects (space), such that there is an apparent juxtaposition between its accidental elements and its eidetic core. This occurs in various aesthetically significant experiences (e.g., *cuteness, beauty, humour, embarrassment, humility, disappointment, loyalty*),[7] but is most prominently displayed in the use of **metaphor** (e.g., when we frame our experience of the tree by describing it as "a flame"). The latter is **causation**, where it interacts with its own real features (essence), so as to unlock its capacities to affect the withdrawn core of other things. As already indicated, the possibility of causation is thrown into question by withdrawal, and this necessitates the theory of vicarious causation to follow, which will turn upon its relation with allure.

Before getting into this though, we must examine the remaining six categories, which are divided into the **radiations** between qualities and qualities and the **junctions** between objects and objects. Much as there was a rift between one of the tensions and the other three with regard to their role in experience, there is a crucial difference between the roles that radiations and junctions play therein. On the one hand, the radiations cover the way that qualities are related *within* experience by the sensual objects that populate it: the relation between two sensual qualities (SQ-SQ) is their **emanation** through the same object of experience, the relation between two real qualities (RQ-RQ) is their **contraction** behind this same object, and the relation between the sensual qualities and the real qualities (SQ-RQ) is their **duplicity** in the way they differ from one another. On the other hand, the conjunctions cover the way that relations between objects constitute experience in relation to ourselves *qua* real objects: the relation between two sensual objects (SO-SO) can only take place as **continguity** within our experience, the relation between two real objects (RO-RO) is the **withdrawal** of the corresponding real objects behind our experience, and the relation between a real object and a sensual object (RO-SO) is the **sincerity** that constitutes this experience itself. Together, the three radiations and three conjunctions provide the framework

---

[7] Harman, *Guerilla Metaphysics*, 212-213.

in which the three experiential tensions can unfold. They give us an abstract map of the phenomenal realms that lie between infernal kingdoms of execution—the borderlands through which they smuggle causal contraband, or the embassies through which they communicate.

c) Vicarious Causation

We can now turn to the problem of *how* this communication occurs. The independence of real objects from one another demands such an explanation: how can mutually withdrawn objects possibly interact, so as to produce **real changes** in one another? These are quite distinct from the mere **phenomenal variations** that sensual objects undergo in experience, because they can reconfigure the intentional space in which experience occurs. Yet it is only within these intentional spaces that a real object can encounter the variable facades projected by other real objects, and only through these **sensual vicars** that any sort of contact can be established between them. The fact that all causal contact arises out of an **intentional relation** between an *experiencing* real object and an *experienced* sensual object that mediates between it and its real counterpart implies that the **causal relation** is not just vicarious, but also **asymmetrical** and **buffered**. It is asymmetrical because the relation has **direction**, proceeding from the object the vicar conceals to the object the vicar appears to. This means that causation can occur one-way between real objects, without reciprocation (e.g., when a bee is hit by an oncoming car, the bee may be destroyed while the car is entirely unscathed). It is buffered because there are many *contiguous* sensual objects present in the same experience, and this does not result in interactions between the real objects they hide (e.g., the bee may be drawn into the path of the truck by an enticing flower, but the truck and the flower may be entirely unrelated). This means that a real object's *sincerity* in encountering a sensual object is the condition of that object's **receptivity**.

However, we are not causally affected by every object we experience. The phenomenal realms that real objects find themselves immersed in are filled to the brim with myriad sensual unities, many of which have no impact upon them at all. This means that intentional relations are not automatically causal relations. The question is thus what more there is to causal contact than mere sincerity. Harman responds by drawing the link between *causation* and *allure* mentioned above. Genuine change is *internal* to a real object, insofar as it only occurs when a real object becomes connected to its qualities in regenerating its *essence*, but this nevertheless requires an *external* trigger, which can only take the form of some variation within the intentional space it's immersed in. Harman proposes that the *confrontations* usually precipitated by such variation are insufficient to trigger causal contact, because the qualities encountered therein are still tied to the facade that hides the *triggering* object from the *triggered* object. It is only in *allusion* that these ties are broken, and the qualities are allowed to orbit the real object underlying them (e.g., when the metaphorical comparison of the tree with a flame highlights the relevant qualities in a way that makes them alien to it as we are familiar with it). Allure lets reality obliquely slide into appearance, striking the object that experiences it in a way that surpasses the sensual flux it is accustomed to, so that the accidental features of the *affecting* object catalyse the reshuffling of essential features within the *affected* object.

Nevertheless, the latter does not strictly *see* the former, even if it *feels* it in some specific **aesthetic mode** (e.g., as *humorous*) and to some specific degree of **aesthetic intensity** (e.g., as only *mildly* humorous). The brief suspension of *causal independence* that occurs in causal connection never really overcomes the corresponding *epistemic excess*. Allure may play an important role in enabling us to reconfigure the ways we think about entities, but it never amounts to knowledge of them. This is why Harman grants aesthetics a special philosophical privilege. In examining the varieties of allure and their relationships it gives us insight into the metaphysical structure of reality that forever escapes the stale practice of epistemology. With the tenfold categorical schema derived from the fourfold,

Harman has provided a *general* theory of objects, which he calls **ontography**, capable of application to the various *specific* domains of objects that compose the cosmos. Yet it is only through extending of the sorts of aesthetic analysis indicated by his theory of allure that these domains can be fleshed out. Ultimately, Harman proposes an alliance of aesthetics and metaphysics that promises to lay bare the various regions of the cosmos to renewed philosophical inquiry. It now falls to us to assess this proposal, and its worth.

2. The Withdrawal of Arguments

Having looked into the "what" of OOP, it's time to concern ourselves with the "why." This means locating the various arguments that Harman presents for each of the different aspects of his metaphysical system that we've distinguished. As I hinted in the introduction, this is by no means an easy task. Although Harman's work is peppered with phrases such as "I will show…," "I have already argued…," or "As argued repeatedly…," these do not often refer to specific arguments as much as to the overarching dramatisation of a given idea that takes place throughout the work.[8] There are a few notable exceptions to this, as we will see, but what arguments there are in Harman's work tend to be blended together in ways that make them hard to tease apart—a task which is vital if they are to be properly assessed. To draw on Harman's own preferred metaphors once more, the arguments often seem to *withdraw* into themselves, leaving textual vicars that tantalise one's cognitive faculties by *alluding* to their real logical depths. Our current task is thus to draw them out of hiding and expose them to the light of reason.[9]

---

[8] These examples are all taken from *Tool-Being* (Chicago and la Salle: Open Court, 2002), 19, 61, 70, but one can find many similar phrases in all his works. It is very rare to find such a phrase that is tied to a specific chain of inferences, such as by referencing the pages upon which the supposed argument takes place.

[9] Harman himself looks down on this sort of critical engagement with the arguments underlying a philosophical position for various reasons (cf.

Of course, Harman also has his own (fairly derogatory) opinions about the role of argument within philosophy, as part of his wider concerns with the importance of philosophical style, and these must be taken into account.[10] However, we will address these later on in the present essay. For now, our aim is to *delineate* and perhaps even *repair* as much as is feasible of the justificatory tissue holding together the skeletal structure of Harman's corpus which we've already revealed. This is a delicate operation that requires exegetical care, logical skill, and not a small amount of discursive charity. Returning to the medical metaphor opening the first section, we are about to move from *exploratory* to *reconstructive* surgery. In order to facilitate this, I'm going to draw a threefold distinction articulating the different ways in which Harman frames his ideas with an eye to their justification: **historical narrative**, **phenomenological description**, and **metaphysical argument**.

Historical narratives introduce an idea by reconstructing its *genesis* within a particular historical dialectic; usually constituted by a series of different thinkers, each of which makes some important contribution to the problematic in which the idea gestates, only to emerge fully formed in the author's own work. These rational reconstructions are an important philosophical tool deployed by many of the great figures in the history of philosophy.[11] The philosophies of Hegel, Hei-

---

Guerilla Metaphysics, §12A), some of which are curiously intertwined with elements of his own position. He would rather that, instead of systematically critiquing a position on the basis of flaws in its argumentation, we strove to present counter-narratives that construct *suggestive* alternatives to it. Even while Harman admits that "such debunking may be necessary work at times," he nevertheless maintains that "we should not forget that it is mainly the work of dogs (*cynics*, to say it in Greek)." (Ibid.) Even if we grant this, it cannot get in the way of the work that *respect* demands. Mere preference has no say upon when the dogs must be released. Woof.

[10] Cf. Graham Harman, *Prince of Networks* (Melbourne: re.press, 2009), 169-175.

[11] For an account of the logic of this process reconstruction, see Brandom's work on the historical dimension of rationality in the introduction to *Tales of the Mighty Dead* (Cambridge, MA: Harvard University Press, 2002) and his own reconstruction of Hegel in *Reason in Philosophy* (Cambridge, MA: Harvard University Press, 2009), ch. 3.

degger and Deleuze would not be as compelling or even as accessible without the thematic vectors they trace through their forebears in the direction of their own work. Harman is thus to be commended for wielding this method of exposition with some skill. However, the danger associated with this method is that it can easily slip from licit *exposition* to illicit *justification* in the form of arguments from authority. Such arguments can be useful as shorthand forms of justification (equivalent to saying "you need to go read Aristotle/Hegel/Heidegger/etc. before we can talk seriously about this"), but they wither under more sustained forms of philosophical scrutiny. The issue is exacerbated if the readings of the figures in question are particularly controversial, such as Harman's reading of Heidegger, which forms a crucial part of his own object-oriented history.[12] As such, in separating out these narratives from the other forms of exposition and argument in Harman's work, my primary goal will be to ensure that they play no such illicit justificatory role.

Phenomenological descriptions play an important part in Harman's work, insofar as his metaphysics is thoroughly influenced by an appropriation of the ideas of Husserl and Heidegger. His is a metaphysics of intentional relation, and his account of intentionality is fundamentally culled from the phenomenological tradition and its methodology of immanent description. However, the methodological questions regarding the *nature* and *status* of phenomenological description that were of such concern to Husserl and Heidegger receive little attention in Harman's work. He is often all too eager to delve directly into phenomenological analysis without clarifying precisely *what it is* he is doing in doing so. Where Husserl devotes a enormous amount of time and effort to elaborating the various aspects of the phenomenological

---

[12] This is an area in which I can speak with at least enough authority to be taken seriously, given the fact that my PhD thesis (*The Question of Being: Heidegger and Beyond*) presents a synoptic reading of Heidegger's work that, while diverging from both the standard analytic and continental readings much as Harman's does, comes to radically different (and, I would argue, far more nuanced) conclusions than Harman's own.

reduction, and Heidegger devotes a serious (if not necessarily comparable) effort to modifying this within his own existential-hermeneutic framework, Harman gives us little in the way of phenomenological methodology. This not only makes the precise content of many of his phenomenological claims unclear, but more worryingly brings into question the *metaphysical* conclusions that are leveraged on the basis of these claims. It is thus of the utmost importance to identify precisely which of Harman's claims are motivated by phenomenological analysis, and how they are deployed in the attempt to justify his more contentious metaphysical claims.

This brings us to the third form of exposition: metaphysical argument itself. Specifically, it raises the question of what qualifies either a philosophical claim or its justification as metaphysical. Put differently: just *what is* metaphysics anyway? This question should weigh heavily on the shoulders of anyone intending to engage in renewed metaphysical speculation regardless of their preferred method, but this weight becomes particularly acute when one intends to derive metaphysical *conclusions* from phenomenological *premises*. Although it is possible to find his account wanting, one can't say that Heidegger merely identifies phenomenology and ontology without addressing and attempting to justify this quite radical divergence from the metaphysical tradition.[13] Heidegger's detailed historical and methodological work on the problem of metaphysics and the question of Being garners almost no attention in Harman's work, nor is it supplemented by any detailed alternative schema. Indeed, the most sustained engagement with the question I have been able to locate dismisses the possibility of even addressing the methodological task of clarifying the question of Being prior to answering it: "...the question of [B]eing cannot be elucidated until the meaning of [B]eing itself has already somehow been clarified, prior to any special description of Dasein."[14] This sidelining of methodological issues is very

---

[13] For details, consult my aforementioned PhD thesis (http://deontologistics.wordpress.com/thesis/).

[14] Harman, *Tool-Being*, 40.

worrying given Harman's unapologetic calls to return to the problems of pre-critical metaphysics.[15]

All this indicates just how important it is to separate out the roles these different forms of exposition play in the more or less *explicit* arguments within Harman's work, and the way overlaps between them further complicate many of the *implicit* assumptions undergirding the latter. However, the critical purchase upon Harman's work this would provide requires an *exhaustive* approach that has some of its own problems. First, the ideal of exhaustiveness places *exegetical* demands upon a commentator (and critic) that are often unrealistic, and this can easily lead to accusations of impropriety. I have gone out of my way to read as much of Harman's extant work as I can, in order to forestall such accusations, but I expect them nonetheless.[16] Second, it places *hermeneutic* demands on those who would read (and perhaps respond to) the commentary that are substantial, if not always unreasonable. Not only must they be willing to cover the same exegetical ground as the commentator, but they must keep track of

---

[15] It is also helpful to note that despite using the term "being" quite extensively throughout *Tool-Being*, Harman never provides any generic definition or analysis of the term that goes beyond his own metaphysical account of it. If pushed to provide a quick analysis of his usage of the term, I would say that he uses it in one of two senses: A) in the *particular* sense to refer to the being of a given object (cf. 85), or B) in the *singular* sense to refer to the totality of objects (cf. 294). This almost entirely elides the *general* sense referring to the Being of objects *as such* that Heidegger himself is principally concerned with (as the subject of the question of Being). In addition, in accordance with his own metaphysical proclivities, the senses in which Harman does use the term are almost universally deployed in opposition to *seeming* (cf. 26), which is only one of the major oppositions that Heidegger outlines (and indeed, questions) in the course of his career (cf. *Introduction to Metaphysics* [New Haven: Yale University Press, 2000], 103-122).

[16] I have read all published books and essay collections, but I have not read all of Harman's published papers, nor any unpublished material that may be circulating. I have also followed his writings on his blog (http://doctorzamalek2.wordpress.com) rather extensively, though I have refrained from referencing them in justifying any of the substantial points in this paper, for obvious reasons. I consider this to be an eminently reasonable level of work to justify the present essay, even if I cannot completely rule out the possibility that I have missed something crucial in the writings I have not read.

multiple different arguments and their intersection. I have endeavoured to organise the present essay in as accessible a manner as possible, but this can only ameliorate these problems to some extent. Third, it often has profoundly counterproductive *psychological* effects. It's an unfortunate fact that it is often easier to convince someone of the falsity of a theory or the wrongness of a policy by focusing upon a single objection to it, rather than aiming to present several equally serious objections. We all have a finite amount of attention, and thus a limited ability to cope with barrages of arguments, and these unavoidable limitations can often lead to us dismissing arguments that overload our attentional capacities. This phenomenon is a serious problem in many mainstream political debates, where certain multifariously flawed ideas often survive precisely because no unitary line of attack upon them is obvious. I will beg the reader to pay attention (ironically enough) to this phenomenon, and endeavour not to take the lack of a singular criticism as a point in favour of the position criticised.

This brings me to the last substantive point in the current prolegomena, regarding the nature of philosophical disagreement and its presentation. Harman has complained to me before that I fail to follow the proper procedure for engaging with a discursive opponent in my more informal debates with him: first outlining the areas in which one agrees with one's interlocutor, before proceeding to outline the relevant disagreements.[17] My response to this criticism is that, sometimes, there simply aren't enough points of agreement to make this more than an empty gesture. My own commitments, which I have endeavoured to keep out of the present paper wherever possible,[18] are quite radically different from Harman's, and this leaves little ground for praise on my part. Nevertheless,

---

[17] This was written in private correspondence.

[18] For an unpolished overview of my own position, I recommend reading the available draft of my *Essay on Transcendental Realism* (http://deontologistics.wordpress.com/2010/05/essay-on-transcendental-realism.pdf). This is a rough draft that has yet to be revised and expanded for publication, but it does a reasonable job of outlining the central themes of my work.

I will mention six areas in which there is something resembling agreement between us: (i) we both think that **correlationism** is problematic; (ii) we both hold that **individuality** is an important metaphysical topic; (iii) we agree that there is more to **panpsychism** than is often thought; (iv) we each take it that **aesthetics** is an important philosophical field with wider ramifications than commonly accepted; (v) we are jointly committed to both the possibility and necessity of **metaphysics** in some form; and (vi) we strongly agree that **realism** is essential if it is to be pursued properly.

The problem is that once we begin to define what is meant by the core terms in each case (correlationism, individuality, panpsychism, aesthetics, metaphysics, and realism) the agreements are revealed as fairly superficial: (i) I agree with Meillassoux[19] that the essence of correlationism is *epistemological* rather than *metaphysical*, and that it must be challenged on this terrain rather than dismissed as ontologically arrogant; (ii) I think that there can be no study of the *metaphysics* of individuality that does not begin with its *logic* (e.g., identification, quantification, existential commitment, etc.) rather than leaping headlong into intuitive speculation; (iii) the features of the history of panpsychism I am concerned with (e.g., Spinoza, Leibniz, Nietzsche, Whitehead, and Deleuze) consist in their generalisation of *non-intentional* features of thought (i.e., conation and sensation); (iv) I'm convinced that aesthetics, as the study of a certain kind of value, has less to do with the *sensations* and *feelings* that signal its presence than the *actions* this demands of us; (v) I predict that a return to metaphysical speculation without the *methodological* awareness accompanying an answer to the question "what is metaphysics?" is doomed to failure; and (vi) I think that there can be no viable "realism" without a *definition* of "real" more subtle than "that which is always other than our knowledge of it."

This is all I will say about these disagreements for now. The criticisms upon which they turn will be revealed as we

---

[19] "Speculative Realism" in *Collapse III: Unknown Deleuze*, 445-446, in conversation with Peter Hallward.

look at Harman's arguments themselves. I will group these arguments on the basis of the aspect of his system that they underpin (withdrawal, the fourfold, and vicarious causation, respectively), such that the order of the following subsections corresponds directly to the order of those in the previous section. Each subsection will deal with a number of different arguments of varying strength and complexity, with varying degrees of reconstruction on my part. Each will also be smaller than the last, as the relevant arguments build upon one another. I will do my best to indicate exegetical concerns surrounding my reconstructions, but my aim is to present the strongest possible forms of each argument, so as to make the corresponding criticisms as strong as possible. This is the core feature of the respect owed to OOP discussed in the introduction.

a) Tools, Knowledge, and Distinctness

Harman has a several arguments for his account of withdrawal. By far the most famous is the reading of Heidegger's tool-analysis, presented in his first book: *Tool-Being*. However, despite the fact that the tool-analysis is referred to and summarised to different degrees all over Harman's work, it remains fairly opaque in its logical structure.[20] This is principally because, as much as it gets referred to as if it were a single argument, it is really a blend of a number of distinct arguments, mixing all three forms of exposition discussed above: historical, phenomenological, and metaphysical. Disentangling these expository and justificatory strands is difficult enough when focusing on one text, but its manifold presentation confronts us with some serious choices about how to go about doing so. I have decided to focus upon two presentations of the analysis: the original and most detailed presentation of it in *Tool-Being*, and a more recent and concise

---

[20] To give a representative example, in the collection *Towards Speculative Realism* (Winchester: Zero Books, 2010), 8 out of 11 essays contain truncated summaries of the tool-analysis.

presentation of it in Harman's *Meillassoux* book.[21] I highly recommend reading the relevant sections of these texts along with my reconstruction of the tool-analysis, so as to confirm the fidelity of my reconstruction. These preliminaries aside, I will break the tool-analysis down into two separate parts. I call these the argument from **execution** and the argument from **excess**. This will be followed by an examination of an additional argument that often accompanies them, which I call the argument from **identity**.

i) Harman's Heidegger

Before delving into the details of the tool-analysis, it's necessary to address the exegetical elephant in the room. I have already announced my disagreement with Harman's reading of Heidegger. Harman is very clear that his version of the tool-analysis is not one that Heidegger would himself endorse, and that as such it must be assessed on its own merits. This is precisely what I intend to do. However, in line with the earlier remarks about the role of historical narrative, it will be helpful to present the crucial errors of Harman's reading of Heidegger as I see them. On the one hand, this inoculates against any illicit slip from exposition to justification, and, on the other, it helps to situate many of the issues Harman is dealing with within their correct historical context. There are five principal aspects of Harman's reading with which I disagree: (i) he reads Heidegger's critique of **presence** as championing a complementary notion of **execution**; (ii) he takes the distinction between the **ontological** and the **ontic** to be equivalent to the distinction between the **ready-to-hand** and the **present-at-hand**, respectively; (iii) he claims that the "world" should not be understood as a **phenomenological horizon**; (iv) he holds that Dasein is not **central** to Heidegger's ontology; and (v) he identifies the encounter with the **broken tool** with the **as-structure**. I'm going to tackle these disagreements by addressing several characteristic criticisms that Harman

---

[21] Graham Harman, *Quentin Meillassoux*, 135-136.

deploys liberally against other interpreters of Heidegger. If understanding these exegetical points is of little interest to you, you might wish to skip the rest of this section, though I don't recommend it.

To begin with, Harman repeatedly criticises other interpreters for mistaking the significance of the distinction between readiness-to-hand (*Zuhandenheit*) and presence-at-hand (*Vorhandenheit*) for a distinction between *types* of entity. He zealously reminds his readers that ready-to-hand entities are not those specific things that happen to be used as tools by humans, but rather that any extant entity may be taken as ready-to-hand or present-at-hand.[22] This point is certainly misunderstood by a number of interpreters. However, even when combined with his reading of Heidegger's use of the word "mere" (*Bloß*) to denigrate the status of *presence (Anweisenheit)*,[23] this does not show that Heidegger is championing a complementary notion of *execution (Vollzug)* as the real meaning of "Being" that the metaphysical tradition overlooked. On the contrary, it is possible to view this as a distinction between different **modes** of Being (*Seinsarten/Seinsweisen*) without reducing it to a distinction between mutually exclusive **types** of beings. This is precisely how Heidegger describes the distinction, and it will connect to the other exegetical points still to be made.[24] Moreover, the fact that Harman develops this notion of execution into a new conception of *substance (ousia)*, bemoaning the inability of Heidegger commentators to see the connection between *Zuhandenheit* and *ousia*,[25] indicates he has diverged from Heidegger somewhere earlier down the line.[26]

---

[22] Cf. Harman, *Tool-Being*, 38.

[23] Ibid., 48-49.

[24] Cf. Martin Heidegger, *Basic Problems of Phenomenology* (Bloomington and Indianapolis: Indiana University Press, 1988), 305; Martin Heidegger, *Metaphysical Foundations of Logic* (Bloomington and Indianapolis: Indiana University Press, 1984), 151-152.

[25] Harman, *Tool-Being*, 270.

[26] Heidegger's criticism of presence is inexorably tied up with his critique of substance, at least in his most systematic presentations of it (Cf. *Introduction to Metaphysics*).

Secondly, Harman claims that Heidegger's insights cannot be truly *ontological* ones if they are taken to be understood in terms of the *intelligibility* of entities to Dasein. The argument for this essentially boils down to the idea that intelligibility to Dasein is *seeming* for Dasein, and Harman defines "Being" as opposed to seeming.[27] For Harman, ontology is the study of beings as they are *in themselves*, as distinct from their appearances. This is almost the opposite move made by most orthodox Heidegger scholars, who define "Being" as the intelligibility of beings as distinct from any "metaphysical" conception of the underlying *grounds* of this intelligibility. For them, ontology is the study of *appearances* freed from the mistaken metaphysical search for *substantial* basis of these appearances. Both of these readings are seriously misguided insofar as Heidegger does not *define* "Being" in either way. However, each has an element of truth to it. In line with the orthodox interpretation, he tries to *argue* against the metaphysical tradition that Being is to be understood in terms of intelligibility (**unconcealing**). In line with Harman's interpretation, he also thinks that something must be said about that which resists or escapes intelligibility (**concealing**). His later work in particular attempts to show that the revelation of each entity to our understanding is tempered by its situation within a broader field of meaning (**world**) which is always in tension with reality in itself (**earth**). Every entity thus appears as a local modification of this global struggle (**strife/truth**).

Thirdly, this brings us to Harman's criticism that, in interpreting Heidegger's use of "world" as a phenomenological horizon within which entities appear to each given Dasein, Heidegger scholars have stumbled into a disastrous regress towards ever deeper unitary grounds (e.g., *Zeitlichkeit, Temporalität, Ereignis*, etc.). He even parodies this regress by way of a children's sleepover game.[28] However, again, as much as this is a legitimate lampooning of the stylistic and exegetical excesses of much Heidegger scholarship, this does not amount

---

[27] See fn. 15.
[28] Harman, *Tool-Being*, 27.

to a proof that there is no well defined regress of unitary grounds in Heidegger. Even if there is a certain overworn argumentative trope in Heidegger, this does not excuse us from examining the specificities of its instances. It is thus entirely possible (and desirable) to determine that there are only a specific number of steps in Heidegger's analyses, and that they actually have an end point in some more or less well delimited unitary structure (e.g., *Temporalität* in the early work, or *Ereignis* in the later work). Harman's alternative is to read "world" as a complete totality of entities rather than a phenomenological horizon in which they appear. This is a disastrous misreading, and is explicitly counselled against by Heidegger.[29]

Fourthly, this sets the stage for Harman's attack on anthropocentric readings of Heidegger. Although Harman recognises that Heidegger himself grants Dasein ontological privilege, he takes this to be entirely unnecessary, insofar as every entity can be interpreted as a **for-the-sake-of-which** engaging with other things in terms of **projective understanding**.[30] Harman explicitly claims that although Heidegger uses the term "understanding" (*Verstand*) here, this can be interpreted non-anthropocentrically as covering all interactions between things. This is indicative of a really pernicious misunderstanding of Heidegger's project that underlies the other points addressed so far. To briefly summarise Heidegger's account of understanding: he thinks that Dasein relates to the things it encounters in terms of the possibilities for **action** that they provide it, and that what characterises Dasein *qua* Dasein (*Existenz*) is that set of conditions (*Existentiale*) without which Dasein could not count as freely **choosing**, and thus acting in any real sense. Harman is fond of ridiculing Heidegger's analysis of the mode of Being of *animality* as distinct from Dasein's mode of *existence*, precisely because he fails to see that Heidegger is describing entities that have similar be-

---

[29] Cf. Martin Heidegger, *Fundamental Concepts of Metaphysics* (Bloomington and Indianapolis: Indiana University Press, 1994), §67.

[30] Harman, *Tool-Being*, 41-42.

havioural capacities to Dasein (*drives*) that nevertheless lack the specific conditions of organisation that enable choice (as opposed to mere *disinhibition*).[31]

This ties back to the third point: Harman cannot see what it would be to be world-poor insofar as he does not see what it would be for something to have a world in Heidegger's sense: an internally articulated space of possible action (i.e., the *projection* of what is possible), involving a grasp of both **generality** and **particularity** (e.g., the possibilities of pens *as such*, and the possibilities of *this* pen, respectively), in **isolation** and **situation** (e.g., the possibilities of this pen in relation to paper *as such*, and the possibilities of *this* pen in relation to *that* piece of paper, respectively), organised in terms of a **hierarchy of ends** (e.g., the end of writing a letter, itself a means to maintaining a friendship, itself a means to… etc.) united by the **fundamental goal** of becoming oneself (i.e., Dasein as its own *for-the-sake-of-which*). Entities appear in the world for Heidegger insofar as they modify this space of possibility: their **actuality** consists in the way they *open up* certain specific possibilities for action while *closing down* others. This in turn ties back to the second point: Harman cannot see that differences in modes of Being (e.g., *Zuhandenheit, Vorhandenheit, Existenz*, etc.) are not simple differences between types of beings, insofar as he does not see the different ways they are supposed to be **individuated** as actualities within the world *qua* space of possibility. So, it is true that all spatio-temporally located particulars are *both* ready-to-hand and present-at-hand in some sense (even if the *space* and *time* in question are not straightforwardly identical), but this is a matter of the difference between our grasp of possibilities as tied to the everyday forms of activity we inherit from the culture we are *thrown* into (e.g., pens *qua* writing implements), and our grasp of possibilities as *abstracted* from these activities (e.g., pens *qua* ink-filled molded plastic), respectively.

Fifthly, then, this brings us to Harman's persistent criticisms of pragmatist readings of Heidegger in general, and of the

---

[31] Cf. Heidegger, *Fundamental Concepts of Metaphysics*, part 2, ch. 3-6.

tool-analysis more specifically. These are inexorably bound up with the other criticisms already presented, but there is an important additional dimension here: his claim that Heidegger's concern with the **use** of equipment has nothing to do with use as we normally understand it, but should be understood as a matter of **reliance** upon equipment.[32] It is the fact that reliance is an essentially *causal* notion that underpins his claim that all interactions between entities can be described as entities "understanding" one another "as" something, and the development of this into the claim that all such interactions are analogous to the encounter with the broken-tool. We'll return to the independent methodological problems with this claim, but for now it serves to point out the sheer extent to which this misunderstands Heidegger's account of the as-structure and its relation to the broken-tool encounter. The crucial point is that Heidegger distinguishes between the **hermeneutic** "as" and the **apophantic** "as," and associates these with the ready-to-hand and the present-at-hand, respectively. The relationship between the former thereby circumscribes the relationship between the latter, and it is essentially a matter of the relation between **implicitness** and **explicitness**, respectively.

It is important to understand that the "as" is indicative of generality. We grasp something "as" something insofar as we grasp a particular as an **instance** of a general type. The idea behind the split in the as-structure is that the grasp of generality involved here can be articulated in two distinct ways, even if these forms of articulation are fundamentally inseparable and always combined in different degrees. We grasp the entities around us principally through the hermeneutic "as" insofar as the specific possibilities we are immediately presented with by them (e.g., writing a letter) are articulated by an implicit grasp of the general types of equipment they instantiate (e.g., pens and paper *qua* equipment for writing). This implicit grasp is the condition of **interpretation**, which is the process through which we reconsider these immedi-

---

[32] Harman, *Tool-Being*, 18-21.

ate possibilities, taking them apart and bringing forth the generalities that articulate them. However, this process of interpretation is not yet linguistic: it is the move to making **assertions** about entities that transforms the hermeneutic "as" into the apophantic "as." These involve the use of special linguistic equipment to isolate and then re-articulate the general possibilities that constitute these types. This enables a process of progressive abstraction which extricates the **causal capacities** of entities from the **normative functions** through which our everyday understanding grasps them. The present-at-hand is nothing but the correlate of the limit-case of this process of abstraction. It is not constituted by *pure presence*, or actuality devoid of possibility, but rather by *pure capacity*, or possibility devoid of function. The exemplars of the present-at-hand are those entities posited by science independently of any role they could have in everyday practices (e.g., electrons, black holes, mitochondria, etc.). Science is thus hardly the domain of pure presence in this vacuous sense, but rather the forefront of our attempt to work out what is *really* possible, over and above the expectations implicit in our parochial forms of life.

The encounter with the broken-tool must be understood in terms of this complex interplay between causal capacity and normative function. The important thing to realise is that the tool cannot break unless it behaves in a way it is not *supposed* to: there is no **malfunction** without proper function. It is the fact that we grasp equipment (e.g., pen and paper) in terms of a set of normatively articulated everyday activities (e.g., letter writing, drawing, doodling, etc.) that enables it to surprise us by *failing* to behave as it should in the context of those activities (e.g., the pen leaking ink all over the paper). This means that we must already encounter the equipment *as* equipment: without a prior hermeneutic "as," nothing can break. This prior "as" forms the basis of the response to the encounter, insofar as the surprise malfunction incites us to re-interpret our grasp of the tool's possibilities. This interpretation can then either stay at the hermeneutic level, or be developed apophantically by using assertions to draw out the causal capacities the tool possesses independently of its functional role; or rather, independently of its status *as a tool*. It is in this sense that the encounter with the broken-tool amounts to a *transition* between the tool as ready-to-hand and the tool as present-at-hand: it is an *invitation* to a different form of understanding.

What all this reveals is that Harman's reading cannot be an interpretation of the substance of Heidegger's ideas, even one that Heidegger himself would disagree with. It is possible to read thinkers against themselves, but this requires that there is some essential element present in their work that the work itself fails to live up to.[33] The element that Harman tries to unearth in Heidegger's tool-analysis simply isn't there.[34] The only reason he can propose to extend the intentional relation between Dasein and its tools to cover all interactions between entities is that he has stripped this relation of everything that makes it recognisably Heideggerian. He has excised the structure of projective understanding wholesale, and thereby completely abandoned the semantic and epistemological framework within which the encounter with the tool is described. This becomes clear once we ask the question: just what would it be for a screen door to encounter a knife *as* a knife?[35] To say that this is for it to be affected by it in a way that is common to all knives is to say nothing that warrants using the word "encounter" in an intentional

---

[33] This is a hermeneutic strategy that Brandom calls *de re* interpretation, as opposed to *de dicto* interpretation: the attempt to be faithful to the subject matter, rather than the words used to express it (*Tales of the Mighty Dead*, ch. 1).

[34] Another point to make here about Harman's reading qua reading is that even if there were some evidence that Heidegger did see the tool-analysis in something resembling this way, then it would still be far fetched, given the extent of the other aspects of Heidegger's work it invalidates: theory, mood, space, time, etc. (cf. *Tool-Being*, §4-7) Harman gives us a long list of features of his thought that Heidegger can say nothing specific about despite his sincere and extensive attempts to do so. The sheer amount of Heidegger's work that Harman's reading disqualifies thus constitutes a pretty good *reductio ad absurdum* of it as a reading of Heidegger, even if we ignore the misunderstandings just discussed.

[35] This is Harman's own example (*Tool-Being*, 30-32).

sense. The screen door has nothing that could qualify it as having anything like an **awareness** of generality. There is no hermeneutic "as" circumscribing its engagements with things. This leaves us saying that what it is for a screen door to interact with a knife *qua* knife is for it to be affected in the way that knives affect screen doors. This is an empty tautology unworthy of metaphysical scrutiny.[36]

ii) The Argument from Execution

The principal argument derived from the tool-analysis in *Tool-Being* is what I have called the argument from execution. This argument aims to establish that the reality of entities consists in their execution (or tool-being), and on this basis to demonstrate that they withdraw from all *epistemic* and *causal* contact. Harman takes the method of the argument to be a matter of phenomenological description, insofar as it is a purported reconstruction of Heidegger's own phenomenological analysis.[37] The point of this analysis is to reveal the **absolute invisibility** of objects *qua* execution, by presenting three interrelated characterisations of execution: as **causal capacity** (or "effect"), as **pure action** (or "impact"), and as **functional role** (or "reference"). However, as we've already noted, Harman provides no clarification regarding the nature of his phenomenological method, or how it can be expected to yield metaphysical results. This is complicated by the fact that many of Harman's claims are patently more metaphysical than phenomenological. This raises the possibility that in some cases he has simply imported metaphysical assumptions instead of collecting phenomenological evidence. We will thus have to be very careful to keep all the elements of his analyses separate in reconstructing their logical form.

Harman's take on Heidegger's phenomenological analysis opens by specifying its object: our ubiquitous encounters

---

[36] For a further example of Harman's attempt to universalise the as-structure in this way, see his discussion of tectonic plates towards the end of *Tool-Being* (221-222).

[37] Harman, *Tool-Being*, 18.

with the entities that we "use" in the course of living. His break with Heidegger's analysis occurs already in this first paragraph:

> Heidegger demonstrates that our primary interaction with beings comes through "using" them, through simply *counting on them* in an unthematic way. For the most part, objects are implements taken for granted, a vast environmental backdrop supporting the thin and volatile layer of our explicit activities. All human action finds itself lodged amidst countless items of supporting equipment: the most nuanced debates in a laboratory stand at the mercy of a silent bedrock of floorboards, bolts, ventilators, gravity, and atmospheric oxygen.[38]

This break is subtle, and does not become completely apparent until a few pages later, when he explicitly substitutes the word "rely" for "use."[39] The examples that Harman focuses on are indicative of this shift. Gone is the emphasis upon equipment *actively deployed* toward a goal (e.g., hammers, cars, signals, etc.), to be replaced with a focus upon "equipment" necessary to *passively sustain* a given state (e.g., ventilators, gravity, oxygen, etc.). It is not that Heidegger is not concerned with some examples of this kind—*sustaining* a state is as eligible a goal as *achieving* one—but rather that Harman narrows the scope of the analysis by collapsing *active use* into *passive reliance*, while simultaneously expanding its scope to include cases of dependence that lack anything that could be construed as *awareness* of the thing depended upon. This move both enables execution to take on the role of *persistence* we saw earlier, and facilitates the *universalisation* of intentionality to encompass all objects and the flaying of Heidegger's account of intentionality that accompanies it.

We can already see the pretence of phenomenology slipping here. Harman has subtly shifted the focus of his analysis from our practical comportment toward things to our **causal dependence** upon them. We are invited to conclude that phe-

---

[38] Harman, *Tool-Being*, 18.
[39] Ibid., 20.

nomenological description is apt to describe my relation to my internal organs, the geological strata that I stand upon, or the delicate balance of environmental factors necessary for life on earth in a manner analogous to my relation to the various socially delineated props I passively engage in carrying out everyday tasks. Harman balances this shift upon a delicate ambiguity in the sense in which encounters with things can be "unconscious" or "unthematic."[40] It consists in misunderstanding what Heidegger calls *circumspection* (*Umsicht*). Heidegger's concern with this sort of "unthematic" understanding was to provide a phenomenological analysis of comportments that lacked a *specific kind* of awareness, rather than lacking awareness *as such*. He would not consider my relation to my internal organs to be an intentional relation unless it consisted in some *implicit grasp* of general ways in which they are involved within practical activities, either as obstacles (e.g. an awareness of my fickle digestive system) or resources (e.g., the metabolic control some yogic masters have achieved), or some *explicit grasp* of their general modal features (e.g., the theoretical understanding of a biologist or surgeon). Harman essentially substitutes Heidegger's concern with the "unconscious" encounter as *awareness without attention*, for a concern with it as *dependence without awareness*.

Bearing all this in mind, we can turn to the first step in Harman's analysis. This is his claim that *what* we encounter in relying upon equipment is its *causal capacity* to produce the specific effect that we rely upon. This is his first characterisation of the execution that constitutes the reality of the tool, and he vehemently opposes it to the idea that the tool consists in the ways humans expect to use it: "Equipment is not effective 'because people use it;' on the contrary, it can only be used because it is *capable of an effect*, of inflicting some kind of blow on reality. In short, the tool isn't 'used'—it *is*."[41]

---

[40] It is also helped by an ambiguity in the sense of "reliance," which can be read either as an intentional relation involving an *expectation* regarding whatever is relied upon, or as a matter of brute causal dependence.

[41] Harman, *Tool-Being*, 20.

On the face of it, this is a perfectly good inference—successful reliance upon a thing demands that it possess the causal capacity to produce the effect relied upon—but the way it is introduced and used by Harman is questionable precisely insofar as it is metaphysical rather than phenomenological. Harman is already straying into metaphysics in describing the thing as *consisting* in this capacity, rather than simply *possessing* it, and he will stray further when he fleshes out his characterisation of this capacity *qua* execution. He does not linger in this register though. He rapidly returns to phenomenology when he insists upon the invisibility of this capacity.[42] However, invisibility is apparent only insofar as we focus upon precisely those un-Heideggerian cases that Harman has smuggled in. This paradoxical **revelation of invisibility** essentially consists in our discovery that we *really* have no awareness of those things we depend upon without awareness—at least that is, until we turn our phenomenological gaze upon them. This has no force whatsoever, because there is no correlation between dependence and awareness either way. *Prima facie*, it is entirely possible for me to be aware or not aware of the things I depend on, to varying degrees.[43]

Let us move deeper into the nature of execution and its purported invisibility then. The second characterisation of execution is its status as *pure action*, and it has two aspects. First, the equipment is never what it is simply because it is *capable* of an effect, but must also *enact* this effect at every moment: "Equipment is forever *in action*, constructing each moment the sustaining habitat where our explicit awareness is on the move."[44] Second, this perpetual action is *unitary*, insofar as its effect cannot be broken down into subsidiary actions that might be held in reserve. It must be "an agent

---

[42] Harman, *Tool-Being*, 21.

[43] No doubt some will claim that although there may indeed be *degrees* of awareness, this never amounts to complete awareness, and that this is sufficient to underwrite the putatively "absolute" character of invisibility. This is a entirely separate argument, which I will deal with in the next section as the argument from excess.

[44] Ibid., 18.

thoroughly deployed in reality, as an *impact* irreducible to any list of properties that might be tabulated by an observer."[45] There are at least two distinct tensions inherent in this characterisation: a **modal tension** between *possibility* and *actuality*, and a **temporal tension** between *dynamism* and *stasis*. The former comes from the contrast between this and the first characterisation of execution in terms of capacity, insofar as it flattens whatever possible effects a thing might have into its current actual effects. The latter comes from the characterisation of the thing as *always already* in action, an act whose occurrence is such that we only encounter it in a state of *silent repose*, or *diachronic transition* so pure it is the very essence of *synchronic persistence*. These tensions are seemingly constitutive for the invisibility of equipment. Try as we might to understand any specific capacity, we never reach the unitary effect that silently whirs behind it:

> Whatever is visible of the table in any given instant can *never* be its tool-being, *never* its readiness-to-hand. However deeply we meditate on the table's act of supporting solid weights, however tenaciously we monitor its presence, any insight that is yielded will always be something quite distinct from *this act itself*.[46]

Try as we might to understand the way an occurrence unfolds, the things it involves are events already past yet ongoing: "A tool exists in the manner of enacting itself; only derivatively can it be discussed or otherwise mulled over. Try as hard as we might to capture the hidden execution of equipment, we will always lag behind."[47] Harman provokes us like a zen master wielding a koan: a pure act rests behind all superficial acts, a pure actuality grounds all potential actualities. One hand claps slowly.[48]

It now seems we may have gone too deep after all. What

---

[45] Harman, *Tool-Being*, 21.

[46] Ibid.

[47] Ibid., 22.

[48] Before withdrawing into itself, and disappearing in a puff of *metaphysics*.

should we make of these tensions within the account of execution from the perspective of the split between phenomenology and metaphysics? At best, they constitute a brute phenomenological description of dubious plausibility. Despite the *general paradox* of the accessibility of inaccessibility, and the more *specific paradoxes* of modality and temporality it poses us with, we might simply have to throw up our arms and admit: "Well, things do *seem* this way, just like he says!" Even so, we would have to be receptive to any analysis that could dissolve these seeming paradoxes, as opposed to simply harnessing them. At worst, they constitute a series of strange and strained metaphysical assumptions extending the reification of capacity carried out by the first characterisation, assumptions we are given *anything but* good reason to endorse. Just what is really going on here? Harman seems to have transposed the phenomenological analysis of tools as deployed *in* actions—which he otherwise ignored in favour *passive dependence*—into a metaphysics of tools *as* actions. This has a peculiar effect that can best be described as **performative phenomenology**. The revelation of invisibility is an artefact of the way in which it is introduced. The general paradox is underwritten by the specific ones. We encounter the invisibility of equipment as the **ineffability** engendered by the impossible tensions in the ways in which it is described. The supposed demonstration of epistemic inaccessibility is actually an elaborate numbing of our epistemic faculties, performed by multiplying the incompatible aspects of the mysterious withdrawn tool. Single hands don't clap after all.[49]

We now turn to the third and final characterisation of execution: as *functional role*. This builds upon the previous two characterisations by articulating the *effect* which the capacity produces in its pure action as a *means* to an *end* of some sort. This is how Harman cashes out Heidegger's account of *reference (Verweis)*: he takes every entity to *refer* to those things the persistence of which *depends* upon its own persistence. The reference of a thing's execution is another thing whose

---

[49] It turns out to have been a puff of *logic*, after all.

execution it *sustains*. Reference and dependence are thus unified into a single relation of **functional dependence**. This is responsible for Harman's machinic descriptions of entities, insofar as it underwrites his discussion of dependence relations in mereological terms, not merely as between *part* and *whole*, but as between *component* and *system*. What happens here is that the *causal capacities* actualised in composition get transformed into *normative functions* through being normatively underwritten by the whole they *actually* compose. The various girders, nuts, and bolts that compose a bridge are simultaneously depended upon by the bridge and captured in executing their functional role in sustaining the bridge as a systematic effect on which further things depend.[50] It is this interpretation of reference relations that collapses Heidegger's account of world into a simple totality, insofar as it takes them to hold exclusively between *individuals*, understood in terms of their *actual states*, rather than a complex horizon that involves relations between both *types* and *instances*, understood in terms of their *possible states*.

According to Harman, this characterisation implies the second fundamental aspect of Heidegger's tool-analysis: what he calls the tool's **totality** as opposed to its invisibility. To understand this, it's important to see that Harman takes functional dependence to extend beyond intuitive forms of *mereological* dependence (e.g., dependence upon my *internal* organs), to include things like *environmental* dependence (e.g., my dependence upon *external factors* such as gravity and oxygen), and even goes so far as to incorporate *negative* dependence relations (e.g., my dependence on a meteorite *not* falling from space into me). Moreover, although both dependence and reference are *asymmetric* relations, they go in opposite directions: if x depends on y then y refers to x, and each relation is *transitive*, meaning that: if x depends on y and y depends on z, then x depends on z, and therefore also that z refers to x. Given all this, the world becomes a network of functional dependence relations, in which each specific

---

[50] Harman, *Tool-Being*, 22-25.

entity is individuated through its location relative to everything else. The bridge is what it is in virtue of depending upon precisely what it actually depends upon, and supporting precisely what it actually supports; the same is true for every nut, bolt, girder, and environmental condition upon which it depends, which includes everything upon which they depend, *ad infinitum*, and for every passing traveller, supply chain, or local business it exists in aid of, and everything they in turn support, *ad infinitum*. This converts the world from a simple totality of disparate individuals into a unified individual in its own right: the plurality of *local* systems of execution become an integrated network of components in a single *global* system, or "world-machine."[51] The numerous ends at which execution aims are subsumed within a single system of ends, the ultimate purpose of which can only be to sustain the system itself.

This produces a **relational tension** alongside the modal and temporal tensions we have already uncovered, but it is more complicated insofar as it arises from a conflict between the relational **holism** Harman attributes to Heidegger and the radical **individualism** that he aims to derive from the principles on which it is founded. The tension consists in Harman's attempt to convert holism into individualism by transforming execution from something *individuated through* the functional dependence relations it is bound up in, to something *prior to* these relations which makes them possible. It becomes manifest in the way he connects totality and invisibility through the characterisation of execution as functional role. His attempt to derive invisibility from functionality is far more reminiscent of Heidegger than the other arguments for invisibility we've discussed: "The function or reference of the tool is effective not as an explicit sign or symbol, but as something that *vanishes into* the work to which it is assigned."[52] For Heidegger, our *attention* is inevitably drawn towards the immediate ends of our activity, rather than the

---

[51] Harman, *Tool-Being*, 33.

[52] Ibid., 25, my emphasis.

various subordinate tasks and the means they involve. We focus upon what we're doing with the hammer—putting up shelves—rather than the mechanics of the hammer and our use of it. Nevertheless, this phenomenological insight is not meant to preclude the possibility of turning our attention to any of these easily overlooked details. Our *awareness* of the task as an articulated whole enables us to shift our attention back to any aspect of it. We shift focus to our grip upon the hammer, thereby adjusting it to optimise the force we can achieve at the odd angle the space allows us. Harman's reading warps this insight: the *activity* becomes the *thing*, and the *focus* of our attention *upon* the end of the activity becomes the *vanishing* of our awareness of the thing *into* whatever it sustains. This mutates further when exposed to his totalising logic of reference: all awareness vanishes into the world-machine, as the unitary activity in which everything plays its sustaining role.[53]

So far then, Harman appears to have derived the invisibility of everything but the world as a whole from his functional account of individuation. Perhaps the strangest move is still to come though, because he converts this claim about invisibility back into a claim about individuation: "Every being is entirely absorbed into this world-system, assigned to further possibilities in such a way that there could never be any singular end-point within the contexture of reference. *In the strict sense, the world has no parts.*"[54] It is not merely the *visibility* of the parts but their *distinctness* which collapses into the whole—*vanishing* becomes *absorption*. This is highly problematic, because it uses an account of the articulation of systems into distinct components to deny that there is any such articulation at all. It presupposes the fact that there are distinct entities with differentiated capacities that can be combined and configured in a variety of ways, only to interpret this combination and configuration in such a way as to deny the distinctness that it is predicated upon. We would be

---

[53] Harman, *Tool-Being*, 32-33.
[54] Ibid., 43.

forgiven for insisting upon a *reductio ad absurdum* of some, if not most, of Harman's premises at this point. He does indeed intend to perform a *reductio* of sorts, but it is not the one we might expect, and indeed, should insist upon.[55] He ignores the inconsistency at the heart of his account of functionality in favour of the contradiction between his account of invisibility and the "existence of objects as a glaring experiential fact."[56] He in turn allies this with a further apparent contradiction implied by the account: "If [it] were the case, physical causation could never occur, since there would be no individual objects, but only a single system, with no explanations for why this system should ever alter..."[57] The issues of *diachronic* causal interaction (as opposed to *synchronic* causal dependence) and the *appearance* of a multiplicity of distinct objects (as opposed to the *reality* of unitary execution) are hereby intertwined.

What is Harman's *reductio* then? What is it that converts Heidegger's purported holism into his radical individualism? The answer is the introduction of the break between the *real* and the *sensual*—which is to say, the core of the account of withdrawal. This emerges in his interpretation of the as-structure and the way he identifies it with the broken-tool encounter.[58] The principal motivation for this theoretical supplement is its ability to diffuse the live contradictions hovering in the background. However, it will only be warranted if it can integrate the three facets of the account of execution into the individualist account of substance, at least in outline, and thereby dissolve the relational tension between this and its functional foundations. How this is supposed to work, and whether it can also dissolve the accompanying modal and temporal tensions is now our principal concern. I'll tackle it one contradiction at a time.

On the one hand, Harman aims to resolve the contradiction between functional totality and apparent individuality

---

[55] Harman, *Tool-Being*, 43.

[56] Ibid.

[57] Ibid., 34.

[58] Ibid., §4.

by re-conceiving the very notion of appearance itself. Harman's concern with invisibility up until this point has turned upon an *implicit* conception of awareness, which, as we have seen, has not yet been made *explicit* through the provision of a phenomenological methodology. Nevertheless, the invisibility of things has been "shown" through purportedly phenomenological analyses of the scope of this awareness. What now changes is that the **phenomenal aspect** of this implicit conception is explicitly severed from the **epistemic aspect**: awareness is split in two, so that multiple individuals may *phenomenally appear*, even while the singular whole from which they appear *epistemically withdraws*. We can *see* the hammer, but we can never *know* the intricate system that harbours its hidden essence. This rift constitutes the difference between the hammer as *presence* and the hammer as *execution*, the hammer *as* hammer and the hammer *in itself*, and the *malfunctioning* hammer and the *functioning* hammer, respectively. It permits the conversion from invisible to visible in the encounter with the broken tool precisely because the underlying execution of the tool is not *really* made visible. The malfunction throws off an epistemically irrelevant husk that can at best hint at the silent reality of proper functioning.

On the other hand, Harman aims to resolve the contradiction between functional fixity and apparent change by uniting the question of causal interaction and the question of phenomenal presence. Although this is often hinted at, it only becomes completely explicit towards the end of *Tool-Being* itself:

> the time has come to admit to the reader that I have been guilty of a deliberate over-simplification...In fact, it is impermissible to replace the tool/broken tool distinction with the difference between causality and visibility. For it turns out that *even brute causation already belongs to the realm of presence-at-hand*.[59]

---

[59] Harman, *Tool-Being*, 221.

If we accept Harman's identification of presence with malfunction, then this makes a certain amount of sense. If the world is taken to have a fixed order insofar as it is constituted by a network of functional dependence relations, then any change to this order must amount to a break with these relations, and thus to a malfunction of some sort. This would make the question of interaction/presence a matter of explaining how components rebel against the systems in which they are seemingly subsumed, so as to generate the abundance of individuality in our phenomenal experience. This is not a question Harman takes the tool-analysis to answer. He simply takes it to have posed the problem in the correct terms. Nevertheless, he insists that the analysis implies that any solution must move beyond the *appearance* of individuality to the *reality* of individuality, because entities can break with the functional order in which they are enmeshed only if they hold something in reserve that is not determined by this order.[60] This is where the relational tension becomes most acute: just how is the account of execution that implies holism to be modified so as to permit the individualism it seemingly demands?

The tension is more serious than might be initially apparent. This is because Harman extends the identification of presence with causality beyond diachronic interaction to include the cases of synchronic dependence upon which his initial characterisations of execution were built. This can be seen in his example of a bulky metal appliance sitting upon a frozen lake: "When the lake supports the appliance, this act of supporting unfolds entirely within the as-structure, not within the kingdom of tool-being."[61] It is this move that enables Harman to convert the distinction between *execution* and *presence* into the distinction between **substance** and **relation**, insofar as it enables him to treat all causal relations in the same way. Whatever is held in reserve in order to change

---

[60] Harman, *Tool-Being*, 229-230.
[61] Ibid., 223.

the relations of functional (and thus causal) dependence that entities are bound up in withdraws from all current relations, as the substance that underlies them. However, as Harman continues: "This raises the following question: if the fact that the frozen lake supports an object is *not* its tool-being, then *what is*?"[62] As he puts it slightly earlier: "In short, tool-being is not at all what we have thought it was up till now. It must lie at a still deeper level than that of force or relation. It is no longer an effect as opposed to an appearance, but rather an executant *being* that is neither of these."[63] We are once more told what execution *is not*, but we are still none the wiser about just what it *is*.

Here is where we stand then. The relational tension consists in the fact that Harman's individualist conception of execution as *substance* is incompatible with the holistic conception of execution as *functional role* from which it is derived, but he does not make clear which aspects of the latter conception are abandoned, and thus precisely how the former differs from it, apart from its purported individualism. He does not stop characterising execution in terms of function.[64] He continues to think of objects in terms of systematic unity.[65] When he needs to talk about the substantial reserve that necessitates individuality, he simply turns to his earlier characterisations of execution: it stands independent of all relations as an actuality "richer than all possibility"[66] and prior to all effects as a "real execution, silently resting in its vacuum-sealed actuality"[67] Far from dissolving the modal and temporal tensions discussed above, he intensifies them, and he nowhere provides us an account of how the functional character of execution is to be curtailed, let alone how it is to be integrated with its status as capacity and act. When they are acknowledged, the three

---

[62] Harman, *Tool-Being*, 223.
[63] Ibid., 222.
[64] Cf. Ibid., 285.
[65] Cf. Ibid., 288.
[66] Ibid., 229.
[67] Ibid., 283.

tensions we have located (modal, temporal, and relational) are presented as paradoxical intuitions that open up room for further metaphysical speculation, but, at best, they are an argument left hanging.[68] Harman has not yet succeeded in discharging the contradictions that arise from his assumptions. He has failed to provide us with a good reason to adopt his partial reconstruction of what he takes to be Heidegger's inconsistent system, rather than simply rejecting its core presuppositions.

How does this reflect upon the relation between phenomenology and metaphysics? Let's take one last look. I think the core methodological issues emerge from the attempt to provide an account of **modality**. Here it is useful to contrast Harman's approach with the brief summary of Heidegger we provided earlier. Heidegger provides us with is an intricate **modal epistemology**. He builds a phenomenological framework within which he analyses both our understanding of the entities we encounter in terms of the *normative features* they acquire through the practices we are socialised into, the unthematic understanding of the *causal features* of these entities that is implicit in this, and the various levels of thematic understanding that can be developed out of this. His analysis of the encounter with the broken-tool is a subtle demonstration of the interface between these levels of modal understanding.

By contrast, Harman's approach can only be described as **modal mysterianism**. It begins with *phenomenological descriptions* of our experience of things, from which it derives a pseudo-Heideggerian functional vocabulary, but almost immediately converts this into a *metaphysical inquiry* into our causal relations with things, in the process hypostatising this functional vocabulary into a **metaphysical teleology**. It is important to emphasise how contentious this move is. There are deep and divisive arguments about the reality of functions running from Plato and Aristotle, through Leibniz

---

[68] Harman explicitly presents two unresolved paradoxes at the end of *Tool-Being* (287-288), but they are not the tensions I have outlined here, which emerge more sporadically throughout the work.

and Spinoza, Kant and Hegel, all the way to contemporary debates regarding the correct interpretation of Darwin. Harman makes this move not by providing a compelling reason for it, but by simply ignoring an important methodological distinction. As we have seen, the other claims he makes about the metaphysical basis of causal capacities are equally methodologically suspect. Where Heidegger does his best to delineate the modal relations between normative functions and causal capacities, showing both how they connect and pull apart, Harman systematically conflates them under the single heading of execution, which he then fails to sufficiently integrate. His purported justification of epistemic inaccessibility on the basis of these modal features (excess) is thus stuck halfway between a questionable attempt to *phenomenologically delimit* phenomenal access (the revelation of invisibility), and a dubious *metaphysical reinterpretation* of phenomenal access itself that simultaneously undercuts his phenomenological pretensions (the split in awareness) and fails to provide a coherent account of the inaccessible (the unresolved tensions). The philosophical framework he builds in *Tool-Being* leaves us with no grasp of what tool-being *is*, and simply decreeing "that's the point!" is to lapse into mysterianism.

iii) The Argument from Excess

The other argument that Harman associates with the tool-analysis, which I have called the argument from excess, can be found intermingled with elements of the argument from execution at several points in *Tool-Being* and elsewhere,[69] but it becomes the dominant strain of the analysis by the time of his presentation of the tool-analysis in his book on Meillassoux.[70] It is fairly brief, and its conclusion is more often

---

[69] Cf. *Tool-Being*, 96, 98, 223; "A Fresh Look at Zuhandenheit," in *Towards Speculative Realism*, 54-55; "The Revival of Metaphysics in Continental Philosophy," in *Towards Speculative Realism*, 116-117.

[70] Harman, *Quentin Meillassoux*, 135-136.

simply asserted than properly derived from its premises, but it is possible to reconstruct a reasonably concise version of it on the basis of these examples. I will first quote the relevant sections from the Meillassoux book, to provide a basis for reconstruction:

> In Heideggerian terms it is true that phenomena in consciousness fail to do justice to the full depths of things, to their inscrutable being withdrawn from all presence. Yet it is *also* the case that the practical handling of entities fails to do them justice as well...human theory and human praxis are both translations or distortions of the subterranean reality of [tool-being], which is no more exhausted by sentient action than by sentient thought.[71]

He thus opens with an outright assertion of the thesis of withdrawal, but he frames it in two important ways. He articulates it as a matter of the **inexhaustibility** of tool-being, and he identifies theoretical understanding and practical use in terms of their inability to exhaust it. The framing of withdrawal in terms of inexhaustibility will form the centrepiece of the argument, whereas the identification of theory and praxis paves the way for the more controversial identification of knowledge and causation. This is followed by a sort of retroactive argument for withdrawal that works from within this frame:

> All of these activities could possibly be linked under the term "intentionality," but whereas the intentionality of Brentano and Husserl is a matter of *immanent* objectivity, we are now concerned with a transcendent kind of object. It is true that the hammer takes on a specific configuration both for the construction worker and for the scientific specialist on hammers (assuming the latter person exists). But what is most relevant here is the *transcendent* hammer that startles us with surprises, shattering in our hands or rotting and rusting more quickly than expected. The present-at-hand hammer cannot explain these sudden surprises, and hence by subtraction we arrive at the notion of

---

[71] Harman, *Quentin Meillassoux*, 135.

a withdrawn, subterranean tool that enters into relation with me and other animate and inanimate entities as well.[72]

What we have here is an argument that aims to proceed from the *obvious fact* that the causal capacities of an object can exceed our understanding of them (and thereby "surprise" us) to the *contentious claim* that we cannot encounter the real objects in which this excess consists, but only the distinct sensual objects that they withdraw behind.

What follows is my best attempt to reconstruct the transition between the two. I'll begin by splitting the obvious fact into two fairly uncontentious claims:

i) Our knowledge of things does not exhaust all their features. There is more to them than we *actually* know.
ii) Our causal interactions with things do not exhaust all their capacities. There is more to them than we *actualise*.

The example of something's causal capacities exceeding our grasp of them is obviously taken from the analysis of the broken-tool, but its real import comes in straddling the divide between (i) and (ii). Although other presentations will emphasise one or the other, the justification of the thesis of withdrawal depends upon equivocating between these two claims in some fashion, be it by leaning upon aspects of the argument from execution (e.g., interpreting praxis as reliance) or simply treating the identity of intentional and causal relations as a given. This equivocation exemplifies the collapse of phenomenology and metaphysics into one another discussed earlier. What is important is that the combination of (i) and (ii) gets interpreted in a somewhat more contentious way than either of them:

iii) Our knowledge/interactions can *never* exhaust all the features/capacities of things. There is more to them than we could *possibly* encounter.

---

[72] Harman, *Quentin Meillassoux*, 136.

This move converts a **factual excess** of features/capacities into an **essential excess**. The move is strictly illicit, but, although it leads to a stronger claim than either (i) or (ii), it is still not all that contentious. There are many who would agree with (iii) for independent reasons, or simply because it is reasonably intuitive. The really contentious claims are those that get inferred from (iii):

> iv) Our knowledge/interactions can never exhaust *all* the features of a thing, because there is *some* feature of every thing *qua* thing that we can never encounter.

This move aims to explain the necessity of excess by locating it in a feature common to all things, as opposed to something which varies from thing to thing. It holds that excess is essential because there is an essential feature of entities that is excessive. This makes sense if one demands an **intrinsic** explanation of excess, which locates the reason for the excess in the *encountered object*, as opposed to an **extrinsic** one, which locates it in the *encountering object*. When the latter is understood as a *knowing subject*, the extrinsic explanation of excess has traditionally taken the name of **finitude**. This posits an internal limit upon the cognitive abilities of the subject that precludes it from knowing objects in full. This limit needn't be interpreted in terms of some common **qualitative excess**, but could be seen as a disparate **quantitative excess**. It could simply be the case that the subject can only grasp a finite number of the infinity of features belonging to each thing, but that there is no particular feature that is in principle ungraspable.

Harman insists upon an intrinsic explanation, as can be seen in the above quote, but it's important to recognise that this is underwritten by the equivocation between knowledge and causation: "I am convinced that objects far exceed their interactions with other objects, and the question is both *what* this excess is, and *where* it is."[73] In other words, he takes the

---

[73] Harman, "The Revival of Metaphysics in Continental Philosophy," in

issue of essential excess to be equivalent to the issue of *substantial reserve* discussed in the argument from execution.[74] The localisation of **epistemic excess** is thus predicated upon the localisation of **causal excess**. This sets the stage for the final (and most contentious) inference:

> v) Our knowledge/interactions can never exhaust a thing, because we can never encounter the *essence* of the thing. We only encounter the *(sensual) appearance* of the thing, never its *(real) being*.

This move converts the essential excess into an **excessive essence**. Harman takes the common essential feature of all things that cannot be encountered to be *what things are in themselves*, or essence *as such*. This is supposed to warrant the absolute distinction between the real and the sensual, insofar as it implies that whatever epistemic/causal contact there is with a thing must be contact with something *other* than what it really is. It thereby moves from *localisation* to *isolation*. However, this exploits the same equivocation as (iv), albeit in reverse, insofar as it makes sense of **causal isolation** in terms of **epistemic isolation**. While it is easy to understand withdrawal as the impossibility of *direct epistemic access*, it is much less clear how we are to understand independence as the impossibility of *direct causal contact*. There is a clear quantitative line from *some* access to *no* access, because we can intuitively grasp what it would be to completely fail to know anything about a thing despite seeming to, but there is no such clear line from *some* contact to *no* contact, because we cannot intuitively grasp what it would be to completely fail to activate any of a thing's capacities, despite seeming to. Of course, this is not how Harman conceives of independence. He bypasses quantitative considerations involved in (i) to (iv) by treating that which underlies causal interaction as a unitary execution as opposed to a multiplicity of distinct

---

Towards Speculative Realism, 117.

[74] This is precisely how the arguments intertwine in *Tool-Being*, 223.

capacities. The actualisation of capacities through causal contact is then treated as something qualitatively distinct from the *independent substance* which underlies them, much as the appearance of features through phenomenal access is treated as qualitatively distinct from the *withdrawn essence* which underlies them. This qualitative break is what divides execution and causation into distinct forms of actuality (modal tension) and activity (temporal tension). The equivocation between knowledge and causation thus disguises an illicit leap from quantitative to qualitative excess, along with the mysterian tensions it invokes.

The overall shape of this argument is thus another *reductio ad absurdum* of sorts. It begins by assuming that there is **partial** contact between objects only to try and demonstrate that its essentially partial character implies the impossibility of any contact at all. It slides easily from quantity to quality on the back of Harman's characteristic universalisation of intentional relation, but as with the argument from execution, this conceals problems that warrant rejecting the terms in which it is framed. However, there is a further aspect of the move from quantity to quality worth considering:

> But the following objection to this theory often arises: why exaggerate and say that things cannot touch at all? Does it not seem instead that things *partly* make contact with each other?...The problem is that objects cannot be touched "in part," because there is a sense in which objects have no parts.[75]

Harman is very insistent withdrawal is complete. Our knowledge of things is not merely limited, but entirely inadequate. Objects are foreclosed to us. But here he presents the mereological missing link in his reasoning from quantitative excess to qualitative excess. It seems that he takes the idea that a whole is *more* than its parts to imply that the whole is *entirely distinct* from its parts, such that to know the parts is not to know the whole, not even partially, as it were. This is

---

[75] Harman, *The Quadruple Object* (Zero Books, 2010), 73.

somewhat questionable, but it is not the whole story, as it only works if we treat the features and/or capacities of objects as if they are parts. This provides a path between (iv) and (v), but it is highly dubious.

iv) The Argument from Identity

The final argument, which I call the argument from identity, will require even more reconstruction than the argument from excess. This is because, although it is frequently invoked, it is usually presented without a detailed analysis of how it is supposed to work. Though it does appear in the context of the tool-analysis,[76] usually in conjunction with some form of the argument from excess, it also appears independently,[77] as the snappiest and most condensed statement of the case for withdrawal. The most explicit presentation it has so far received is in Harman's criticism of James Ladyman and Don Ross' *Every Thing Must Go*, which I will quote at length:

> Let's imagine that we were able to gain exhaustive knowledge of all properties of a tree (which I hold to be impossible, but never mind that for the moment). It should go without saying that even such knowledge would not itself be a tree. Our knowledge would not grow roots or bear fruit or shed leaves, at least not in a literal sense. Even in the case of God, the exhaustive knowledge of a tree and creation of a tree would have to be two separate acts. Now, it has sometimes been objected to this point that it is a straw man. After all, who confuses knowledge of a tree with an actual tree? The answer, of course, is that no one does, since no one could openly identify a thing with knowledge of it and still keep a straight face. Yet the point is not that people defend this view openly, which they do not. Rather, the point is that many people uphold a model of the real that *entails* that knowledge of a tree and a real tree would be one and the same, and hence their views are refuted

---

[76] Cf. Harman, *Tool-Being*, 224; Harman, *Quentin Meillassoux: Philosophy in the Making*, 136.

[77] Cf. Harman, *Guerilla Metaphysics*, 83, 103; Harman, *Prince of Networks*, 132; Harman, *The Quadruple Object*, 28, 73.

by *reductio ad absurdum*. Namely, if someone holds that there is an isomorphic relationship between knowledge and reality, such that reality can be fully mathematized, then it also follows that a perfect mathematical model of a thing should be able to step into the world and do the labor of that thing. But this is absurd.[78]

The essence of this argument is the attempt to derive the impossibility of **complete knowledge** of a thing from the **ontological distinction** between a thing and our knowledge of it. Although it sometimes appears that this invocation of non-identity is an argument for withdrawal proper, it is really an argument for the epistemic component of premise (iii) of the argument from excess. The rejection of *complete* knowledge must then be leveraged into a rejection of *partial* knowledge, as is clear from the article just quoted, which finishes the above section with a short appeal to the mereological component of the argument from excess discussed above.[79]

The inference from ontological distinction to the impossibility of complete knowledge once more takes the form of a *reductio ad absurdum*. The principle that underlies it is the claim that complete knowledge of a thing would somehow have to be identical to the thing, thereby contradicting ontological distinction. It is this principle which is nowhere given a detailed analysis, and which we must therefore reconstruct. The major problem we face here is that Harman's use of the term "knowledge" is never really backed up by an **epistemology** that could answer questions about the distinction between *completeness* and *incompleteness*, how this relates to the distinction between *correctness* and *incorrectness*, and whether knowledge of an object is *composed* of distinct representations. I have thus endeavoured to reconstruct the argument on the basis of reasonable assumptions about what Harman means by knowledge, the most important of which is that although Harman tends to simply talk about knowledge of an object

---

[78] Harman, "I am also of the opinion that materialism must be destroyed," in *Society and Space*, volume 28 (2010), 788-789.

[79] Ibid., 789.

as a unitary phenomenon (e.g., knowing a tree), the notion of completeness/incompleteness implies that this must be composed out of correct representations of distinct features of the object (e.g., its species, size, shape, colouration, location, etc.). I'll thus begin with some premises that codify this implicit epistemology:

i) For any representation of an object to be *correct*, the object must in some sense be *the same* as it is represented as being: I know the tree is an elm only if I represent it as being an elm *and* the tree is actually an elm, or if the *tree-for-me* and the *tree-in-itself* are the same in the relevant respect.

ii) For a *composite* representation of an object to be correct, every distinct *piece* of it must be correct: my representation of the tree will not amount to knowing the tree if I misrepresent its structure, despite correctly representing its species, or if there is a *difference* between the *tree-for-me* and the *tree-in-itself*.

iii) For a composite representation of an object to be *complete*, it must be both *correct* and *exhaustive*: I know the tree completely only if there is no feature of the tree that is not accurately represented by some component of my representation of it as a whole.

From these premises it is then possible to infer the following claim:

iv) For any knowledge of an object to be complete, the *object-for-us* and the *object-in-itself* must be *the same in every respect*.

We now only require Leibniz's principle of the **identity of indiscernibles** to reach the principle from which our contradiction is derived:

v) For any knowledge of an object to be complete, the *object-for-us* and the *object-in-itself* must be *identical*.

This means that as long as we have good reason to think that the object-for-us and the object-in-itself must be ontologically distinct, the *reductio* will work. Harman's argument depends upon the obviousness of this fact.

However, if we dig into this obviousness, we'll find that all is not as straightforward as it might initially seem. I take the intuitive basis for ontological distinction to be the conjunction of two ideas: what I'll call the **possibility of error** and the **necessity of identity**. The former is the idea that for any representation to *be* a representation there must be the possibility that it could be incorrect, because correctness makes no sense without the possibility of incorrectness. The latter is the generally accepted principle that if two things are identical it is not possible that they could have been distinct. If we add these to (v) we can derive ontological distinction by *reductio ad absurdum*. This is because, if the object-for-us and the object-in-itself were identical, then our knowledge of the object would be necessarily complete, and therefore its component representations would have to be infallible, thereby violating the possibility of error. However, the fact that this demonstration includes (v) should give us pause for thought. It indicates that there is something fishy about the connection between (v) and ontological distinction that should be pursued further. What it indicates is that (v) already has some ontological content. Some potentially questionable metaphysical assumptions have been snuck in via the back door.[80]

---

[80] It should be noted that to reject these questionable assumptions and the hasty proof of ontological distinction given above is not necessarily to reject the brute fact of ontological distinction. Another way of looking at the issue is to say that our knowledge (or its *representational content*) and its object are distinct by *default*, insofar as, *pace* Harman, the question of their identity simply cannot arise. To give a parallel example, Julius Caesar is distinct from the number 9, because, although we have procedures for determining whether numbers are identical, and whether people are identical, we have no procedures that cross the number/person divide. We have similar ways of determining whether representational contents are identical (e.g., whether you and I are saying *the same* thing in speaking the same sentence), and these need not be compatible with our procedures for identifying the objects they represent.

However, there is an illicit assumption concealed in (i) that only becomes explicit with the invocation of the identity of indiscernibles in inferring (v) from (iv). It all comes down to how the notion of *sameness* is interpreted. In order for the inference from (iv) to (v) to work, the uncontroversial idea that a correct representation must somehow *represent* the object as being the same as it actually is needs to be converted into the much more controversial idea that a correct representation must somehow *be* the same as the object is. This means that correctly representing some feature of an object is interpreted as standing in some relation to *another* object that also possesses that feature. Knowing that the tree-in-itself is an elm involves standing in some curious relation to a tree-for-me that is an elm *in precisely the same sense* as the tree-in-itself. For the principle of the identity of indiscernibles to work, the object-for-us and the object-in-itself must not only be able to have the same features, they must also possess these features in the same sense. What this shows is that the argument from identity can only contribute to the proof of withdrawal if Harman is allowed to base his epistemology upon a metaphysical distinction (object-for-us/object-in-itself) closely resembling the distinction between the sensual object and the real object it is intended to demonstrate. The *fact* of a distinction between types of object is already given, even if its *character* is not.[81] To call this epistemology idiosyncratic would be an understatement.

b) Heidegger, Husserl, and Kripke

Harman's fourfold obviously emerges from the combination of the real/sensual distinction provided by the arguments

---

[81] This is an interesting contrast to the way the distinction between types of object emerges in *Tool-Being*, which sees it as a consequence of his reconstruction of the tool-analysis, rather than something already implicit in the analysis (258-259). However, the argument of this particular section is suspect (essence must itself have essence, *ad infinitum*) and does not seem to be repeated in any of the subsequent work.

for withdrawal with the object/quality distinction. There are a number of different ways in which Harman introduces the latter distinction and thereby facilitates this emergence. However, the fourfold lacks an obvious counterpart of withdrawal's tool-analysis: there is no single argument which stands out above all others. Rather, there is a mix of the three forms of exposition, which although it can be broken down into two core arguments: the argument from **eidos** (taken from Husserl) and the argument from **essence** (taken from Leibniz, Zubiri, and Kripke), is principally organised by Harman's interpretation of Heidegger's famous fourfold (*das Geviert*) of **earth** (*Erde*), **sky** (*Himmel*), **gods** (*Göttlichen*) and **mortals** (*Sterblingen*). As such, we must once more preface our examination of Harman's own arguments with a brief analysis of his reading of Heidegger.

i) Harman's Heidegger Revisited

Harman's reading of the fourfold is to be praised for refusing to either sideline it as an unimportant feature of Heidegger's work, or deny the numerical specificity of the categories constituting it. Moreover, it is to be commended for interpreting these categories as the result of the intersection of two distinctions that it basically gets right: **cleared/concealed**, and **multiple/unitary**. It is in the interpretation of these distinctions that everything goes wrong. The most serious problem is that he identifies the more famous fourfold discussed above with another fourfold schema found earlier in Heidegger's works—in his course during the Freiburg Emergency War Semester of 1919. This is the intersection of a distinction between the **pre-theoretical** (*vortheoretische*) and the **theoretical** (*theoretische*) and a distinction between the **generic** and the **specific**, producing these four categories: the **pre-worldly something** (*Das vorweltliche Etwas*), the **world-laden something** (*Welthaftes Etwas*), the **formal-logical objective something** (*Formallogische gegenständliche Etwas*), and the **object-type something** (*Objektartiges Etwas*).[82] This is complicated by the fact that Harman also misreads the 1919 schema, reading its concern with the "something" as a matter of **singularity** as opposed to **universality**, or a matter of beings as opposed to Being.

It is understandable that Harman takes the pre-theoretical/theoretical distinction to correspond to his own real/sensual distinction, but, as we've already shown, this is a misreading of Heidegger's concern with the difference between the ready-to-hand and the present-at-hand. It is not a distinction between that which is understood (the sensual) and that which exceeds understanding (the real), but a distinction between theoretical (apophantic) and pre-theoretical (hermeneutic) modes of understanding. The more serious error is that he confuses the distinction between beings considered *generically* (beings *qua* beings) and beings considered *specifically* (e.g., this pen, that piece of paper, etc.) with the distinction between the *unitary* bearer of qualities (e.g., this pen, *qua this*) and the *multiplicity* of its qualities (e.g., this pen *qua* pen, *qua* plastic, *qua* blue, etc.). Although in considering something as a generic something we are indeed abstracting away from its specific determinations, we are not thereby moving from multiplicity to unity: the object-type something is already unitary, it is simply a unit of a specific type (e.g., a pen) with many other specific features (e.g., it is made of plastic, it is blue, etc.). The point is not to investigate the *singularity* of each being as distinct from the *plurality* of its qualities, but to investigate the *universality* of its Being as distinct from the *particularity* of its type and its other features. In essence, the 1919 schema is an early articulation of the connection between projective understanding and the question of Being: it circumscribes the relationship between the general structure of our theoretical understanding of beings (formal-logical objective something) and the primordial source

---

[82] Theodore Kiesel, *The Genesis of Heidegger's Being and Time* (University of California Press, 1992), 21-25.

of our understanding (pre-worldly something). This is just what Heidegger will later characterise as the relationship between Being and time.[83]

The later fourfold most famously appears in an essay entitled "The Thing" in Heidegger's analysis of the conditions under which a humble jug appears to us, but the themes that compose it are hinted at at least as early as his masterful "On the Origin of the Work of Art" and run rampant across the jumble of musings that compose *Contributions to Philosophy*. Harman overlooks these for the most part, in favour of his attempt to read a continuity with the 1919 schema. It is ironic then that his interpretation of the twin distinctions that constitute the fourfold gains more traction here. This is because it is essentially a modification and extension of the account of the strife between earth and world briefly discussed earlier. The important differences are that: a) world *qua* projected space of possibility is renamed *sky*; b) Dasein's role in the projection of this space is made explicit in the form of *mortals*; and c) the enigmatic *gods* are added as a counterpart to mortals. This leaves us with a split between a unitary *horizon* of appearance (sky), multiple agents who *clear* this horizon (mortals), a unitary locus of *resistance* to this clearing (earth), and multiple foci where this resistance is *hinted* at within the horizon itself (gods). The **mirror play** between these four is then nothing but an extended account of strife: the process through which we attempt to negotiate a **coherent** and **comprehensive** grasp of reality by wrestling with that reality itself.

Harman underplays Heidegger's version of the cleared/concealed and multiple/unitary axes in order to draw a

---

[83] Of course, Heidegger never provided a complete account of his analysis of Being in terms of time. The third division of part one of *Being and Time* which was supposed to contain this analysis was never published, although we have fragments of the ideas that would have made it up in the form of *Basic Problems of Phenomenology*, which provides the most extensive version of the analysis, along with the best account the projection of Being upon the primordial source of temporal understanding (*Temporalität*).

continuity with his own fourfold.[84] The crucial difference between them is that Heidegger interprets the multiple/unitary axis as a distinction between beings *as such* (the plurality of beings) and beings *as a whole* (the totality of beings), whereas Harman interprets it as the distinction between the multiplicity of a being's *qualities* and its singularity as *bearer* of these qualities. This reflects their differing interpretation of the other axis, insofar as the later Heidegger understands concealing principally in terms of the whole (earth), of which particular concealings (gods) are derivative, whereas Harman takes particular concealing to not only be primary, but to be the only real form of concealing (withdrawal). Harman does not think the whole conceals itself as much as that it doesn't exist. It is nothing but the mutual withdrawal of every being from every other.[85] This raises the issue of the relation between the multiple/unitary distinction and the part/whole distinction. Harman's rejection of the whole turns on interpreting it not merely as the totality of beings, but as a single being composed out of all other beings. As we have seen, this is precisely how he interprets Heidegger's account of totality. This makes Heidegger's position into a variant of what he would call **onto-theology**, insofar as it comprehends Being in terms of a single privileged being. This misinterpretation reveals a deeper issue though, insofar as Harman seems to blend these two distinctions in explaining his own schema. Specifically, the multiplicity of a thing's real qualities and its unity as bearer of these qualities is often exchanged for the distinction between the thing's real parts and its unity as the whole these parts compose.[86] This conflation sometimes

---

[84] I say "underplay" here because there are points at which he seems to recognise that Heidegger's later schema simply does not fit his own. This is somewhat implicit in *Tool-Being* (266), but it is explicit by the time of *The Quadruple Object* (87-88).

[85] Harman, *Tool-Being*, 294-296.

[86] This is most explicit in the section of *Tool-Being* where he explains the distinction between real objects and real qualities by way of Zubiri's account of essence: "The object lives with a dual tension in its breast. On the one hand it fluctuates between the vacuum of its tool-being and the power of

comes out into the open, only to disappear once more.[87] We must be careful not to let it pass without notice.

ii) The Argument from Eidos

It is clear that any argument Harman presents for his fourfold schema and the categorical structures he derives from it will inevitably depend upon the arguments for withdrawal we have already presented. Beyond this, Harman does not really need to argue for the distinction between objects and qualities, at least insofar as it is a correlate of the intuitive distinction between **subjects** and **predicates**. Rather, what must be argued for is his interpretation of the way this distinction intersects with the distinction between the real and the sensual to create a divide between two kinds of quality. The first such argument we will consider, from *The Quadruple Object*, attempts to reverse engineer this distinction by independently deriving one of the categories that emerges out of it. It aims to demonstrate the divide between kinds of quality from within experience itself by appropriating Husserl's phenomenological analysis of *eidos*. Harman is fond of remarking that despite the avowedly *idealist character* of Husserlian phenomenology, it nevertheless has a distinctly *realist flavour*.[88] He finds this flavour concentrated in the analysis of eidos, where he attempts to separate it out from the bitter overtones of Husserl's idealism.

Harman begins by introducing Husserl's theory of **ad-**

---

its impact on neighbouring beings. *On the other hand it is itself a systematic empire swarming with interior parts.*" (266, my emphasis).

[87] The sheer extent of this is dramatised across *Guerilla Metaphysics*, in which the distinction between parts and qualities finally becomes evident, as if suddenly discovered, only to metamorphose through a number of different forms (cf. §7B, §10, §11) before finally settling upon a rejection of the plurality of qualities in favour of the plurality of parts (228-229). A detailed commentary upon these convoluted transitions is beyond the scope even of this extensive essay, but the need for one is ameliorated by the subsequent fading of this bold position in the formulation of the object/quality distinction presented in *The Quadruple Object* (cf. 88).

[88] Harman, *The Quadruple Object*, 20.

umbration (*Abschattung*).[89] The basic idea underlying this phenomenological concept is that in ordinary perception we encounter things from different perspectives, and that the way the thing is presented may vary between them, highlighting some features and concealing others, despite the object remaining the same. We can stand outside a house and view it from various angles, and even walk within it, touching its walls and smelling its scents, but we are always encountering the same house, even if the encounters themselves are distinct. From this, Harman draws the phenomenological insight that the object is distinct from the qualities that it presents in these adumbrations, not because it is *more* than them, but because there is some sense in which it is *less* than them. This is because it is possible to *subtract* them from the object without it ceasing to be the same object. However, there is a limit upon subtraction, because if we could subtract all of a sensual object's qualities there would be nothing to distinguish it from other such objects.[90] There are some *essential* features without which the sensual object cannot be what it is, and it is possible to compare different adumbrations of the same object and strip away the *inessential* features they present, in order to leave these behind. Husserl calls this process **eidetic variation** and its result *eidos*.

Harman then claims that, according to Husserl, eidetic qualities are never revealed in perceptual adumbrations in the way that accidental ones are, but only through the process of eidetic variation, or the **categorial intuition** that arises from it. Harman then criticises Husserl, and amends his account in the following way:

> Husserl is wrong to distinguish between the sensual and the intellectual here; both sensual and categorial intuition are forms of intuition, and to intuit something *is not the same as to be it*. Hence the eidetic features of any object can never be made present even through the intellect, but

---

[89] Harman, *The Quadruple Object* §1B.
[90] Ibid., §1C.

can only be approached indirectly by way of allusion, whether in the arts or in the sciences.[91]

The argument from identity thus makes a reappearance here to invoke the split between the real and the sensual. However, what is more important is the way this is configured in relation to the analysis of eidetic variation. Harman draws a distinction between sensual and intellectual modes of engagement with a thing's eidetic features only to collapse it, and thereby insist that these features must lie beyond both. He thus converts the distinction between accidental and eidetic features into his distinction between sensual and real qualities: "For the qualities of its eidos are also withdrawn from all access, and 'real' is the only possible name for such a feature."[92] Here we once again encounter the strange interface between metaphysics and phenomenology in his work. Just what is eidetic variation if the features it was supposed to reveal can never actually be revealed?

The truth of the matter is that Harman has parted ways with Husserl long before this move is made. Husserl's concept of eidos is an account of **general essence**, as opposed to the account of **individual essence** that Harman is attempting to develop. Husserl principally talks about eidetic hierarchies of *genus* and *species* (e.g., the eidetic features of trees as opposed to those of elms) which eidetic variation and its corresponding modes of intuition allow us to traverse on the basis of our intuitions of individuals.[93] He insists that all eidetic features "*belonging to the essence of the individuum another individuum can have too,*"[94] in contrast to the idea that eidos could be *unique* to a given sensual object. However, this claim is not just in conflict with Harman's take on essence, but with his take on the qualities that compose it: "qualities

---

[91] Harman, *The Quadruple Object*, 28, my emphasis.

[92] Ibid., 28.

[93] Edmund Husserl, *Ideas I* (Kluwer Academic Publishers, 1982), 8-15.

[94] Ibid., 8.

as described in this book are always individualised by the object to which they belong."[95] Harman not only thinks that the process of eidetic variation aims at what makes a sensual object the unique individual that it is, but he thinks that it does so by considering qualities that are unique to it *qua* individual. This dearth of generality means that there is no basis for the process of comparison, insofar as there are no qualities that could possibly be shared.[96] This makes the basis of the process of subtraction entirely mysterious, as there are no criteria for sorting accidents from eidos.[97]

In essence, what Harman does here is capitalise upon this mystery, in a manner similar to that we've seen in the arguments from execution and excess. He converts the absence of criteria for *differentiating* between essential and inessential qualities in any given case into an *absolute difference* between essential and inessential qualities in all cases. That there are no conceivable features that could be the end point of the process of determining eidos so described is used as a reason to treat eidetic features as inconceivable. Ultimately, the paucity of Harman's account of eidetic variation is actually best indicated by the way he appeals to *allusion* to fill it in. Not only does this bear no resemblance to the Husserlian phenomenological method on which the argument is supposedly founded, but it raises difficult questions about the categorical schema derived from the fourfold, insofar as it

---

[95] Harman, *The Quadruple Object*, 30.

[96] We have already seen this dearth of generality in Harman's interpretation of Heidegger's phenomenology (cf. *Tool-Being*, 84-85), but it is equally present in his reading of Husserl's. For instance, the example of the phenomenological reduction he presents in *Guerilla Metaphysics* (§10B) never moves beyond the level of the individual, but simply decomposes sensual wholes into sensual parts and explores the relations between them.

[97] Going further than this, in "On Vicarious Causation" Harman claims that Husserl's method is superficial, because it cannot analyse eidetic qualities without turning them into "something like accidents" (214). He even goes so far as to claim that, not only are qualities individualised, but there is really only one quality—the singular eidos. He thus sees eidetic variation as a sort of frantic scrabbling to unwrap a present in which we never reach the gift itself, only ever more layers of wrapping paper.

seemingly conflates *allure* (space-fusion) with *theory* (time-fission).

iii) The Argument from Essence

The second argument for the distinction between sensual qualities and real qualities is less localised. It must be reconstructed out of two components that are liberally spread throughout Harman's work, one associated with Kripke's work on **rigid designators**,[98] and one associated with Leibniz and Zubiri's work on individuation and essence.[99] When taken together, these components allow for a reverse engineering of the distinction similar to that of the argument from eidos, by deriving the corresponding category of *essence*. Also like the argument from eidos, it depends upon the distinction between sensual and real established by the arguments for withdrawal. This is because it needs to conceive the relation between the sensual object and the real object in terms of **reference**. This does not mean that it must be described in terms of Heideggerian functional relations between *things* and *things* (*Verweis*), but rather that it must be described in terms amenable to the debates regarding how *words* relate to *things* inaugurated by Frege's theory of sense (*Sinn*) and reference (*Bedeutung*). This is facilitated by the fact that the Husserlian terms in which Harman couches his theory of sensual objects were developed in dialogue with Frege. It is this concern with the *intentional basis* of reference that connects his work with the issues that Kripke raises for the theory of **names**.[100]

To explain further, Harman draws on Husserl's concept of **nominal acts** to explain the relationship between the sensual

---

[98] Cf. Harman, *Tool-Being*, 124, 213-215; Harman, *Guerilla Metaphysics*, 28-29, 108-110, 197-198; Harman, *Prince of Networks*, 175; Harman, *The Quadruple Object*, 67.

[99] Cf. Harman, *Tool-Being*, §23-24; Harman, *Guerilla Metaphysics*, 82-83, 147, 162, 192; Harman, *The Quadruple Object*, 48-49.

[100] Saul Kripke, *Naming and Necessity*, (Oxford: Blackwell, 1981).

object and its real counterpart.[101] He interprets Husserl's claim that all other intentional acts are founded upon nominal acts as saying that in any intentional relation we are **acquainted** with an immediate "this" (sensual object) that in turn *refers* to a shadowy "this" (real object). Names are attached to the former as if they are the *senses* that determine their references. This means that *distinct* sensual objects can refer to the *same* real object insofar as one thing can have many names. The crucial point is that, although Harman thinks that we can become acquainted with a sensual object by means of a **description** of the object that would draw our attention to it, and thus that we can learn how to use names through using descriptions (e.g., "'Pete' refers to the person who wrote the paper you're currently reading"), he does not think that this is necessary for acquaintance. As he explains in his reading of Ortega y Gasset, our acquaintance with the sensual object is a sort of **feeling**, and the object a sort of **feeling-thing**, which any particular description can never completely capture.[102]

However, this inability of descriptions to capture the *feel* of sensual objects is not yet the inability to capture the *meaning* of names that Kripke reveals. Harman takes the latter inability to consist in the relation between the name and its reference rather than the name and its sense: "For Kripke, names are 'rigid designators' that point to (or stipulate) realities beyond all possible descriptions of them."[103] Whereas the immediate "this" is something *more* than the *particular descriptions* that give us purchase upon it, the shadowy "this" is something *other* than every *possible description*. It's helpful to quote Harman at some length on this point:

> Kripke's "rigid designator" is meant to serve as a proper name pointing to something that remains identical even when all known features of the thing are altered, so that the moon remains the moon even if we turn out at some future point to have been catastrophically wrong about all its properties…However, the question for us is whether the invio-

---

[101] Harmen, *Guerilla Metaphysics*, 28-29.
[102] Ibid., 108-110.
[103] Harman, *The Quadruple Object*, 67.

late "this" beneath all apparent properties is something lying within perception, or is instead a real object lying somewhere beneath it.[104]

Harman obviously answers this question in the affirmative, but it is important to see that he does so for *epistemological* reasons. He thinks that because we can use names to talk about the same thing regardless of any *possible disagreements* about how we should describe it, every name must therefore refer to a mysterious "inaccessible 'x' lying behind any descriptions that might be given of it."[105] What this means is that because Kripke shows that the *reference* of names is somehow independent of our beliefs about their qualities, the *individuation* of the objects they refer to cannot have anything to do with these beliefs. This is the first component of the argument.

The second component is much simpler. It amounts to a rather straightforward claim about the nature of individuation, which enables us to draw consequences regarding how the individuation of real objects does work from the above claim about how it doesn't. Harman discusses this in relation to Zubiri's work, but his simplest statements of it are always his remarks on Leibniz: "[Leibniz] observes that even though each monad must be one monad, each also needs a multitude of qualities to be what it is, to differ from other monads rather than being interchangeable with them."[106]

For real objects to be distinct from one another they must possess some qualities that distinguish them. There can be no individuation without qualities. This claim interacts with the Kripkean component in the following way:

> The basic point is that we can no longer simply distinguish between a sensual world of properties and a deeper hidden core of the essential "this"...The "this" may be separable from all sorts of specific and falsifiable features, but it is never separable from a specific essence, and is therefore no "bare particular."[107]

---

[104] Harman, *Guerilla Metaphysics*, 197-198.

[105] Harman, *Tool-Being*, 213.

[106] Harman, *The Quadruple Object*, 49.

[107] Harman, *Guerilla Metaphysics*, 197-198.

Real objects must have *individual essences* that distinguish them from all other things, even if these cannot be adequately described in terms of any sensual qualities whatsoever. Therefore, if sensual qualities are unable to compose these essences, there must be an entirely distinct type of quality capable of doing so. The need for essence thus demonstrates the need for a distinction between real qualities and sensual qualities.

The issue with this argument is that, much as we saw with Husserl in the argument from eidos, Harman's attempt to integrate Kripke's insights into his metaphysical framework ends up seriously warping them. We could focus on the fact that Kripke would not endorse the account of indirect reference that Harman's division between sensual and real objects implies, but this is a tortuous point, given the intricacies of neo-Fregean attempts to account for names as rigid designators.[108] A more salient point is that although Kripke also develops a conception of individual essence out of his account of rigid designation, it is remarkably different from Harman's. Kripke does not take his account of rigid designation to imply that the essential properties of things must be of a completely different kind to their inessential ones.[109] For him, it is entirely possible for one thing to possess a property *essentially* (e.g., a living cell's salinity, which must remain within a narrow range for it to function) and another to possess the same property *accidentally* (e.g., a cooked piece of pasta's salinity, which can vary well outside of this range without dissolution). Of course, he might simply have failed to recognise the implications of his own theory, but it should give us pause for thought. As such, we should take a look at his argument against descriptivism.

Kripke claims that the meaning of a name such as "Aristotle" cannot be composed out of descriptions such as "the most

---

[108] I have in mind the work of Gareth Evans, John McDowell and Robert Brandom. I personally endorse Brandom's own anaphoric approach to integrating the Fregean sense/reference distinction and rigid designation, which he calls "tactile Fregeanism," cf. Robert Brandom, *Making It Explicit* (Harvard University Press, 1994), ch. 7-8.

[109] Cf. *Naming and Necessity*, 39-53, 110-115.

famous student of Plato," "the tutor of Alexander the great," or "a Greek philosopher with an impressive beard," even if these descriptions *uniquely* pick out the relevant object, either individually or in conjunction. Put in its simplest form, the argument for this claim is that we would otherwise be unable to make sense of statements such as "Aristotle *might not* have been the greatest student of Plato," "Aristotle *could* have died before Alexander was born," or "It was possible for Aristotle to shave off his beard and abandon philosophy." For any descriptive feature that is supposed to belong to the meaning of a name, we can construct a seemingly reasonable **counterfactual** statement involving that name in which the object lacks it, thereby producing a contradiction. The important contrast to draw with Harman's presentation of the argument is that this is straightforwardly *modal* rather than *epistemic*: it involves differences between the way the world *actually* is and ways it *could* have been, rather than differences between the way the world *really* is and ways we *take it* to be. What Kripke means when he says that names are rigid designators is simply that they pick out the same thing in all counterfactual scenarios. Moreover, he does not think that the name successfully refers to an object in every proposed scenario. He holds that some counterfactual statements (e.g., "Aristotle could have been a pig") are false precisely because there are some essential features (e.g., humanity) that could not be absent from a scenario without the object being absent. He thus does not think that grasping the *essence* of a thing is impossible, but simply that it is distinct from grasping the *meaning* of a name that refers to it. There may be independent reasons not to endorse Kripke's essentialism, but they are not necessarily reasons to endorse Harman's alternative.

Harman's account of rigid designation has thus mutated into **stubborn designation**, insofar as names not only refer to the same thing throughout counterfactual variations, but across *all* possible appearances. For Kripke and those who attempt to incorporate his insights, there is still at least some role for descriptions of the features and history of the objects our names refer to in determining whether two different names refer to the same thing. There can be entirely separate causal histories (or anaphoric chains) determining the reference of different names (e.g., "morning star" and "evening star") and yet facts about these can help determine whether they have been referring to the same thing all along (e.g., "the morning star is the evening star," as both are names for Venus). For Harman, we can at best use descriptions to determine whether the sensual objects our names are attached to are the same, but never whether distinct sensual objects might refer to the same real object. This makes the boundaries between real objects as mysterious as their qualities.[110] The sensual chair I am sitting on and the sensual tree I am staring at are *sensually distinct*, but they might not be *really distinct*. The sun, the sea, and the strudel I had for breakfast may *really* have been the same thing all along. The messy business of working out just what it is we're talking *about* can only be given over to allure in the same fashion that the *theorisation* of eidos seems to have been. It therefore seems as if the whole issue of reference from which the argument begins has gone out the window.

Even more worryingly perhaps, we are left wondering why me must affirm the reality of discreteness at all, rather than some singular *Apeiron* underlying a plurality of discrete appearances. Harman's own analysis of appearance cannot but dissolve the "glaringly obvious fact" of discreteness that he himself held up against Heidegger's purported holism. His radical dissociation of the individuation of sensual objects from the individuation of real objects precludes appealing to apparent discreteness to prove real discreteness, and thereby undermines his seemingly radical individualism. If we cannot know anything about the criteria of individuation of real objects, then we are left with the real possibility that there might just be one.

---

[110] I owe this point to Daniel Sacilotto.

c) Occasionalism, Independence, and Supplementation

In considering the arguments for the final aspect of Harman's system, we are put in a similar position to our examination of the arguments for the fourfold, only more so. Though Harman devotes a considerable amount of space to elaborating his account of allure,[111] and presents some additional reasons why we should want such an account of causation, the principal motivation for the account is provided by the arguments we have already considered and rejected. Harman issues the following challenge to those who would assess his account of causation in *Guerilla Metaphysics*:

> Once it was conceded that the world is made up of withdrawn objects, utterly sealed in private vacuums but also unleashing forces upon one another, all the other problems follow in quick succession. Let anyone who does not agree with the strategies of guerilla metaphysics specify clearly which of its initial steps is invalid.[112]

This is precisely what I have done. None of these initial steps has proved valid, let alone all of them. This seems to rule out vicarious causation by default. Still, there are some more probative reasons that Harman presents for his account of causation. He provides a further historical narrative regarding the tradition of **occasionalism** about causation, which is meant to suggest that the problem his theory responds to emerges from a broader range of concerns than his own. He also suggests that the scientific account of causation demands **supplementation** by a metaphysical theory of causation of precisely the kind he provides. I will now address both of these, but will divide them with a final statement of the core of Harman's argument for vicarity, on the basis of the **independence** of objects from one another. This provides a proper contrast with the motivations of the occasionalists as well as contextualising the demand for supplementation.

---

[111] Cf. Harman *Guerilla Metaphysics* §8-12; Harman "On Vicarious Causation."
[112] Harman, *Guerilla Metaphysics*, p. 97.

Speculations III

i) Harman's Occasionalist Tradition

According to Harman, the problem of how distinct things can causally interact has a long lineage.[113] On the one hand, he sees it being raised within explicitly metaphysical terms in the Islamic occasionalism of the Ash'arite school, the modern occasionalism of Descartes, Malebranch, and Leibniz, and in the more contemporary occasionalism of Whitehead. All of these thinkers invoke **God** as a mediator capable of overcoming what they see as the causal gap between entities, be it as the source of all causal power (the Ash'arites), the source of the connection between different kinds of substance (Descartes), or the medium through which entities are able to encounter one another (Malebranch, Leibniz, and Whitehead). On the other, he has sees it being raised implicitly in the epistemological skepticism/critique of Hume and Kant. He reads these thinkers as invoking the **mind** as a mediator which provides the causal connections between appearances, be it through mere habit (Hume), or through transcendental necessity (Kant). Harman criticises both of these trends for advocating a **global occasionalism**, insofar as they require all causal relations to be mediated by the same thing, be it God in the former or the mind in the latter, and proposes, along with Latour, a **local occasionalism**, in which causal relations between entities are mediated by further entities.

Now, although this strikes me as presenting a somewhat perverse reading of Kant and Hume, insofar as it reads their epistemological concerns in metaphysical terms they would abjure, there are definite continuities here. There are overlapping themes that seem to motivate similar accounts of causation, insofar as they all demand some form of **causal mediation**. However, this demand does not arise from a single problem held in common between the various sub-traditions that make up this narrative. For instance, Islamic occasionalism did not only provide a *theological solution*, but was motivated by a *theological problem* about the power of God. This is

---

[113] Cf. Harman, "On Vicarious Causation," 188, 202, 218-219; Harman, *Prince of Networks*, §5C.

remarkably different from Descartes' problem concerning the split between thought and extension, Leibniz's problem concerning compossibility, and lightyears from the concerns with the nature of explanation that motivate Latour's occasionalism. If we do not share any of these diverse concerns, then this problem has no hold on us. Harman hardly takes the theological concerns of the Ash'arites to be pressing, so he cannot lean upon them to motivate his own theory of causation. In short, we still need some good reasons to accept the problematic status of unmediated causal relations above and beyond this narrative.

ii) The Argument from Independence

Harman's own reasons for taking unmediated causal relations to be impossible all stem from his claims about the independence of objects from their relations to one another. These turn up at various different points in the three arguments for withdrawal we've considered, but they are never motivated independently of claims about the excess of objects over our grasp of them, be there an explicit connection between them or an implicit conflation of them. This should be unsurprising given the dominance of phenomenological themes throughout these arguments, even when they are illicitly intertwined with metaphysical ones. My aim is now to make this tangle of claims about epistemic access and causal interaction a bit clearer, not by reconstructing a further argument, but by unearthing a non sequitur underlying the other arguments. This amounts to a final attempt at cutting the Gordian knot of methodological issues underlying Harman's project before we consider his ideas about the relationship between philosophy and science.

    I think the key here is Harman's offhand remark that "despite its various degrees of efficacy, [physical causation] must ultimately either work or fail to work."[114] This is made in the context of displaying the parallels between causation and allure, which he similarly takes to either succeed or fail

---

[114] Harman, *Guerilla Metaphysics*, 176.

in this binary fashion. This adds an extra layer of depth the to the picture of vicarious causation presented above, insofar as not only is sincerity insufficient for causal interaction, but that allure is sometimes insufficient too. Successful causation requires successful allure. However, what is really interesting is the claim that causal interaction should be understood in terms of success *at all*. If the problem of how one object can *affect* another is actually the problem of how one object can *successfully* affect another, then this tells us something more about the implicit motivations of the problem. This is because knowledge can be understood in terms of representational success. If one conflates representation and causation by treating causation in intentional terms, then one can seemingly infer the impossibility of successful causation (causal independence) from the impossibility of knowledge (epistemic excess). This conflation can only be held together by the sort of functional language that Harman refuses to abandon at the end of the argument from execution, as it lets us treat things as *striving* for ends. We can say that things *try* to affect one another, even if they always *fail*.

Of course, there still must be some way in which causation can succeed. The absolute ban upon causal contact is thus qualified using the notion of **directness**: all *direct* access fails, therefore all *direct* causation fails. The hope of an *indirect* form of access (if no longer strictly epistemic in character) thus holds open the hope of an *indirect* from of causation. This hope is answered in both cases by allure. It provides a supposedly non-representational way for us to *access* the real, and in doing so provides a way for the real to *affect* us. However, the fact that these relations proceed in *opposite* directions should give us pause for thought. The object that tries to affect is the object hiding behind the sensual object, whereas the object that tries to access is the object encountering this facade. What's going on here then?

The crucial question is this: in precisely what way can allure be said to *succeed* where representation *fails*? It is the equivocation between the standards of representational success and causal success that allows us to convert epistemic excess into causal independence. If there is no sense in which allure is held to the former standard, or to some deeper standard that it shares with representation, then there is no good sense in which it can overcome causal independence. The problem is that the only concrete standards of success that Harman ever deploys in his discussions of allure concern how the allure *affects* the one who experiences it.[115] Does the joke make me laugh? Does my mistake embarrass me? Does the metaphor make me think? The fact that these are the questions that determine the success of allure indicates why successful allure is a model for successful causation. These allusions can only succeed or fail insofar as there is some *effect* they are *supposed* to produce upon us. They are thus more like access to *narcotics* than access to *information*. It doesn't *seem* to matter that there is no substantive comparison with representational success, only because it is *already* understood in causal terms. The non sequitur is hidden by blatant circularity. Harman's aesthetics is an introspective theory of **emotional affection**.

iii) The Argument from Supplementation

Finally, we come to Harman's defence of the importance of his theory of vicarious causation by way of his thoughts on the relationship between philosophy and science. Let's jump straight in at the deep end:

> For several centuries, philosophy has been on the defensive against the natural sciences, and now occupies a point of lower social prestige and, surprisingly, narrower subject matter. A brief glance at history shows that this was not always the case. To resume the offensive, we need only reverse the long-standing trends of renouncing all speculation on objects and volunteering for curfew in an ever-tinier ghetto of solely human realities: language, texts, political power. Vicarious causation frees us from such imprisonment by returning us to the heart of the inanimate world, whether natural or artificial. The uniqueness of philosophy is secured, not by walling off a zone of precious human

---

[115] Cf. Harman, *Guerilla Metaphysics*, §8-9, 211-213.

reality that science cannot touch, but by dealing with the same world as the various sciences but in a different manner.[116]

He thus sees his metaphysical system as an attempt to return philosophy to its rightful subject matter. He defends philosophy's right to tackle the same topics as the sciences by claiming that it can approach them through other means. Given the difficulties we've had in determining Harman's methodology up till now, we are entitled to some curiosity regarding just what these means are, and how they are supposed to differ from those of the sciences. This is where the theory of vicarious causation is supposed to shine, by providing us with an exemplar of the divergence between the scientific and philosophical approaches:

> From the naturalistic standpoint, ignoring for now whatever complications one might wish to infer from the quantum theory, causation is essentially a physical problem of two material masses slamming into each other or mutually affected through fields. One object becomes directly present to the other, whether through physical contact or some other form of intimacy. But there is also a *metaphysical* problem of causation.[117]

The initial problem with this is that all of the contrasts Harman makes between the supposed scientific understanding of causality and his own metaphysical one present an incredibly crude version of the sciences.[118] Although he pays lip service to the implications quantum mechanics, he entirely ignores the advanced mathematical techniques (e.g., phase space modelling, statistical analysis, information theory, etc.) that the sciences have developed to model phenomena since Hume talked about billiard ball dynamics, along with the intricate theoretical questions regarding the nature of causation that these have spawned, both in the sciences and

---

[116] Harman, "On Vicarious Causation," 190.
[117] Harman, *Guerilla Metaphysics*, 18.
[118] Cf. Harman, *Tool-Being*, 19, 209 ; Harman, *Guerilla Metaphysics*, 79.

the philosophy of science (e.g., emergent capacities, statistical causality, information transmission, etc.).[119] However, on second thought, the real problem is that Harman's approach precludes him from paying any attention to these things anyway. As far as he is concerned, the sciences don't tell us anything about *reality*. They only talk about it as it *seems*, whereas philosophy can talk about it as it *is*. This isn't to say science is useless, but simply that the truth is entirely inaccessible to it. Maybe this truth will be relevant to the sciences, maybe it won't, but there's no real debate to be had here, even if there might be mutual inspiration.

There is a tremendous irony in this, insofar as the strange methodological hybrid of phenomenological description and metaphysical argument that Harman adopts amounts to the practice of **introspective metaphysics**. It is important to understand that this is different from what is often called "armchair metaphysics" insofar as it has nothing to do with the *a priori* as traditionally understood. It is not a matter of retreating from observation to contemplate and reason about the fundamental concepts that underpin observation, but a matter of seeking out a special kind of intuition unknown to the sciences. Harman claims to get at the reality that the sciences can never describe by closely describing the structure of seeming. Far from challenging the retreat of philosophers from the world into the bastion of consciousness, he has simply extended the domain of consciousness into the world. On this basis, he provides us with an introspective theory of causation modelled upon emotional intensity. This theory is independent of the sciences insofar as it is based on a form of evidence entirely alien to the sciences, but it strikes me as equally alien to the proper practice of philosophy. The phenomenological trappings in which Harman's metaphysical introspection is clothed are at best a bad disguise, like a tasteless rubber Nixon mask, only formed into a bizarre

---

[119] This is evident in the way he approaches the work of Ladyman and Ross in "I am also of the opinion that materialism must be destroyed," where he all but explicitly refuses to consider the scientific issues that motivate many of their crucial metaphysical choices.

caricature of Husserl's face instead. What they hide is a series of questionable assumptions and sometimes outright misunderstandings regarding important epistemological and metaphysical issues. Our next task must be to peal back this mask and bring these assumptions into the open, in order to better understand why one might be tempted to endorse OOP despite the convoluted and deeply flawed arguments presented for it.[120]

---

[120] This argument will be continued in a second part which will be published in a forthcoming issue of *Speculations*.

Of Realist Turns
A conversation with Stathis Psillos
Fabio Gironi

STATHIS PSILLOS IS PROFESSOR OF Philosophy of Science and Metaphysics in the Department of Philosophy and History of Science in the University of Athens, former president of the European Philosophy of Science Association and editor of the review journal *Metascience*. Psillos is one of the most prominent defenders of scientific realism in contemporary philosophy of science, and he formulated his arguments in defense of realism in two important monographs: *Scientific Realism: How Science Tracks Truth* (1999) and *Knowing the Structure of Nature: Essays on Realism and Explanation* (2009). Psillos' investigation begins with the identification of three core theses of scientific realism:[1]

- *The Metaphysical Thesis*: the world has a definite and mind-independent natural-kind structure;

---

[1] See Stathis Psillos, *Scientific Realism: How Science Tracks Truth* (London and New York: Routledge, 1999), xvii and Stathis Psillos, *Knowing the Structure of Nature: Essays on Realism and Explanation* (Basingstoke: Palgrave Macmillian, 2009), 4.

- *The Semantic Thesis*: scientific theories should be taken at face-value, being truth-conditioned descriptions of their intended domain, both observable and unobservable;

- *The Epistemic Thesis*: mature and predictively successful scientific theories are to be considered well-confirmed and approximately true descriptions of the world.

He proceeds by offering an articulation of the so called "no-miracles argument" for scientific realism as the crucial argument supporting this realist worldview, taking it as an instance of inference to the best explanation and defusing the attacks of vicious circularity moved against it. He has also defended scientific realism from a range of other anti-realist arguments, including Larry Laudan's pessimistic meta-induction, the argument from underdetermination of theory by evidence (the so-called Quine-Duhem thesis), and the constructive empiricism of Bas Van Fraassen. Psillos's scientific realism conjoins a positive epistemic attitude towards a fully knowable natural-kind structure of the universe with a robust, non-epistemic conception of truth, constructing a realist stance which is (as famously phrased by Crispin Wright)[2] both metaphysically modest (there is an external world which is in every way independent from us) and epistemically presumptuous (this world can be known, to a good approximation of truth-likeness by our best epistemic practice, i.e., science).

There is thus no better dialogue partner than Prof. Psillos to discuss realism, especially for those interested in "bridging the gap" between the continental and the analytic philosophical traditions. I take it to be an integral part of the mandate of *Speculations* to promote this cross-contamination: those interested in the resurgence of realist concerns from within the continental tradition ignore the vast analytic philo-

---

[2] See Crispin Wright, *Truth and Objectivity* (Cambridge, MA: Harvard University Press, 1992), 1-2.

sophical production on this topic at their peril. An informed understanding of how the realist stance has evolved in the last few decades of philosophical research in philosophy of science in dialectical engagement with a variety of anti-realist positions and how it has worked towards the clarification of concepts like causation, explanation, truth, and reference to unobservable entities, will offer precious conceptual resources for realists of all stripes and backgrounds.[3]

As readers of *Speculations* will know, in the last few years we have witnessed a return of realist concerns within the continental tradition: this has taken shape in both readings of figures from the history of continental philosophy on the background to the problem of realism and antirealism (often in relationship with their understanding of the natural sciences)[4] and of formulations of new, original realist positions. Many of these new theoretical orientations have been grouped under the term "speculative realism," a rather loose category which can be characterized, for brevity's sake (and indeed in the attempt to find a minimum common de-

---

[3] Some thinkers within the continental realist movement are aware of this necessity, and it is not uncommon, in their work, to find reference to a range of analytic figures including Wilfrid Sellars, John McDowell, Robert Brandom, Nancy Cartwright and Paul and Patricia Churchland.

[4] See, for example, Lee Braver's historical narration of antirealism in continental philosophy (Lee Braver, *A Thing of This World: A History of Continental Anti-Realism* [Evanston, IL: Northwestern University Press, 2007]), Iain Hamilton Grant's defense of a materialist/vitalist Schelling (Iain Hamilton Grant, *Philosophies of Nature After Schelling* [London and New York: Continuum, 2006]), Trish Glazebrook's account of the evolution of Heidegger's opinions about science throughout his philosophical career (Trish Glazebrook, *Heidegger's Philosophy of Science*, [New York: Fordham University Press, 2000]), Manuel DeLanda reconstruction of Gilles Deleuze's realism through his engagement with complexity theory and differential geometry (Manuel DeLanda, *Intensive Science and Virtual Philosophy* [London and New York: Continuum, 2002]), Martin Hägglund's and Michael Marder's materialist/realist reading of Jacques Derrida's philosophy (Martin Hägglund, *Radical Atheism: Derrida and the Time of Life* [Stanford, CA: Stanford University Press, 2008] and Michael Marder, *The Event of the Thing: Derrida's Post-Deconstructive Realism* [Toronto, Buffalo, London: University of Toronto Press. 2009]). It is worth noting that many of these texts have the programmatic intent of presenting the work of continental figures in terms appreciable by an analytic audience.

nominator in a range of often widely different approaches), by a reaction against and rejection of all those boundaries (Kantian-transcendental, phenomenological, cultural relativist, postmodern) posed between the human subject and "things-in-themselves" independent from human epistemic access. The criticized stance can be reduced to what Quentin Meillassoux has christened "correlationism," the thesis defending the viciously circular impossibility of thinking an entity x as independent of thought, a stance which always reinscribes (correlates) the independent dimension of an entity within the limited horizon of a language, of consciousness, or of any other transcendental condition. These new forms of realism share the belief in the possibility of constructing a philosophy which can reclaim the right to deal with things in themselves, but to do so in a "speculative" manner. One should be cautious in defining what "speculative" means here. Roughly, new continental realisms are "speculative" insofar as they either 1) reject the mandatory grounding of a realist metaphysics on purely empirical foundations and thus promote the reactivation of the possibility of a rationalism of a pre-Kantian kind (reclaiming the possibility of "first philosophy" and, to a certain extent, carrying forward the continental ambition of doing *fundamental ontology*) or 2) even when embracing the natural sciences' results as a starting point (without caricaturizing or simplifying them), intervene precisely where the sciences themselves are unable to find an internal explanation of their results by revising their metaphysical conceputal apparatus. As a general point one can say that it is precisely the negotiation of a new relationship between (continental) philosophy and science which is at stake in speculative realism, and thus that different orientations along this realist "spectrum" are to be distinguished on the basis of their degree of allegiance to the natural sciences or—if we consider the comparative dimension that we will pursue in this interview—the degree to which they reject the strict naturalism which dominates the analytic field.

Stathis Psillos – *Of Realist Turns*

Fabio Gironi: *I would like to begin by asking you how you developed your philosophical interests. You started your academic education in Greece with a degree in Physics. What pushed you to philosophy and specifically to the philosophy of science?*

Stathis Psillos: Part of the reason why I was drawn to the study of the natural sciences and of physics in particular was disillusionment with the way philosophy was conceived of, and practiced, in Greece back in the 1980s (and until not too long ago—perhaps even today in certain traditional circles). Philosophy was taken to be an essentially philological discipline constitutively engaged with the interpretation of the texts of the great dead philosophers (especially the ancient Greeks) and with an attempt at a grand historical narrative of philosophical ideas; as if philosophical ideas were developed in an epistemic vacuum independently of what was going on in science and in general culture. Actually, philosophy was taken to be a discipline which has evolved in opposition to science. Studying philosophy *this* way was extremely unattractive to me (even though, unbeknownst to me back then, there were pockets in a couple of philosophy departments in Greek universities that resisted this conception of philosophy). I was therefore led to physics, but it was quite clear to me from quite early in my studies that I was looking for a window of opportunity to engage with philosophy in a systematic manner. My turn to philosophy of science was a natural outcome of my engagement with physics and my tendency to look for philosophical problems that arise within physics as well as from what physics tells us about the world. I wrote my first degree dissertation on issues in the philosophy of quantum mechanics (trying—in vain, I am afraid—to understand the rich Aristotelian notion of potentiality and its possible relevance to the stochastic conception of the world, as this is depicted in the standard interpretation of quantum mechanics). Back then (in the late 1980s) it was quite hard to find any serious literature in Greece and I was lucky to be given by a teacher of mine the typescript of the yet unpublished book of Michael Redhead's *Incompleteness, Non-Locality and Realism*, which excited my interest in realism.

My commitment to realism (admittedly in a naïve and perhaps vague way, and mainly conceived of as materialism) was already there because of my theoretical engagement with Marx. In fact, this engagement kept my philosophical awareness alive throughout my University studies and led me to try to understand both the idealist and the empiricist opposition to realism (perhaps, unwittingly, conflating them back then). Reflection on Marx's second thesis on Feuerbach ("The question whether objective truth can be attributed to human thinking is not a question of theory but is a practical question. Man must prove the truth—i.e. the reality and power, the this-sidedness of his thinking in practice. The dispute over the reality or non-reality of thinking that is isolated from practice is a purely *scholastic* question.") was leading me towards a conception of realism that was meant to enable the task of transforming the world. I was feeling quite satisfied by the fact that this task was meant to be the *proper* mission of philosophers, as Marx, I thought, was claiming in the famous eleventh thesis on Feuerbach: "The philosophers have only interpreted the world, in various ways; the point is to change it." But I soon realised that I was fooling myself. Contrary to Marx's eleventh thesis, the point was *still* to interpret the world—if we are to know what we are doing when we try to change it. In this endeavour to interpret the world, science, I thought, was the bastion of rationality and progress; the *terra firma* upon which one could base all hopes for a better world. I believed back then—and still believe now—that science is the best way we humans have invented to push back the frontiers of ignorance and error, to achieve a deep understanding of the world and of our place in it, and to make the world a better place to live. What I now add is that science is *not* a faultless, value-neutral and interest-free way to understand and change the world.

But science and its claim to truth and knowledge are not immune to criticism; hence, they need justification and defence. To me, looking into the scientific realism debate was no longer optional. It amounted to taking a *standpoint*: the scientific realist standpoint. When I went to King's College London for graduate studies in philosophy of science (having gratefully received a state's scholarship, without which I would have been unable to pursue my philosophical studies in the UK), I came into the scientific realism debate with no neutrality. I wanted to defend scientific realism, along with the objectivity and rationality of science and its method. This was both an intellectual and, I thought, a *political* goal. Back in the 1990s, there was a pervasive thought, especially among left-wing American and continental European intellectuals, that undermining the alleged epistemic authority of science, challenging its claims to objectivity and knowledge, was an act of emancipation from the strangling authority of Reason. I was never persuaded by this rhetoric. It conflated intellectual authority with authoritarianism and, at least to all of us who learned our basic philosophy and politics in the European south, intellectual authority (and objectivity and criticism and the search for truth) were the arch enemies of any kind of authoritarianism.

FG: *Indeed. Considering the paradigm of "charismatic" populist authoritarianism that has been steering politics in my own country in the last decades, I couldn't agree more. I'd like now to introduce readers not acquainted with them to discussions taking place in the analytic philosophy of science (since enthusiasts of the continental "realist turn" often tend to overlook the fact that a similar turn has occurred in the analytic tradition roughly between the 1960s and the 1970s, and has developed vigorously ever since) and, second, to expose you to some recent realist developments in continental philosophy. As for the first point, can you clarify how the "scientific" qualifier differentiates "scientific realism" from the more general "realism" part of philosophical vocabulary since medieval scholasticism? And can you offer a brief historical narrative guiding us from the realist turn which lifted the embargo on the reference to unobservable, theoretical entities—originating in the work of philosophers such as Wilfrid Sellars, J.C.C. Smart and Richard Boyd—to the present state of the scientific realism debate?*[5]

SP: Historically, realism has been taken to be a doctrine about the independent and distinct reality of universals (*qua* attributes or species). It was opposed to nominalism, viz., the view that only particulars exist. Nominalists argued that general terms and predicates are merely names for classifying particulars in terms of their similarities and differences. Realists—who, historically, came first—claimed that universals are real entities referred to by abstract terms, general names and predicates, and argued that they are necessary for knowledge and for grounding the similarities and differences among particulars. There have been transcendent realists (those who think that universals—*qua* Platonic forms—are apart from, and prior to, the particulars) and immanent realists (those, like Aristotle, who think that though a universal is the one over the many and "imperishable," it is not apart from the many).

It's an interesting question when and under what circumstances the term "realism" started to acquire philosophical currency. I have not looked into the matter with any seriousness. The term appears in Kant's first critique (quite late in the text) joined with the qualifiers "transcendental" and "empirical." Kant contrasts realism to idealism; in particular to his own transcendental idealism. Kant claims that transcendental realism takes the phenomena (outer appearances/objects of the senses) as real and as existing independently of us and our sensibility, thereby taking them as things-in-themselves. It is transcendental realism that he famously denies and to which he opposes his transcendental idealism, viz., the view

---

[5] "The Present State of the Scientific Realism Debate" is the title of the first chapter in Psillos' *Knowing the Structure of Nature*. Readers seeking a fully detailed account of this debate should turn to it or, for an even broader perspective, to Psillos' exhaustive historical survey of the entirety of twentieth-century philosophy of science in chapter fourteen of Dermot Moran, *The Routledge Companion to Twentieth Century Philosophy* (London and New York: Routledge, 2008).

that the objects of knowledge are not the things-in-themselves, but the phenomena as they are constituted by their epistemic conditions for their knowledge (the categories and the forms of pure intuition). But transcendental idealism, he insists, makes room for *empirical* realism, meaning that the objects of the senses are material things that are to be found in space, even though space (and time) are *a priori* forms of sensible intuition. The fact is that Kant's way to cure the "scandal of philosophy" (recall: "it must still remain a scandal to philosophy and to the general human reason to be obliged to assume, as an article of mere belief, the existence of things external to ourselves…and not to be able to oppose a satisfactory proof to anyone who may call it in question"[6]), created another scandal: the inherent unknowability of things as they are in themselves (by beings like us anyway, who are bounded by sensible intuition).

The Kantian dichotomy between the noumena and the phenomena (an epistemic dichotomy, to be sure) made any robust realist position having to face an uphill struggle: to save the independence of the world from the human mind while avoiding scepticism or agnosticism. Denying the very distinction between the noumena and the phenomena, the Hegelian idealist tradition compromised the independence of reality from thought, thereby securing its knowability. It's not clear to me there were any strong realist voices in the nineteenth century. Perhaps the strongest was Gottlob Frege's who took it that the truths of arithmetic are fully objective, mind-independent and about numbers *qua* abstract objects. Bertrand Russell, in the early twentieth century, developed what came to be known as (a version of) structural realism in an attempt to argue that, given various quite plausible causal assumptions, the structure of the things-in-themselves (that is of the world as-it-is-in-itself) is inferable from, and hence knowable on the basis of, the structure of the phenomena. Rudolf Carnap famously argued that the issue of the reality (and mind-independence) of the world is a pseudo problem,

---

[6] Kant, *Critique of Pure Reason*, B XXXIX.

but following Moritz Schlick he made room for empirical (as opposed to metaphysical) realism. The spectre of metaphysical realism, as Schlick put it, was the phantom of a world "somehow standing behind the empirical world, where the word 'behind' indicates that it cannot be known in the same sense as the empirical world, that it lies behind a boundary which separates the accessible from the inaccessible."[7] It was the specter of the Kantian noumena, perhaps under the illusion that there is a special non-empirical method of knowing them. Rejecting metaphysical realism, Schlick and co. were striving for a position which would leave metaphysics behind, without however abandoning the rich conception of the world, as this is described by the sciences—a world populated by atoms and fields and whatever else our best science tells there is. Science advances by revealing the constituents of things that we encounter in perception and the fact that these are (typically) invisible is no reason to suppose they are not real. Hence, Schlick and co. were aiming to articulate an empiricism-friendly philosophical stance towards science which is distinct from instrumentalism but not committed to a metaphysically-loaded sense of reality.

By the 1920s, the classical Newtonian conception of the world was giving way to a new theoretical framework dominated by Einstein's theories of Relativity and Quantum Mechanics. What is more, the atomic conception of matter was gaining wide acceptance—it had become the new paradigm. With it, this conception brought the issue of the ontic status of the various invisible entities posited by theories to explain the various observable phenomena. By the turn of the twentieth century, there was a rather heated debate concerning the status of explanatory hypotheses in science—those that posited the existence of unobservable entities. The resistance to explanation-by-postulation was motivated by philosophical arguments, mostly driven by what was taken to be commitment to empiricist theses. One line of resistance had to do

---

[7] Moritz Schlick, "Positivismus und Realismus," *Erkenntnis*, 3, 1-31, 1932. Translated as "Positivism and Realism" in *Logical Positivism*, Alfred J. Ayer, ed. (Glencoe, NY: Free Press, 1960).

with semantics: how can we render language to refer successfully to things that are not given in experience? Another line of resistance had to do with epistemology: how can we possibly come to know anything about the unobservable, if the basis of this knowledge is not rooted in experience? A third line had to do with metaphysics: what exactly is it to be committed to the reality of unobservable entities? Perhaps, a final line was methodological: in trying to understand science as a practice that involves theory and observation, do we need (and do we have) to read theories as if they aim to tell a true story about the unobservable world behind or beyond the phenomena? In practice, these four lines of resistance were mixed and conflated. But the fact is that very many eminent scientists who had philosophical motivation and acumen (from Ernst Mach, to Pierre Duhem, to Henri Poincaré, to Wilhelm Ostwald) took it that there is something deeply problematic with explanation-by-postulation and its promise to take our epistemic grasp beyond the limits of (immediate/sensory) experience. It turns out that the key to shifting scientific opinion in favour of the reality of atoms was Jean Perrin's theoretical and experimental work (roughly around 1910) on the causes of the Brownian motion, which drove home the message that explanatory hypotheses can be highly confirmed by empirical evidence (provided they acquire characteristics that make them definite and testable). It was in this period that the first versions of a major argument for scientific realism were drafted, by the likes of Poincaré, Duhem and Ludwig Boltzmann—viz., that the predictive success of scientific theories cannot be a feat of chance, but that it is best explained by (and hence gives us reason to accept) facts involving unobservable entities which, according to the theories, are causally responsible for the generation of the relevant empirical phenomena. It was also in this period, however, that an important argument against scientific realism started to take shape: the argument from theory-change in science. This is based on the historical fact that there are radical revisions in the scientific image of the world; that past theories were abandoned and replaced by substantially different ones. This fact caught the public eye in France, in the beginning of the twentieth century, under the rubric "the bankruptcy of science." If current theories will have the fate of the past ones (if they too become part of the future history of science books), what is the reason to take them seriously as revealing to us the way the world is? Faced with the problem of radical discontinuity in theory-change, Poincaré and Duhem argued that there is, nonetheless, some substantial continuity at the level of the mathematical equations that represent empirical as well as theoretical relations. From this, they concluded that these retained mathematical equations—together with the retained empirical content—fully capture the objective content of scientific theories. By and large, they thought, the theoretical content of scientific theories is structural: if successful, a theory represents correctly the structure of the world. It is noteworthy that at least in Poincaré's case, his structuralism had a Kantian origin. He took it that science could never offer knowledge of things as they were in themselves. But he did add to this that their relations could nonetheless be revealed by structurally-convergent scientific theories.

These two major arguments (one from the success of scientific theories and the other from the existence of revolutions in science) were destined to define most of the logical space within which the scientific realism debate would take place later on in the century. Neither of these arguments were at the forefront during the heyday of logical positivism. It was Herbert Feigl's liberating critique of the main tenets of logical positivism that set the agenda for the realist turn of the 1950s. He argued that the empiricist programme had been a hostage to verificationism for too long. Verificationism runs together two separate issues: the evidential basis for the truth of the assertion and the semantic relation of designation (i.e., reference). It thereby conflates the issue of what constitutes evidence for the truth of an assertion with the issue of what make this assertion true. If theoretical statements cannot be given truth-conditions in an ontology that dispenses with theoretical entities, then a full and just explication of scientific theories simply requires commitment to the irreducible reality of unobservable entities, no less than it requires commitment to observable entities.

Perhaps the first full-blown defence of scientific realism was Jack Smart's *Philosophy and Scientific Realism*—published in 1963, though his key papers on the reality of theoretical entities were published in the middle of 1950s. Smart rebutted various views that treated theoretical entities as fictions or phenomenal constructs or mere concepts. Smart put the defence of scientific realism in proper perspective by arguing that it rests on an abductive argument, *aka* inference to the best explanation. Smart argued against instrumentalists that they must believe in cosmic coincidence. Scientific realism, on the other hand, leaves no space for a cosmic-scale coincidence: it is because theories are true and because the unobservable entities they posit exist that the phenomena are, and are related to one another, the way they are. It is fair to say that the realist turn in the philosophy of science was greatly facilitated by Wilfrid Sellars's attack on the myth of the levels. This myth rested on the following image. There is the bottom level of observable entities. Then, there is the intermediate level of the observational framework, which consists of empirical generalisations about observable entities. And finally, there is yet another (higher) level: the theoretical framework of scientific theories, which posits unobservable entities and laws about them. It is part of this image that while the observational framework is explanatory of observable entities, the theoretical framework explains the inductively established generalisations of the observational framework. But then, Sellars says, the empiricist will rightly protest that the higher level is dispensable. For all the explanatory work vis-à-vis the bottom level is done by the observational framework and its inductive generalisations. Why then posit a higher level in the first place? Sellars's reply was that the unobservables posited by a theory explain directly why (the individual) observable entities behave the way they do and obey the empirical laws they do (to the extent that they do obey such laws). He, therefore, offered an indispensability argument for the existence of unobservable entities: they are indispensable elements of scientific explanation of singular observable phenomena.

In his brief review of Smart's book in 1964, Quine exclaimed: "With science dominating our lives and progressing ever faster on even more frontiers, it is strange that such a view [the realistic view of fundamental particles of physics] needs urging. Strange but true." But by then, the tide had started to move the scientific realists' way. Putnam expressed this by his famous slogan, which has become known as the "no miracles argument": "The positive argument for realism is that it is the only philosophy that does not make the success of science a miracle." In his widely circulated and discussed, but still unpublished, manuscript *Realism and Scientific Epistemology*, Richard Boyd tied the defence of scientific realism with the best explanation of the fact that scientific methodology has succeeded in producing predictively reliable theories. Boyd viewed scientific realism as an historical thesis about the "operation of scientific methodology and the relation between scientific theories and the world." As such, realism is not a thesis only about current science; it is also a thesis about the historical record of science: it claims that there has been convergence to a truer image of the world, even though past theories have been known to have been mistaken in some respects. This historical dimension is necessary if the truth (or partial truth, or significant truth) of scientific theories is to be admitted as the best explanation of the predictive reliability of methodology. For, as noted already, unless continuity-in-theory-change and convergence are established, past failures of scientific theories will act as defeaters of the view that current science is currently on the right track. If, however, realism aims to explain an historical truth—viz., that scientific theories have been remarkably successful in the prediction and control of natural phenomena—the defence of scientific realism can only be *a posteriori* and broadly empirical.

Couldn't scientific realism be lightweight? Would it not be enough for someone to accept the reality of unobservable entities without also rendering them mind-independent?

And wouldn't this move bring scientific realism in contact with empirical realism and in freedom from metaphysical realism and/or transcendental realism? Well, a lot depends on how exactly the claim of mind-independence should best be understood. I take it that the sense in which realists claim that the world is independent of theories, beliefs, warrants, epistemic practices, etc. is best captured by admitting the possibility of divergence between what there is in the world and what is issued as existing by an epistemically right theory, which is licensed by the (best or even ideal) evidence or other epistemic criteria. It is precisely for this reason that realists need to rely on a non-epistemic conception of truth (the most popular, and controversial, of which is that truth is correspondence with the facts), which does allow for the foregoing possibility. When truth is attributed to the theory, this is a substantive attribution which is meant to imply that the theory is made true by the world, which, in its turn, is taken to imply that it is logically possible that an accepted and well-confirmed theory might be false simply because the world might not conform to it. A realist non-epistemic conception of truth, and in particular the possibility of divergence, does justice to the hard-won fact of empirical success and convergence of scientific theories. Given that there is no guarantee that science converges to the truth, or that whatever scientists come to accept in the ideal limit of inquiry or under suitably ideal epistemic conditions will (have to) be true, the claim that science does get to the truth (based mostly on explanatory considerations of the sort we have already seen) is quite substantive and highly non-trivial. If, on the other hand, the possibility of divergence is denied, the explanation of the success of science becomes almost trivial: success is guaranteed by a suitably chosen epistemic notion of truth, since—ultimately—science will reach a point in which it will make no sense to even raise the question of whether there is possible gap between the way the world is described by scientific theories and the way the world is.

FG: *Thanks, that was an excellent survey indeed! Now, for the second point. To start with, as a philosopher of science with an analytic background what is your relationship, if any, to the continental tradition? You authored a* Philosophy of Science A-Z *text,[8] which includes entries on notable philosophers of science: the closest one of these gets to being considered "continental" is perhaps Pierre Duhem, hardly a central figure in the continental canon. I take your choices not as prejudiced or idiosyncratic, but dictated by the necessity of faithfully representing the discipline as it is practiced, with its themes and central figures. Are students trained in the analytic tradition of philosophy of science exposed to any non-analytic material?*

SP: A lot depends on how we should understand the so-called *continental* tradition. As you have seen from my previous answer, I have been influenced by many continental thinkers, though they are not in the canon of what is called *continental philosophy*. But what exactly is continental philosophy? Are we thinking in terms of the Franco-German tradition in contradistinction to the Anglo-American one? But let us not forget that analytic philosophy, let alone analytic philosophy of science, would be nowhere if it were not for certain strands within the Franco-German tradition: from Frege, to the neo-Kantians, to Wittgenstein, to the French conventionalists, to the Logical Positivists. When I try to picture the so-called continental tradition, I see some schools of philosophy, like phenomenology, existentialism, structuralism, hermeneutics and post-modernism. Is there anything that unifies them into a single tradition? Perhaps it is that they are subject-centered; perhaps it is that they are based on narratives rather than rigorous arguments and conceptual analysis; perhaps it is that they are anti-science (in the sense that they bracket—to say the least—the scientific image of the world and are indifferent to the possible relevance of scientific findings to

---

[8] Stathis Psillos, *Philosophy of Science A-Z* (Edinburgh: Edinburgh University Press, 2007).

philosophy and its methods); perhaps it is they take the key task of philosophy to be to unravel how the subject is related to the world of experience and what categories constitute this relation; perhaps it is the thought that there are no external (non-subjective, non-textual, non-what-have-you) standards of correctness of philosophical theory; perhaps it is all (or some) of the above in various blends. I do not think this kind of search (for the blueprint of *continental* philosophy) is either profitable or interesting. I prefer to look into individual thinkers and schools (with some order of preference—I would never bother much with Heidegger!), and to try to find out whether what they say, or argue for, can help us better to understand some philosophical problem. I am deeply impressed, for instance, by Hegel's critique of mechanism and I have argued that the key problem he raised, viz., that mechanisms are individuated functionally and hence that their boundaries and composition are relative to the function they are taken to perform, is significant for the current debate about mechanisms in the philosophy of science. Or take Husserl's *The Crisis of the European Sciences and Transcendental Phenomenology*. This is a really significant piece. Husserl was very critical of the "bottomless theorising" that characterised the exact sciences. His criticism of the modern (post-Galilean) science and of the mathematisation of nature on which it was basing its search for objectivity is that in this process, science lost contact with the world of subjective experience. He took as the task of his own philosophy to rehabilitate subjectivity. He then urged that scientific objectivism be bracketed and that philosophy (that is, his own phenomenology) focuses on the life-world; the "actually intuited, actually experienced and experienceable world."[9] I happen to disagree with the way Husserl prioritises the life-world. But the problem he raises—the relation between the world as it is described by science and the world as we experience it—is profound and you can find variations of it both Carnap's *The Logical Structure*

---

[9] Edmund Husserl, *The Crisis of European Sciences and Transcendental Phenomenology* (Evanston, IL: Northwestern University Press, 1970), 50.

of the World and in Sellars's famous discussion of the relation between the scientific image and the manifest image—where the category of "person" is ineliminable. Here we are talking about three different perspectives on the same philosophical issue and the classification of these perspectives in the categories "continental" and "analytic" would simply distort their significance. Or take Althusserian Marxism and its insistence on the structure over the subject as well as the need for science to break free from ideology (though, as Althusser himself admitted, his early distinction was too theoretical). This is not the place to go into details, but my view is that modern structuralist tendencies in the philosophy of science have a lot to learn from the French structuralist tradition (especially when it comes to the social world and the social sciences).

It is true, however, that there is little communication between analytic philosophers and continental philosophers and that this is partly due to the fact that philosophical training has been identified with the immersion within a tradition and its own ways to raise and to articulate philosophical problems and to determine what counts as the right approach or answer to them. I would not surprise anyone if I said that I simply cannot get a grip on what some "continental" philosophers say, though I can more easily associate with them when what they argue is translated (perhaps by someone conversant in both traditions) into the language of the philosophical conceptual framework I relate with.

In recent years, there have been systematic attempts by various "analytic" philosophers to immerse themselves into the views of the continental thinkers—and this is quite heartening, if only because, if you think of it, the split between the so-called analytic and the so-called continental philosophy is a historical event that took place *within* a single philosophical framework. It is related (to some extent at least) to the split of Kantianism into two neo-Kantian schools who disagreed as to how best they were supposed to develop the key Kantian points after the collapse of the neat way in which Kant's described how knowledge is possible. Those in Marburg took mathematics and the natural sciences as the models of objectivity and knowledge and aimed to remove all intuition from knowledge, while those in Baden focused on values and their role in knowledge, turning their attention to history and the human sciences and aiming to unveil their peculiarities vis-à-vis the natural sciences. Whichever way to look at it, both the analytic and the continental traditions are heirs to the network of problems, concepts, methods and theories that constitute the lore of philosophy from Plato to old Kant.

When it comes to philosophy of science in particular, it is significant that analytic philosophers of science have started to take notice of the tradition of historical epistemology—what is simply called "epistemology" in many continental countries—which is a genuinely historical and contextual approach to conceptual and philosophical problems in the sciences. This encounter should ideally lead to a new synthesis between historical approaches to science and philosophy of science.

FG: *Right, let's pursue this further. I feel that it's still reasonable to say that this "neat" disciplinary division in the philosophy of science can perhaps be traced along two lines. First, as you just mentioned, the importance (or lack thereof) attributed to historical concerns. This might be a sweeping statement if we consider the analytic tradition as a whole, but it seems to be fair if we consider the philosophy of science (moreover, I think that there is some truth in the claim that historical interests in analytic philosophy, while not absent, tend to be located on the meta-philosophical level rather than organic parts of the construction of an argument). This is arguably a consequence of the logical empiricist collapsing of the traditional disciplinary distinction between* Naturwissenschaften *and* Geisteswissenschaften *(essentially in favour of the former), one which took shape in the Carnapian "unity of science" program and which strictly confined "cultural objects" outside of the mandate of science. Little more than a decade later Edmund Husserl laments precisely this positivistic reduction of philosophy (and science itself, both somewhat subsumed in the German term* Wissenschaft*) to a narrow concern with a factual objectivity ex-*

punged of the concern for "human questions" and, in a memorable line, claims that "Positivism, in a manner of speaking, decapitates philosophy."[10] He goes on to denounce the "naïvete through which objectivist science takes what it calls the objective world for the universe of all that is, without noticing that no objective science can do justice to the [very] subjectivity which accomplishes science."[11] Scientific objectivity, an ethical imperative to be reached for the Husserl of the Crisis, is ultimately grounded in a lifeworld (Lebenswelt) of intersubjectively, historically constituted cultural formations. Even outside the Husserlian phenomenological legacy, continental philosophy of science, in particular the French epistemological tradition running (roughly) from Emile Meyerson to Michel Foucault through Leon Brunscvicg, Gaston Bachelard and Georges Canguilhem, was composed by thinkers with a scientific background who put a premium on a philosophico-historical analysis that would emphasize the discontinuities of science. These would be often caused by those psychological, (inter-)subjective preconceptions ("epistemological obstacles" as Bachelard named them) which are to be accounted for if we are to offer an account of science as actually practiced by human subjects. A far cry from Carnap's antipsychologism guiding, in the Aufbau, his "rational reconstruction [rationale Nachkonstruktion] of the concepts of all fields of knowledge on the basis of concepts that refer to the immediately given."[12] Canguilhem well synthesizes the spirit of French épistémologie in one paragraph:

> The history of sciences is not the progress of sciences in reverse, i.e. the putting into perspective of outmoded stages whose truth is today on the point of disappearing. It is an effort to enquire into and give an understanding of the extent to which outmoded notions or attitudes or methods were, in their time, successful; and consequently of the respect in which the outmoded past remains the past of an activity for which it is necessary to retain the term

---

[10] Edmund Husserl, *The Crisis of European Sciences and Transcendental Phenomenology* (Evanston, IL: Northwestern University Press, 1970), 9.

[11] Ibid., 294-295.

[12] Rudolf Carnap, *The Logical Structure of the World and Pseudoproblems in Philosophy* (Chicago and La Salle, IL: Open Court, 2003), v.

"scientific." To understand what gave instruction in its time is as important as exposing the reasons for its destruction by what followed.[13]

Of course, Thomas Kuhn acknowledged Meyerson among his key influences, but the Kuhn-inspired historical turn seems to have de-legitimized itself (in the eyes of most philosophers of science) with what were perceived as post-Kuhnian relativist excesses (from Paul Feyerabend's methodological anarchism to David Bloor and Barry Barnes' "strong programme" in the sociology of scientific knowledge) with the result that today mainstream philosophy of science remains well insulated from those projects of "science studies" that aim at placing science in its historical (but also gendered and social) context. I personally think this is for the worse, and I see much value in the recent, more regulated, return to a merging of history and philosophy of science (HPS) in the so called "Integrated HPS" (or &HPS) projects,[14] (in which I think you are personally involved, being among the organizers of the 4th international Integrated HPS Conference, which was held in Athens last March). HPS can help re-conceptualize episodes and concepts from the history of science from being the province of antiquarian interest to the living field of original philosophical work. As Hasok Chang recently put it "history-writing can be a very effective method of philosophical discovery."[15] What is your position regarding this split along historicist lines? Does the HPS trend hold the promise to effectively integrate analytic philosophy of science with historical research, and could this be an occasion for rapprochement between the two traditions?

SP: It's obvious from what I said above that we agree on quite a bit. But I disagree with Husserl's judgement on Positivism.

---

[13] Georges Canguilhem in Gary Gutting, *Continental Philosophy of Science* (Oxford: Blackwell, 2005), 201.

[14] For an overview of this project, see Seymour Mauskopf and Tad Schmaltz, *Integrating History and Philosophy of Science. Problems and Prospects* (Dordrecht, Heidelberg, London, New York: Springer, 2011) and the issue of *Isis* (199:1, 2008) with a focus on "Changing Directions in History and Philosophy of Science."

[15] Hasok Chang in *Integrating History and Philosophy of Science*, 111.

Recall that his claim was against positivism as the dominant *ideology* for doing science: science is only concerned with experience and with getting the facts right. I am not sure any serious philosopher (not even Comte himself) held this view. Clearly this was *not* the view of the Logical Positivists and Husserl was aware of this. So if we take the "in a manner of speaking" seriously in his dictum, he might well be making a good point! But he too felt that the Logical Positivists' approach was a weapon against irrationalism. Their criticism of traditional speculative metaphysics was meant to reshape philosophy in such a way that it is brought (again) in contact with science and rigorous conceptual tools and methods (broadly borrowed from logic and mathematics). So I'd say that positivism, in a manner of speaking, liberated philosophy. It's true though that the Logical Positivists had had little time for history (though not for subjectivity and its place in the theory of knowledge). This is somewhat ironic since, at least until they were forced, by the rise of the Nazi's in power, to leave the Continent (Schlick, as is well known, was assassinated in the staircase of the University of Vienna), they were the true heirs of the philosophies of science of Poincaré, Duhem and Mach; philosophies of science which were deeply immersed in history. But the insensitivity to history was, in a sense, necessary for what the logical positivists took as their immediate task, which is this: how to reconcile the emerging new scientific image of the world with the collapse of the Kantian theory of knowledge, without at the same time jettisoning the Kantian idea of the spontaneity of understanding. Fulfilling this task requires an orchestrated philosophical act, one key element of which is clarifying the conceptual foundations of the new scientific theories (so that what they say of the world—their factual content—becomes as clear as possible), the other key element being the need to reformulate and reshape the standard philosophical categories by means of which the analysis and criticism of knowledge is effected. In this process, the very idea of intuition and of synthetic *a priori* knowledge of the world had to go; better: synthetic *a priori* principles were reconceived as analytic and yet revisable framework-dependent principles. It was in this context that Schlick attacked Husserl's *Wesenschau* (intuition of essences). He thought that empiricism could accommodate subjectivity without having recourse to sense-intuition or to substantive synthetic *a priori* principles. No special intuition of essences was necessary for knowing the structure of experience. The so-called "phenomenological propositions," far from being part of the structure of the life-world, were analytic principles having to do with the structure of language. However, the very idea that the remnant of the Kantian spontaneity of understanding was to be found in framework-dependent and hence revisable general principles had a deep (if implicit) historical motivation, viz. the presence of revolutions in science. The synchronic logical analysis of the language and concepts of science that the positivists pursued was predicated on the thought that the form of the scientific method (*aka* inductive logic) is diachronic (and hence, essentially historically invariant), while its content is historically variable.

Philosophy abhors vacuum, so the historical method that Duhem and Poincaré (as well as Mach) had followed in their philosophies of science was picked up by the French epistemologists of the school of Gaston Bachelard. But I take it that there was a lot of uncertainty as to how exactly history should be an integral part to philosophy of science. Back in 1906, Duhem was quite clear about the importance of the historical method:

> The legitimate, sure, and fruitful method of preparing a student to receive a physical hypothesis is the historical method. To retrace the transformations through which the empirical matter accrued while the theoretical form was first sketched; to describe the long collaboration by means of which common sense and deductive logic analysed this matter and modelled that form until one was exactly adapted to the other; that is the best way, surely even the only way, to give to those studying physics a correct and clear view of the very complex and living organization of this science.[16]

---

[16] Duhem, Pierre, *The aim and structure of physical theory*, trans. P. Wiener

The historical method—the historical investigation of the conceptual processes that led to an adaptation between matter (empirical laws) and form (mathematics)—was taken to be an essential way to do philosophy of science. This is because the historical point-of-view unravels the constitutive interplay between empirical-factual investigations and mathematical-formal frameworks in the development of scientific theories. Admittedly, Duhem tied his historical turn to a certain historiography of science, viz. one that stressed the elements of continuity and rejected the view of theory-change as the way Athena emerging fully armed from Zeus's head. Hence, he was using history as a guide to the *future*: as a way to show how there can be revolutions without incommensurability; how the physics of each epoch "is nourished" by past physics and "is pregnant with the physics of the future."

The view of the role of history shaped by the French epistemologists seems to me to be far more radical than Duhem's. I think its forebear is Emile Boutroux, who argued for the presence of "genuine irreducible contingency" in the world and took it that according to this doctrine "it is erroneous and chimerical to attempt to reduce history to a simple deduction." Furthermore, he argued that "it is not...the nature of things that should be the final object of our scientific investigations, it is their history,"[17] which, incidentally, he took it to be the locus of objectivity. The French epistemologists extended these ideas to the very nature of science, arguing that science is essentially historical (no core themes, methods, etc.), the object of science (and concomitantly) the object of philosophy of science being *historically variable*. This way to view science leads to particularism, and particularism (when fully developed) is self-defeating. Unless all these activities that are classified under science have some general and shareable characteristics, it is hard to see what makes them science; what unites them under a common rubric?

(Princeton: Princeton University Press, 1906), 268-269. It is clear from the context that Duhem meant it as a general method for the study of science.

[17] Emile Boutroux, *The Contingency of the Laws of Nature*. (Chicago and London: Open Court, 1920), 166,167.

Stathis Psillos – *Of Realist Turns*

When Thomas Kuhn pleaded for "a role of history" in the introductory chapter of *The Structure of Scientific Revolutions*, he was fully aware that history did already have a role—especially among the French *epistemologists*. So, his plea was for a *new* role for history, and in particular one that was based on the rejection of the cumulative-developmental model of science. There is, certainly, a way in which history was assigned a *new* role within general philosophy of science and this was related to the structure and the testing of the macro-models of scientific growth that became popular in the 1960s and 1970s. Models of scientific growth, such as Kuhn's and Lakatos's, presented the unit of scientific appraisal (the scientific paradigm, the scientific research programme) as an evolving dynamic structure that follows a rather tight historical pattern. Kuhn emphasised both the element of historical tradition that characterises normal science (seen primarily as a rule-governed—or exemplar governed—activity) as well as the element of change that characterises revolutionary episodes (seen primarily as an abrupt change not-fully-accounted-for in terms of reason and evidence). Lakatos stressed the element of continuity and looked for clear-cut criteria of progressiveness in the transition from one research programme to another, which could underpin a notion of developmental rationality of science. But both took issue with a conception of science in general which had taken it to be subject to rules by means of which theories are appraised (e.g., a formal system of inductive logic and degrees of confirmation). And both took it that their macro-models of science reflected—and hence were licensed by—the actual *historical* development and succession of scientific theories.

The genie of history was out of the bottle but I feel there still a lot of uncertainty—among philosophers of science—as to what wishes to make. If we were to think of the matter a bit abstractly, we could distinguish the following ways in which history of science and philosophy of science can be related. (1) Philosophy of science is an essentially ahistorical discipline dealing with the logical analysis of the structure and concepts of science. If there is any role for history of science, it is merely its role as the *past of science*: it is either a narrative as to how concepts evolve or a source of examples. (2) Philosophy of science is the theory of historically individuated macro-models of theory development. History of science is then conceived of as the domain of application (and testing) of these models. (3) Philosophy of science involves a historical dimension in searching (in an *a posteriori* fashion) for the forms and justification of general rules and methods of science—what came to be known as methodological naturalism. (4) Philosophy of science is the rational reconstruction of the history of science and as such it relies on the history of science for warranted descriptions of how past scientists have actually practised science. I am not claiming that this list is exhaustive. Nor it is the case that these four points of view are totally independent from each other (especially the approaches 2 to 4). But what they all have in common is that they promote a kind of philosophy-infested history of science; that is, a reading of the history of science in which that criteria of relevance are fixed by philosophical considerations.

It's time for a renegotiation and re-appraisal of the relations between the history of science and the philosophy of science. It's not the case that there should be just one correct way in which history of science should be related to philosophy of science and a lot of insight will be gained by exploring the various ways in which philosophy of science and history of science could interact. I have tried to clear some of the ground for a renegotiation of the relation between philosophy of science and history of science in a very recent piece of mine called "What is General Philosophy of Science?," which appeared in a special issue of the *Journal for General Philosophy of Science*. I would recommend a New Deal. The model I would promote is based, roughly, on the dipole idealisation/de-idealisation. Much of philosophy of science involves idealisations—what Alexander Koyré aptly called "structural schemata." This is inevitable if a general view about science, its structure, methods and concepts is to be had. It is inevitable if we move beyond particularism and have a view of *science-in-general*. This is the proper subject matter of philosophy of science. But this drive towards idealization and abstraction, towards an idealized view of science, is essentially incomplete; it leaves out of the picture a lot of the fine structure of science. An important way to reveal this fine structure, I think, is to use history of science as a de-idealiser, thereby getting a more accurate representation of the cluster of activities (and the various determinants) that constitute science. To put it bluntly, idealized (philosophical) models explain but do not represent; while de-idealised (historical) models represent but do not explain. Ideally, we need a new balanced relation. When you do philosophy of science, it is inevitable that the reading of history will be based, ultimately, on philosophical criteria of relevance. But this does not entail that a proper understanding of the history of science—one licensed by historical methods—will leave our philosophical conception of science intact. Integrated HPS is certainly on the right track. I feel, however, that it has not yet managed to mobilise historians of science to the extent that it is necessary for a partnership of equals to get off the ground.

FG: *I guess that from a more properly philosophical standpoint the question is: to what extent, if at all, does historical awareness in philosophy of science undermine our faith in the correctness of our theories, the reliability of our methods or even in our theories' ability to refer to an external, theory-independent world? Does such an historical reconstruction inevitably lead into a Laudan-like pessimistic meta-induction and ultimately to some form of anti-realism?*

SP: This is a good guess! Note, though, that things were not like that in the beginning of the twentieth century, when what should be properly called *historical philosophy of science* was formed. I have spoken already about the "bankruptcy of science" debate and how Poincaré and Duhem were trying to restore some warranted belief in scientific rationality and progress. The point is that the study of the history of science does not necessarily undermine the philosophical view that as science advances there is convergence to a stable network of principles and theories about the deep structure of the world; to truer theories, as I would put it. In fact, a proper appreciation of the history of science delivers a mixed message: there is change and continuity; rupture and stability. This is no news, of course. Already in 1900, Boltzmann addressed the "historical principle" employed by the phenomenologists, viz., that hypotheses are essentially insecure because they tend to be abandoned and replaced by other, "totally different" ones. Against this "historical principle," he argued that despite the presence of "revolutions" in science, there is enough continuity in theory change to warrant the claim that some "achievements may possibly remain the possession of science for all time."[18] To be sure, we realists need to do a bit more work here. Two moves are really important. The first is to make the claim of convergence plausible, viz., to show that there is continuity in theory-change and that this is not merely empirical continuity; substantive theoretical claims that featured in past theories and played a key role in their successes (especially novel predictions) have been incorporated in subsequent theories and continue to play an important role in making them empirically successful. But making this first move does not establish that the convergence is to the truth. For this claim to be made plausible a second move is needed, viz., that the emergence of this stable network of theoretical assertions is best explained by the assumption that it is, by and large, approximately true. This is, roughly put, the role of the no-miracles argument. In doing all this, current theories constitute the vantage point from which we examine old ones—could there be any other vantage point? Yet, the identification of the sources of success of past theories need not be performed from this vantage point.

Note that those who think that the history of science will necessarily lead to a pessimistic conclusion, viz., that current theories too are likely to be false and abandoned, rely on various illicit philosophical assumptions that can be unearthed

---

[18] Ludwig Boltzmann "The Recent Development of Method in Theoretical Physics," *The Monist* 11 (1900): 253.

and challenged. One of them is an uncompromising holism regarding the confirmation of theories; another is a theory of meaning and reference that leaves no room for semantic bridges between distinct theories. The point that I am trying to make is that in this debate there is no neutral use of the history of science—the history of science does not speak with the voice of an angel. I take seriously Canguilhem's dictum that "Without epistemology, it would thus be impossible to distinguish two kinds of history of science, that of superseded knowledge and that of sanctioned, that is, still actual because acting, knowledge."

FG: *Back to the division between the two traditions. I think that a second split line can be traced back to the notorious Carnap-Heidegger controversy about the role that modern logic should play in the development of future philosophy, about the legitimate employment of language (and arguably, about the political nature of the social reform that both perceived as necessary) but mostly about what the overcoming/abandonment of metaphysics really should amount to.[19] Even after the abandonment of the logical empiricist program, and the consequent rehabilitation of a range of metaphysical concerns, analytic philosophy still presents an hostility (or indifference) to that tradition of fundamental ontology, that kind of Aristotelian "first philosophy" concerned with being qua being, that came back to the fore in the wake of Heidegger's project of answering "the question of the meaning of Being." Today's analytic metaphysics is organized around the problems of modality, of defining space and time, of causation, personal identity and free will, and hardly address the issue of "Being" (indeed, I think that a rough but efficient rule of thumb to distinguish a piece of analytic philosophy from a continental one is to count the occurrences of*

---

[19] The classic reference for this debate remains Michael Friedman, *A Parting of Ways: Carnap, Cassirer and Heidegger* (Chicago and La Salle, IL: Open Court, 1990), but Abraham Stone recently proposed a slightly different take on the disagreement between the two philosophers, downplaying their disagreement over issues of logical consistency and emphasizing those regarding the allowed uses of language in his "Heidegger and Carnap on the Overcoming of Metaphysics" in *Martin Heidegger*, ed. Stephen Mulhall (Aldershot: Ashgate, 2006).

"Being" as a noun). In Heidegger's eyes, what contemporary philosophy of science refers to as "metaphysical commitments" would amount to a mere ontic project of identifying existent entities, rather than a properly ontological inquiry of Being itself. On the other hand, post-Heideggerian continental philosophy has kept referring to "Being" in its ontological (but post-metaphysical) projects, especially in the work of "realist" thinkers such as Gilles Deleuze and Alain Badiou, the former reactivating a tradition of "univocity of Being" which runs back to Duns Scotus, the latter reformulating the question of being in mathematical terms. This disagreement regarding the possibility of ontology can be seen as rooted in a different relationship with the natural sciences. From your standpoint, does it make any sense, today, to pursue the question of what "Being" is or means over and above what current best science tells us about the fundamental constituents of the universe, or is such a question a vestigial problem, a relic of medieval scholasticism or a "Heideggerian hangover?"[20]

SP: I would not trust Heidegger too much! And I doubt he should be given too much credit anyway. If one were to answer the question "what is metaphysics?" by trying to read Heidegger's homonymous lecture, one would get a very distorted and perplexing idea of what it is all about. I'd say: if you want to do metaphysics (and to see metaphysics at its best) start straight from its source: Aristotle. The question of being is central to his *Metaphysics*. But more importantly, Aristotle suggests that there are two questions to be asked. One is what kinds of things there are (what kinds of being are), while the other is what it is for something to be: what is being. It might well turn out that these two questions are interconnected. But their conceptual separation makes metaphysics possible as a distinct and distinctive enterprise. For the second question can be asked only *within* metaphysics; it arises from a genuine metaphysical *aporia*. It transcends the

---

[20] I borrow this expression from Adrian Johnston, "Hume's Revenge: À Diex Meillassoux?" in *The Speculative Turn: Continental Materialism and Realism* edited by Levi Bryant, Nick Srnicek and Graham Harman (Melbourne: Re.Press, 2010), 110.

bounds of the individual sciences, since the latter investigate the being-under-a-description, and hence some part of it, say the physical or the biological world (1003a22-26). Metaphysics is the science of essence; of being *qua* being. But Aristotle wanted to put metaphysics in the service of science—what he called *episteme*. The fundamental structure of reality (ultimately comprising primary substances, essences (or essential properties *qua* universals) and accidental properties (*symvevikota*) grounded the possibility of episteme and made episteme a distinctive kind of knowing (*qua* general, explanatory and necessary). His account of scientific knowledge (in *Posterior Analytics*) goes hand in hand with his account of the fundamental structure or being (in *Metaphysics*). If we take Aristotle seriously, adding the adjective "analytic" to metaphysics is a pleonasm.

I take it that the immediate rival to "analytic" metaphysicians (would it not be better to be called "metaphysicists?") is the metaphysics-free tradition within analytic philosophy that was associated with Humean empiricism and later on with logical positivism. Could it then be that the addition of "analytic" is meant to make (pre-Kantian) metaphysics more palatable? Metaphysics is inevitable—the only question is: how much of it is necessary? Now, one may ask: necessary for what? To put it poetically, metaphysics fills the cracks of the scientific image of the world (in its totality and interconnectedness). To put it more theoretically, metaphysics secures the coherence of the scientific image of the world. I very much doubt that it makes sense to do metaphysics in complete isolation from what science tells us about the world, but I also think that science does *not* dictate a unique conception of the metaphysical structure of the world; of the kinds of beings there are; of the kinds of connections there are among them; of the basic characteristics that they have to have in order for the world to have unity and coherence. Science goes a long way, but not all the way (ultimately, it cannot settle the question of being *qua* being). Think of the question of what, and how many distinct, categories of being need to be presupposed by a coherent conception of reality—this is the problem of nominalism versus realism about universals. Or think of the question of whether there is *sui generis* power in the world which grounds and explains the regularity there is in it, or whether it is regularities all the way down, as I am fond of saying—this is the problem of the nature of causation. Or think of the question of whether some kinds of properties are constitutive of the kind of being something that there *is* or whether all properties are on a par—this is the question of essentialism. These are typically metaphysical questions whose answer should certainly be constrained by what we know of the world via science; but they are clearly underdetermined by what science tells us about the world.

If you think of it, this situation is not terribly odd or unfamiliar. Scientific theories themselves are underdetermined by the empirical evidence and yet there are plausible criteria to break ties of empirical equivalence: empirical equivalence does not entail epistemic equivalence. The situation is essentially the same with metaphysics: the name of the game is "inference to the best explanation." Metaphysical hypotheses about the structure of the world might not explain in precisely the same way in which scientific hypotheses about unobservables explain, but they do play an important explanatory role by enhancing the unity and coherence of the scientific image of the world. When the logical positivists attacked metaphysics, they were not in the business of taking explanatory criteria as decisive. A.J. Ayer famously took it that what's wrong with metaphysics is that it promises knowledge of reality which transcended the world of experience. He was right that there is no special non-empirical method of acquiring knowledge of the world. But he was wrong to restrict the empirical methods of science to those allowed by verificationism. Be that as it may, verificationism was a natural (if exaggerated) reaction to the speculative metaphysics of German idealism and its successors. Heidegger, for instance, thought that the inquiry about what he called THE nothing (the non-being) is a central preoccupation of metaphysics, which sets it apart from science (of which Heidegger said that it "wishes to know nothing about the nothing"). Carnap was fully justified to take on *this* conception of metaphysics and to argue that it fails to express genuine propositions. Here again, Carnap was taking metaphysics to be an endeavor to "discover and formulate a kind of knowledge which is not accessible to empirical science," perhaps by means of *special inferences* that may begin from experience but transcending experience. This is something that Heidegger and co. may well have been fond of. But explanatory methods (which are legitimately employed in science) might well take us beyond experience without transcending it (at least in the technical philosophical sense of "transcendence"). In 1957, when Carnap added some remarks to the English translation of "The Elimination of Metaphysics through the Logical Analysis of Language" he noted that his early reactions to metaphysics did not apply to attempts "towards a synthesis and generalization of the results of the various sciences." When philosophers like Quine (and Sellars) made room for explanation, metaphysics (properly understood as not relying on *sui generis* methods and inferences) started to become legitimate again. Quine was sharply critical of Carnap's point that ontological questions could be asked in two distinct ways: as external questions and as internal ones. Carnap, famously, excluded *external theoretical questions*: questions about the reality of a general *type* (or category) of entity which are supposed to be settled by looking for (empirical) evidence for the reality of this type or by insight into the metaphysical structure of the world. Questions concerning the reality of a type of entity, Carnap argued, are legitimate and have content, but only if they are taken to be *either* external *practical* questions concerning the benefits of adopting a certain framework which includes this type of entity in its basis ontic inventory *or* as *internal* theoretical questions concerning the evidence there is for (or other reasons for accepting the reality of) certain tokens of this type, but only after a framework has been adopted. Despite his trenchant criticism of Carnap's dichotomy, Quine did agree with Carnap on a fundamental point, viz., that there is no theory-free standpoint from which what there is can be viewed. But he took this denial of a theory-free vantage point to imply that there is no sharp line between theoretical issues (or questions) and practical ones. Ontological questions (questions about what there is) are theoretical questions *as well as* practical ones: they are answered by our best theory and there is no extra-theoretical court of appeal. Already in *Two Dogmas of Empiricism*, Quine had argued for the "blurring of the supposed boundary between speculative metaphysics and natural science."

If explanation-based metaphysics is allowed, where does one stop? Should, for example, a scientific realist adopt neo-Aristotelianism simply on the basis that it is the best explanation of, say, the neo-Humean account of the world? My own view on this matter comes to this. We should certainly take IBE seriously, but it can be contested that neo-Aristotelianism does indeed meet the best explanation test. One particularly acute problem is that all the denizens of the neo-Aristotelian world (powers, metaphysical necessities, dispositional essences and the like) are themselves unexplained explainers. Though everyone should accept *some* unexplained explainers, in this particular case, they are more poorly understood than the Humean facts that they are supposed to explain. Another problem, noted above, is that it is not clear at all how all these heavy metaphysical commitments are related to current scientific theories. The fact is that this kind of neo-Aristotelianism—and its commitment to heavy-duty metaphysics—has become a major force in current analytic metaphysics. And it also true that it is being developed (to a large extent at least) in close connection with science. Unfortunately, not all current analytic metaphysics is in contact with current science. This raises a serious issue: what are the criteria of success in metaphysical theorising? It cannot be merely internal consistency; the metaphysical theory must also be plausible. Since there is no *a priori* insight into plausibility, I think the plausibility ranking must be based on the ordinary defeasible criteria that are used in science to rank and evaluate competing theories. If all this sounds too shaky a ground for metaphysics, so be it!

FG: *I largely agree with you here, even though I think that some forms of rationalism or a priori forms of reasoning can be salvaged if articulated within a Darwinian framework, defending a kind of naturalized rationalism which in my opinion is the most interesting path of inquiry taken by up by some "continental naturalizers." However, going back to your indictment of neo-Aristotelian metaphysical options like powers or dispositional essences (and in general your scepticism towards any sort of "crowded" metaphysics) I would like to probe your opinions a little deeper with a "limit case." How do you react to the recent renaissance of panpsychism (seen both as an approach to the "hard problem" of consciousness[21] but also as a respectable general metaphysical option[22] for a description of reality as a whole)? On the one hand, what I find interesting is that it seems to be an option which cuts transversally across the "two traditions" drawing in metaphysicians of both purely analytic breed and those inspired by German idealism or phenomenology. On the other, it seems to me to be a hopelessly wrongheaded stance, one that fails your test of plausibility as being the best explanation, and that makes a rather odd use of otherwise correct anti-anthropocentric guidelines—it's alleged to be a sign of human-centered narcissism to assume that humans are the only entities in the universe endowed with "mind" or some form of intentionality. The most famous argument here is the Galen Strawson thesis that "real physicalism" (as opposed to a reductionist, dogmatically scientistic "physicSalism") actually implies panpsychism.[23] Your "scientific realism with a Humean face" is open-minded enough to not be a dogmatically, "old-fashioned" physicalist one (or indeed invested in any other strong metaphysical commitment) because it is defensible independently from naturalism, but isn't panpsychism a prime example of*

---

[21] See Michael Blamauer, *The Mental as Fundamental: New Perspectives on Panpsychism* (Heusenstamm: Ontos Verlag, 2011) and David Chalmers, *The Conscious Mind: In Search of a Fundamental Theory* (Oxford: Oxford University Press, 1996), 297-299.

[22] See *Mind that Abides: Panpsychism in the New Millennium* edited by David Skrbina (Amsterdam and Philadelphia: John Benjamins Publishing Company, 2009).

[23] See Galen Strawson "Realistic Monism: why Physicalism entails Panpsychism," in *Mind that Abides: Panpsychism in the New Millennium*.

an explanans *which is far less clear than the* explanandum? *Is this not a clear case where "empirical equivalence does not entail epistemic equivalence?" Personally, I am particularly interested in the metaphysical clashes behind the science vs. religion debates, and to take as an example another path-breaking panpsychism-friendly philosopher—Thomas Nagel—I think a clear point can be made regarding all this. The* argumentum ad ignorantiam *that proceeds from our sketchy understanding of consciousness to the plausibility of some form of conscious activity in non-human entities, essentially defended in his 1979 essay,*[24] *seems to me to lead directly to the theses he puts forward in a later essay called "Secular Philosophy and the Religious Temperament." Here, he seeks a "secular alternative" to reductive naturalism and identifies it in a kind of natural teleological process wherein "each of us…is a part of the lengthy process of the universe gradually waking up"*[25] *How far does your Humean/empiricist outlook allow you to go in the refutation of a thesis like this, which seems to fly in the face of some central, historically hard-won, steps towards the goal of a full(er) scientific knowledge of nature (here, the rejection of Aristotelian teleology and the physics it produced)?*

SP: There are endless possibilities in philosophy, given time and world enough. I have not followed the literature on panpsychism (at least the recent one, since a form of it is supposed to be present in Spinoza), but I feel there are two readings of it, one weaker (and relatively plausible) and another stronger (and I think implausible). The weaker reading, I take it, is an attempt to dethrone the human mind from the centre of the universe, opposing the Protagorean idea that the human being is the measure of everything. In this sense, panpsychism would say that the mind and the mental life is not the prerogative of the human animals. But note well: this conception does not entail a special view about the soul

---

[24] Thomas Nagel, *Mortal Questions* (Cambridge: Cambridge University Press, 1979), Chapter 13.

[25] Thomas Nagel, *Secular Philosophy and the Religious Temperament* (Oxford: Oxford University Press, 2010), 16,17.

or the mind, or the spirit. In the history of philosophy, these have been the various candidates (typically, but not invariably, taken to be the same "thing") for the uniqueness of the humans among the "created" beings. This individuating factor has been taken to be imperishable, in constant motion, the locus of thought and mental activity, the subject of salvation and others. Weak panpsychism need not be committed to all this and is consistent with the scientific image of the world (if we take it to imply that the mental life is not uniquely human). The stronger version of panpsychism, in my view, would be committed to the implausible hypostatisation of the soul, albeit extending it to other animals (or even to non-animals). Why is this view implausible? Precisely because it does not sit well with what we know about the mind and its functions. It feels good to believe that there is an immortal soul; that the mind is a substance; that there is a set of non-natural properties that constitute the mental economy. It gives reassurance. But does it do good? I see no intellectual benefit in accepting this view. I still endorse non-reductive physicalism (though it is not entailed by scientific realism) which is essentially the same as naturalism. Sober—that is non-eliminative—naturalism puts a pressure on everything that is (supposed to be) non-natural to show that it has what it takes to be included in the natural world. So, all *prima facie sui generis* entities (or states, or attitudes) that are needed to explain Moorean facts (which include facts about colours and epistemic norms and evaluative attitudes and beliefs and pains) need to *earn their right* to be included in the natural world. They don't earn this right automatically (by featuring, say, in potential explanations—cf. animistic or vitalistic explanations). Nor do they enter the natural world autonomously. And to earn this right is, a naturalist would say, to be suitably dependent on the natural. There are notorious problems with this notion of dependence. But the central characterisation, I think, should be in terms of physical constitution. Naturalism need not be imperialistic, but is has to be *elitist*. Even so, it's *not* arrogant elitism that characterises it. Anything that is *prima facie sui generis* can earn the right for inclusion in the elite club, but they have to do some work to achieve that. It is a contingent fact about the world that all spatio-temporal entities are physically constituted. This does not, on its own, exclude the possibility of a property-dualism (or, better, property-pluralism.) But perhaps all that is needed to be added is that given the physical constitution of all spatio-temporal objects, whatever properties they have—and whatever causal powers they endow these objects with—are controlled from *within* "and are not imposed upon then from without" (cf. Dewey, Hook & Nagel 1945, 109).[26]

Naturalism excludes supernaturalism. Perhaps, Dewey, Hook and Nagel (1945, 116) can help here too. The *horror supernaturae* is indeed the horror of naturalists. But this horror is the expression of a methodological policy: it is the firm refusal to accept that for which there is no evidence (or, in some cases, that for which there is overwhelming evidence against). In a certain sense, the naturalists' *horror supernaturae* is the outcome of the following principle: if something is not acceptable, then it should be avoided, which is the contrapositive of the sound principle: What cannot be avoided, is to be accepted.

There is an issue I want to touch upon and this is the role of *a priori* within naturalism. Philosophical tradition has wavered between two conceptions of the *a priori*: the absolute conception and the absolute rejection. The absolute conception is exemplified in Kant. According to the Kantian conception, the possibility of human knowledge requires placing *a priori* restrictions on the admissible models of the experienced world—only those models are admissible that conform to a set of synthetic *a priori* principles. This captures a sense of *constitutive a priori*: some principles are necessary presuppositions for knowledge (and for doing science)—necessary in the sense of being *sine qua non* for understanding the world. Since those principles that are necessary for experi-

---

[26] John Dewey, Sidney Hook & Ernst Nagel "Are Naturalists Materialists?," *Journal of Philosophy*, 42 (1945), 515-30, reprinted in *American Philosophical Naturalism in the Twentieth Century*, edited by J. Ryder (New York: Prometheus Books, 1994).

ence precede experience, they cannot be defeated by it; they are permanent and *unrevisable*; they are *necessarily true*. Kant thought that these two senses of being necessary—necessary presuppositions for doing science and necessary as permanent and unrevisable—ought to *coincide* if some principles properly were taken to be independent of experience. This coincidence is the kernel of the absolute conception. According to the Millian-Quinean absolute rejection of the *a priori*, there cannot be any justification independently of experience. Mill's chief point was that *all* justification, even justification of the laws of arithmetic, is inductive. Quine's chief point was that *everything* can be revised or abandoned in light of experience. Since, according to the absolute conception, statements that are supposed to be *a priori* are unrevisable, Quine drew the conclusion that there are simply no *a priori* principles. The logical empiricists (capitalizing on an empiricist tradition that arguably goes back to Locke and Hume) thought that there is a middle way: some truths (notably the truths of logic and maths) were meaning-constitutive analytic truths; hence they tried to secure the *a priori* by tying it to analyticity (and to necessity, by implication, since all and only analytic truths were supposed to be necessary). Quine's arguments against analyticity have conclusively shown that there is no non-circular way to characterise analyticity. This, of course, does not show that there are no analytic truths—but it does question that we have a coherent idea of what we attribute to them when we call them analytic.

There is another way to defend a middle position between the absolute conception and the absolute rejection, without being committed to analyticity. This is to drive a wedge between the elements of *a priori* knowledge: constitutivity and necessity. The *locus classicus* of driving this wedge is found in Hans Reichenbach's *The Theory of Relativity and A Priori Knowledge* (1921). He drew a distinction between two elements in the Kantian conception: *a priori* principles are meant to be necessarily true; and they are meant to be constitutive of the object of knowledge. Reichenbach accepted the second dimension but denied that *a priori* principles were necessarily true and unrevisable—rather, being framework-dependent, they are abandoned when the framework they are constitutive of is abandoned. I have tried to develop this middle ground in joint work with my ex-student and current colleague Demtera Christopoulou.[27] The point I want to make now is that this relativised conception of the *a priori* seems compatible with a broader naturalistic perspective in the sense that naturalism does not obliterate the spontaneity of the understanding; nor is it committed to the rejection of the view that some principles are constitutive of the object of knowledge. In a rather marvelous passage, Poincaré drew a fine distinction between contradiction and condemnation. He was quite firm in that no experiments can ever contradict a constitutive principle (what he called "conventions"). For no experiment can conclusively *refute* such a principle. Yet, experiments can *condemn* a constitutive principle, or even a whole framework, in that persistent failure to account for new facts renders a particular principle or a whole framework no longer convenient. What a *realist* naturalist should retain at all costs is obviously the possibility of friction between our conceptual schemes and the world, which friction (making itself present in persistent and recurring anomalies) is (to a large extent) responsible for the replacement of conceptual frameworks by others.

FG: *The analytic/continental divide is active on several dimensions: professional, stylistic, methodological and thematic. I take the first to have little of philosophical merit, boiling down to a matter of safeguarding one's own academic turf. Are the other dimensions crystallized enough to impede hopes of reconciliation, and is reconciliation a desirable outcome to start with? I think there can be three possible approaches: 1) bridging the gap, possibly through an interpretative work aimed at demonstrating how behind different methods and styles there can be identified*

---

[27] Stathis Psillos and Demetra Christopoulou "The A Priori: Between conventions and implicit definitions." In N. Kompa, C. Nimtz, and C. Suhm (eds.), *The a priori and Its Role in Philosophy* (Paderborn: Mentis Verlag, 2009).

common concerns;[28] 2) preserving the gap, in the name of either the preservation of "essential traits" (analytic virtues of problem-solving and clarity vs. continental "breadth of vision" and "existential relevance") whose disappearance is deemed dangerous[29] or in view of an inherent value of a fragmentation of viewpoints and approaches, or 3) ignoring it. What would this latter option amount to? I take it to be a real possibility that the divide will gradually vanish with generational change: as the "old guard" dies out, a new generation of philosophers will achieve intellectual maturity having ignored institutional divisions and having simply read–and thought through–the work of philosophers from both camps. Here I agree with part of Richard Rorty's diagnosis, identifying the institutional origin of the split at the "graduate student level." Rorty argued that

> graduate students trying to shape themselves into plausible job candidates for teaching positions in philosophy only have time to read so much. They can please only so many potential employers....No matter how much intellectual curiosity a student has...there just is not enough time. So if she develops am-

---

[28] One can think of the work of Christopher Norris and (more recently) of Samuel Wheeler to present Derridean deconstruction (and, in Norris' case, Alain Badiou's philosophy) in terms understandable to analytic philosophers, or of Lee Braver's and Jeff Malpas's comparison of the work of Davidson with Heidegger's and Gadamer's (see Christopher Norris, *Language, Logic and Epistemology: A Modal-Realist Approach* [Basingstoke: Palgrave, 2004]; Christopher Norris, "Tractatus Mathematicus-Politicus: on Alain Badiou's *Being and Event*" in *Speculations* II (2011), 7-48; Samuel Wheeler, *Deconstruction as Analytic Philosophy* [Stanford: Stanford University Press, 2000]; Braver, *A Thing of This World*, and *Dialogues with Davidson: Acting, Interpreting, Understanding*, edited by Jeff Malpas [Cambdidge, MA and London: MIT Press, 2011]. Also several chapters of *A House Divided: Comparing Analytic and Continental Philosophy* edited by G.C. Prado, (Amherst, NY, Humanity Books, 2003) seem to adopt this "contrast and compare" strategy over selected philosophical themes.

[29] An example from the analytic camp is Timothy Williamson, who in the appendix of his *The Philosophy of Philosophy* (Oxford: Blackwell, 2007), 289, recommended that contemporary analytic philosophy as a whole should "do better," guilty, in his eyes, of forsaking its mandate of argumentative clarity, rigor and precision and indulging in "ugly, convoluted, ramshackle definitions of concepts and theses."

> bidexterity [Rorty's term for proficiency in both traditions], it will usually be in later life—usually after she gets tenure. Then she can afford to start following her nose rather than pleasing interviewers or senior colleagues.[30]

However, I think that we are witnessing today the emergence of a significant minority of graduate students reckless enough to take the risk and attempt to develop "ambidexterity." Do you see some form of reconciliation as necessary, and would you encourage students to ignore traditional boundaries? And would you say that a realist *philosophy of science can be at the forefront of such reconciliation, the two traditions having, so to speak, to be judged equally by the standards of an external reality independent of the philosophical style one uses to examine it?*

SP: Hume used to say that philosophy arises out of intellectual curiosity and that the philosophical problems will keep cropping up and boggle the investigative mind even if we try to lay them to rest by an appeal to common sense. There are different ways to address the very same philosophical problems; there are different prioritizations of their urgency; and, ultimately, there are different problems for which philosophers are curious about. This, schematically put, explains the dichotomy between the two traditions, but also highlights that they are traditions within *the very same intellectual enterprise.* As I noted in my reply to an earlier question, what we call "the two traditions" have emerged from the very same womb and they share a common ancestry. In practice, things are more complicated of course, and no-one should be oblivious to this. There is a certain philosophical ideology associated with each tradition and until fairly recently there have been important linguistic, stylistic and methodological hurdles that had to be jumped if one were to immerse oneself in both traditions. Even nowadays, it's hard to understand a thinker from the "opposite tradition" unless you read stuff that ex-

---

[30] Rorty in Prado *A House Divided: Comparing Analytic and Continental Philosophy*, 18.

plains what they were supposed to be doing in the language of the tradition you are duly immersed. Immersion is part of the philosophical training and it depends, at least partly, on contingent factors. Given this, I doubt that the matter has to do with an "old guard" and its resistance to rapprochement. In the European continent, where the "continental tradition" was dominant for decades, there is a younger and very dynamic generation of philosophers which conscientiously inscribe themselves within the analytic tradition and pursue analytic themes vigorously and with flair. There are vibrant societies for analytic philosophy and plenty of congresses and workshops. This might be ironic since it happens in an age in which the original divide tends to fade away in the Anglo-american philosophical community. This might well have to do with the fact that the history of philosophy has become a hot topic in the analytic tradition in the English-speaking world. But on the European continent, analytic philosophy still plays the role of an identity-maker among young academic philosophers. To promote analytic philosophy is to make a statement about what philosophy is; what philosophical problems are important; what methods pertain to philosophy; how philosophy is connected with science, etc. I am part of this tradition in my own country, even though I understand its limitations. Reconciliation will take time. Developing a *rapport* is much more manageable and welcome. The form that this will take is hard to tell. I would encourage philosophy students to engage with the writings of the major thinkers of the twentieth century and to try to identify the problems they were grappling with and how these problems re-appear and are re-shaped in the work of various past and present philosophers of various schools and traditions.

Can realism facilitate this rapport? The very issue of realism and its rivals is constitutive of philosophy and present in both traditions, perhaps in different forms. In this sense, it could provide a platform for thinking that philosophy is ultimately one and its fundamental problems the same for all. I was very glad to see (in the material you sent me and in the claims made in your questions) that there is a "realist turn" happening presently in the continental tradition. It was even more heartening to learn that this turn is a self-conscious attempt to reclaim the realist ground and to recoil from the dominant neo-idealist and anti-realist tendencies within this tradition. I feel that what you call "correlationism" (the view that the only thing that can be accessed is the relation between thought and being and not the relata in isolation of this relation) has had a strong grip on the tradition that obscured the fact that a) the relata can be posited (and get their identity) independently of their relation; and b) if the (cognitive) access to reality were independent of thought, language, concepts, etc. we would not *need* thought, language, concepts, etc. to access reality. It is precisely because the cognitive access to the *independent* reality is mediated by epistemic categories, that the very question of the conditions and credentials of this access becomes philosophically exciting and pressing. If there is a problem that "correlationism" points to, (the problem of how thought is related to reality), it is *not* solved by collapsing the two relata to one. It cannot be solved by making thought spinning in the void. There are various issues that can provide a fertile ground for the growth of the discussion between the various realist tendencies in both traditions; to name but a few: the relation between realism and materialism, the issue of reductionism, the role and function of mathematics and the question of truth.

FG: *Let us pursue the theme of the continental "realist turn" then. As I've tried to sketch in the opening remarks, a common trait of these new continental approaches to realism is the insistence on considering reality in-itself as not reducible to our cognitive capacities and to our metaphysical categories. Their return to realism associates a rejection of Kantian dichotomies between the humanly knowable and the unknowable (or even of the postmodern, relativist, or linguistic denial of any noumenal reality) with informed allegiance to contemporary science. These philosophers are especially interested in the counter-intuitiveness and irreducible character of the reality presented to us in the Sellarsian "scientific image." Consequently, metaphysics is not seen as limited* to Strawsonian "descriptive" tasks but allowed to be thoroughly "speculative," i.e. legitimately operating on a purely philosophical ground to offer an account of those consequences and presuppositions which science cannot account for intrascientifically. Adrian Johnston (a critic of some "speculative realist" positions, but part of the broader resurgence of continental realism nonetheless) summarizes this spirit when he argues, referring back to Hegel, that "the sciences produce out of themselves, on their own grounds, an internal delimitation of their explanatory jurisdictions"[31] while a physicist like Gabriel Catren proposes a "speculative physics" aimed at deducing the rational necessity of scientific theories.[32] As I noted above, an economical way to say this is that these kinds of "speculative" realisms offer only a conditional submission to naturalism: the natural sciences are the most reliable epistemic enterprise which humans have managed to come up with, but there are real features of the world which a method regulated by strict empiricist scruples cannot fully account for. Herein lies the subtle but crucial divergence between the continental and the analytic realist stance. You are strongly against what you call "principled epistemic divisions" between what can be known and what cannot, and indeed claim that it is possible to know the structure of nature (that is what current best science offers us), but in your Humean-flavoured realism you have a naturalist skepticism of those inflationary neo-Aristotelian metaphysics which postulate natural kinds, powers, metaphysically necessary laws and so on, since they rely too much on a priori postulation of what the world must be like. How do you feel about attempts to reintroduce some forms of rational speculation in the context of our scientific worldview, a philosophy that, starting from the natural sciences, attempts to employ their results as speculative opportunities for a reconceptualization of our metaphysical categories, included those which were employed by science in the first place? To focus this further, you wrote that "only science can tell us what the world

---

[31] Adrian Johnston, "Materialism, Subjectivity and the Outcome of French Philosophy," interview by Michael Burns and Brian Smith in *Cosmos and History*, 7:1 (2011), 177.

[32] Gabriel Catren "A Throw of the Quantum Dice Will Never Abolish the Copernican Revolution," *Collapse V* (2009), 459.

is like. Philosophy can only raise some principled challenges to the ability of science to tell us what the world is like."[33] *How far, in your view, can these challenges go? Are there reasons to place some boundaries on the epistemic audacity of science, and its ability to answer, without philosophical aid, meta-scientific questions about science's own foundational assumptions or are these questions to be considered (in positivist fashion) meaningless?*

SP: Science is far from sacrosanct! But it is also by far the best way we humans have invented to know the world. This does not mean that philosophy is the handmaiden of science; nor does it imply that the scientific image of the world is free from deep and controversial philosophical assumptions. In my most recent book, *Knowing the Structure of Nature*, I indeed argued against the view that there is a principled epistemic division between what can be known of nature and what cannot; hence that there is a principled limit to the scientific knowledge of the world. This limit is different in the assorted positions that I argued against, but it is supposed always to be *principled, definite* and drawn by philosophical reflection and argument. I am not claiming that science will discover everything there is to know. Science might, in the end, not reveal us what the world is like. It might be able to disclose only part of the structure and furniture of the world. But this is as it should be. It would be a totally different matter if there were good reasons—mostly drawn by philosophical reflection on science, its methods and its limits—to believe that we *qua* cognitive beings, or science *qua* an epistemic enterprise, are cognitively closed to some aspects of the unobservable world. What I do claim is that though there might be parts of nature that science might never be able to map out, these do not fall nicely within a conceptual category which captures one side of a sharp epistemic dichotomy (the unknown x: the things in themselves; the unobservable; the non-structure; the intrinsic properties, or what have you).

---

[33] Psillos in *The Continuum Companion to the Philosophy of Science*, edited by Steven French and Juha Saatsi, (London and New York: Continuum, 2011), 88.

Naturally, there are significant philosophical motivations for raising these epistemic barriers that science is supposed to be unable to cross. It might be ironic but one important recent motivation is that (a form of) realism is best defended if it lowers its epistemic optimism. Hence, there are weaker versions of realism on the market such as structural realism or semirealism. The challenges to realism come from various sources, but perhaps the most significant (as we have already seen) comes from the history of science, and has the form of the pessimistic induction. Another challenge (with some empiricist credentials) comes from the claim that the explanation by reference to unobservable entities and mechanisms (what I call explanation-by-postulation) leads to inflationary metaphysics. There is a sense in which this is obviously true: realism takes science to proceed by positing further entities that are meant to *explain* the life-world and its (typically non-strict) laws. But in another sense, the inflation is metaphysically harmless. For, if you think of it, science proceeds by positing micro-constituents of macro-objects, whose main difference from them is that they are, typically, unobservable. That a putative entity is unobservable is, if anything, a relational property of this entity and has to do with the presence of observers with certain sensory modalities (of the kind we have) and not others. No interesting metaphysical conclusions follow from this fact; nor any seriously controversial ontological inflation.

As I have noted already above, the attempt to marry realism with a neo-Aristotelian conception of the metaphysical structure of the world is a different matter. There I side with neo-Humeanism, which I take to involve the following three negative theses:

A There are no necessary connections between distinct existences (No necessity enforcers).
B There are no universals as distinct from classes of resembling particulars (No resemblance enforcers).
C There are no powers as distinct from their manifestations (No regularity enforcers).

It might be thought that neo-Humeanism is anti-metaphysics altogether, but this is wrong. As I said already, metaphysics—that is, a view about the deep structure of reality and its fundamental constituents—is not optional. The only serious issue, I believe, is how *deeply* this view should be digging; how rich the conception of the fundamental structure of reality ought to be. Neo-Humeanism promotes a rather thin—or sparse—view of the fundamental structure of reality, according to which there are irreducible regularities in nature (regularities all the way down, so to speak) which involve patterns of dependence among members of natural classes (natural properties) and which underpin the causal and generally modal relations there are between them. But buying into the idea that the world is characterised by regular patterns of co-existence and succession of property-instances is metaphysics enough!

Does science need the help of philosophy? Clearly yes! There are certain issues that can be raised only within a proper philosophical perspective on science. These include the status of first principles in science; the relation of science to reality; the epistemic credentials of scientific theories; the fabric of the deep structure of the world as it is described by science; and the very possibility of a unified (but not necessarily reductive) account of it. Actually, these are issues that cannot be successfully dealt with at the level of individual sciences. We have to look at *science as such*. The individual sciences, as well as their philosophies, lack the conceptual resources and the power of abstraction that are required for a more global perspective on reality—for seeing the whole picture. They are limited by the fact that they focus on aspects or layers of reality. Putting together the scientific image of the world, looking at the various interconnections among the "partial" images generated by the individual sciences, and clearing up tensions and conflicts is precisely the kind of job that philosophy of science is meant to do. To put it in Sellarsian terms, philosophy of science offers the space in which the various images of the world provided by the individual sciences are fused together into a stereoscopic view of reality.

FG: *A similar question but put in terms of truth rather than ontology. A stance defended by some recent figures of continental realist philosophy, inspired by the work of Alain Badiou, is that we need to reconceive the concept of truth as that which by definition breaks the boundaries of our current-best knowledge and that which introduces radical novelty in our worldview. A wedge must be firmly put between knowledge and truth, since the latter will have the power to completely rearrange the structure of the former. You think that a verification-transcendent conception of truth is a cardinal pillar of the realist position, and that true assertions have truth-makers which are independent of our current opinion (or lack thereof) about them and that we shouldn't be shackled by the epistemic criteria of warranted assertability or trapped in our linguistic horizon. Yet I suspect you would be cautious of claiming that new truths can be discovered through purely rational, logico-deductive means rather than by ampliative inference grounded on empirical observations. Do you consider it possible for our truth-tracking enterprises to go, to use Graham Priest's formula, "beyond the limits of thought,"[34] to those boundaries that cannot be crossed, and yet are crossed? And do you consider the total set of truth-makers in the universe (the known and the unknown existents) to be a closed totality that doesn"t allow for novelty? Or is this, once again, a meta-scientific question that the empirically-minded realist can refuse to answer?*

SP: As I noted above, I take a non-epistemic conception of truth to be an essential realist commitment because this is the best way to capture the standard realist assertion that the world is mind-independent. Traditionally, the opponents of realism (idealism and phenomenalism) expressed their antagonism to realism by claiming that there is only mental stuff in the world. So the realist declaration of independence might be seen as a commitment to the view that there is material stuff in the world and, in particular, that the entities posited by scientific theories are non-mental (material). I do not think this

---

[34] See Graham Priest, *Beyond the Limits of Thought* (Cambridge: Cambridge University Press, 1995).

is a useful way to think of the realism issue any more. There is an anti-realist tradition which argues for something more complicated and interesting. It centres on the conditions that must be in place for legitimate commitment to the existence of whatever entities are said to make up the world. According to this long anti-realist philosophical tradition, it makes no sense to be committed to the existence (or reality) of some entities unless this commitment is understood as implying (and being predicated on) the fulfilment of certain *epistemic/ conceptual* conditions, the most popular of which is Michael Dummett's warranted assertibility. Very much like realism, this tradition opposes idealism and phenomenalism. But it does render the world (or a set of entities) mind-dependent, albeit in a subtler sense: it forges a logical-conceptual link between what there is in the world and what is licensed as existing on the basis of the satisfaction of suitable epistemic conditions; hence, this kind of anti-realism renders what there is (whatever kind of stuff it may consist in) exhaustible by what can be known in principle (verified, warrantedly asserted and the like) to exist. Opposing this kind of mind-dependence, the realist claim of mind-independence should be understood as logical or conceptual independence: what the world is like does not logically or conceptually depend on the epistemic means and conceptualisations used to get to know it.

As I stressed above, this commits realism to the possibility of a *divergence* between what there is in the world and what is licensed as existing by a suitable set of conceptualisations and epistemic conditions. Modern anti-realism (let's call it verificationist anti-realism) precludes (*a priori*) this possibility of divergence by adopting an epistemic conception of truth. What, ultimately, is at stake in the scientific realism debate is a robust sense of objectivity, according to which the world as it is independently of our changing and evolving conceptualisations of it is the final arbiter of their correctness. Verificationist anti-realism cannot, however, dissociate objectivity completely from the obtaining of some or other (however idealised and inter-subjective) epistemic condition. The result is that the final arbiter of the correctness of our conceptualisations is not the world but the fact, if it is a fact, that some but not other conceptualisations satisfy certain epistemic conditions and therefore are licensed by them.

Some care is needed here, however. The claim that truth is evidence-transcendent is a claim about the nature of truth; a claim about what makes a truth true. It is not an epistemic claim about the knowledge of truth; it does not lead to scepticism (though it does leave its possibility open). Attaining truth very much depends on our truth-tracking methods and their reliability. These are ampliative and hence defeasible. Their success requires epistemic luck, but it is *not* due to luck; it requires (and gives us evidence for) a co-operative world.

I would certainly not contrast truth to knowledge. Truth is required for knowledge, but there may well be unknown truths. Whatever else it is, truth is something that has no expiry date. Unlike dairy products, truth cannot go off. If a belief is *true* now, it is true atemporally: it has been true in the past and will stay true in the future. In this sense, truth cannot be equated with acceptance or kindred epistemic notions. Nor can it be equated with what communities or individuals agree on, or with what the present evidence licences. If we made these equations, truth would not be a stable property of beliefs. It could come and go all too easily. Besides, if we made these equations, we would end up with a thoroughly relativised conception of truth. But relativism about truth, viz., the claim that truth ascriptions are always relative to a person or a community, is ugly and self-refuting, anyway. Even those who think that truth is, ultimately, an evaluative concept, have to think of the norms that govern its use as objective (or ideal). Similarly for knowledge. Knowledge is not something than can be lost in the sense that something can be *known* now but not known tomorrow. Sometimes we use the term "knowledge" colloquially, equating it with whatever we have evidence to accept or whatever we believe today. Then we say that our knowledge of the world has changed; or that what it was known in the past is considered false today. This is loose (and incorrect) talk. Once possessed, knowledge is not lost.

(Clearly, knowledge can be "lost" in the unproblematic sense that some kind of truth that was known in the past has not survived in what is known today.) So truth and knowledge are intimately connected. There is simply no guarantee that all truths are knowable; and in any case, realism allows for the *possibility* that there are unknowable truths. Suppose that, as a matter of fact, all truths are knowable and that there is a coincidence between whatever is licensed by an epistemically right theory of the world (that is, a theory that satisfies certain epistemic conditions) and what *really* exists in the world. This need not compromise the realist commitment to the mind-independence of the world. Nor, of course, does it commit realism to an epistemic account of truth. All the realist needs to claim is that there is a certain direction of fit or order of dependence. This can be made plain by being put in terms of a Socratic Euthyphro-type contrast. Suppose there is a coincidence between what there is in the world and what is licensed as existing by an epistemically right theory (that is, a theory that meets certain epistemic conditions). Is the world what it is because it is described as thus-and-so by an epistemically right theory *or* is a theory epistemically right because the world is the way it is? Scientific realists can and should go for the second disjunct, while verificationist anti-realism goes, ultimately, for the first.

I am not quite sure how to understand your request for novelty. The world is the totality of what there is; part of what there is is known and part of it is (and may remain) unknown. If the request for novelty were the request for a kind of openness, I would agree. The world is *transformed* by human action (for better or for worse) and not just by human action, so new things are brought into existence and other cease to exist. Truth-makers come and go. There has been a traditional worry about the independence of the world: how can it be interfered with (known, manipulated etc.) if it is independent of the subject? To this worry I juxtapose another one: what worth would the interference have if the world was not independent of us?

FG: *But can there be novelty independently from human interference? I suppose I'm asking if in your view it makes any sense to claim that there is some incompleteness at the ontological, mind-independent level. This is probably what you would call speculative metaphysics, but is there any necessary principle regulating the actual totality of all that is the case (the known and the unknown) to remain the same, or modally constraining the possible to a limited set of configurations? I am hinting here towards worldviews that admit (or require) some form of ontological contingency. You mentioned Émile Boutroux, who, in his* The Contingency of the Laws of Nature,[35] *defended the thesis that modern science, in its reliance on fixed laws of nature, offers only a partial understanding of the universe, that limited part where stability reigns, since the latter is really governed by a "principle of creation" and "permeated by contingency."[36] Similar arguments were offered by other philosophers and scientists after him, including at least C.S. Pierce, A.N. Whitehead, and J.A. Wheeler. These theses are often (certainly in Boutroux's case) motivated by theological/spiritualist leanings, and yet today it is not uncommon, in "continental" circles, to see "contingency" defended as a secular notion, indeed a radicalization of "Hume's problem" which rejects any metaphysical necessity, ontological unity and universal laws (but I suppose we could at least tangentially include someone like Nancy Cartwright's work in this trend).[37] Is this idea of contingency and ontological novelty something that, from your own Humean perspective, cannot be excluded or does it undermine the reliability of scientific knowledge in a way that forces us to discard it? To phrase it differently, how far is your Humean "regularities all the way down" from Bas Van Fraassen's claims that "[t]here are no necessary connections in nature, no laws of nature, no real natural bounds on possibility" and*

---

[35] Émile Boutroux, *The Contingency of the Laws of Nature* (Chicago and London: Open Court, 1920)

[36] Ibid., 160.

[37] See Nancy Cartwright, *How the Laws of Physics Lie* (Oxford: Clarendon Press, 1983) and Nancy Cartwright, *The Dappled World* (Cambridge: Cambridge University Press, 1999).

that "[r]eally, nothing is necessary, and everything is possible"?[38]
Can one be a realist rejecting any *natural necessity?*

SP: I agree that contingency should be defended as a secular notion and part of the reason for my adherence to it is that I believe there is no external (super-natural) law-maker and law-giver. But this does not mean there are no laws! I defend the view that laws are a species of regularity and I deny the claim that there are regularity-enforcers of a distinct metaphysical kind. I have commented on this issue in a previous answer, so what I want to add here is that denying the existence of enforcers (metaphysical entailment; universals; powers) does not imply that anything goes! It does not imply that there are no non-trivial actual relations between the regularities there are in the world; that there are no actual objective relations of similarity and difference in the objects in the world. Denying the existence of enforcers implies that these relations are not metaphysically necessary; they do not have a grounding in metaphyisically distinct layers of facts. Those philosophers who think that laws are contingent necessitating relations among universals (David Armstrong, Michael Tooley and Fred Dretske) are right in claiming contingency, but I think we do not have a clue as to what exactly this necessitating relation is; hence it is an extra burden in our attempt to understand the presence of regularity in nature. But the price of metaphysical necessity is even heavier, especially if it's taken together with the currently very popular dispositional essentialism (and power realism). On this view, it is not clear any more whether there are laws! They are either summaries of the potencies of related powers or nothing at all. Worst, there can be all the power in the world and nothing happening in it. I have recently tried to do some work on the notion of pattern, in order to explain the presence of regularity and to differentiate laws from accidentally true generalisations.

---

[38] Bas Van Fraassen in Jan Hilgevoord, *Physics and Our View of the World* (Cambridge: Cambridge University Press, 1994), 124.

My views have not matured yet (I must say it is really hard to do any serious philosophical thinking under the present situation in Greece). But in broad outline the idea is that a pattern is a repeatable and recurring network of differences and similarities among entities and that those regularities are laws that are characterised by the unity of a (natural) pattern. Patterns seem to have the following advantages: a) they can be characterised in terms of their naturalness; b) they may occur within other patterns; hence they may form networks and c) there need not be a pattern-enforcer (of distinct metaphysical type). I do hope that when this work matures it will show how there are non-trivial actual relations between the regularities there are in the world and hence that the contingency of the laws of nature is far from being a threat to the objectivity of scientific knowledge. This commitment to necessity in nature is, to paraphrase Elizabeth Anscombe, the dogmatic slumbers of the day.

FG: *Whatever the details and the arguments employed to defend one's position, what is at stake in being a realist? Both positivists and postmodernists coated their (differently motivated) rejection of realism with ethical concerns. As we've seen, Bas Van Fraassen—arguably the most prominent critic of scientific realism today—still argues along these lines when he claims that metaphysical realists are deluding themselves, guided by a naïve metaphysical reassurance given by "deep" explanations going beyond the phenomenal surface, and presents his own "empirical stance" as the only intellectually responsible, truly "disenchanted" one to assume.[39] On the other hand, a number of philosophers have defended realism precisely against the moral dangers of a reduction of reality to opinion (be it individual or collective, be it about scientific entities or political events)—Richard Boyd, for example was equally engaged in the defence of both scientific and moral realism, while Christopher Norris has attacked the postmodern suspension of belief in reality in the wake of very real events like the first Gulf War. Today, think-*

---

[39] See Ibid., and Bas Van Fraassen, *The Empirical Stance* (New Haven and London: Yale University Press, 2002).

ers within the continental tradition are mobilizing continental sources (from Hegel to Lacan, from Deleuze to Derrida) to build more or less direct bridges between a renewed materialism and leftist emancipatory politics (Slavoj Žižek probably being the most prominent figure). Are there ethico-political grounds on which you embrace and defend your realist stance?

SP: This takes us back to the first question. Of course there are ethico-political grounds for realism (at least the kind of realism I want to defend). To be a realist, in my book, is to occupy a certain standpoint according to which there are objective criteria of rightness and wrongness and external facts-of-matter as to what is right to believe and what not. This, to be sure, is an external constraint on our belief systems and in very many typical cases, we might not be able to say or warrantedly assert that we know these external facts-of-the-matter or the grounds of objectivity in judgement. This predicament—the human predicament—does not invalidate the role (sometimes, the regulative role) of this standpoint. The realist standpoint and its commitment to objectivity need not (and should not) be confused with a claim that there is a royal road to truth and that some already possess it. Well, science is the best road we have invented so far and we should be quite confident that it tends to lead to truths (though not to the whole truth and nothing but the truth)! But even there, truth emerges from theoretical pluralism, failed theories and defeasible methods. In my mind, the realist standpoint makes possible the battle against relativism. Relativism should not be confused with pluralism and open-mindedness. It is as ugly as its opposite: authoritarianism. It's hard to see how relativism can be avoided without having external standards of objectivity and rightness. It's even harder to think how one can oppose oppression and war and injustice without taking an anti-relativist stance. I cannot go into this now, but a robust realist stance in ethics and society (one that takes it that an underlying social reality grounds social appearances and that ethical conduct has an objective—though not necessarily abstract and ideal—ground) can help human emancipation.

The realist standpoint need not be associated with the impossible view from nowhere. Representation is always perspectival, but the represented is not. In fact, it can emerge as the invariant element in various representations. Nor should we confuse the lack of certainty in knowledge with the lack of objectivity of our knowledge of the world. Objectivity without certainty is possible!

FG: *That's a slogan to keep in mind! So, to conclude, I would like to ask you about the repercussions on academia of the current economic situation in Greece. Are you encountering problems when it comes to funding for students or for the organization of academic events? Is the country losing a generation of scholars, emigrating elsewhere in the hope of finding more promising prospects for an employment? Have you or your colleagues considered moving abroad after the radical cuts to the salary of academic staff?*

SP: Greece is in a terrible mess currently and will be like this for quite a while. The causes of the crisis is a matter of dispute (there is, broadly, a right-wing and a left-wing account of them), but the working people of Greece—who have heavily suffered from the unprecedented wave of austerity—are not among the causes. We are living through the dismantling of welfare state in Greece—a state that was built slowly but steadily (and not without deep structural problems and deficiencies) after the collapse of the military junta in 1974 and especially in the early 1980s. Deep and persistent recession; rising unemployment (dangerously high among the youth); more than 30% reduction of the annual income of civil servants and most other employees (including the University teachers); slashing of all pensions and benefits; high prices and mounting inflation; one capital tax piling upon another; disappearance of state investments; slashing of the budgets of hospitals, schools, universities, the police... This is Greece nowadays. And on top of it, there is a growing recognition of the obvious: that the recipe prescribed by the IMF (taken from its outdated rulebook) for getting Greece back on track was simply disastrous; a non-starter. After two years of ruthless policies that were supposed to take Greece out of the zone of bankruptcy (predicated on the thought that the welfare state is too costly to maintain and that an internal devaluation of "human capital" would make Greece competitive), Greece is still on the brink of default—things have gone worse; almost out of control. But the fiscal deficit (and the crazy policy of diminishing it whilst economy is in massive contraction) is the tip of the iceberg; the social deficit that the relentless austerity has created is far more serious and dangerous. There is an increasing number of dispossessed and disaffected especially in the big cities; there are families with no parent in employment; there is a rise in crime and violence; even in the number of suicides. Poverty and desolation are visible in the streets and the neighbourhoods of Athens. A whole generation will be lost. There is a democratic deficit too, which puts the role of the democratic institutions at stake; but this is a different (and ugly) story.

And as if all this was not enough, the previous government decided to reform the universities, passing a bill which will render them less democratic and more authoritarian institutions. The new ideology of "excellence" is implemented from above and in an environment in which austerity and cutbacks have almost brought the universities to their knees. Disintegrating infrastructure is left to its own devices. Research funds have become scarce. Research grants that have been awarded after a national competition (one of them to my group; the only one in philosophy, I must say) have been frozen and are drowning in a wave of delays and redtape. More than 800 junior members of staff that have been elected in university positions were on the waiting list to be officially appointed; 300 of them were appointed recently after an almost three-year wait, but the prospects for the remaining 500 are not good. An increasing number of students have to look for some kind of part-time job to support themselves. The really sad thing is that the Greek universities are on the brink of stagnation—Greece's intellectual capital will be wasted. It's not uncommon that academics or PhDs look for employment abroad; the prospects of intellectual flourishing in Greece are dim.

My colleagues and I took pride in that, in precisely this atmosphere, we successfully organized in October 2011 in Athens the third conference of the European Philosophy of Science Association. It was an act of intellectual defiance and we were deeply moved by the determination of philosophers of science to come to Athens for the conference, despite the fact that a strike of the air-traffic controllers hit Greece on the first day of the conference. My feeling—call me a pessimist—is that Greece won't make it in the end; really dark days lie ahead of us. The Greek academics (and philosophers in particular) who have contributed to the advancement and the rising international standing of the Greek universities have an intellectual obligation to resist all this; to make values prominent and to show that human beings and their prosperity are above profits.

FG: *Thanks a lot for your time, I believe that we covered quite a lot of material and readers of the journal will surely enjoy our conversation. As a parting gift, could you just whet our appetite with a quick description of the book you are working on at the moment? I believe you are preparing something on empiricism, trying to rediscover a certain line of realism-friendly thinkers from within the Logical Positivist movement—is that correct?*

SP: Yes, I want to reclaim a tradition within empiricism which took it that the critique of metaphysics should leave intact the world as this is described by science; a world populated by atoms, and fields and DNA molecules, but also by natural kinds and social classes. If time and energy permit, I want to write a book about the history of the philosophy of science in the twentieth century focusing on the transition from views that allowed a priori principles to play a role in the constitution of the object of scientific knowledge to more naturalistic views.

Levi Bryant, *The Democracy of Objects*
Ann Arbor, Open Humanities Press, 2011
314 pages

In Defense of Unfashionable Causes

Daniel Sacilotto

University of California, Los Angeles

T*HE DEMOCRACY OF OBJECTS* IS LEVI Bryant's first full-blown monograph since enlisting in the ranks of the recent philosophical movement known as Object Oriented Philosophy (OOP). It offers an outline of what is a broadly novel metaphysical system which, following the work of Graham Harman, describes a reality composed of objects all throughout, and nothing besides. Seeking to displace the primacy of the relation between the human and the world, OOP follows the basic intuitions of Quentin Meillassoux's work in proposing an alternative to idealist and correlationist philosophies, in the arduous process of stepping out of the post-Kantian shadow of critique, wherein Continental theory and thought is said to have circularly roamed, imprisoned, for the past few centuries.[1] However, unlike some of its fellow Continental realists, OOP's approach for overcoming the putative force of the "circle of correlation" is to adopt a deflationary strategy, in which the question about how humans access the world is construed as being just one more relation

---

[1] Quentin Meillassoux, *After Finitude*, trans. Ray Brassier (London: Continuum, 2006).

between objects in a metaphysical account. In that regard OOP is not entirely new, in that it remains continuous with the trivialization of epistemology sought by many Continental thinkers during the 20th Century, promoting rather the restitution of the primacy of ontological questioning, i.e. the kind of radicalization of the critique of metaphysics of which Heidegger, Deleuze, and more recently Badiou, are perhaps the tradition's most emblematic figures. However, rather than exacerbating the epistemological question of access to the point where strict epistemology becomes displaced in favor of an examination of its linguistic, historical, or socio-cultural conditions, OOP proposes to dislodge philosophy from its human cohort altogether, the better to rehabilitate an exploration of "the great outdoors" philosophy had sown shut in favor of critique, making the world relative to our own faculties in some form or other.

In what follows, I concentrate on evaluating Bryant's proposal for a new metaphysics from two perspectives. First, I present and evaluate Bryant's case for the *methodological* primacy of ontology over epistemology, which is chiefly indebted to the work of Roy Bhaskar, and which is the focus of the first chapter of the book. In doing so I seek to isolate the core motivations for the prospect of a metaphysics of objects that is supposed to be propadeutic to any kind of epistemological enquiry. In that regard, it is important to notice that however "exhausted" the problematic of access is taken to be for OOP, this shouldn't dissuade us from questioning whether the displacement of epistemology is in fact tenable, and whether such exhaustion has in fact taken place. For even if critical philosophy succeeded in tightening the correlationist leash and casting an unforeseen anthropocentric myopia, one might insist that such a predicament follows from the philosophical *difficulties* that the injunction to proscribe any principled harmony between thought and reality bestow upon thought: thought is not guaranteed access to being, just as being cannot be straightforwardly described without first clarifying on what grounds one is entitled to provide such a description. If thought is potentially refractory to being, and if the former's access to the latter is not to be construed in epistemological terms, but rather in metaphysical ones, then we will surely still need a story about how to resolve the critical quandary of the relation between thought and reality, in the process of legitimating the purchase that our theories might bear on the world they are allegedly in a position to tell us about. The first section will thus allow us to see the main thrust behind Bryant's OOP and his case for a new metaphysics. I shall suggest that the case against the primacy of epistemology, inspired principally by Bhaskar, is insufficient to motivate the kind of metaphysics that Bryant admirably defends, in failing to dissolve the primacy of *representation* in favor of *practice*.

Second, I propose to examine the internal conceptual coherency of Bryant's metaphysical system, and his multifaceted account of objects. This is of course the core of his project, and constitutes a remarkable attempt to draw insights from various disciplines, not restricted to philosophy: Bruno Latour's theory of collectives and actants, a Deleuzean-inspired metaphysics of the virtual, Niklas Luhmann's autopoietic systems theory, Lacanian psychoanalysis, just to name a few. We shall briefly consider how this varied assortment of theoretical frameworks comes to bear within Bryant's system, by evaluating their articulation. For reasons of space, our analysis shall be restricted to assessing what I take to be the main theses in Bryant's ontology of objects: the twofold structure of *substance* as virtual and actual, the complex account of *withdrawal* which affects all objects, the account of *relation* inspired by autopoietic-systems theory, and the defense of a "flat" ontology which purports to make all objects as being finally in the same metaphysical footing, without compromising their difference.

Given that Bryant's account is rich and filled to the brim with content, I set myself the task to open up a space for discussing the more salient features of his overall system, rather than to seek an exhaustive delineation of the virtues and flaws in his philosophy, or to evaluate in rigorous fashion the justice he does to the theories that inspire his account. Thus, I shall obviate, at present, many intriguing attempts throughout the book to apply his major ontological insights in the form of varied examinations of psychoanalytic, political, and social situations. These are all valuable facets of Bryant's project, and merit consideration in themselves, which I reserve perhaps for a future occasion. In the end, this precautionary paucity is strategic, since the plausibility of OOP as proposed by Bryant cannot but supervene on how the methodological and metaphysical theses hang together; and so without further ado I propose to focus on these.

I - Methodological Quandaries
Epistemology or Ontology, Representation or Practice?

At the outset of the book, Bryant sets the itinerary for an audacious challenge to the ubiquity of post-Kantian "philosophies of access," which purport to examine the relation between mind and world, as opposed to the structure of world as such.[2] This tradition, we are told, has somewhat uniformly maintained that the category of the *object* ought to be thought of as being correlative to that of the *subject*, and so that a philosophical examination of former must be in principle understood as pertaining to something which is in *relation* to the latter. In short, they constitute what Bryant calls *epistemological realisms* (ER).[3] The core feature that Bryant seeks to isolate from every iteration of ER is the latter's characterization of the relation between subject and object as being one of *representational* nature, i.e. the subject stands to the object as *representing* agency stands to *represented* content. This representational link is to be understood in the sense in which the intentionality of thoughts, mental states, signifiers or propositions are supposed to "mirror" states of affairs wherein objects are potentially known, making thus all object-related content relative

---

[2] For an account of the expression "philosophies of access," see Graham Harman, *Guerrilla Metaphysics: Phenomenology and the Carpentry of Things* (Chicago: Open Court, 2005).

[3] Levi Bryant, *The Democracy of Objects* (Ann Arbor: Open Humanities Press, 2011), 13-14.

to the faculties and powers of the subject.[4] We should note that the reference to "mirroring," which obviously brings to mind Rorty's famous moniker for certain brands of analytic epistemology, strongly suggests that Bryant understands ER as involving a *correspondence* theory of truth and meaning, where objects take place as arguments in the representation of semantically determinate facts. The result is that for ER "... the question of the object becomes a question about whether or not we adequately represent the object."[5]

In contrast, Bryant proposes an *ontological realism* (OR), where the task becomes to describe the being of objects themselves, as opposed to their being in relation to us. Whereas ER cannot but subordinate the being of the object to its relation to the human knowing subject, quickly paving the way for the anti-realist evisceration of all exteriority, OR purports to access the structural features of objects and their relations, which include, albeit not exclusively nor especially, the human. Bryant wittily calls his system an *onticology*, obviously playing on the Heideggerean *ontological difference* between beings and being.[6] The term indexes the key maneuver in OOP through which philosophy is to be delivered back to the task of providing an inventory of the items and features that populate a multifaceted reality and their objectual, general structure, thereby folding the ontological back into the ontic. In that regard, OOP is a "revisionary Aristotelian" position, insofar as it thinks of the explanatory primacy of metaphysics, within the scope of an account of substances *qua* objects, as first philosophy. Indeed, the "return to Aristotle" is one of the motifs that Harman himself has set for OOP in general in its reactivation of the category of *substance* understood as autonomous, discretely individuated entities, that exist independently of the relations they might have to other substances.

---

[4] Bryant, *The Democracy of Objects*, 14-15

[5] Ibid., 14.

[6] Martin Heidegger, *Being and Time*, trans. John Macquarrie and Edward Robinson (San Francisco: Harper, 1962).

We should underline that Bryant does *not* mean to say that the relationship between humans and the world has no bearing for OOP, but merely that *subject-object* relations are to be construed as a *species* of *object-object* relations. Having said this, let us note that although ER is characterized by Bryant as being a kind of realism, the more subtle point is that it paves the way for an anti-realism about objects, where the ontological determinacy and constitution of the latter are rendered dependent on the subject's faculties/operations, however broadly understood. Thus, while ER is still a realism, it is one only in the sense that it acknowledges the reality of *relations* between subject and object in some form or other, since it already shuns from the philosophical imaginary the possibility of thinking of objects *independently* of anthropocentric determinants. In that regard, Bryant's OOP is in perfect continuity with both the deflationary position endorsed by Harman, insofar as they both seek to supplant the centrality of the human in order to "flatten" the latter into the category of object and with Meillassoux's own diagnosis against the correlationist reification of relation as displacing the (classical) realist avowal of the in-itself.

At this juncture, several questions appear urgent: are there no further alternatives besides ER, anti-realisms, and OR? Is the construal of ER as tethered to a correspondence-theory a fair characterization of those who insist on the priority of epistemology and the primacy of representation? Why should we choose in favor of OR and the displacement of epistemology, and particularly the version that Bryant's OOP advances, over its alternatives? In what follows I assess some of Bryant's arguments in response to the questions suggested above, and argue that the cogency of these answers conditions the feasibility of his onticological program.

The first crucial issue concerns the motivations for the choice in favor of OR over ER. To make his case, Bryant follows George Spencer-Brown in order to qualify the difference between metaphysical and epistemological realisms, through the difference between *distinction* and *indication*.[7] The latter

---

[7] Bryant, *The Democracy of Objects*, 20.

is said to presuppose the former, i.e. in order to be able to *indicate* anything whatsoever, we must begin by making a prior *distinction* which separates that which can be located and differentiated within a given domain from that which the distinction leaves out altogether. Once we make *use* of a distinction, we can only *indicate* that which is within its demarcating space, while the primary distinction itself is rendered invisible to those who use it. Yet, since every indication presupposes that a distinction has already been made, the interesting question becomes the one about *which distinctions ought to be made, and on which basis*. The main point that Bryant seeks to draw from this is that ER and anti-realisms begin by *distinguishing* within their internal domain that which is determined by subjective or cultural operations, with the result that the "great outdoors" wherein non-human objects abound is excluded from taking part as the domain's proper content. Thus, every posterior *indication* performed within the space of ER or anti-realism will enforce seclusion within the cohorts of the human or the cultural, and their manifold contents: ideas, representations, signifiers, sensations, etc. These denominations are supposed to be broad enough to cover the emphasis on epistemology and propositional analysis motivated by the linguistic turn in the analytic tradition, as well as the exacerbation of the critical turn carried out by the Continental tradition which, despite its manifold claims against epistemology, ends up reinforcing the priority of the human. The alternative that Bryant proposes is to begin rather by marking *objects* as the distinguished domain within which every posterior indication will take place, thereby rendering human and non-human factors univocally accounted for as possible contents for indication.

Subjects are objects *among* objects, rather than constant points of reference related to all other objects. As a consequence, we get the beginnings of what a proper anti-humanism and post-humanism *ought* to be, insofar as these theoretical orientations are no longer the thesis that the world is constructed through annonymous and impersonal social forces rather than through an individual subject. Rather, we get a variety of nonhuman actants unleashed in the world as autonomous agencies in their own right, freed from any constant reference to the human where they are reduced to our representations.[8]

Bryant argues that whereas ER is forced into the enclosure of the subjective, since it concerns itself with how *propositions* relate to facts in the enterprise *acquiring* knowledge, OOP factors in non-human entities by thinking of the *production* of knowledge. By the same token, anti-realisms cannot but concern themselves with exclusively human factors and properties, such as signifiers or ideal contents, since they have proscribed the possibility of thinking robustly of any externality, rendering material production and knowledge entirely subservient to the straightjacket of the human. The suggestion then seems to be that if we want to account for our relation to non-human factors in the production of knowledge, as well as for the relation between non-human objects themselves, we cannot endorse ER or anti-realism. Now, it is a truism to say that in order to be realists and so to endorse the mind-independence of a world we cannot be anti-realists; that can hardly be an argument for a realism of any kind. Rather, the motivation for realism would have to come from considering what allegedly anti-realism leaves out. And the idea is that anti-realism prevents us from thinking about how entities that are ontologically independent from each other interact and play a part in the *production* of new beings, forms and events, and not just exclusively for the *acquisition* of human knowledge which ER emphasizes. In that regard, Bryant is surely correct in suggesting that insofar as anti-realisms cannot but subordinate the ontological valence of non-human factors to the human, their capacity to explain interactions as involving entities that are wholly autonomous to the human is necessarily shut.

The more difficult question comes however with regard to ER. For it is far from clear that representational accounts that try to explain how we understand the world in terms of propositional content are in principle incapable of accounting for such things as non-human factors, the relations between

---

[8] Bryant, *The Democracy of Objects*, 22-23.

humans and other non-human factors, the relations between non-human factors themselves, or the experimental conditions under which knowledge is produced and not just acquired. For although accounts which favor some kind of correspondence theory, if successful, ought to describe how the properties and existence of beings in the world is within our cognitive and linguistic grasp, this does not seem in principle to rule out the possibility of giving an ontology for the world thus accessed. Indeed, many proponents of the analytic philosophical tradition, which could be characterized as endorsing a form of ER by Bryant's own lights, actively defend various metaphysical accounts. It is therefore unlikely that a *methodological* primacy or autonomy reserved for epistemology should *in principle* destine thought towards the "death of ontology," as Bryant calls it.[9] Notwithstanding the fact that much epistemology in recent decades has thoroughly *rejected* representational models tethered to correspondence-theories, it is not even clear that approaches that defend the latter must result in the anthropocentrism that Bryant deems inescapable.

The implicit worry seems to be that if we concentrate on the semantic properties of propositions we are bound to remain caught in talk about language. As Bryant claims:

> Were the world the totality of true *propositions* or constructed by language, this activity would be most peculiar indeed as there would be no *unknown* generative mechanisms to uncover in the experimental setting. In other words, the intelligibility of experimental practice is premised on the *ontological* supposition of generative mechanisms or objects *independent* of that activity.[10]

However, we must note, that this is to confuse *sentences* and *propositions*: the former are linguistic items and are fundamental in explaining how human communication and sapient thought takes place, while the latter provide a logical grammar for the *formal* structure of thoughts and the states of

---

[9] Bryant, *The Democracy of Objects*, 34.
[10] Ibid., 50.

affairs *represented* thereby. The link between the two is to be construed in terms of how propositions relate the *declarative force* of sentences.

Yet the *propositional content* or "descriptive content" associated with a sentence or a linguistic item need not be constrained to human entities in principle, or indeed to the properties of linguistic items or mental states; certainly not any more than Bryant's own roster of theoretical *claims* must be *about* linguistic items simply because they take the form of expressions in English.[11] To say that propositional or descriptive content is taken to be "correlative" to whatever can be asserted through the use of declarative sentences (classically, those expressions which complete *that*-clauses) is just to say that sentences are usually taken to express some state-of-affairs in the world which can be *formalized* by a proposition, and *not* that sentences are *about* propositions, or that propositions are *about* sentences.[12] And it is certainly not to say that the subjects and predicates, entities and properties, as expressed in propositional or sentential form, must be ontologically indistinguishable from their expressions. To claim otherwise would be to incur in an instance of Stove's Gem: the fallacy that seeks to derive from a) the tautological *epistemic* dependence of any knowledge to our capacities to know, b) the *ontological* dependence of that which knowledge is supposed to be *about* such capacities/faculties. In other words, the metaphysical status of propositional content is quite controversial, and cannot be straightforwardly identified with mental or linguistic entities.

---

[11] The term "descriptive content" is Sellars' own coinage to isolate the non-conceptual element of experience, in which the knower becomes tethered to causal processes, in relation to its surrounding environment. See Wilfrid Sellars, *Empiricism and the Philosophy of Mind*, (Harvard: Harvard University Press, 1997).

[12] It is important to notice that although Bryant wants to emphasize the importance of knowing-how over knowing-that, or practice over theorizing, it still becomes necessary to account for the former within any framework that presumes to disambiguate between the claims one makes and the things the claims are supposed to be about. This concern is hardly palliated by appeals to the priority of human practice.

In short, propositional analysis is not linguistics or psychology, and propositions with mental content are not in principle proscribed from relating to a mind-independent world. Even inferentialist approaches to philosophical semantics which do away with ontology, constraining *meaning* to inferential-role and *truth* to that which is preserved by inference, are not for this reason incapable of pursuing realism in an analysis of objectual evaluability, i.e. semantic holism does not entail idealism.[13] In general, to insist in that propositional contents are *representational* in any case is simply to say that such content is to be understood as formally expressing states of affairs which compose the world, i.e. we must understand questions about the nature of *intentional* content and the precise ways in which features of the world are cognized by isolating the formal structure of such features. But what kinds of relations and items we offer as candidates for representational contents and how semantic value is determined is highly disputed within epistemological schools, and here usually questions proper to ontology come to bear as well.[14] Since Bryant surely thinks that our *thoughts of things* are not themselves *the things that are thought*, and that we can think *about things* which are not for this reason *ontologically dependent on thought*, the idea that the contents of propositions must be restricted to human-relative items or else make everything ontologically dependent on the human strikes me as rather odd. If all it takes for an account to become representational is the belief that one's claims stand in some sort of relation or other to

---

[13] For an excellent debate on whether inferentialism can support robust representationalism in terms of objectual evaluability see the exchange between Robert Brandom and Michael Kramer in Bernhard Weiss and Jeremy Wanderer, *Reading Brandom: On Making it Explicit* (New York: Routledge, 2010)

[14] In particular, contemporary naturalisms have yielded light into the difficulties involving the task of understanding representation: computationalism, eliminativism, ontic structural realism, and instrumentalism all being examples of this sort. It would therefore be extremely misleading and oversimplifying to say that contemporary epistemology seeks to transform questions of ontology into its own terms or to dissolve ontology altogether; the porous frontier between epistemology and ontology, our understanding of the structure of thought and reason and the structure of the world, is one of perpetual negotiation and which must be understood carefully.

the things they purport to describe, whether these be mind-dependent or not, then even Bryant's account would have to be deemed implicitly representational in claiming to provide a suitable account of the metaphysical structure of reality.

But the more worrying gesture seems to be the implicit ban on explanatory necessity: what Bryant finds reproachable about ER is not that its proponents hold that thought and claims *can* potentially stand in some relation or other to the world, but the demand that one *ought* to explain what this relation consists in order to legitimate one's metaphysical claims. For Bryant's argument to have the strength it presumes to have he would need to show not only that ER concerns itself with questions of access to the world in virtue of dealing with propositions, but that in doing so it elides the possibility of a realist metaphysics. Needless to say, such a bold accusation would require much further argument to be persuasive for anyone looking to see whether the displacement of ER is tenable. This is, however, precisely the kind of confrontation with the tradition that Bryant declares he is able to avoid, arguing instead that philosophical progress is not made through the successful resolution of arguments following deliberation, but rather that what matters in the end is how fashionable positions gather sufficient supporters across generations, leaving those unresolved dilemmas to whither on the vine:

> New innovations in philosophy do not so much refute their opponents as simply cease being preoccupied by certain questions and problems. In many respects, object-oriented ontology, following the advice of Richard Rorty, simply tries to step out of the debate altogether. Object-oriented ontologists have grown weary of a debate that has gone on for over two centuries, believe that the possible variations of these positions have exhausted themselves, and want to move on to talking about other things. If this is not good enough for the epistemology police, we are more than happy to confess our guilt and embrace our alleged lack of rigor and continue in harboring our illusions that we can speak of a reality independent of humans.[15]

---

[15] Bryant, *The Democracy of Objects*, 29.

The suggestion made above threatens to compromise the rational grounds on which philosophical issues are decided. For if "growing weary" of a particular problem, however fastidious, is sufficient to obviate it rather than to motivate its urgency, then nothing prevents the philosopher to *ignore* arguments presented to them, as opposed to having the rational obligation to respond to them. Of course, one cannot exhaustively "fight off" every possible objection and interlocutor; indeed, no philosopher, however worthy of the name, has ever done such a thing. But it seems quite tendentious to claim that the questions that drive philosophers and research programs all around the world are "exhausted" to the point of vacuity without further ado. This is particularly grave, considering that the characterization Bryant gives of ER is meant to be a diagnosis of the global state of the discipline, rather than narrowing down a particular school. But epistemological realism is unfortunately not precise enough a denomination to cover the depth of the field it presumably disqualifies, failing even in establishing that one could not achieve the kinds of things Bryant expects from a metaphysics unless such a disqualification were to take place. Without curbing one's affirmative enthusiasm by policing the extent to which we are deemed capable of describing a mind-independent world, one risks blurring the line between fiction and philosophy, between imaginative freedom and rational obligation.

However, the more important question is whether the positive arguments for the primacy of ontology over epistemology in fact work, and for this Bryant devotes the entirety of the first chapter of the book. This is a particularly important issue, because the difference between distinction and indication that Bryant draws upon to suggest the prerogative of ontology is later in Chapter four characterized by Luhmann as being a *contingent* matter, so that every identity ascribed to beings in ontological terms will be grounded in a *decision*: "Luhmann effectively shows how this distinction is *contingent* such that identity is no longer the ground of being, but an effect of a distinction that enables observation."[16] Thus, we must ask if

---

[16] Bryant, *The Democracy of Objects*, 139.

the distinction which decides in favor of objects isn't finally tacitly subordinated to a subjective whim, in which case we are either back with anti-realism, or else we must explain *why* such a distinction is in fact not contingent upon voluntarist caprice, but suggested on rational grounds. In other words: what sets constraints on our capacity to make distinctions so that onticology can be something besides an arbitrary thought experiment, and without making ontology impossible, like Luhmann claims?

For these purposes, Bryant takes on the work of Roy Bhaskar's transcendental realism, which is set to provide the "sufficient reason" to think of the methodological primacy of ontology.[17] In particular, he suggests that we should extrapolate the ontological aspect from the transcendental argument that Bhaskar offers for scientific realism. At core, the argument proceeds as follows: rather than imagining what the mind must be like for knowledge of the world to be possible, Bhaskar inverts the question and asks what the world must be like in order for the experimental activity of science to be possible.[18] Second, given that through experimental activity we learn that objects may have qualities or powers which they do not exhibit at a given time, we must stipulate that there are such things as *intransitive objects*, i.e. an object is intransitive if and only if objects are real structures whose powers may be "out-of-phase" with the actual patterns or events that they manifest at a given time.[19] For Bryant, this constitutes a crucial rejoinder to the traditional *empiricist* argument which relativizes any knowledge of the object to our sensory impressions that obtain in *actual* manifestations. This "empiricist" view quickly leads to the Humean consideration that causality is not real, but a mere projection illegitimately drawn to support an imaginary necessity from what are mere associations between perceptual events. The idea is thus that scientific experimentation must acknowledge that objects can be intransitive, since if it

---

[17] Bryant, *The Democracy of Objects*, 39-52

[18] Ibid., 40-43

[19] Ibid., 44-45.

didn't it would have no reason to suppose that objects have causal powers hidden from what they evince at a given time. Furthermore, considering that conjunctions of events are exceptions rather than rules, experimental practice is tenable precisely insofar as it teases the capacities that an object has but might not exhibit regularly, through repetition in controlled settings. This will turn out to be a crucial element for Bryant's thesis of *withdrawal*, i.e. objects always have structural features that are not manifested at a given time, but which upon repeated testing might become evinced, illuminating the object's nature:

> We thus have an ontological distinction between objects or generative mechanisms on the one hand, and events, on the other. If experimental activity is necessary, then this is because generative mechanisms can be dormant, inactive, or veiled by the agency of other objects or generative mechanisms. Nonetheless, it is generative mechanisms or objects that are responsible for the production of events.[20]

As we shall see below, the distinction between generative mechanisms and events is reproduced in an assortment of other distinctions from different theoretical sources: virtual proper being and actual manifestation (Deleuze), substance and qualities (Aristotle), system and information (Maturana, Varela, Luhmann), being the main ones as far as I can gauge. For the moment, let us note that Bhaskar's transcendental argument is meant to reinforce the necessity of a mind-independent world not just for *scientific practice* to be possible, but more generally for *ontology* to get off the ground. In that regard, the argument for the existence of physical objects is generalized to infer the existence of intransitive objects, which for Bryant are *not* taken to be necessarily of physical nature. This is important, since Bhaskar's argument suggests that intransitive objects exist in order for *scientific* practice to be understood; but, accordingly, these objects are meant to conform to our understanding of *physical* phenomena, and not just an unqualified domain of objects-in-general. It is

---

[20] Bryant, *The Democracy of Objects*, 48.

therefore not clear just how far Bryant's commitment to materialism can make use of the scientific grounds in Bhaskar's argument to support his more general claims about objects. This is not trivial, seeing that Bryant intends to extend the distinction between objects and events to argue for the existence of *all kinds* of objects, and not only for the physical beings whose existence is supported by the transcendental argument. Although the latter is meant to give warrant to the claim that all existing objects can be out-of-phase with regard to their powers, and even assuming that the argument works in determining the autonomy of physical phenomena, it surely wouldn't follow from the latter that there are objects outside the concern of scientific experimentation that either exist or exhibit these same features. We will later see how Bryant develops the thesis of withdrawal as being a general feature of objects, which are not taken to be by necessity physical.

The more interesting question is whether Bhaskar's transcendental argument effectively works to ground a realism of any given sort, and here a few provisory observations are pertinent. First, it is not clear that pointing to the empiricist conflation between causal powers and sensible manifestations suffices to establish the existence of causally autonomous objects. Rather, what it seems to show is that *if* objective properties are reduced to sense-data, and *if* causal laws are taken to be *ontologically* relative to such data, then causality is either epiphenomenal or epistemically foreclosed. Therefore, it suggests that *if* causal powers exist then these cannot be reduced to *salient* features in sense-data, and so that traditional empiricism won't work to motivate realism. However, the argument does *not* show that other accounts that think of an epistemological relation between mind and world reserving a role for perception to yeild objective knowledge couldn't successfully avoid the perils of traditional empiricism.

Indeed, revisionist approaches to naturalism have challenged sense-datum theories, and not just or exclusively against traditional empiricism, by insisting that *perception* should be understood as a thoroughly conceptual achievement proper to rational behavior, while *sensibility* can be given a perfectly intelligible account as a *causal*, non-conceptual process nevertheless.[21] For these roughly post-Sellarsian accounts, one must reject the reification of sense-data or phenomenological givenness in their attempt to play the part of 'presentationalist' anchors for representation on experience, i.e. the claim that sensibilia present themselves to us immediately, and so that we have privileged access. They thus reject that representation must be anchored on anything like 'immediate experience', or that acquaintance with sensation by itself yields knowledge, and in that regard they follow the Hegelian trivialization of givenness or sensible intuition. These, they argue, must be deflated in favor of integrating perception a formal analysis of the inferential structure of *representation* in its conceptual envelopment. Thus, perceptual *judgments* are to be understood in terms of the distinctive inferential role that they play within a conceptual economy (distinctively as language-entry transitions) and must be subject to defeasibility conditions relative to the causal onsets that trigger them, in order for them to play the epistemic role they do.[22] Blunt experience is epistemically mute; conceptual rationality is the mark of sapience.

Other externalist approaches, such as Tyler Burge's (2010), suggest that while perception is the most primitive form of representation, anchoring the organism's relation to its environment, it does so through (fallible) subpersonal mechanisms for objective individuation, which exhibit strict conditions for *veridicality*, i.e. conditions for the success of failure of a perceptual faculty in representing its environment.[23] Furthermore, "nativist" approaches argue against the exclusive

---

[21] Wilfrid Sellars, *Empiricism and the Philosophy of Mind*.

[22] This is not to claim that all *knowledge* is necessarily *causally* acquired by means of an inference, or that there cannot be non-inferential knowledge. It is simply to say that all knowledge, in order to count as *knowledge*, must be *justifiable* independently by another proposition(s) on the basis of the goodness of the inference from the latter to the former, even if the belief thus justified wasn't *formed* or *acquired* through a process of inference.

[23] Tyler Burge, *The Origins of Objectivity*, (New York: Oxford University Press, 2010).

primitiveness of perception and sensation, claiming that there are also *modular* representational states which conform to conceptual core-cognitive *acquisitions* or "triggerings," and which condition the *central* development of full-blown conceptual projection through which learning properly takes place.[24] Such contemporary models for perception need not assume that those representations which enter into modular perceptual computations be consciously accessible; they are computed through subpersonal mechanisms that require the appropriate, causally instantiated environmental triggers.[25]

Crucially, following Piaget and Quine, nativist approaches explicitly challenge traditional empiricism in emphasizing that the primitive representation of persisting objects *cannot* be circumscribed to perceptual contents, since the former are multimodal while the latter are modally-specific to the organism's sensory-analyzer capacities to register data.[26] Multi-modality is therefore taken as an epistemological route to anchor realism, on the basis of what a persistent, perception-independent object *must* be like in order for their representations to obtain. All of this to say that the conceptual onsets required for the representation of objects are taken to be fundamentally distinct from the computations of actual sensory outputs, and that only the former require conceptual envelopment to some degree. Thus, the instantiation of these conceptual capacities must be described *causally* by relating the organism to its environmental stimuli, and independently of any appeals to the putative conscious transparency of sensible "ideas" that traditional empiricists used in order to fold causation inwardly into the "contents" of perception.

---

[24] For an example of these approaches and an explanation of the modular/central distinction for representational-state acquisition see Susan Carey, *The Origins of Concepts* (New York: Oxford University Press, 2009); also Jerry Fodor, *The Language of Thought* (USA: Thomas Y. Cromwell Company, 1975). For a more recent account see Jerry Fodor, *LOT 2: The Language of Thought Revisited,* (New York: Oxford University Press, 2008).

[25] Carey, *The Origins of Concepts*, 31.

[26] Indeed, nativist accounts argue that the ontological commitments which anchor our capacity to represent objective reality are innate, and triggered by brute causal processes as opposed to "learnt."

In dispute with these variegated approaches, Burge insists that although perceptual representation is pre-conceptual, it nevertheless suffices for objectual representation, insisting that the latter need not be tethered to multimodality, but that anticipatory mechanisms that come with the organism as base cognitive functions suffice to do the trick (and indeed, such abilities are taken to be present in non-sapient organisms such as insects).[27]

In any case, the point here is not to argue whether any of these alternatives is better suited for realism, but to point out that the suggestion that we're forced either into an OR of the sort supported by Bhaskar's transcendental argument, or else faced with the quandaries of traditional empiricism wed to the putative "givenness" of sense-data, is a false one. Clearly, much work in recent epistemology goes far beyond classical empiricism, and it is far from clear how Bhaskar's arguments motivate the ontological prerogative against these alternatives.

The most salient worry is, however, is that the transcendental argument begs the question about why non-manifestness should entail mind-independence. Certainly, one could claim that phenomenally individuated particulars bear properties that are not, at a given time, manifested or transparently available to consciousness. One of Harman's own frequent examples is that of Husserl's inflection of the phenomenal/noumenal distinction to phenomenal: the intentional object *of consciousness* retains a unified being irrespective of its contingent *adumbrations*.[28] Similarly, for Heidegger, epistemic opaqueness is the norm rather than the exception; for the most part we deal with the world practically, without explicitly construing its contents as having propositionally determinate, explicitly salient properties.[29] Yet this is not to say that such properties are taken to be independent of their

---

[27] Additionally, Burge construes conceptuality in narrower terms than Carey, by taking it to be a distinctive feature of sapient organisms equipped with the capacity for *linguistic* representation. See Tyler Burge, *The Origins of Objectivity*.

[28] Edmund Husserl, *Ideas: General Introduction to a Pure Phenomenology*, trans. Fred Kersten (The Hague: Nijhoff, 1982).

[29] Martin Heidegger, *Being and Time*, 103.

mode of apprehension, given that for Heidegger the realm of present-at-hand particulars and their properties is taken to be a function of the breakdown of ready-to-hand equipment in practice, while the latter remains tethered to Dasein's comportments within a correlationally constituted world.[30] The inference from out-of-phasing to mind-independence seems less persuasive once we realize that science can be explained on instrumentalist grounds, while accepting out-of-phasing as a constitutive feature of the objects proper to empirical study. Indeed, the status of causality within contemporary debates in the philosophy of science and metaphysics is also highly disputed. Proponents of instrumentalist approaches, insist in that ontic determinacy is ultimately a matter of pragmatic convention, while accepting that experimentation runs on the background of non-manifest, non-theorized states, i.e. the specificity of the latter can be accounted for without biting the realist bullet. These considerations lead me to suggest that Bryant's reading of Bhaskar runs on a very narrow conception on what the contents of perceptually triggered mental states can be like. More specifically, it seems like Bryant thinks that the causal autonomy of objects must follow from the following two requirements for perceptual content:

(Luminosity): For any perceptually triggered mental state x, I can know that I'm in x. If $P(x)$ is true at t_1, then I can know that $P(x)$ is true at t_1.

---

[30] A similar confusion is repeated towards the end of the third chapter where Bryant claims that "it is difficult to see how language could ever have the power to divide or parcel in the way suggested by the linguistic idealists were it not for the fact that the world is itself structured and differentiated. Absent a world that is structured and differentiated, the surface of the world, as a sort of formless flux, would be too slippery, too smooth, for the signifier to structure at all." See Levi Bryant, *The Democracy of Objects*, 132. Again, it is not clear that differentiation need be mind-independent in order to occur, since one can easily hold that it is the realm of appearance which is differentiated and split, and which the signifier works upon to make its secondary differentiations. The point is not that this would not still be correlationism or idealism, for it would clearly be one of the two, but that the transcendental argument from Bhaskar does not help assuage the possibility of this scenario.

(Actualism): For any perceptually triggered mental state x at a time t1, there is no property P(x) manifest at t1 that is not manifest at a later time t2.

These two theses taken together underlie Bryant's idea that so long as we don't postulate a mind-independent roster of objects we will not be able to explain why an object can fail to manifest all of its qualities, i.e. why objects must be intransitive if open-systems obtain. As I suggested above, there is no independent argument to support either luminosity or actualism about perceptual states, and so the inference from epistemic opacity to mind-independence is in my estimation not a good one. With this in mind, I conclude that appeals to Bhaskar's transcendental argument to motivate the prerogative of OR against ER are not adequate.

Before moving on to assess the composition of Bryant's ontological system, we should make a few cursory remarks on his general contentions against correlationism, idealism, and the epistemological inflections of contemporary philosophy that are offered towards the end of the first chapter. Following a brief excursus through the history of correlationism, Bryant goes on to reassert what he takes to be a fatal complicity between epistemologically oriented accounts and experiential givenness:

> Wherever claims about the being of beings are transposed into questions about our access to beings, we end up with givenness legislating what exists and what doesn't exist based on what is given or accessible, and we thereby find ourselves trapped in a self-defeating self-referential paradox where we simultaneously concede the existence of objects while denying their existence.
>
> As a consequence, claims about the being of entities are arrived at in an entirely different manner than the epistemological question of access. We do not begin with our access to beings, but instead ask what the world must be like for certain practices to be possible. The object-oriented ontologist is not claiming that we have access to beings, that they are given, or that our perception is identical to the way the world is, but that the existence of substance is a necessary premise for a whole

slew of our practices to be intelligible. In other words, the onticological thesis is that the world must be a particular way for certain practices and activities like perception, experimentation, discourse, and so on, to be possible and that the world would be this way regardless of whether we perceived, experimented, or discoursed about it."[31]

As I have been suggesting above, the complicity between perceptual data and givenness is vastly challenged by epistemologists everywhere, and cannot be taken seriously as an Achilles heel bound to force one into pragmatic contradictions, or to anthropocentric claustrophobia. The claim that questions about access are bound to be transformed into questions of givenness is therefore a strawman against the arguments proposed by those who insist on the methodological priority of epistemology, and the viability of grounding realism through the latter.

Granted, to transform questions proper to ontology into questions of epistemology would be to fold the contents of the world into the human. But this is clearly not what is at stake for epistemologists: the question is not whether we *ought* to construe the world as a function of human knowledge, but rather to specify how the fallible and revisable structure of the latter makes possibly intelligible the existence and structure of the former. When Bryant suggests that we *ought* to shift the starting point from epistemology to ontology to ground realism, he is thus in fact obviating rather than addressing the pertinence of the critical filter against *dogmatic* metaphysics, a precaution emblematic of modernity which is advanced in order to rule out appeals to any given pre-established harmony between thinking and being, concepts and objects. Given that the support for realism that Bryant draws from Bhaskar does not settle the case in favor of ontology, one may be forgiven for being skeptical about the thesis that epistemology must have exhausted its speculative resources to the point of warranting its destitution.

So to answer Bryant's question: "Why not begin with amoeba?,"

---

[31] Bryant, *The Democracy of Objects*, 64-65.

we can simply answer "Because the problem of access remains, and unless we enact a regression to dogmatic metaphysics, we better have a story to tell about *how* the structure of the world is within our cognitive grasp!" Indeed, anything less would surely compromise the "democratic" pretences of OOP, subjecting its metaphysical account to prescriptions based on authority rather than argument. And if such grounds ensue as feasible criteria for entitlement to one's own philosophical position, then we inadvertently restitute the prerogative of our pragmatic interests and contingent proclivities over the force of reasons. It is precisely such a displacement of our critical standards that surrenders philosophy to the whims of the human, to the enclosure of the subjective, and which should be taken to be in complicity with correlationism and anti-realism, and not the work of those who insist on the importance of clarifying the gulf that persists between mind and world.[32] Realism in any relevant sense is not something

---

[32] It should be remarked that it is actually those philosophers devoted to exploring the gulf that persists between mind and world that have been most attentive to the "vast outdoors" of non-human actants and factors, rather than our veritable stock of Continental theorists which dismiss the problematic, "materialists" or not. It is usually those who work on the kinds of issues epistemologists concern themselves with that indeed contribute to the numerous empirical explorations carried forth by the empirical sciences, and not those who routinely patronize the necessity to leave one's armchair in the name of a more fundamental understanding, ontological or otherwise.

This is not to indulge in some facile "scientism," to claim that philosophy is the "handmaiden" of the sciences, or to disavow the philosophical valence of other domains of investigation and practice besides science. It is just to recall that philosophers who ally themselves to the post-Heideggerean suspicion against "epistemology" for being a kind of metaphysics are for the same reasons usually dismissive of scientific insight, the better to staple themselves to their cozy armchairs. To Bryant's credit, his concern with developmental biology, however brief or cursory, is already rather exceptional among Continental theorists, and in this he certainly does justice to some of his intellectual heroes, like Deleuze and DeLanda, who are also exceptional in that regard.

The patronizing dismissal of the scientific exploration of the world, which is proudly regurgitated and reenacted to this day by many leading theorists, has resulted in an incalculably pernicious aloofness and mystification for generations of philosophers, severing the discipline from the very world it was allegedly committed to think about. With this in mind it should prove

we *ought* to innocently *assume* for philosophy to be possible, but is rather something that *may* be a *result* following from philosophical questioning. If Bryant's earnest wish to decentralize the focus on the human is to be carried out without facile obviations, then one must perhaps realize that in asking about the limits of knowledge one begins by modestly accepting that intelligibility comes at a price, that we are quite fallible in bringing the real before us, and that we need to understand *how* we may have the capacity to know this real before unabashedly proclaiming that we do.

Having said this, Bryant's enterprise is nevertheless laudable insofar as it raises the fundamental question about whether philosophy ought to assign methodological priority to ontology, or to epistemology. And if epistemological realisms which opt for the latter option can be endorsed, then the challenge will be to show that such an enterprise is possible without running along presupposed *metaphysical* precepts, readily awaiting the deconstructive scavengers to ruin the day. The suggestion that Bryant advances closing on the first chapter is that epistemology-driven accounts must at the very least presuppose the metaphysical reification of the knower that thinks, and must therefore invariably run on a tacit ontological footing:

> Those who advise us to observe the observer somehow seem to miss the point that the very act of observing the observer or observing how other observers observe presupposes the existence of an observer that is doing the observing of other observers. Far from undermining the thesis that substances or objects exist, in other words, this move presupposes

---

surprising to see OOP perform a similarly facile dismissal of the epistemological tradition which has occupied philosophers of mind during the last century, by no means restricted in scope to an exploration of the human, but rather devoted to thinking along the intricacies of scientific experimentation and practice to this day. Specialization at the price of synthetic capaciousness surely renders philosophy dull and myopic; but synthetic ambition without curiosity and discipline for learning delivers philosophy to quixotic banality and shallowness, however disguised in appeasing rhetoric.

the existence of at least one substance or object. And as a consequence, this move is incapable of consistently maintaining the thesis that the world is a product of how observers perceive other objects.[33]

We should note that even if one restricts the scope of the correlationist obsession with access to only imply the being of the one who thinks and does the observing (and not *other* observers), the question about whether ontology can be deferred or suspended lingers on. Bryant is correct in detecting that an epistemological destitution of ontology *in principle* would just beg the question, and become directly complicit with anti-realism, or else forced to endorse a reification of the knowing subject as a minimal ontological commitment, enacting a kind of Cartesianism run amok. Yet this would surely jeopardize the claim that epistemology could get off the ground without any prior ontological decision or reflection.

However, to claim that it would be on any account *impossible* to begin with anything but ontology, since one must run with some metaphysical commitment or other, strikes me as eliding the *possibility* of distinguishing between a *methodological dualism* which defines the semantics of rationality *functionally*, and a *metaphysical dualism* which begins by reifying rationality *metaphysically*. It rejects the possibility that we may avoid the ontological circle by way of methodologically suspending the metaphysical status of thought in the process of engaging in an epistemological investigation of reason. The charge against such a possibility obviously calls into question the viability of all post-Sellarsian approaches that claim for a methodological separation of the normative from the natural, and which do *not* reify this difference in a metaphysical dualism of mind and world.[34] This is not some arcane conceit that occupies stale epistemologists, but forms part of the Kantian legacy which Bryant wages against. By attempting to secure the distinctiveness of rationality for

---

[33] Bryant, *The Democracy of Objects*, 66.

[34] Wilfrid Sellars, *Empiricism and the Philosophy of Mind.*

the normative purchase that allows for subjects to engage in *commitments* and hold *endorsements* for which they are *responsible*, the "inferentialist" program seeks precisely to extirpate any residual metaphysical baggage that came with primitive characterizations of judgment as predication, in the way of explaining what constitutes the intentionality of the mental. This is what Brandom, following Sellars, crucially takes to be already at work in the Kantian "jurisprudential" account of representation and the construal of reason as a "tribunal": "Kant's most basic idea is that minded creatures are to be distinguished from unminded ones not by a matter-of-fact ontological distinction (the presence of mind-stuff), but by a normative *deontological* one. This is his *normative characterization* of the mental."[35] In continuity with this account, what transcendental idealism continued to reify from aesthetic experience in the ideal structures of space-time, is deflated by revisionary approaches which, while retaining the prerogative of giving a formal account of the inferential structure of representation, deny the valence of intellectual intuition and experiential givenness. Bryant's excursus therefore implicitly suggests that these accounts cannot but run on metaphysical endorsements of the sort that vitiate the purported ontological neutrality of the normative.

However, even if we had to accept (and it is not clear that we do) that we are forced into an ontological decision prior to any pretence to epistemological questioning, this still wouldn't by itself suffice to legitimize ontological realism *about objects*, or about any other *particular* ontological option for hypothesizing a mind-independent reality. And it certainly won't suffice to elide the prerogative of the question of knowledge or representation to deny the claim that rational agency must be recognized. For we *might* think, in continuity with the modern legacy castigated by Bryant and his Continental predecessors, that the minimal commitment to which thought is forced into acknowledging is that of *itself*

---

[35] Robert Brandom, *Reason in Philosophy: Animating Ideas*, (USA: Belknap Press of University of Harvard Press, 2009), 32-33.

as that being who is gripped by the force of reasons, and that such a commitment immediately solicits an investigation into reason's structure, whether this be called transcendental, deontological, or ontologically "regional." Such an explanatory exigency haunts those who inhabit the logical space of reasons *in any case*; it holds irrespective of whether we must assign to the latter's inferentially governed structure a metaphysical status or not. For even if we must endow rationality a minimal metaphysical character, then we still have to acknowledge that our being as knowers delivers us into a reflection about the structure of the reason through which the knowing takes place.

This is the idea that has motivated philosophical modernity, from Descartes to contemporary epistemology; a possibility that ceases to appear as the antiquated and exhausted option OOP deems as long as one remembers that its *critical* exigency came about in order to defuse dogmatic claims to metaphysical knowledge. In looking past the importance of critique in the name of theoretical vanguardism, OOP risks enacting a profound philosophical regression, throwing away, along with the prudential discipline of the post-Kantian legacy, both the rationalist baby along the anti-realist bathwater. Worse still, if OR fails in its methodological motivations, then it is not clear that OOP can even abjure the anti-realist side of critique, as it proclaims. But on any account, Bryant's opening chapter evinces the difficulty facing anyone's claims to realism: how to reconcile the *critical* necessity to adjudicate our purchase on a world which is by itself not designed to be intelligible, while explaining how the purposeful thought that rationally enjoins itself as the will to know arises out from such a purposeless world.

II - Mereological Quandaries
Withdrawal, Structure, Relation

Although both Harman and Bryant seem crucially indebted to the work of Bruno Latour, whereas the former's account develops closer to the phenomenological tradition, the latter looks in the direction of Deleuze, Luhmann, and Lacan, among others. On both accounts, the basic task is to think of an ontology of self-subsistent objects, while nevertheless providing an adequate account of relation and change that doesn't relapse into a pre-Darwinian avowal of fixed essences or ideal forms, as in classical realist accounts and traditional Aristotelian/Platonist position. Although Harman becomes explicitly a dualist in his distinction between real and sensuous objects, Bryant follows Deleuze in proposing ontological univocity and a "flat" ontology, claiming instead that objects have two distinct dimensions as part of the same ontological domain: the virtual and the actual. As we shall see, however, this distinction remains continuous with Harman's account insofar as both accept that one must separate between what an entity *is* and how an entity *appears* within a given situation or to another being in relation.

These propadeutic insights allow us to observe two major aspects of what Bryant calls the thesis of *withdrawal*: objects are ontologically independent from their relations by possessing an internal structure of their own, and objects have non-manifest potentialities proper to their structure which in every case are irreducible to what their actual states reveal.[36] The second and third chapters of the book propose thus to lay the foundations for a new account of substance, distinguishing for every object an internal structure (its "endo-relations"), and the qualities or events that they manifest in actuality as a result of entering in relation with other objects, which Bryant calls the "exo-relations" of substance.[37] This distinction is analogous to the one developed in the third chapter between the *virtual proper being* of the object and its *local manifestations*, between the powers that the object has *qua* generative mechanism, and the events or qualities that it manifests *at a given time*.[38] In other words, qualities are to be understood as events that *happen to* objects and aspects manifested by objects, rather than as *features in* objects.

---

[36] Bryant, *The Democracy of Objects*, 68-69.

[37] Ibid.

[38] Ibid., 87-88.

Speculations III

With this in mind, Bryant goes on to introduce the two major aspects of what he calls the thesis of withdrawal in the following passage:

> Within the framework of onticology, the claim that objects are withdrawn from other objects is the claim that 1) substances are independent of or are not constituted by their relations to other objects, and 2) that objects are not identical to any qualities they happen to locally manifest. The substantiality of objects is never to be equated with the qualities they produce.[39]

The two aspects of the thesis are obviously linked together: objects are ontologically independent from their qualities precisely insofar as they are always capable of doing things that exceed that which they actually do. The capacity of the object to produce effects relative to its virtual structure is thus the obverse of the claim that every manifestation is necessarily the manifestation *of* a power proper to the object; or else it wouldn't make sense to say that powers are in excess *to* their manifestations. With this in mind, I propose the following formulation for the *excess* condition that Bryant gives as follows:

(Excess): For any substance x, if xRy makes x manifest a local quality a at t, then there is a power b of x such that xRy does not manifest b at t.

Bryant goes on to tie in his account of withdrawal with his distinction between object and parts. As one might expect, he claims that an object is ontologically irreducible to its parts. This is yet another dimension of the withdrawal thesis: objects are not only independent from the qualities they manifest, but also from the parts that compose them. The latter are taken to be objects in their own right. We should note that with regards to the relation between objects and parts, excess would have to mean something quite different than we surmised above;

---

[39] Bryant, *The Democracy of Objects*, 70.

namely, it should entail that objects always have powers which their parts themselves don't possess. Or stated differently, it ought to be possible to predicate of objects features that are not equivalent to those of their parts, or else the former would be the sum of what is predicated of the latter:

> Were objects identical to their parts, then this would entail that objects are predicates of their parts. This, in turn, would undermine the autonomy or independence of objects. Consequently, while substances certainly cannot exist without their parts, substantiality must be something *other* than the parts of which an object is composed.[40]

At this juncture, however, the Aristotelian and Deleuzean sides of Bryant's account are, if not in conflict, at least unclear in their articulation. For if every object has a virtual structure which *can* subsist without having *any* qualities (objects can be "dormant"), then it must be equally true that objects *cannot* exist without their parts, which plainly suggests parts are not qualities. However, it is equally unlikely that the parts of an object must belong to what Bryant calls the object's virtual structure, or its potentialities, since the latter are taken to be essential to its being, while parts are said to be accidental. It is difficult to understand how parts are articulated within the dual structure of the object, since the intrication between parts and virtual structures is not rendered transparent in Bryant's account, albeit it is clear that whatever parts are they must have a virtual structure of their own, being objects themselves. Indeed, Bryant claims that "...substantiality must be something *other* than the parts of which an object is composed," thereby suggesting that parts are not parts *of* the *proper being* of the object.[41] But then in what sense can parts be *of* objects, if not "properly"? To what extent can an object depend on its parts without indexing the latter to its internal structure, but without splitting the object into two? It seems therefore as if we must distinguish not just between

---

[40] Bryant, *The Democracy of Objects*, 68.
[41] Ibid., 70.

the endo-relations of the object's virtual proper being and the exo-relations which it has with other objects in producing qualitative states, but also between the virtual proper being of an object defining its autonomous and necessary structure, and its contingent parts. In this regard, parts are like qualities in that they are contingent or accidental features apart from the proper being of the object, while they are like the virtual proper being in that they condition the possibility of the existence of the object.

However, it remains unclear just why we should call such accidental components "parts" *of* an object as opposed to merely autonomous objects with which that object enters in exo-relations, as argued above. And the intuitive answer is that although parts are *independent* insofar as they are objects themselves, the object of which they are parts of couldn't *exist* without them. There is thus a crucial disjunction tacitly at work in Bryant's account between an object's *ontological independence* and its *existential independence*: the former requires that one's virtual structure be defined in terms of powers that are autonomous to the relations into which the object enters, while the latter implies that the virtual structure of the object couldn't continue to subsist as such without support from its parts. It is the account of existential independence, however, which remains opaque in Bryant's account, since it is just not clear how the virtual proper being of an object must relate to the parts which compose it so as to render the former existentially dependent on the latter. With this in mind, the intrication between the three aspects of the object (virtual proper being, qualities, and parts) as articulated through the withdrawal thesis, is unclear.

In any case, the manifold sides of withdrawal are closely knit to Bryant's account of relation, and of how entities manage to *perturb* one another. Before we go on to provide a brief assessment of these however, we should provide a few remarks about how Bryant develops the dyad between an object's virtual proper being and its local manifestations, mainly through Deleuze and the work of Manuel DeLanda. The virtual/actual distinction maps two thoroughly dissimilar

Daniel Sacilotto – *Review of* Democracy of Objects

aspects of the object: a *topological* aspect which defines its potentialities across a *vector field*, and a *geometrical* aspect which defines its actual states and the qualitative transformations it undergoes in *phase space*.[42] The most important qualification that Bryant proposes as a corrective to Deleuze's account is to treat the virtual as what defines *discrete objects,* as opposed to a *pre-individuated continuum* composed of *singularities* which fall short of being individuals. This corrective is necessary since, in Bryant's estimation, Deleuze lacks an account of non-qualitative individuation that would be adequate to his antipathy to substances and objects:

> By treating the domain of the virtual as the pre-individual and the domain of the actual as an *effect* of the virtual, Deleuze is left without an account of why the virtual actualizes itself at all (despite his impressive efforts to the contrary), and is led to treat the actual as a mere product, an excrescence, that itself has no efficacy within being. What is required, by contrast, is an account of the virtual that treats it as a dimension of primary substances or discrete individuals, where substance precedes the virtual (transcendentally, not temporally) not the reverse, and where *actual* entities are capable of interacting with one another.[43]

Yet Bryant seems to oscillate between the claim that Deleuze has no account of individuation, and the claim that such an account is given but is unsuccessful. This turns out to be an important issue, because the ontological decision in favor of an ontology of objects is supposed to come out of the insufficiency of thinking of the virtual as being pre-objectual or pre-individual. It seems clear that Deleuze, at the very least, did provide a theory of morphogenesis as *intensive individuation* through his account of larval subjectivity, and the syntheses of space and time, which culminate in his account of psychic

---

[42] Bryant, *The Democracy of Objects*, 91.
[43] Ibid., 104.

individuation.[44] It is far less obvious, however, what exactly Bryant finds to be lacking in Deleuze's account, besides the fact that it is said to fail when accounting for objectual discreteness.

In that regard, it is not clear how the suggestion that an account which explains individuation starting from pre-individual singularities is necessarily incapable of accounting for individual differences in being. Considering that Deleuze's entire project constitutes allegedly an effort to think of virtual singularities as the unequal-in-itself, or difference-in-itself, how exactly the *multiplicity* of virtual singularities and their actualizations relapses into an undifferentiated *continuum* is left unexplained.[45] Without such an explanation, it is far less clear either that we ought to choose in favor of the restitution of substances, or that the Deleuzean account is incapable of accounting for individuation, as the argument proposes.

Second, performing a similar maneuver to his extrapolation of Bhaskar's transcendental argument, Bryant dislodges DeLanda's allotment of the virtual to the spatial domain of the topological, to argue instead that the division between the virtual and the actual is of an ontological dimension which might hold for all objects in general. In order to cash out the more intuitive appeal of Deleuze's notion of the virtual as involving "singularities," he proposes to follow DeLanda thus in treating the latter as *attractors*, i.e. singularities are to be understood as the potentialities which define variable tendencies in a system/object, and which preside any specific

---

[44] Gilles Deleuze, *Difference and Repetition*, trans. Paul Patton (New York: Columbia University Press: 1995), Chapter II, pp. 78-85.

[45] One possible way of understanding Bryant's argument is that he follows Badiou's reading of Deleuze that claims that Deleuze's notion of multiplicity is subordinated to the notion of the "One," in the sense in which fails to rise to a purely extensional domain of the pure multiple. This kind of argument is, however, foreclosed to Bryant, since he himself has a notion of self-constituted objects which are entirely defined by internal relations, and which would constitute prime examples of the kind of "Oneness" extensional approaches proscribe in principle.

actual state which the latter might manifest at any given time. Thus, Bryant wants to thinks of potentialities as that which persists and underlies every actualization for an object, i.e. it becomes part of how to understand the withdrawal thesis:

> Yet, above all, the distinction between virtual proper being and local manifestation teaches us that objects are *plastic*. As a function of the exo-relations objects enter into with other objects, the attractors defining the virtual space of a substance can be activated in a variety of different ways, actualizing objects in a variety of different ways at the level of local manifestations. It is for this reason that the confusion of objects with their actualization in local manifestations always spells theoretical disaster, for in doing so we foreclose the volcanic potentials harbored in the depths of objects.[46]

But Bryant illegitimately detaches a theoretical model from its proper domain of application: whereas vector spaces wherein attractors are defined serve to model the topological properties of spatial systems for DeLanda, Bryant wants to define every object's virtual proper being as composed of singularities or attractors without thereby attributing to them spatial being. However, how things such as numbers, Popeye and parties are supposed to be formalized in terms of actualizations from vector fields to phase space is missing from the account. It is straightforward enough to claim virtual powers and actual manifestations differ; but from this it seems a long way to claim one that can successfully model a non-spatial account of objects on a procedure that maps specifically relational, homeomorphic-independent features such as continuity, neighborhood, disjunction, connection, etc. Specifically, attractors are supposed to define systemic *tendencies* in extended space without temporal variables, and so singularities are supposed to be understood as limit-points for changes within the system. Although Bryant seeks to draw ontological lessons from what is restricted in a scientific explanatory framework to account for spatial events, it is anyone's

---

[46] Bryant, *The Democracy of Objects*, 114.

guess just in what sense one could say that an object's actual manifestations are *trajectories* in the process of *approaching* their own powers. The latter make sense within the scope of morphogenetic processes and topological thinking because trajectories can be mapped onto a spatial field wherein homeomorphic transformations can take place, and thus through which spatial relations specifically are understood. But the claim that objectual powers are in excess to actual states and to all relations *without qualification* cannot be bluntly identified with the claim that there are trajectories in phase space developing in relation to attractors. Bryant claims:

> The virtual proper being of objects consists not of qualities, but of powers and these powers are never exhausted by local manifestations. In this regard, there is never a complete mapping of any phase space, but rather only ever a limited mapping of a phase space dependent on the exo-relations into which the object has been placed.[47]

With these divergences kept in mind, the continuity between the Aristotelian and Deleuzian aspects of Bryant's account in terms of the presumed isomorphy between substance/qualities binary on the one hand, and between the virtual/actual one on the other, is not secure. The idea that substances are constituted by a virtual proper being which is in turn defined in terms of vector spaces seems to be at this point merely a metaphor to reinforce the notion of withdrawal outside the stillness of the classical theory of substance, and towards a dynamic account of individuation. But becoming untethered from the spatial, virtual powers qua attractors start to sound oddly abstract, to the point where one begins to wonder whether Bryant has compromised his alleged commitment to univocity in favor of a kind of dualism. Yet it is not even clear that by accepting dualism one can nest withdrawal, thinking of the virtual as parts of objects, for the reasons mentioned above. In that regard, the idea that qualities are somehow *creatively* instantiated differentiations which can be internal

---

[47] Bryant, *The Democracy of Objects*, 121.

to the system (endo-qualities) or external to it (exo-qualities), while nevertheless "not resembling" the powers they are instantiations of, is left also unclear within this framework. At that juncture, it seems that Bryant's excess condition inexplicably shifts from an argument from *quantitative* difference to *qualitative* difference, from the numerical excess of powers over manifestations, to constitutive ontological gulf separating them beyond repair.

Having said this, and in order to continue to assess how the notion of withdrawal is supposed to work, I now focus on the intricate account Bryant provides of objectual constitution and relations, which takes up the core of chapters four and five. It is here that Bryant specifically deploys resources from autopoietic systems theory, and more specifically from the work of Maturana, Varela, and Luhmann. The point I will focus on is his account of how different objects relate to each other by *translating* that which is received from other entities in the form of *perturbations*, by transforming the latter into *information* which selects *system states*, and which result in an object manifesting a quality/having a local manifestation. The interplay between these three interrelated concepts is difficult to disentangle from the text. Bryant states from the start that what he finds most attractive from autopoietic systems theory is the notion of *operational closure* which define the autonomy of a given system or object.[48]

The two major aspects of such systems are: 1) *self-referentiality*—the outputs of every system are a product of their own internal structure; 2) *operational closure*—every system must relate to its exteriority by virtue of translating whatever perturbations it receives from other objects into information, in order to select a system state/actualize itself.[49] Taken together, both claims are strongly resonant with Bryant's withdrawal theses: an object's contingent manifestations are the result of its endogenous structure, and the manifestations that an object obtains by entering in relation with other objects are

---

[48] Bryant, *The Democracy of Objects*, 140.
[49] Ibid., 140, 146.

relative to the structural powers that it has. Having said this, we can approximate that for Bryant a perturbation is that which for any object (may) trigger a given manifestation when relating to other objects. The term *translation* is thus meant to capture that every object reacts to relational encounters in accordance with the parameters set by their internal structure, i.e. information is not transmitted between objects, but is rather what an object *produces* from the perturbations it receives from other objects.

It is important to notice that information is not yet equivalent with a local manifestation or a system state, but rather that it is that which allows an object to *select* a system state within its range of potential variations. In this regard, insofar as an object can only be susceptible to be affected by certain perturbations it can translate into information, given parameters defined by its own internal structure, there is a sense in which the environment of an object is constituted by how the latter selects system states from translated information:

> An environment is thus an environment *only* for the *interior* of an object or substance. Two consequences follow from this: First, the environment is not a *container* of substances or systems that precedes the existence of substances or systems. There is no environment "as such" existing out there in the world. Put otherwise, there is no *pre-established* or pre-given environment to which a system must "adapt."[50]

This becomes also the focus in the fifth chapter of the book for an account of why objects, despite being autonomous and generative of their environments, are not for this reason unlimited in their creative power. This is plainly because an object's capacities to interact with other objects, which Bryant calls the object's *regime of attraction*, run against the higher complexity of the environment it unifies in relation, which can perhaps be taken to be yet another dimension of the withdrawal thesis, i.e. an object's capacity to be perturbed by other objects and to perturb other objects is limited not just by its own internal structure, but by the structure of those

---

[50] Bryant, *The Democracy of Objects*, 146.

objects with which it enters in relations and which must be invariably more complex than it. So, Bryant claims:

> Just as other substances in a substance's environment can only *perturb* the substance without determining what information events will be produced on the basis of these perturbations, the most the substance can do is attempt to perturb other substances without being able to control what sort of information-events are produced in the other substances. And these attempted perturbations can always, of course, fail.[51]

Having laid our rough account of the basic features Bryant borrows from systems theory, some questions are in order. First, what is the precise ontological status of a perturbation? Are they objects, local manifestations in objects, parts of objects, or something to be understood quite differently from these distinctions? This might seem like a fastidious question, but it seems relevant for Bryant's account of relation without transmission, and of operational closure as constraining the translation into information by a virtual structure, leading to the choice of system states. Although it is clear that it is *objects* that perturb other objects, we must remember that given the withdrawal thesis it must follow that any object that perturbs another must do so in virtue of being in an actual state. However, given operational closure, it follows that one couldn't say that the perturbed object *receives* a local manifestation or a quality, since no transmission ever occurs between entities. The question then becomes one about *ourselves* as objects, in the process of providing a description of the world which we know of in practice as much as theory, if we are invariably translating our world into terms that are relative to us. That is, how are we supposed to characterize the features in other objects as being proper to the object's themselves, if there is a good sense in which every characterization is rendered relative in its determinate specificity to our own internal structure? That is, how do we know that the features we attribute to objects are in *the objects themselves* if we must accept

---

[51] Bryant, *The Democracy of Objects*, 205.

that information is relative to our own structure? How do objects can ever come to *know* of other objects, and not just *produce* knowledge through relations? The following few passages provoke this concern:

> However, here we must proceed with caution, for information is not something that *exists* out there in the environment waiting to be received or detected. Moreover, information is not something that is *exchanged* between systems. Often we think of information as something that is transmitted from a sender to a receiver. The question here becomes that of how it is possible for the receiver to decode the information received as identical to the information transmitted. However, insofar as substances are closed in the sense discussed in the last section, it follows that there can be no question of information as exchange. Rather, information is purely system-specific, exists only within a particular system or substance, and exists only *for* that system or substance. In short, there is no pre-existent information.[52]
>
> ...
>
> Perturbations are never identical to information precisely because information is object-specific, whereas the same perturbation can affect a variety of different objects while producing very different information for each object perturbed. Finally...events of information link difference to difference through a linkage of different withdrawn objects to one another. No object directly encounters another object precisely because all objects are operationally closed. As a consequence, no object is capable of representing another object or of functioning as a pure carrier of the perturbations issued from another object. This is because objects always transform or translate perturbations. Nonetheless, information links the different to the different in a substance-specific manner wherever substances relate to one another.[53]

Here we find a potentially unwarranted corollary of the withdrawal thesis: if one only is capable of relating to the world by translating unspecific perturbations into information, then there is a sense in which not only the object's virtual

---

[52] Bryant, *The Democracy of Objects*, 153.
[53] Ibid, 156.

proper being withdraws from relation, but even their local manifestations are *in themselves* intractable. In other words, it seems as if every feature we could attribute to other objects would be a function of *how we translate* an otherwise unspecified perturbation, and so that the actual states whereby we characterize object could at best be construed as a case of what the object is *for-us*. But this is to reintroduce the skeptical quandaries associated with epistemic foreclosure proper to correlationism, and which Bryant surely wants to avoid. By the same token, if Bryant wants to say that however relative the information translated by each system is endogenously specified, this does not rule out that such information allows us to infer that objects exist outside of such delimitations. Bryant in fact suggests that this much may be accomplished through experimental activity:

> Knowledge of an object does not reside in a list of qualities possessed by objects, but rather in a diagram of the powers hidden within objects. However, in order to form a diagram of an object we have to vary the exo-relations of an object to determine that of which it is capable. And here, of course, the point is that knowledge is gained not by *representing*, but...by *doing*.[54]

In the previous section I suggested that the appeals to experimentation inspired by Bhaskar did not suffice to ground ontological realism, and now we are in a position to see why the problem is configured more acutely within Bryant's ontological system. Within the onticological framework, knowledge as a practice ought to be understood in relation to an object's *regime of attraction*, i.e. in order to know an object one must vary the exo-relations into which it enters so as to tease out its potentialities which might otherwise not be manifest. But the problem is that knowledge of objects must be capable of construing the latter *qua* virtual structures in their own right and not just *as translated* into our own terms. In other words, although knowledge will necessarily be produced *on*

---

[54] Bryant, *The Democracy of Objects*, 170.

the basis of how the perturbing object becomes translated by the perturbed object's virtual proper being, the resulting state must yield knowledge *of* the object *as it is in itself* and not just as it is *for us* through our manifest knowledge-states. If one cannot do this, then all talk about mind-independent *objects* becomes suspect, and the distinction between direct knowledge (which is impossible) and indirect knowledge (which is possible) becomes unintelligible at a loss for epistemic criteria for distinguishing *what* we are relating to, and *how* it is that we relate to this same entity so that we *know* of it. However, in order to make such a distinction, Bryant must be able to show that our knowledge is related not just to a mind independent *reality*, but to *objects specifically*, and more still, to objects whose inherent potentials may be inferred as having the content we attribute to them *from* our translations. As we saw earlier, the possibility of a wholesale qualitative gap between the virtual and the actual, and not just a quantitative one, makes it exceedingly difficult to understand how an actual manifestation could ever be *of* a corresponding power. But now this ontological gulf seems redoubled by an epistemological gulf, wherein even the manifestations of the object are only accessible via a process of translation which invariably renders them relative to our endogenous capacities. An account of how these translations could ever suffice to inform us of the extraneous objects that populate the much coveted "great outdoors" is well in order.

However, this means that Bryant requires an account of how an object's operationally-closed translations and knowledge track the powers and qualities in other objects which emit perturbations, and how these can affect different objects in different ways. Thus, the *information* we translate must yield content through which one must be able to access a foreign object's endogenous structure and powers, in order to make sense of the claim that these are capacities proper to autonomous objects, and not just relative to us or our faculties. Such an account couldn't but be *representational*, by definition, and so this spells obvious problems for a theory which has abjured the valence of representational explanation altogether. Indeed, in spite of the dismissive attitude against empiricist accounts which cling to presentational givenness, the onticological argument proceeds as if the manifest content which constitutes an object's privately constituted information serves as the basis for the ulterior inference that mind-independent objects populate the world, without clarifying how it is that such states map the structural features of this world. This threatens to reactivate appeals to the experiential transparency which Bryant castigated earlier as an empiricist corollary knit to correlationism. It would thus seem that although Bryant refuses to explain how representation *works*, it nonetheless remains implicitly presupposed in his account. But it then seems that it is not so much that we *cannot* or *should* not seek to explain our relation to the world in epistemological terms, but simply that Bryant *does not* provide such an explanation. And yet, failing in the task to provide an account of how thought tracks the world by saying that such an account is untenable in principle, onticology distorts a philosophical *deficiency* to a principled philosophical *impossibility*. As a result, Bryant incurs in an instance of Dennett's so-called philosopher's fallacy: to camouflage a failure of imagination or argument by claiming that one is dealing with an impossibility for thought.

With this in mind, the two possible scenarios facing Bryant are equally at odds with the aims of his project. First, one insists in saying that nothing gets "transferred" between systems, that knowledge is system relative and that the information produced by a system is only intelligible within its own parameters, and so that knowledge is by definition knowledge of reality as it is *for us*. The same would hold for every object, presumed existent, which enters in relation to another. In this case we obtain either a version of idealism which makes system-independence utterly *unthinkable*, or a version of weak correlationism where knowledge of the real is *unknowable*, albeit thinkable. This scenario leaves it open that *if* an external world exists, then it may be the repudiated formless *apeiron*, the much coveted universe of objects, or any thinkable assortment of ontological options. Whether any notion of a "flat" ontology is tenable or not seems, on this account, a question that becomes impossible to answer in principle.

Alternatively, one admits that translated information may nevertheless index inferable features about a mind-independent reality, while insisting in that this knowledge is acquired through our own epistemic parameters, in which case we rehabilitate representation and the question of *how* we know the world in accordance to our own faculties. The question of how our own virtual structures produce this information would necessarily be methodologically propadeutic to any account purporting to describe the structure of other objects, their own proper capacities for translating information, and their regimes of attraction. This option inadvertently reactivates the necessity and methodological priority of epistemological questioning for realism about the external world, the very exigency which was allegedly disavowed in favor of the priority of ontology from the start. To claim that one can *have* knowledge of external objects without a representational account, while insisting in that operational closure constrains intelligible information to the native structure of the host-object which translates an otherwise amorphous perturbation appears, on these grounds, to want to have one's cake and eat it.

Before closing up on our discussion, a few remarks cursory should be made about the developments that Bryant pursues in the last two chapters of the book. The fifth chapter seeks to emphasize the intrication between systems and environments, so as to explain how objects can be autonomous and creative of their own openness to other objects, while not "dominating" the latter, i.e. how it is that constraints limit the development that an object goes through, and so the relations it enters into and the powers it actualizes.[55] This feeds right back into the problem we have been exploring, since by departing from Maturana and Varela's strict theory, Bryant wants to resist the claim that objects *create* other objects, while admitting of

---

[55] Bryant, *The Democracy of Objects*, 204-205.

operational closure, and so that each object's environment is relative to its own powers. As we emphasized above, this relative autonomy was accounted for in terms of the higher complexity of the environment in contrast to the organism which construes such an environment. Following Luhmann, Bryant emphasizes that an object's openness to the environment it constitutes does not have control over what happens in this environment just because it is *for* the object that such an environment is constructed. To quote again from Bryant's original account of substance:

> Just as other substances in a substance's environment can only *perturb* the substance without determining what information events will be produced on the basis of these perturbations, the most the substance can do is attempt to perturb other substances without being able to control what sort of information-events are produced in the other substances.[56]

Crucially, this seems to suggest that environments are not just the *perturbations* that objects receive from other objects, or the collection of objects with which an object may interact at a time, but rather the "space" wherein different objects can perturb one another. For it is within *an* environment that an object is said to be capable of being affected or of affecting others. Now, this seems rather strange, since it suggests that environmental openness is metaphysically prior to the actual perturbations that take place between objects. Yet Bryant insists repeatedly that environments are to be understood in terms of how an entity's regime of attraction determines its exo-relations, by sorting out what it "relevant" to it, i.e. by reacting in accordance to what its virtual powers allow it to do. The question is then simply about what it means to say that an object constructs its "openness" to the environment. In what sense can an object A, which is *not* relating to another object B, nevertheless be *within* object A's "openness" to the environment, or vice versa? In other words, in what sense

---

[56] Bryant, *The Democracy of Objects*, 205.

can the "openness" that an object exhibits include within its scope other objects which it has *not yet* entered in relation to. Since there is no information *prior* to the translation of a perturbation from another object, and since the environment constructs the openness from which environments are woven through such reactions, in what sense can things be within the reach of an object, falling short of relation? If objects have only *relations* to that which they are *selectively open* to, and this is to count as an explanation of how objects do not *ontologically* determine that which they relate to, then the notion of openness *to* other objects must not be simply reiterative an object's virtual proper being, in excess to external relations and its own manifestations:

> Of course, this openness to the environment can shift with changing events within the system such that the system becomes open to events that it was previously closed to, but the point is that at any point in time the system only maintains selective relations to its environment.[57]

In other words, if one claims that an object is open to that which its internal powers allow it to relate, then it makes no difference to say that an object is capable of doing something, and it being open to something. And yet this is to elide the distinction between what an object can do *at a given time*, and what its virtual powers delimit it to do *in general*. However, how are we to construe selective openness? Bryant suggests that this should be understood in terms of the *anticipatory* capacity of the object, at least for autopoietic systems:

> Because structures operate within the framework of system/environment distinctions, they are selectively open to their environment and can therefore evolve and develop as a result of that openness to their environment. Objects constrain the sort of events to which they're open from their environment through their distinctions or organization. In the case of autopoietic objects, this entails that structures are

---

[57] Bryant, *The Democracy of Objects*, 235.

anticipatory of what the future will bring. When events issue from the environment, information-events are produced selecting system-states within the system. This leads to the production of further events within the system, unfolding within a particular order and structured in a particular way.[58]

This claims that the selection process *precedes* the openness of the object, and that the latter is determined in part by the former. Nevertheless it remains exceedingly opaque what exactly openness is meant to entail, and how it constructs a field of potentialities which are neither those native to the object's structure, nor actual relations to other objects. My contention is that without being able to clarify exactly how selective openness is irreducible to translated information or to virtual powers, then it won't help to appeal to it in order to clarify how an object is potentially constrained by its environment. Since it is precisely the space for an interaction between autonomous entities which is in dispute and which must be accounted for, Bryant needs to tell us how it is that an object can have something like a non-relational apprehension or exclusion of other objects which does not require translation, and which therefore places the object within an environmental space which it does not dominate on its own without constituting it as internal information. As far as I can gauge, such an account is missing from the book and so it does not help resolve the major worry about how objects are capable of individuating features which map other objects through their translations, both powers and their qualities. In fact, it is not even clear how translated information can numerically map an object to a single perturbing object, given that every registered instance of information is necessarily already processed through the host-object's internal structure. Perhaps this can be assuaged with an amplified story of how relation and translation works, but I shall leave this issue for the moment.

---

[58] Ibid., 237.

Speculations III

Conclusion

When all is said and done, Bryant's first attempt to develop an ontological system remains a commendable one, bringing to the fore many crucial questions for anyone interested in the issues once associated with the brand name of "speculative realism." Our critical overview of the core theses of the book should nevertheless point towards what is a problematic attempt to resolve the correlationist quandaries that Quentin Meillassoux admirably set for Continental philosophy. Bryant's work virtuously displays stylistic lucidity and clarity, and a sincere attempt to comprehensively tackle a field muddled by debates and terminology under a guiding idea: philosophy is more than a narcissistic exercise with ourselves, and we must open for thought, once again, that "great outdoors" which has been, for long, exiled from our reach. These two guiding principles remain a part for any serious concern with realism, whether it be called Continental, epistemological, ontological, speculative, or whatever else.

Only the sustained antipathy to anti-realism can survive the polarization that has somewhat dissolved whatever valence the term "speculative realism" was meant to unify. This disintegration must be, however, indicative not of philosophical sectarianism, but of the inevitable rupture that comes with rational dissonance between positions. And if this is the case, then it becomes increasingly evident that it is not so much the antipathy to correlationism that guides us uniformly as a principle, but the *way* in which this battle is pursued that ultimately matters. For if realism deserves to be taken as a philosophical quandary, rather than a pleonasm knit to thought, as Heidegger believed, then it all turns to what the term could mean and require from us today. Or, put somewhat differently, and not without an air of bombast, the task is perhaps not just to leave the cave and shadows behind, but rather to make sure that in our zealous desire to *see* we don't rush against the force of the blinding sun, bouncing back, sightless into the dark.

Christpher Watkin, *Difficult Atheism: Post-theological thought in Badiou, Nancy and Meillassoux*
Edinburgh, Edinburgh University Press, 2011
281 pages

Assessing the French Atheistic Turn

Fabio Gironi

Cardiff University

IN UNDER A DECADE WE HAVE witnessed a proliferation of texts on "atheism," so much so that the term "New Atheism"[1] has become a widely employed label to describe the discourse of this intellectual current, and books propounding or opposing it compete on the shelves of bookstores. Mostly, unfortunately, the tone of this discourse ranges from the patronisingly sarcastic to the irresponsibly uninformed (in the case of atheism-friendly authors) and from the wisely condescending to the virulently obscurantist (in the case of religious apologists). Most commonly associated with this movement are the naturalising reductions of religion by Daniel Dennett, the militant, neo-positivist Darwinism of Richard Dawkins, the pedantically cultured work of Christopher Hitchens and the populist, mouth-foaming Islamophobia and self-righteous outbursts of Sam Harris (these four authors are often grouped together as the "Four Horsemen" of atheism) and—to quote at least one author

---

[1] One might legitimately wonder what exactly would be "new" about it. Many "new Atheists" bring less to the intellectual table (and with poorer style) than Celsus' strident *Logos Alethes* did in the 2nd or 3rd century CE (see Celsus, *On the True Doctrine: A Discourse Against the Christians*, [Oxford: OUP, 1987]).

from the other side of the intellectual barricade—the natural theology *redux* of Alister McGrath. With the exception of the best moments of Dennett's work these publications usually suffer from a deficit of philosophically informed argumentation and (even in Dennett's work) of actual engagement with the historico-theological heritage that is part and parcel of our conceptual toolbox.

This is of course a rather lengthy introduction to the fact that Watkins' book has nothing to do with this kind of literature: the object of Watkins' study is a completely different tradition of atheist thought, and the title already suggests so. Watkins' focus is the *difficult* atheism sought by three contemporary French philosophers (Alain Badiou, Jean-Luc Nancy and Quentin Meillassoux), not the relatively *easy* (which does not *necessarily* mean facile) atheism matter-of-factly presented by Dawkins and his associates. To do justice to these two different styles, it would be correct to claim that the basic methodological difference between them lies in the gap between a *naturalising*, science-first approach of the new atheists and the (eminently French) *rationalist* propensities of the protagonists of Watkins' book. Indeed, *Difficult Atheism* is best seen as part of a recent series of studies—whose unrelatedness demonstrates their timeliness—concentrating on the development of a certain constellation of approaches to atheism developed in twentieth- (and in *Difficult Atheism*'s case, twenty-first-) century French philosophy. The first (in order of publication) of these works is Martin Hägglund's *Radical Atheism: Derrida and the Time of Life* (2008), a powerful (re)reading of Jacques Derrida aimed at reclaiming (at times violently so) his philosophy from theological appropriations. Hägglund does so by interpreting Derrida's structure of the trace in the atheist key of an inescapable complication of time and space of all beings, privileging the aporetic, inescapable radical finitude of survival over the soteriological notions of infinity, immortality or eternal self-subsistence. Hägglund's work has significantly contributed towards the correction of the facile stereotype (largely diffused even in certain "speculative realist" circles) of a Derrida irremediably compromised by narrow linguistic-ethical concerns and thus dispensable for philosophers interested in the (re)construction of metaphysics, and has shown how the logic of deconstruction is a precious methodological ally (if not something of a forerunner) of post-ontotheological materialists[2] (note, however, that the radically atheist Derrida presented by Hägglund is at odds with the brief treatment Watkins gives of him).

The second important publication in this area is Stephanos Geroulanos' outstanding (yet somewhat underestimated),[3] *An Atheism that Is Not Humanist Emerges in French Thought* (2010). This text draws the genealogy of a non-humanist atheism parallel with the development of a negative philosophical anthropology and the political critique of humanism in French culture between the 1930s and the 1950s. It maps the under-examined intellectual ground that allowed in subsequent

---

[2] Admittedly, this thesis is far from uncontroversial. John Caputo, in his detailed (if somewhat repetitive) 93-page (!) long review of *Radical Atheism* (John Caputo "The Return of Anti-Religion: From Radical Atheism to Radical Theology," *Journal for Cultural and Religious Theory* 11:2 (2011): 32-125) responded to Hägglund's direct attacks by defining the book as offering an "abridged edition of Derrida" (Ibid., 33) and "a torso of deconstruction" (Ibid., 34). In the space of this brief footnote I cannot do justice to the hermeneutical nuances underlying this debate over Derrida's legacy, but it will suffice to say that what is at stake are two different understandings of deconstruction, neither of which is necessarily incorrect: Hägglund's paradigmatic Derrida is the early one, the (post-structuralist) philosopher of aporetic origins and of the *logic* of the trace as that which comes before the founding question of Being, excluding the possibility of an answer in the language of presence; Caputo's Derrida is the later one, the Kierkegaardian philosopher of the impossibility of fore-seeing the *a-venir*, of a messianism without a Messiah, of a *poetics* of *difference* casting everyone (and everything) into an inescapable, structural, "fear and trembling" in the face of the risky business of existence. If Caputo probably offers a more "complete" version of Derrida, it shouldn't be forgotten that he was instrumental in forging a certain understanding of Derrida's thought through a sustained personal interaction with Derrida himself. One could only speculate what Derrida's reaction would have been to Hägglund's book, but I suspect it would have been less hostile than Caputo's is and that it might have pushed him to take a clearer stand on issues that, in the later years of his life, simply occupied less of his philosophical engagement.

[3] Perhaps because it is too much a work of careful intellectual history for the contemporary, largely anti-historicist philosophical climate.

decades for the emergence of full-blown post-structuralist antihumanism and the announcement of the "death of Man." Geroulanos' book offers material of direct relevance for readers of this journal: his first chapter in particular delineates the conceptual traits of what he names "antifoundational realism" through an analysis of thinkers like Gaston Bachelard, Alexandre Kojève, Jean Wahl and Alexandre Koyré. Such a position, derived from a unique encounter of post-1920s (post-"quantum revolution") philosophy of science and the "imported" phenomenology of Martin Heidegger, rejects the neo-Kantian focus on the knowing subject as detached observer and replaces it with a human, finite subject. The subject is *trapped* in a world of immanence whose details are essentially foreclosed, a subject characterised by its lack of (classically interpreted) transcendence upon the world and by its *failure* to concur with a reality-in-itself that is always already a *human reality*. There is no better description of this (all-too often neglected) epoch of epistemological pessimism[4] to put some historical flesh on the bones of Meillassoux's (largely unhistorical) definition of "strong correlationism," and the book as a whole offers an excellent "preface" to Watkin's own treatment of later developments of French atheism.[5]

---

[4] Which was however, it's worth underlining, not conceived as an *antirealism*. In this regard Geroulanos' "antifoundational realism" could be analysed parallel to Lee Braver's description of the ontological modesty which underpins what he names a "transgressive epistemology" (wherein our knowledge of reality is "passively" dependent onto a reality which always partially exceeds our comprehension) in the context of a forthcoming paper on "continental realism." The figure that best links the two accounts is Emmanuel Levinas, the author of the expression that provides the title for Geroulanos' book and a central figure in Lee Braver's narration, responsible for the overturning of the focus of Husserlian phenomenology from the constitutive action of the I to the receptiveness of the subject to the object's "call" (see Braver, "A Brief History of Continental Realism," *Continental Philosophy Review*, 45(2) (2012): 261-289.

[5] Watkin indeed credits Geroulanos's book as "a fine analysis of the relation between humanism and atheism to which the present volume [*Difficult Atheism*] owes a debt" (16, n.3). Note however that the comparison with Geroulanos' narration allows us to somewhat question Watkin's association of Nancy with Badiou and Meillassoux: even when sharing a focus on im-

Fabio Gironi – *Review of* Difficult Atheism

Watkin presents his book as aimed at a survey of the contemporary move towards a thinking after God, a "post-theological thought"[6] which cannot be merely reduced to "atheism" since historical consciousness forces it to go *through* theological thought before disengaging it. This is no concession to Christianity though, since Watkin clarifies that the endgame of post-theological reflection is "to follow the death of God more rigorously than before."[7] In the introduction, Watkin presents a very useful taxonomy of two different "styles" of atheism which will be employed as a key hermeneutic device throughout the book: the first is imitative or *parasitic* atheism (the latter formulation is the most commonly employed by Watkin), a thought that preserves a theological structure replacing divine content with celebratory humanism. This is the atheism of Enlightenment humanists, divinising (at times literally) human reason, hypostatising it as a faculty metaphysically separate from "mere nature" and celebrating the intrinsic dignity of man; an intellectual stance which runs from the Comtean *religion de l'Humanité* straight to the

---

manence, what sets the latter two apart from Nancy is their strong, principled rejection of any commerce with the theme of finitude which characterised post-structuralist thought. In Badiou's case, a further particularity of the dialectical relationship of his thought with post-structuralism resides in what Ed Pluth aptly described as "Badiou's theoretical anti-humanism and practical humanism," which amounts to the splitting of subjectivity into "finite" pre-eventual individuals and "infinite" militant subjects (see Ed Pluth, *Badiou* [Cambridge: Polity, 2010], 12ff.) Watkin is of course well aware of this: I am merely suggesting that from a broader historical perspective the case can be made that Badiou's and Meillassoux's positions represent (if still in embryonic form) a different "stage" (not necessarily progressive!) in French thought. Perhaps more cogently, it could be argued that the inclusion of the "atheist practice without doctrinal atheism" presented by Françoise Laruelle would have been a very important addition to Watkin's survey of immanentist positions in the contemporary French scene, one arguably capable of offering a different avenue for the development of post-theological thought which Watkin seeks to describe (see Françoise Laruelle, *Future Christ: A Lesson in Heresy*. Trans. by Anthony Paul Smith [London and New York: Continuum, 2010]).

[6] Watkin, *Difficult Atheism*, 12.

[7] Ibid., 12.

New Atheists polemicists.[8] This does not amount to a mere borrowing of terms though, as Watkin explains that "an atheism is parasitic upon theology only when it deploys concepts that cannot be accounted for in exclusively atheistic terms but require assumptions proper to theology, whether or not those concepts happen to carry theological labels."[9] Parasitic atheism thus fails to disengage itself fully from theology, but the second tendency scarcely fares better. This second atheism is residual or *ascetic* atheism (again, Watkin seems to favour the second term), which is the post-Nietzschean stance of a world void of any transcendent guarantee, where the same disease that killed God has withered away ideas like Truth, Reason and Humanity, an atheism that finds instantiation in Blanchot and Camus (Watkin's examples) but also in the thinkers analysed by Geroulanos in his own book. Ascetic atheism is an atheism that is not humanist since "far from triumphantly acceding to God's vacated throne, Man finds himself unable to survive the divine demise."[10] The death of God is but the omen of the death of Man. However, bringing together the terminology of different authors,[11] "ascetic atheism" can at best merely ground an "antifoundational realism" as it is too metaphysically anodyne to fend off the resurgence of "fideism." In Watkin's view Derrida's emphasis on the inescapable finitude of our expectation of *a-venir* "presents us with a sophisticated version of ascetic atheism"[12] and indeed ascetic atheism's capitulation is best represented by the theological turn in French phenomenology, and the

---

[8] See for example Dennett's membership of the (somewhat infelicitously named) "international internet constituency" of the "Brights," aimed at "[promoting] the civic understanding and acknowledgment of the naturalistic worldview, which is free of supernatural and mystical elements" (see http://www.the-brights.net), as well as A.C.Grayling's recent publishing of *The Good Book: A Secular Bible* (London: Bloomsbury, 2011. Published in the US with the somewhat more acceptable title of *The Good Book: A Humanist Bible*).

[9] Watkin, *Difficult Atheism*, 3.

[10] Ibid., 6.

[11] Watkin, Geroulanos and Meillassoux, respectively.

[12] Watkin, *Difficult Atheism*, 7.

emergence of post-religious or post-secular faith in a God beyond being (from Levinas to Marion).[13] Residual atheism thus "finds itself unable to refute the turn to religion; in fact it is the very seedbed in which the turn can take root and bloom [and] under the guise of heroically repelling the religious intruder it is in fact an abject accommodation to religion's terms of engagement."[14] We can now understand the meaning of Watkin's title: what is *difficult* is to reach a consistent post-theological stance which does not unwittingly slip into the (ultimately bankrupt) positions of parasitic or ascetic atheism. Watkin has therefore chosen three "case studies"—Badiou, Nancy and Meillassoux—as three prime examples of thinkers attempting a "post-theological integration" whose goal

> is not to oppose theism but to occupy it, not to expel theism but to ingest it, taking terms and patterns of thought previously associated with theism and re-inscribing them in a way that is not to be confused either with parasitism or with asceticism.[15]

Notice however that Watkin almost immediately crushes our hopes: none of these thinkers manages to safely achieve a post-theological position. According to Watkin "neither Badiou nor Nancy unproblematically secures a position that is 'without God'" and "Meillassoux's move beyond atheism does not succeed in freeing itself from the shadow of religion"[16]—although throughout the book we can detect a slight partisanship with Nancy's positions.[17] The failure of these thinkers to actually

---

[13] As Dominic Janicaud put it in his well-known report on "The Theological Turn in French Phenomenology" (in Dominic Janicaud, *Phenomenology and the Theological Turn: The French Debate* [New York: Fordham University Press, 2001]) this turn essentially consisted in a "rupture with immanent phenomenality" and the consequent "opening to the invisible, to the Other, to a pure givenness, or to an 'archi-revelation.'" (Ibid. 17.)

[14] Watkin, *Difficult Atheism*, 11.

[15] Ibid., 14.

[16] Ibid., 15.

[17] Unsurprisingly so, considering that Watkin's previous publication, his

elaborate a successful post-theological integration, however, should not diminish the importance of the "new determination to grapple with the legacy of the death of God in a deeper way than ever before, re-making philosophy from the ground up as a thinking 'without God'"[18] at work in their writings. In contemporary French thought that of post-theological integration (as opposed to an "atheism" which would fall prey of parasitism or asceticism) is more of a research program (a *difficult* atheism) than an accomplished result.

Throughout the book, Watkin displays in-depth familiarity of the whole corpus of published work by the three French philosophers he examines, and he is well up-to-date with (and often critical of) the most significant pieces of secondary literature. The book is neatly organised, and each chapter is divided into sections dedicated to each thinker and contains a useful concluding paragraph summarising the main points which were examined.[19] The first two chapters of the book deal with the theme of the "death of God" in Badiou and Nancy. Watkin borrows the Badiouian taxonomy (from his prologue of his *Court Traite d'Ontologie Transitorie*) of a variety of "deaths": the death of the God of the philosophers

---

Phenomenology or Deconstruction?: The Question of Ontology in Maurice Merleau-Ponty, Paul Ricoeur and Jean-Luc Nancy (Edinburgh: Edinburgh University Press, 2009) (an extension of his PhD thesis) already showed a (critical) propensity towards Nancean positions and indeed had as one of its aims to render justice to the nuances of Nancy's thought ignored by a somewhat selective reception of his work in English-language literature (Ibid. 9, 137.)

[18] Watkin, *Difficult Atheism*, 240.

[19] I have only one minor editorial qualm with Watkin's decision of always quoting the original French and to insert the translation in the endnotes at the close of each chapter. My French is decent enough to manage to understand at least the general meaning of the, at times lengthy, quotes that are often encountered in the book without the need to jump to the endnotes at each occurrence, but as a general rule I'm not sure that an English-language publication should adopt this practice. Given that most of the texts quoted by Watkin are available in English translation, it seems more reasonable to me to offer an English quote in the main text, followed by a double page reference (English and French editions, as Watkin already does) and include the original French passage (a very welcome inclusion indeed!) as an endnote (or—even better—as a footnote).

(chapter one) and that of the God of the poets (chapter two), and introduces the reader to the conversation between the two (particularly through Nancy's intervention on Badiou "Philosophy Without Conditions"[20] and Badiou's *L'Offrande Reservee*) to highlight some crucial differences between their approach to post-theological thought. Chapter one thus stages "a productive encounter between Nancean finitude and Badiouian infinitude"[21] by counterposing Badiou's axiomatic, dichotomising "Platonism of the multiple" to Nancy's "deconstruction of Christianity": whereas for Badiou a true detheologised thought can only be the one which originarily posits an infinite inconsistent multiplicity, axiomatically rejecting the infinite/One of God (and foreclosing any reintroduction of the One, including Nancy's finitude), Nancy stresses the necessity of recognising the historicity of metaphysics and its impure genesis and thus indicates a latent parasitism in Badiou's commitment to a singular break of mathematism from mytho-poetic thought. However, Watkin concludes, "neither of these positions can, in the final account,...banish the ghost of parasitism."[22]

Chapter two proceeds by explicating the rejection of the "God of the poets" and romanticist aesthetics through Badiou's and Nancy's reading of the Hegelian difference between "bad" (interminable repetition of finite instances) and "good" (actual) infinity: agreeing in the rejection of the negative finitude characterising bad infinity, Badiou opts for a positive (mathematically detheologised) infinity, while Nancy for a positive finitude, a finitude that opens unto infinite without falling into theological thought. The contrast drawn here is once again that between an immanent, rational infinity without theological reminders and a work-in-progress, "yet-without" infinity of the finite.

---

[20] In Peter Hallward, *Think Again: Alain Badiou and the Future of Philosophy* (London: Continuum, 2004).

[21] Watkin, *Difficult Atheism*, 23.

[22] Ibid., 47.

Chapter three brings Badiou and Nancy together by examining the key methodological articulations of their post-theological thought: Badiou's deployment of axioms and Nancy's movement of dis-enclosure and spacing. This is a crucial chapter of the book which resists a quick summary: most interestingly (in my view) Watkin here defends Badiou's employment of mathematical (set-theoretical) axioms against a range of accusations highlighting the "arbitrary" character of this choice, by highlighting how in Badiou's own understanding the founding (existential) axioms of set theory respond to "a certain historical necessity,"[23] an historical injunction to come to ontological terms with modernity's (along with Koyré's well-known thesis)[24] rejection of a finite, enchanted cosmos and the adoption of a secularised infinity. Watkin is quite right here in observing that Badiou's axioms are neither inevitable (responding to a strict, quasi-Hegelian necessary stage of philosophical development) nor arbitrary (a mere unjustifiable fetishism for matehmatisation), but are strictly *undecidable*, an undecidability necessarily collapsed by the very axiomatic decision which decides them. This leads to one of the most interesting problems raised by this book: what Watkin calls Badiou's "axiology of the Good."[25] Badiou's philosophical choice of axiomatic thought cannot be justified by either an eternal necessity or as belonging to a contingent, and transitory, historical moment: Watkin therefore argues that "Badiou's axioms are worthy (*axios*) because they promote the implicit Good in Badiou's philosophy."[26] Watkin argues that this normative commitment is at work since the founding gesture of Badiou's thought, and that "the Good for Badiou can be construed as atheism itself."[27] As in Lucretius' (and the

---

[23] Watkin, *Difficult Atheism*, 103.

[24] See Alexandre Koyré, *From the Closed world to the Infinite Universe* (Baltimore: The John Hopkins Press, 1957).

[25] Watkin, *Difficult Atheism*, 107.

[26] Ibid., 107.

[27] Ibid., 109.

Epicurus of the *Letter to Herodotus*) case, an ethico-existential concern precedes and orientates ontological commitments, and Badiou's choice of an axiomatic method is meant "to be worthy of the secularised, generic, universal notion of being that propels his thought,"[28] buttressing a materialist and immanentist worldview. Watkin calls this an ultimately "therapeutic moment in Badiou's axiomatisation"[29]: the Good is to set oneself free from the tyranny of the One (in all its—always "parasitic"—forms), through adherence to the purely rational, mathematical, edifice built on a founding decision which axiomatically rejects the existence of any such One in favour of the primacy of multiplicity. This, however, introduces an element of circularity in Badiou's atheism since "secularisation itself becomes the promise which decides the axioms of his mathematised universe in the first place"[30] and thus demonstrates, for Watkin, that Badiou's atheism "must inevitably fall either into parasitism or into asceticism, an atheism that, like all great philosophies, is inaccessible to itself, and in that admission finally becomes consistent, as it makes room for fidelity to ontological *ataraxia*."[31] Once again, the chapter—which also examines Nancy's faith as a *supplement* for reason and his rejection of the theism/atheism dichotomy in his "atheology"—closes with the diagnosis that both thinkers "come up short of a post-theological integration."[32]

Chapter four discontinues the parallel analysis of Badiou and Nancy by introducing the thought of Quentin Meillassoux and his rejection of the dichotomy of theism and atheism in favour of "philosophy." *Difficult Atheism* thus holds the record (if only by a few months) of being the first English-language publication which examines the entirety of Meillassoux's published works to date. And not only the published ones: Watkin refers to (and quotes extensively from) Meilassoux's unpublished doctoral thesis *De L'Inexistence Divine*. Watkin

---

[28] Watkin, *Difficult Atheism*, 109.

[29] Ibid., 109.

[30] Ibid., 123.

[31] Ibid., 123.

[32] Ibid., 123.

does an excellent job in unpacking for the reader the nuances of both Meillassoux's argument for a rational belief in a non-existent (or inexistent) God, and his defense of the "principle of factiality" offering critical commentary of central nodes of this thought (often employing a Nancean deconstructive line). Once again, I want to focus here on some of the most interesting (especially for readers of this journal) of these points of critique. Repeating the structure of his commentary to Badiou, Watkin defends Meillassoux's hyperchaos from accusations of crypto-theological miraculousness but the goes on to argue that "hyperchaos is the undoing of the principle of factiality, and the exposure of Meillassoux's philosophy as parasitic after all,"[33] by offering arguments against factuality and Meillassoux's defense of the absoluteness of the law of non-contradiction and uncovering other binary oppositions which undermine Meillassoux's short-circuiting of atheism and theism. Watkin's main strategy is to draw the consequences of hyperchaos itself, a notion whose radicality Meillassoux "underestimates."[34] In what he calls the "split rationality critique" he argues that Meillassoux's

> own thinking must be up for grabs in the contingency of logical laws. In other words, the processes by which he arrives at the notions of "necessity," "contingency" and "factiality" must themselves be able to be replaced by other, currently unimaginable, ways of thinking.[35]

And that therefore

> [t]he very decision as to what may or may not be "rationally legitimate" must not be unaccountably exempted from a possible future contingent rationality that in the present remains radically unforeseeable, on pain once more of fideism in the enduring necessity of rationality *as it is currently understood and practised*.[36]

---

[33] Watkin, *Difficult Atheism*, 150.

[34] Ibid., 153.

[35] Ibid., 150.

[36] Ibid., 151.

Once we recognize the utter unpredictability of the changes brought about by a hyperchaotic shift, nothing is safe from modification, including the very notion of hyperchaos. Further, Watkin deconstructs the crucial Meillassouxian binaries of necessity/contingency and thinkability/unthinkability, possibility/impossibility by arguing that a consistent application of hyperchaos would explode such binaries themselves: no conceptual distinctions can survive hyperchaotic change, and no absoluteness could be predicated in their absence. Therefore, this short-circuiting of logical distinctions makes it impossible to say anything meaningful about hyperchaos:

> The concepts of possibility and impossibility do not begin to account for hyperchaos... The least we can say about hyperchaos (which is also all we can say, and in truth nothing at all) is that it will have been incommensurable with the concepts of possibility and impossibility... and incommensurability.[37]

Watkin pushes his critique even further: not only the logical conceptual apparatus could be collapsed or modified beyond commensurability in the aftermath of hyperchaotic change, but our very ability of recognising or acknowledging this change would be undermined by it, unless our cognitive faculties would be somehow untouchable. His conclusion is that Meillassoux

> has two options: if he affirms that our understanding and the laws of logic cannot have changed in this way, he is making an idol of one, or the other, or both; if he is more circumspectly reckoning that they will not have changed, then he is supplementing his principle of factiality with a faith that, like Nancy's faith, irreducibly makes reason what it is. Meillassoux's factiality is either an idol, or an article of faith. What it cannot be is neither.[38]

Watkins singles out the unjustifiable, pre-philosophical

---

[37] Watkin, *Difficult Atheism*, 153.
[38] Ibid., 155.

decision of rationalism at play in Meillassoux's work and in particular in his insistence on the anhypothetical nature of facticity, a principle given exclusively through demonstrative discourse, a decision which corresponds to an unexplained and "unaccountable act of faith": Meillassoux's arguments repeatedly "[beg] the question of rationality"[39] and this transpires clearly in his unsupported appeal to intellectual intuition. In other words, Meillassoux rejects the ontological validity of the principle of sufficient reason, but preserves its epistemic role: there must be a reason justifying the beliefs we do hold, and that is the immutable deductive power of rationality itself operating according to (immutable) laws of logic. Watkin thus concludes that even Meillassoux does not manage to go beyond a/theism since his own thought ends up either idolising reason (as being "untouchable" by hyperchaos) or postulating it as an article of "reasonable faith"[40] (needing a Nancean supplement of faith to be what it is) hence being guilty, by his own lights, of the very fideism he so vehemently denounces.[41]

The concluding couple of chapters seek to draw ethico-political implications (sketching the relation between the metaphysical and the normative register) of the three forms of post-theological thinking defended by Badiou, Nancy and Meillassoux: chapter five *vis-à-vis* the ethical and political projects as a whole and chapter six examining more specifically the question of Justice. In the former Watkin neatly summarizes Meillasssoux's ethical pronouncements from

---

[39] Watkin, *Difficult Atheism*, 161.

[40] Ibid., 157.

[41] This line of critique is very close to Alberto Toscano's critique of Meillassoux's reintroduction of idealism within his purportedly materialist philosophy. Like Watkin's observation that Meilassoux inconsistently hedges an idolised reason from hyperchaos, Toscano writes that "[i]n trying to maintain the speculative sovereignty of philosophical reason, albeit advocating a principle of unreason and breaking correlationist self-sufficiency, Meillassoux can be seen to reintroduce idealism at the level of form at the same time as he valiantly seeks to defeat it at the level of content." Toscano in Levi Bryant, Nick Srniceck and Graham Harman (eds.), *The Speculative Turn: Continental Materialism and Realism* (Melbourne: re.press, 2011), 91.

L'Inexistence Divine, Nancy's rejection of the (derivative) distinction between ontology and ethics in his concept of archi-originary *ethos,* and Badiou's reconfiguration of ethics outside the Kant vs. Levinas dichotomy of autonomy vs. heteronomy. In the latter, Watkin pursues head-on the question of "whether post-theological integrations can secure a notion of universal justice"[42] including a comparison of Badiou's "Idea of communism" and Nancy's "ontological communism." Worthy of particular notice, in the context of Watkin's description of Meillassoux's advent of a "fourth World of Justice" and the "baroque"[43] evocation of a prophet of contingency (the Child of Man), is his critique of Meillassoux's narrow understanding of justice, restrictively presented in terms of future redemption of past wrongs via the rebirth of bodies. Watkin draws the rather unobjectionable conclusion that "Meillassoux's philosophy has everything in common with religion in general (and, most often, with Christianity in particular) apart from belief in an actually existing God."[44] More provocatively, and in line with his "radicalization of hyperchaos" strategy of critique in the fourth chapter, Watkin presents Meillassoux with an unresolved issue: "[o]n Meillassoux's account, why not hope that the problem of evil will be solved by a change in my understanding of what is just, rather than by a rebirth of humanity?"[45] I find it hard to disagree with Watkin's skepticism regarding the persuasiveness of Meillassoux's ethico-political speculations. Concluding the chapter, Watkin argues that "[t]he notion of universal justice for each of our three thinkers encounters the problem of a latent or unexplained conflation of goodness and equality, or goodness and justice"[46] and this links to a central, if subterranean theme which recurs throughout the book, approached by Watkin more explicitly in the conclusion: the "question

---

[42] Watkin, *Difficult Atheism,* 206.

[43] Ibid., 231.

[44] Ibid., 210.

[45] Ibid., 213.

[46] Ibid., 233

of fundamental philosophical orientation."[47] Watkin argues that even in their common struggle towards a post-theological thought each of the three philosophers in question adopts a different strategy dependent upon a pre-systematic decision of one or another philosophical orientation, a deep methodological conviction serving as fulcrum for their thought: Badiou's preference for (axiomatic) decision, Nancy's for (deconstructive) dis-enclosure and Meillassoux's for (anhypothetical) demonstration. The Badiouian here could perhaps reply: doesn't this admission implicitly favour Badiou's own explicit reliance on a primordial decision? Isn't it the case that to call Badiou's fundamental orientation a decision in favour of decision is a redundant restatement of his founding gesture? And isn't the *aporia* of justifying the content of one's conception of ethical good best resolved by an *imperative* (in the form of "let there be X"), yet not *sovereign* (without the mastery endowed by an eternal necessity, free of *raison d'être*, an-archic), axiomatic decision?

Finally, Watkin diagnoses again the current situation in French thought, summarising his argument as holding that "a consensus has emerged around a desire to move beyond both parasitism and asceticism to a post-theological integration that cuts the theological root of parasitism without renouncing its fruit."[48] As we have already seen however, and as Watkin has repeated throughout the book, no such post-theological integration has been consistently achieved: every atheism seems to slide back into the traps of parasitism or asceticism. In a way, *Difficult Atheism* is the meticulous chronicle of such a failure (Watkin's argument-counterargument structure in presenting the positions of the three French philosophers is thorough and unforgiving) and it might therefore leave the reader with the impression that no *positive* thesis of enduring value was offered throughout the book. It might be however unfair to ask Watkin to singlehandedly provide the successful formula of post-theological thought in this context:

---

[47] Watkin, *Difficult Atheism*, 241.
[48] Ibid., 239.

Fabio Gironi – *Review of* Difficult Atheism

Difficult Atheism is explicitly an exegetical work and a piece of intellectual history of the present, not a theoretical work in its own right. The most resounding message of Watkin's book is that "we can no longer use the term 'atheism'" since

> [i]f we are to avoid a reductive approach to the current re-assessment of the West's theological legacy we will henceforth need to circumscribe the term "atheism" itself much more tightly and see it as but one possible response to the legacy of the death of God.[49]

Watkin's caution is well justified, and his warning against a reductive dismissal of the problem of genuinely post-theological thought is extremely opportune: the dangers of unwittingly sliding into the safety of crypto-theological metaphysics or of replacing God with any allegedly "secular" transcendental signified are to be always guarded from. However, it could be argued that at times he sets the bar for achieving a "real" post-theological thought too high, and that in his account it is all too easy to fall into an either parasitic or ascetic mode of thought. This could in turn be a weapon in the hands of the theologically-minded interpreter: the one between difficult atheism and impossible atheism risks being too thin a line. In today's intellectual climate, there is a distinct urgency to defend a historicist, revisable, self-critical, plastic and yet resilient and substantial atheist stance against those various forms of irrationalism and antirationalism which have been sparring partners of rationalist intellectuals (at least) since what Isaiah Berlin famously termed the reactionary Counter-Enlightenment.[50] I can only tentatively gesture towards an alternative route here: agreeing with Watkin that we should avoid to settle our thought into either the parasitic or the ascetic permutations of atheism, I would propose that the solution is not to sail through an almost impossible strait between them, but on the contrary to dialectically embrace

---

[49] Watkin, Difficult Atheism, 241.

[50] See Isaiah Berlin, *Against the Current: Essays in the History of Ideas*, (New York: Viking Press, 1979)

both at the same time. In more intelligible terms, I think this would entail a commitment to a form of rational naturalism (or naturalised rationalism) capable of defending the knowledge-producing power of human rationality while destroying the idol of a transcendent Reason with a naturalist hammer—thus combining ("parasitic") Enlightenment values with a ("ascetic") post-Darwinian and post-structuralist demotion of (hu)Man.

Having said that, I believe that *Difficult Atheism* will be a precious contribution to the contemporary discussion regarding "atheism" (inverted commas are now of order) precisely by stimulating a more nuanced understanding of this term, and that many of its insightful critiques on particular aspects of the thought of the three French thinkers will need to be taken in consideration as serious challenges[51] by all those interested in pursuing a secular thought impermeable to re-appropriation by post-modern or post-secular theologians.

---

[51] As I already noted above, I believe that Watkin's objections to Meillassoux's theses regarding our rational knowledge of hyperchaos and the possibility of justice are distinctly penetrating. Meillassoux's daring—and still developing—philosophical approach has provoked the coalescing and development of a large philosophical community loosely bound by "realist" concerns, but as the feeling of novelty wanes, and the entry points for a critique of his theses multiply, it is time for him to offer sound defenses to some of these critiques, and Watkin's should be seen among the most pressing ones.

Andy Merrifield, *Magical Marxism: Subversive Politics and the Imagination*
London: Pluto Press, 2011
240 pages

Fight and Flight
Merrifield's Magical Convulsions

Dave Mesing

Villanova University

"TOGETHER, WE MIGHT BE ABLE to do dangerous subversive things, mischievous things."[1] Such is Andy Merrifield's opening promise in his recent book *Magical Marxism: Subversive Politics and the Imagination*. Merrifield situates the work between two poles of people: those who are more or less orthodox Marxists and those who are Marxists but don't know it. Thus, despite the fact that Merrifield toys with central Marxist tenets, he avoids any notion of third-way rhetoric; Merrifield's arguments are unapologetically Marxist, and his attempt to shake the tradition from within requires some working knowledge of Marx's texts. This is not because Merrifield's arguments are obscure. On the contrary, he is to be commended for how deftly he has condensed a wide range of difficult source material. *Magical Marxism* is a joy for the reader, and Merrifield's broad attempt to inject some affirmation into the critical negativity of Marxism is reflected in his prose.

The book requires a slight familiarity with the tradition

---

[1] Andy Merrifield, *Magical Marxism: Subversive Politics and the Imagination* (London: Pluto Press, 2011), xii.

because Merrifield's proposal of a "magical" Marxism is speculative. However, the point of the book is to help further social and political change, and thus Merrifield does not so much assume that all of his readers will be familiar with Marxism as that they will agree with it. As he puts it in the introduction, "Many young people have no difficulty grasping why workers get ripped off and how capital accumulates in the hands of the wealthy. They know capitalism rarely lives up to it promises, to its supposed potential."[2] To such people, Merrifield hopes to introduce a new politics with "a touch of the magical, that brews up some new radical moonshine, a new potion for stirring up our critical concepts, for making us practically intoxicated, that dreams the unimaginable, that goes beyond merely what is, beyond all accepted rules and logic, a politics that plays by its own rules, rules that have little to do with rationality or economic reason."[3] To unfold this politics, Merrifield relies on Gabriel García Márquez, and in particular, his novel *One Hundred Years of Solitude*. In the book, one of the characters says that he does not understand the point of a political contest in which both parties agree on the rules. For Merrifield, moderation or capitulation to the current rules of the game—political representation, for starters—means losing before the battle even gets going.

It is on the basis of this proclamation that Merrifield begins to articulate his new politics. The new rules are tinged with a poetic spirit, and although Merrifield writes that Magical Marxism is "about irrationality [and] not rationality,"[4] he does not veer into irrationalism, although it's plain to the reader that he enjoys dancing near the cliff. Instead, taking his point of departure from Debord's society of the spectacle and framing his discussion around Henri Lefebvre's conception of the everyday, Merrifield argues that "Magical Marxism means creating another fantasy in light of the ruling fantasy; its critical power doesn't come from criticism

---

[2] Merrifield, *Magical Marxism*, 3.

[3] Ibid., 9.

[4] Ibid., 18.

but from an ability to disrupt and reinvent, to create desire and inspire hope."[5]

Following magical realists such as Marquez, Merrifield takes the existing world as the substance for the illusions that he attempts to conjure up. He compares the additional four decades of life in the society of the spectacle after its naming by Debord to the insomnia plague in Macondo, the village of *One Hundred Years of Solitude*. In the story, the expert insomniac is one who forgets the act of dreaming altogether. The point here is that the blurring of reality and illusion in the society of the spectacle sets a different agenda for Marxism. Merrifield notes that Márquez also incorporates the specific, historical reality of a massacre of banana company workers in Cienaga, Columbia in 1928 into *One Hundred Years of Solitude*. According to Merrifield, no one knows exactly how many people were killed, and what the insomnia plague and Marquez's version of the banana workers massacre demonstrate is "how the reality of historical truth and the reality of (possible) subjective illusion *become one and the same*. There is no *real* way to tell either apart."[6] For this reason, Merrifield asks whether it's necessary or desirable for Marxism to play the role of unmasking illusions to get at the real truth. With Debord, Merrifield finds that a Marxism that seeks to dispel illusions "moves in exactly the opposite direction to radical politics."[7] It is retrospective, and Merrifield argues that radical politics must be carried out along a different continuum, "imagining something in the present tense while struggling to realize it in the future, prospectively."[8] Much of the book is wrought with this tension between the theoretician who looks to the past with analysis and the Magical Marxist who looks forward to the dawn.

To this end, Merrifield introduces an extended discussion of automatist and communist activism in Chapter 2, "Subscribing

---

[5] Merrifield, *Magical Marxism*, 18.

[6] Ibid., 35.

[7] Ibid., 37

[8] Ibid., 37.

to the Imaginary Party: Notes on a Politics of Neo-communism." Merrifield discusses the events surrounding the publication of The Invisible Committee's *The Coming Insurrection*, which in addition to *Society of the Spectacle* and *One Hundred Years of Solitude*, serves as a major touchstone for the remainder of the book. Merrifield's central point in this chapter is that direct-action anarchism is more than simply a fellow traveller with classical Marxism, but rather that an alliance is necessary in order to become Magical Marxists. This activism is "grounded in everyday life rather than the workplace,"[9] and Merrifield invokes André Gorz's *Farewell to the Working Class* in order to suggest that the old argument about the dictatorship of the proletariat is moot. "Consequently, anarchists and Marxists have no real reel beef with one another, seemingly concurring with what Henri Lefebvre told us long ago: that there's essentially no distinction between anarchism and Marxism, at least no significant difference that precludes one from practically identifying with the other."[10] As such, Merrifield boldly proposes that a unified non-class can still carry out a kind of class struggle, even in the absence of the proletariat. With the possibility of subversion beyond the workplace, society itself becomes the site of liberation, and Merrifield affirms a politics of friendship which he claims will add muscle to an affective politics that is causal for social formations. "Affinity becomes the cement that bonds people across frontiers and barriers. In desiring another reality, inventing it, dreaming it up, people find their kindred souls, perhaps nearby, perhaps faraway; and in finding one another they struggle together for the realization of their common hopes."[11] The relationship between affect and politics is something that seems to be subterranean throughout the text, and I often wished for a more explicit treatment of this theme by Merrifield.

In the next chapter, Merrfield expands somewhat on these themes by introducing *mística*, a concept that comes from the

---

[9] Merrifield, *Magical Marxism*, 51.

[10] Ibid., 62.

[11] Ibid., 64.

Landless Rural Workers' Movement in Brazil. He compares this to the Spanish poet Frederico García Lorca's notion of *duende*; both exhibit "a militant poetic and a poetics of militancy that makes things possible even when they're impossible, even when you think that all is lost, that everybody is dead and buried."[12] These concepts are both important, rooted in particular struggles, and serve as concrete examples of the type of politics that Merrifield aims to gather under his banner of Magical Marxism. While this discussion could benefit from a more systematic account of affect, the remainder of this chapter nicely begins to tie the book together. Merrifield's reliance on Lefebvre becomes strongest at this point, and his treatment of spontaneity is one of the highlights of the book. He argues that the spontaneous or unpredictable is essential for radical politics; without it, there is no movement. However, he also admits that not all eruptions of spontaneous political passion are progressive, pointing to several examples, including Margaret Thatcher's "bedside read,"[13] Friedrich von Hayek. Merrifield takes a tempered approach, claiming that the drive to reject spontaneity outright is dogmatic, but to take it as an ontological principle or foundation is equally dangerous and capable of degenerating into violence for the sake of violence or "impulsive nihilism."[14] Merrifield advocates a hacker ethic approach to Marxism because "Marxism has the software as well as the hardware needed to engineer new forms of cooperation and solidarity, new forms of spontaneous activism and self-management spanning the world."[15] This comparison with the Free Software movement may well serve as an apt metaphor for Merrifield's entire approach in *Magical Marxism*, and the book continually sways between some conceptual development or explication of high theory and carrion calls for new forms of affirmative engagements between Marxism and various forms of activism. The ex-

---

[12] Merrifield, *Magical Marxism*, 79.

[13] Ibid., 85.

[14] Ibid., 87.

[15] Ibid., 101.

amples that he gives often illustrate that these engagements are already or nearly underway, and with the recent uprisings around the world in 2011, I assume that an updated version of the book that takes these movements into account would be well worth reading. This is perhaps a strange way to praise a book published so recently, and also a moment to recognize that Merrifield would rather have his readers continue to form new alliances and networks of subversion with these movements than wait for his analysis of them.

In the remaining chapters, Merrifield continues to spin out various examples and urgings for a more positive Marxism. The fifth chapter, "Macondos of the Mind: Imagination Seizes Power," opens with the suggestion that one of the characters in *One Hundred Years of Solitude* can be understood to have hedged his bets entirely on "speculative realism,"[16] which he footnotes with some favorable comments. Merrifield is clearly familiar and enthusiastic with the debates surrounding speculative realism, and notes that "the ontological terrain... is a lot more open, a lot more floating than has hitherto been credited,"[17] even though he clearly favors a more mystical and humanist realism than many speculative realist authors. In this chapter, Merrifield also clarifies precisely what he means by imagination, taken from Sartre as "a consciousness for-itself expressing itself in all its liberty."[18] With this, he also follows Sartre's distinction and slippage between a real future and an imagined future. Merrifield then turns to an extensive discussion of the *Grundrisse*, which helps bring together earlier mentions of figures such as Gorz. The imagination has a task of "the most damned seriousness."[19] Arguing that the subsumption of living labor to machines has reduced the time of necessary labor, Merrifield puts a positive spin on an otherwise dismal present wherein plundering of the commons has taken place through increased capital accumulation. The

---

[16] Merrifield, *Magical Marxism*, 139.

[17] Ibid., 209.

[18] Ibid., 145.

[19] Ibid., 152.

fact that many are working less or part-time becomes a fact to be embraced, and time becomes perhaps the most precious asset for the Magical Marxist. Merrifield is not glib about the potential here, as he knows that the situation of precarious work and an ever-widening gap between the rich and poor of the world is not simply a fact to be celebrated and overcome by opting out of work. Instead, the most damn serious task of the imagination becomes a responsibility to align and fight; "this responsibility is and has to be a world away from bourgeoius/neo-liberal ideas about personal responsibility, about being responsible for the exploitation somebody else inflicts upon us. Communist responsibility, by contrast, means being responsible for self-assertion not for self-condemnation."[20]

With *Magical Marxism* then, Merrifield deliberately reaches in utopian directions in order to spur on a new politics. While he reminds us that to banish negativity altogether is to do away with Marxism itself,[21] his overwhelming posture is affirmative, leaning more on figures such as Bloch or Hardt and Negri than Adorno or Marx himself. For all this positivity, however, Merrifield maintains a dialectical balancing act throughout the book, and thus even when he begins to criticize various figures or concepts within Marxism, he does so in order to push them in a direction that he hopes will be more politically subversive. For this reason, *Magical Marxism* is an important and helpful text as we move towards new stages of the Occupy movements, among other unknown spontaneous forms of passionate activism. Merrifield argues that "subversion is the *condition* of human beings in their quest for liberty,"[22] and with this in mind, I offer only one critique of the book, hopefully in the spirit of a Magical Marxist tarrying with the positive.

I have alluded to a desire for a more thorough framework to deal with issues of affect and politics, and this is because I think that a politics that reaches out to the utopian too strongly runs the risk of being co-opted. I agree that to banish

---

[20] Merrifield, *Magical Marxism*, 156.

[21] Ibid., 183.

[22] Ibid., 199.

the utopian, the magical, the absurd, and the affirmative from a radical politics will render it stale and able it to be easily swept under the rug where other people looking backwards with the right analysis are found, out of sight and unable to effectively bring about a decisive change to the status quo. If we are to make an analogy with affect and reason, then the point is that we can never escape the world of the affects. As Magical Marxists, we can never escape the hope for a better society. Even Adorno, a Marxist who is so negative that Merrifield understandably doesn't even mention him, writes at the end of *Minima Moralia* that "the only philosophy which can be responsibly practiced in the face of despair is the attempt to contemplate all things as they would be from the standpoint of redemption."[23] Our collective utopian desire to live in an emancipated time is already underway, but in order to further it, we need more than a politics of hope: we need a politics of joyful and hopeful reasoning. Spinoza handles this relationship between affect and reason expertly in the *Ethics*, because he understood that to banish affects only serves hierarchical power and does nothing for the advancement of our happiness. For this reason, Spinoza brings together the joyful desire to affirm our own striving with reason as our most powerful tool, giving us the material for an affective reasoning to enact our collective emancipation, wherein we operate at the highest pitch of human freedom.[24]

---

[23] Theodor W. Adorno, *Minima Moralia: Reflections on a Damaged Life*, (London: Verso Books 2005), 247.

[24] Baruch Spinoza, *Political Treatise* trans. Samuel Shirley (Indianapolis: Hackett Publishing Company, 2000), 41.

Graham Harman, *Circus Philosophicus*
Winchester, UK: Zero Books, 2010.
83 pages

Maxwell Kennel

University of Waterloo

AFTER FOUR VIVID PAGES SPENT describing "the myth of the ferris wheel" Graham Harman sets into what some have called the most accessible introduction to Object Oriented Ontology to date. At around 25,000 words in length *Circus Philosophicus* reads nicely in one extended sitting, and very readily yields rewards to both the specialist and non-specialist reader. Situated within Harman's expanding oeuvre *Circus Philosophicus* is not readily comparable with any of his other work work, with the possible exception of the forthcoming *Treatise on Objects* (Open Humanities Press), which Harman describes as having a similar sort of prose.[1] The incomparable genre of *Circus Philosophicus* seems to have been the goal from the beginning, a fact made evident by the rear cover blurb which describes the goal to "restore myth to its central place in the discipline." The following review will give a brief summary of the first half of *Circus Philosophicus* highlighting some pertinent details, while offering some closing comments on the interesting placement

---

[1] Graham Harman, "Treatise on Objects," *Object Oriented Philosophy*, http://doctorzamalek2.wordpress.com/2010/12/10/treatise-on-objects/ (accessed January 6, 2011).

of the work within both the genre and the discourse of Object Oriented Ontology.

From the first sentences of Chapter One, Harman quickly does away with the robotic or obscurantist tones that too often proliferate in contemporary philosophical writing. Instead he offers a narrative exposition of his philosophy in a genre somewhere between travel literature and the more accessible end of traditional philosophical prose. The work includes references to both real and fictional events, ranging from Harman's 2008 trip to Chennai described in Chapter Three, to the imaginary myth of a haunted boat in Chapter Five.[2] It is not surprising, given the latitude taken in both the stories and philosophical exposition that Harman calls it "the most satisfying piece of writing I've ever done."[3]

As mentioned above, the work begins with the myth of the ferris wheel which provides the reader with a vivid image of the object relations that so define the system of Object Oriented Ontology. Harman also describes the mythic wheel in terms of "the dramatic interplay of object and network,"[4] defined by events, contexts, and relations.[5] He begins his argument by refuting the framework of the classical division between substance and aggregate, thereby opening the field for a wider definition of objects varying from "steel workers" to "celebration" in keeping with the curious example on page five. The refutation of the substance aggregate distinction is then pursued by dismissing the "familiar criterion of durability"[6] in discerning "what is real and what is accidental."[7] Soon after,

---

[2] Graham Harman, "A relevant Circus Philosophicus excerpt," *Object Oriented Philosophy*, http://doctorzamalek2.wordpress.com/2010/07/23/a-relevant-circus-philosophicus-excerpt/ (accessed January 6, 2011)

[3] Graham Harman, "Circus Philosophicus being printed," *Object Oriented Philosophy*, http://doctorzamalek2.wordpress.com/2010/10/18/circus-philosophicus-being-printed/ (accessed January 6, 2011)

[4] Graham Harman, *Circus Philosophicus* (Winchester, UK: Zero Books, 2010), 4.

[5] Ibid., 5.

[6] Ibid., 5.

[7] Ibid, 6.

the ghost of Meillassoux's "arche-fossil"[8] can be seen looming in the background as human observers are removed from the myth of the ferris wheel in a sweeping illustrative gesture.[9]

After concluding the myth of the ferris wheel Harman transitions from the third person to the first person and confesses that the myth is in fact an apologetic for the object-centric positions of Alfred North Whitehead and Bruno Latour.[10] This myth in defense of Whitehead and Latour's model of object relations quickly turns to a description of its limitations, including a nod to Latour in Harman's claim that no object is "reducible to the events in which it participates."[11]

The episodic narrative picks up again at the beginning of Chapter 2, entitled "The Bridge," with a description of Harman's years as a student in Annapolis. One can only speculate about the factual status of the narrator's described engagement to the character "Olympia, the multilingual heiress to an ancient pharmaceutical fortune."[12] The lengthy dialogue between the narrator and Olympia proceeds to invoke names from Heraclitus through Dante to Simondon, and the chapter sadly resolves with the termination of the engagement.

Harman then moves the small quasi-autobiography to a discussion on, of all things, calliopes. Powered by steam, or more recently compressed air, the calliope is a large musical instrument consisting of a multitude of whistles (making music which can reportedly be heard for miles). This is followed by mention of Harman's 2007-2008 sabbatical leave from the American University in Cairo, part of which was spent in Amsterdam, and another part in India. After voicing his rejection of Thomas Metzinger's reductionist materialism outlined in Metzinger's book *Being No One*, Harman offers his thoughts on Leibniz's *Monadology*. In light of the

---

[8] See Chapter 1 of Quentin Meillassoux, *After Finitude*, trans. Ray Brassier (London & New York: Continuum, 2008).

[9] Harman, *Circus Philosophicus*, 6-7.

[10] Harman, *Circus Philosophicus*, 7.

[11] Ibid., 8.

[12] Ibid., 14.

idea that "the monad (simple substance) is never separated from its body (composite substance)."[13] Harman criticizes the unity and simplicity of Leibniz's concept of the monad stating that there is a "false distinction between ultimate, simple substances and complex, derivative aggregates."[14] The calliope is then implicated as an example of Edmund Husserl's idea that we first encounter the object as a whole, rather than encountering the individual qualities and linking "them together through the gullible myth of an underlying thing."[15] After some further exposition on the calliopic nature of objects Harman connects this view of irreducible objects to the myth of the ferris wheel through the image of "a series of interlocking calliopes, each emitting music into the local sky above it, and thereby combining with others to yield larger machines."[16]

So concludes the limited summary that this review will provide, for to give away much more would be unfair to future readers. What can be said safely is that the three chapters that constitute the second half of the work include a conversation with the science fiction novelist China Miéville on an offshore drilling rig (coincidentally the name of Chapter Four), Husserl's ideas presented alongside an oriental myth in "The Haunted Boat" (Chapter Five), and a fascinating discussion between Harman and Latour over shisha and bad weather in Chapter Six. Let these be a temptation for the reader to buy the fairly priced book or to find it shelved alongside Heidegger's work in your local library.[17]

As is the custom with the discourse arising in the wake of Speculative Realism's splintering, weblogs lit up with responses to *Circus Philosophicus* upon its release in late 2010.

---

[13] Harman, *Circus Philosophicus*, 32.

[14] Ibid., 34.

[15] Ibid., 34.

[16] Ibid., 36.

[17] Graham Harman, "I don't understand library cataloguing," *Object Oriented Philosophy*, http://doctorzamalek2.wordpress.com/2010/12/11/i-dont-understand-library-cataloguing/ (accessed January 6, 2011).

Maxwell Kennel – *Review of* Circus Philosophicus

The first to occur was an exchange between Graham Harman and Levi Bryant concerning "vicarious causation," and the second, an excellent response from Christopher Vitale of *Networkologies*.[18] This review will conclude with a short examination of the nature of these exchanges, and a look at the unusual genre that *Circus Philosophicus* inhabits within an even more unusual discourse.

Levi Bryant (*Difference and Givenness* and *The Democracy of Objects*), who makes a short appearance near the end of Chapter Four, responds at *Larval Subjects* with an excellent post outlining and summarizing Harman's concept of vicarious causation.[19] Developed in *Guerrilla Metaphysics* (2005), vicarious causation is described by Bryant as having three major characteristics: vicarious, asymmetrical, and buffered. In his response to *Circus Philosophicus* Bryant speaks to his difficulty in accepting vicarious causation in the past, and his present appreciation for its depiction in *Circus Philosophicus*. After outlining the three aforementioned aspects of vicarious causation, Bryant gives us a look into his *The Democracy of Objects* where he argues for an "autopoietic" system of objects which includes a corresponding idea to vicarious causation that differs in its emphasis on the translation-perturbation that occurs between objects-as-systems. Bryant's autopoietic mode of causation is then addressed in Harman's response in terms of a desired clarification regarding exactly how direct perturbed object interactions can be.[20]

This exchange between Harman and Bryant captures several fascinating aspects of the discourse now called Object Oriented Ontology, as well as pointing to similar changes in

---

[18] Christopher Vitale, "Circus Philosophicus," *Networkologies*, http://networkologies.wordpress.com/2010/12/31/circus-philosophicus/ (accessed January 6, 2011).

[19] Levi Bryant, "Vicarious Causation," *Larval Subjects*, http://larvalsubjects.wordpress.com/2010/12/24/vicarious-causation-2/#more-4363 (accessed January 6, 2011).

[20] Graham Harman, "Levi's post on vicarious causation," *Object Oriented Philosophy*, http://doctorzamalek2.wordpress.com/2010/12/24/levis-post-on-vicarious-causation/ (accessed January 6, 2011).

genre found in *Circus Philosophicus*. It first points to the speed at which responses occur to both newly published works and other blog posts, and second, the exchange itself occurs in the emerging medium of our time. Responses occur at a speed which far surpasses the lengthy publishing process that the academy has become so accustomed to, and as we can derive from McLuhan's famous statement, the message will change as the medium changes. Even the companies that publish work on Object Oriented Ontology do so quickly—I am thinking here of Re.Press, Open Humanities Press, and Zero Books. *Circus Philosophicus* was published in the space of a year, and Harman remarks elsewhere that Re.Press offered the publication of his own *Prince of Networks* in a fraction of the time offered by a traditional publisher.[21]

The fact that most of Object Oriented Ontology is played out so quickly on blogs and through open access publishers may also be indicative of its networked nature. As a discourse Object Oriented Ontology uses the images of matrixial objects that are connected and complex. The accessibility of the discourse to anyone with an RSS feed reader also points to the emphasis on the democracy between actors that springs from Latour's Actor-Network Theory (ANT). Situated within these networks *Circus Philosophicus* is certainly a feature of the greater discourse in its accessibility, the speed of its publication, and its networked mediation of the objects called "prose" and "narrative."

On the level of *Circus Philosophicus* itself, genre is bent, but perhaps not entirely reinvented. Robert Pirsig's *Zen and the Art of Motorcycle Maintenance*, although quite a bit longer, does preclude *Circus Philosophicus* in its combining of narrative and philosophical prose. To draw a comparison between the two would bow to the tendency to reduce the one to the other, so the two works should remain connected although, with vicarious causation in mind they best not make contact. The philosophical implications of myth and narrative do remain,

---

[21] Graham Harman, "Follow-up on open access," *Object Oriented Philosophy*, http://doctorzamalek2.wordpress.com/2011/01/06/follow-up-on-open-access/ (accessed January 6, 2011).

however, as the following quotation from Richard Kearney's *On Stories* illuminates:

> What works at the level of communal history works also at the level of individual history. When someone asks you *who* you are, you tell your story. That is, you recount your present condition in the light of past memories and future anticipations. You interpret where you are now in terms of where you have come from and where you are going to. And so doing you give a sense of yourself as a *narrative* identity that perdures and coheres over a lifetime. This is what the German philosopher Dilthey called the coming-together-of-a-life (*Zusammenhang des Lebens*), meaning the act of coordinating an existence which would otherwise be scattered over time. In this way, storytelling may be said to *humanise* time by transforming it from an impersonal passing of fragmented moments into a pattern, a plot, a *mythos*.[22]

Kearney speaks to a concept of narrative identity being informed by myth in the humanization of time. *Circus Philosophicus*, in turn, provides the reader with both a philosophical primer on Object Oriented Ontology as well as some insights into the *Zusammenhang des Lebens* of the author himself. In this way, both the philosophical idea and the narrative life of the author are connected. The networked system of objects that constitutes both the content and form of *Circus Philosophicus* is bound up in both philosophical thought and narrative life, making it a picture of non-reductive object relations. Where other works may be strictly narrative prose or strictly philosophical prose, *Circus Philosophicus* asymmetrically mediates between two disparate objects without reducing one to the other.

As was stated at the beginning, *Circus Philosophicus* offers an accessible introduction to Object Oriented Ontology. Christopher Vitale writes that "this is the most accessible presentation of OOO to date,"[23] and Levi Bryant seconds claiming that it is "perhaps the most amusing and accessible introduction

---

[22] Richard Kearney, *On Stories* (London & New York: Routledge, 2002), 10.

[23] Vitale, "Circus Philosophicus."

to Graham's thought published yet."[24] The form and value of *Circus Philosophicus* extends beyond its content to the fact that it serves as a referent to the larger attributes of the discourse in its twisting of genre, and accessible presentation. The only confusion that stands out in the text is the odd nature of the afterword, also pointed out by Christopher Vitale in his response. It seems appropriate to close with the thought that one can only guess at the significance of a surrealist, monk and telepath in the concluding pages of the work.[25] Perhaps the presence of these disparate objects is another feature of the flat ontology of actors that so define Object Oriented Ontology, or merely a reference to some narrative life-world yet unknown to the reader.

---

[24] Bryant, "Vicarious Causation."
[25] Harman, *Circus Philosophicus*, 77.

Joseph Nechvatal's nOise anusmOs installation
Galerie Richard, New York, April 12-May 26, 2012

Yuting Zou

Independent Researcher

"The task of perception entails pulverizing the world, but also one of spiritualizing its dust."[1]

BLACK IS THE "COLOR" OF UNDIVIDED nothingness and simplicity that has yet been penetrated by light. Black is immanent to itself. Entering the Galerie Richard, black was arguably my instant impression of Joseph Nechvatal's nOise anusmOs installation, for most of this new series of paintings are unified by a black background. Against the black backdrop are complicated webs of alternating red and white, they suggest many ambiguous and provocative images of corporeal surfaces. Here, sfumato plays a role in slightly reducing the contrast of colors by adding a smoky and subtle layer to the otherwise pixelated images. The entire room is filled with immersive noise, from the visual noise (digital virus) inside the pictorial frame to its audial extension into the ambient space through the "viral symphony." Bathed in a continuity of noise, it appeared to me that the overall composition of this body of work was more sparse and plural than before, and more speculative.

On the black canvases, the potencies of color start to unfold.

---

[1] Gilles Deleuze, *The Fold: Leibniz and the Baroque*, trans. Tom Conley, (Minneapolis: University of Minnesota Press, 1993).

Speculations III

Each painting is an autonomy of the inside, and it records the life of the tiny automata—artificial viruses. Those automata are equipped with sensory systems that allow them to perceive their local environment, detect enemies, and react accordingly. While, in most of the artist's previous works, the macroscopic corporeality is decomposed by the microscopic into visible or invisible traces, the majority of this new series reverse the scheme, as the microscopic is used to generate the macroscopic, the cosmological. The artificial viruses are creative agents that resemble Leibnizian monads—simple substances that are living mirrors of the entire universe, projections of a phantasmagorical phenomenon, and each an indivisible autonomous enclosure of infinite minute perceptions. A cluster of viruses start from an indiscernibly close vicinity, with almost indistinguishable perceptions, then form infinitesimal differential relations, and unfold the color pixels underneath their paths. As time goes by, the integration of minuscule differentials gives a clear perception of chiaroscuro of varied degrees. By that increasingly sharp chiaroscuro, the two-fold image is made visible: the human anus (or retina) and the black hole (or wormhole). As such, through viruses' own mild (confused) perceptions, their vibrating trajectories become a filter for a distinct perception towards a threshold of consciousness. This process is captured into an actualized work of art. Looking upon them, vision sees vision.

Under dim lighting, the gallery room simulates a universal theater, where various media coexist to form a *bel composto* (beautiful assemblage) of many arts—the electronic "viral symphOny," computer-robotic assisted acrylic on canvas, video animations, and a projection. Nonetheless, the mixed-media unity is a mind-boggling one, a mixture of mystery and indecency, just like the "permanent happening" on the altar stage of the Cornaro chapel. That is, Bernini's marble sculpture *The Ecstasy of St. Teresa*, where St. Teresa is portrayed as a young woman in tunic at the height of her spiritual transport. As she recalled in her autobiography, she experienced both physically and spiritually an intense *sweet pain* that caused her to moan, when all her entrails were penetrated and drawn out by a golden arrow during a gravity-free levitation.[2] Somehow reminiscent of that, the close-ups of human anus or retina are nomadically linked to the black holes or wormholes, through which an imaginative cosmological teleportation takes place. In that silent flight of noise, bodies are pulverized into weightless dusts, becoming a homogeneous whole with the boundless unknown and the inexperienceable, reaching the ultimate ecstasy. Moreover, in the light of his own theory, the typical strategy of Nechvatal's art works is to invoke "an infliction of a *pleasant frustration* that can lead to creative visualization," which can also be observed from the audience's reaction. Unlike his previous style that is characterized by overlapping two incompossible strata of the actual and the virtual, this time, the actual human retina, anus, or cosmological singularities, are progressively weaved into the fabric of the virtual noise, resulting in an emergent "viractual" (a term coined by the artist).[3] It is a pleasure to see how these strands of virtual particles move on to unfold the magic tapestries that depict the moment of creation. However, they diverge quickly, lose their way in the labyrinth of the black chaosmos, and have only a brief existence from the undifferentiated black, back to black. Perhaps, all this echoes with what Francois Laurelle says, "(t)he World is the endless confusion of man and Universe."[4]

Given the expansive, ecstatic, non-hierarchical impression

---

[2] Teresa, *Life of St. Teresa of Jesus, of the Order of Our Lady of Carmel*. Trans. David Lewis, ed. Benedict Zimmerman. 3rd ed. (London: T. Baker; New York: Benziger, 1904).

[3] Joseph Nechvatal, *Immersion Into Noise*, (Ann Arbor: Open Humanities Press in conjunction with the University of Michigan Library's Scholarly Publishing Office, 2011).

[4] FrançoisLaruelle, *Of Black Universe in the Human Foundations of Color*. The original French essay, titled "Du noir univers: dans les fondations humaines de la couleur," was published in La Décision philosophique 5 (April 1988): 107-112. The English edition of this essay was first translated and published by Miguel Abreu as "Of Black Universe in the Human Foundations of Color" in the catalogue *Hyun Soo Choi: Seven Large-Scale Paintings* (New York: Thread Waxing Space, 1991), 2-4.

of the work, the unity of the microscopic and the macroscopic culminates in one's mindscape as that of the infinitely small (infinitesimal) and the infinitely large, reflecting essentially the Leibnizian fractal view of the infinite:

> I did not definitely assert that there are infinitely many degrees of infinities; I merely made certain conjectures, by virtue of which I deemed this to be possible, and indeed probable. My main reason was that there is no reason why God should have willed the existence only of this degree of infinity or order of magnitude, which constitutes our objects, proportioned to our intellects. I can easily conceive that, in the smallest particle of dust, there can exist a world, in which all things have the same relative proportions as in this large world; and, on the other hand, that our world might be nothing but a particle of dust in another, infinitely larger world. This way of conceiving things can be continued upwards and downwards indefinitely.[5]

---

[5] G.W. Leibniz. *Die mathematische schriften von Gottfried Wilheim Leibniz*, vol. III, C. I. Gerhardt (ed), (Berlin & Halle, 1849-55): p 503-4.